AN AMERICAN IN VICTORIAN CAMBRIDGE

CHARLES ASTOR BRISTED'S
"FIVE YEARS IN AN ENGLISH UNIVERSITY"

Five Years in an English University is a richly detailed account of student life in the Cambridge of the 1840s. It belongs to a fascinating nineteenth-century trans-Atlantic publishing genre: travel accounts designed to describe British culture to Americans and vice-versa.

"An edition of real excellence."
Frank M. Turner, Director of the Beinecke Library, Yale University

"He was at one of the two colleges … which were the two powerhouses of the nineteenth century Cambridge scene. He offers a unique insider's account of this, its competitiveness, its camaraderie and its sheer basic mechanics. We begin to see what underpinned so many of the relationships in the world of nineteenth century British government and politics."
Gillian Sutherland, Newnham College, Cambridge University

"There is nothing quite like it … nothing quite so detailed, so inside the institution and so inside what is for Bristed a foreign culture. It was a tour de force by a man whom Christopher Stray describes (accurately) as something of a playboy. The account mixes delightful anecdote with real understanding, and it is always lively."
Sheldon Rothblatt, University of California, Berkeley

Charles Astor Bristed (1820–1874) was the favourite grandson of John Jacob Astor II, the first American multi-millionaire and the Astor of the Waldorf-Astoria; after gaining a degree at Yale, Bristed entered Trinity College, Cambridge in 1840 and graduated in 1845.

Christopher Stray is an Honorary Research Fellow in the Department of Classics, University of Wales Swansea. His previous books include *Classics Transformed: Schools, Universities and Society in England, 1830–1960* (OUP 1998); *Gilbert Murray Reassessed: Hellenism, Theatre, and International Politics* (OUP 2007).

"Bristed's account of his time at Cambridge enthralled me when I first read it many years ago, and I have often wished that this insightful and entertaining book was better known. Thanks to Christopher Stray, who has brought such extraordinary erudition and such indefatigable research to bear on the project, a carefully edited and usefully annotated and indexed edition is now available at last."

"In the nineteenth century, the world's two great Anglophone cultures were separated by barriers a great deal more troublesome and tempest-tossed than mere ocean vastness. From the 1820s through at least the 1860s, Anglo-American relations were wracked with conflict, permeated by suspicion, and enveloped in a fog of mutual incomprehension. With half of their vast country mired in the sin of slavery and the whole a mix of bustling commerce and noisy democracy, Americans laboured under a painful sense of inferiority to the British elites whose books they read so avidly ... For many of the [British], America represented the triumph of mob rule and vulgar money-worship, forces whose corrosive power might one day threaten to overwhelm the vaunted stability and progress even of the world's greatest empire if not kept firmly in check. The result was a continual and escalating series of fierce skirmishes ... Into this ferociously contested cultural no man's land sauntered the dapper, insouciant, improbable figure of Charles Astor Bristed ..."

from Patrick Leary's Foreword to An American in Victorian Cambridge

An American in Victorian Cambridge

Charles Astor Bristed's "Five Years in an English University"

'αλλ' 'απ' 'εχθρῶν δῆτα πολλά μανθάνουσιν οἱ σοφόι
[but of course wise men learn a lot more from their enemies]
Aristophanes, *Birds* 376

edited and with an introduction by
Christopher Stray

foreword by
Patrick Leary

UNIVERSITY
of
EXETER
PRESS

First published in 2008 by
University of Exeter Press
Reed Hall, Streatham Drive
Exeter EX4 4QR
UK

www.exeterpress.co.uk

British Library Cataloguing in Publication Data
A catalogue record for this book is available
from the British Library.

Paperback ISBN 978 0 85989 825 6
Hardback ISBN 978 0 85989 824 9

Typeset in Didot and Bembo
by Carnegie Book Production, Lancaster
Printed in Great Britain by T J International, Padstow

Contents

Illustrations

The illustrations in the text are taken from John Lewis (or Louis) Roget's *Cambridge Scrapbook* (Cambridge, 1859). The book's full title is *A Cambridge Scrap-Book. Containing in a pictorial form a report of the manners, customs, humours and pastimes of the University of Cambridge … By a Special Commissioner, appointed by himself. With an appendix of papers on applied mathematics*. Roget was suggesting, tongue in cheek, that he was gathering information about the University's workings, just as the members of the Royal Commission on the University appointed in 1850 were charged with reporting on it and issuing recommendations for reform. Their report was published in 1852; Roget's earlier publications, brought together in the *Scrap-Book*, were *Familiar illustrations of the language of mathematics: or, a new picture-alphabet for well-behaved undergraduates* (1850) and *Cambridge customs and costumes* (1851). John Roget (Trinity 1846) was the only son of Peter Mark Roget, whose famous *Thesaurus* first appeared in 1852. He graduated in 1850, taking in the Mathematical Tripos exactly the same position as Bristed had in Classics five years before – second in the second class. Roget became a lawyer, but was also a talented and prolific water-colourist.

Charles Astor Bristed.
Library of Congress, Brady-Handy Collection, BH82–5031A.

Foreword

by Patrick Leary

In the nineteenth century, the world's two great Anglophone cultures were separated by barriers a great deal more troublesome and tempest-tossed than mere ocean vastness. From the 1820s through at least the 1860s, Anglo-American relations were wracked with conflict, permeated by suspicion, and enveloped in a fog of mutual incomprehension. With half of their vast country mired in the sin of slavery and the whole a mix of bustling commerce and noisy democracy, Americans laboured under a painful sense of inferiority to the British elites whose books they read so avidly, a burden that too often left them at once absurdly boastful and exquisitely sensitive to any slights from British visitors or commentators. For many of the latter, America represented the triumph of mob rule and vulgar money-worship, forces whose corrosive power might one day threaten to overwhelm the vaunted stability and progress even of the world's greatest empire if not kept firmly in check. The result was a continual and escalating series of fierce skirmishes, in which the aggressive condescension of visitors like Captain Marryat and Mrs Trollope, with their caricatures of ignorant, prudish, tobacco-spitting, psalm-singing provincials, stung Americans to fury at the ill-mannered ingratitude of these obtuse, pompous, aristocrat-worshipping windbags and their fellows. Into this ferociously contested cultural no man's land sauntered the dapper, insouciant, improbable figure of Charles Astor Bristed, possessed of a keen eye for foibles, a passionate amateur devotion to ancient Greek, and what, to his amusement, went far toward conciliating his British hosts: a stock of well-cut trousers.

My own first encounter with Bristed was as an undergraduate, for a term paper about the Cambridge secret society, the Apostles. There was no secondary scholarship about the group at that time, and I found in *Five Years in an English University* one of the handful of vivid firsthand accounts of its workings. Many years later, when I was writing an article for *Publishing History* about how John Stuart Mill's first book became (much to the author's surprise) a standard text at the universities, a development that reflected the growing market for such textbooks in mid-Victorian Britain, I turned again to Bristed for his clear-eyed explanations of what books Cambridge undergraduates of the time were reading, and were expected to have read. Bristed has much to offer not only those scholars and students working on the history of education, but equally those whose field is 'the history of the book', and, more particularly, the history of reading. Because Bristed's prose is so accessible, the book's potential classroom uses are intriguing, as well: I can easily imagine it as an assigned text in a history survey class on Victorian Britain, or, for that matter, in a graduate-level Victorian literature seminar, as background reading for the study of such fictional accounts of student life as Thomas Hughes's *Tom Brown at Oxford* and Cuthbert Bede's *The Adventures of Mr Verdant Green*.

But the main fascinations of the book to those who are not specialists in English university history lie in the manifold ways in which it reflects the tensions and fascinations then existing – and, in many respects, still surviving – between the two great poles of the English-speaking world: Britain and America. No cultural history of the relationship between these societies, from the nineteenth century to the present, can afford to ignore Bristed's account of his years at Cambridge. This aspect of the book will be of particular interest to American readers, as well as to cultural historians of all sorts.

This is not simply a book about English university life, but pre-eminently a book about an *American* student at an *English* university. There is scarcely a page of it that is not imbued with this heightened sense of difference, of a peek inside a mysterious and rarefied world at the heart of an alien culture, by someone whose wealth and privilege have procured him a degree of access vouchsafed only to a favored few. Like all travelers to exotic lands, Bristed noticed and recorded a multitude of things about that world that were either invisible or unremarkable to its native inhabitants, and he did so in the service of a specifically American readership, one that craved insight into the unfamiliar attitudes and rituals of a foreign educated elite whose books and authors still dominated American literary and intellectual life. *Five Years in an English University* belongs to a fascinating trans-Atlantic publishing genre whose heyday ran from about the 1820s through to the end of the American Civil War: the travel account that attempted to describe and explain American culture for Britons, or vice-versa. The British visitors' side of that exchange is better known – Fanny Trollope, Captain Marryat, Basil Hall, Fanny Kemble, Charles Lyell, Dickens, and many others – and American writers, particularly, were very much aware of these. Yet Bristed was not alone. His book should be set alongside titles such as Frederick Law Olmsted's *Walks and Talks of an American Farmer in England* (1850) and Ralph Waldo Emerson's *English Traits* (1857), to name but two. Like Bristed, Olmsted enlivens his observations with set-scenes of dialogue to help convey the flavor of his encounters with individual Britons; Emerson, also like Bristed, moves easily among the educated elite and contrasts their attitudes and institutions with American equivalents. Situating the book in this way points up how very contentious and influential this whole literature was, particularly among the American readers who were Bristed's intended audience.

Being able to see how Bristed's observations participate in an ongoing discussion and debate between the two cultures also makes clearer some of the things that make him so unusual. For of course Bristed also wrote, and published in book form that same year, *The Upper Ten Thousand*, an attempt to depict elite American society for British readers. I can think of no other writer of the nineteenth century who worked both sides of this particular dialogue, let alone one who did so with such panache and insight. (Had his health been more robust, it is easy to imagine Bristed making the rounds of the expanding lecture circuit in both countries, a circuit whose popularity owed much to the mutual fascination he exploits in both books.) The vivid and funny mock-serious account of how he introduced sherry cobbler to Cambridge in the wake of the publication of the anti-American chapters of *Martin Chuzzlewit*, only to have an undergraduate later ask him if they had such a drink in America, wittily encapsulates not only a kind of ironic riposte to Dickens but Bristed's view of his own privileged role in this heated trans-Atlantic exchange. That he, a scion of one of America's wealthiest and most famous families and a cultivated, cosmopolitan figure even in his twenties, evidently saw himself as a kind of interpreter and ambassador, a bridge between the two nations' elites, makes this book that much more remarkable an achievement, and its history of considerably wider interest.

The book has, besides, many more claims on our attention today – its contributions to the understanding and study of the history of education, but also to the histories of reading, Anglo-American relations, the evolution of manners and conversation, early Victorian culture more generally, and so on. But there is more in Bristed than information for historians – there is also great charm, a charm that makes the book, in its best chapters, a lively and delightful reading experience. This is enhanced by the unusual style of the book – its breezy, colloquial quality; its versatility of portraiture; its often self-deprecating wit, all qualities honed in writing for the lively periodical market that had sprung up on both sides of the Atlantic. How many of Bristed's contemporary writers would have attempted such a sentence as, "I was now undergoing for the third time since I entered the University, and the I-don't-know-how-many-eth time in my life, a course of low Mathematics"? How many could have pulled off that astonishing one-act play, in Chapter 13, that takes place in a room twelve feet square – a set-piece for three voices that conveys the experience of a tutorial with such beguiling immediacy? (No wonder that Bowring in his marginal note calls this scene "Uncommonly well told and to the life.") The boat race that takes up Chapter 7, and the Trinity supper party, told entirely in the present tense, that follows, likewise bring these scenes vividly to life in a few deft strokes. This is a young man's book, with a young man's exuberance, sense of fun, and, at times, soul-searching earnestness. It is also the book of a practiced and able writer.

Bristed's account of his time at Cambridge enthralled me when I first encountered it many years ago, and I have often wished that this insightful and entertaining book was better known. Thanks to the University of Exeter Press and to Christopher Stray, who has brought such extraordinary erudition and such indefatigable research to bear on the project, a carefully edited and usefully annotated and indexed scholarly edition is now available at last.

May 2008

Introduction

by Christopher Stray

In December 1910 George Otto Trevelyan, fellow of Trinity College, Cambridge, decided to re-read Charles Astor Bristed's *Five Years in an English University* over the Christmas vacation. On 20 December, having reached the end of the first chapter, he wrote in his copy, 'I think this book, as I always thought it, with all its faults incomparably the best account of an English university in existence.'[1] *Five Years* has indeed a strong claim to be the most perceptive and richly detailed account of the student experience ever written in English. Charles Bristed was a highly intelligent and perceptive observer who made it his business to understand how the system of examination and discipline worked in practice in the Cambridge of the 1840s. Writing for his fellow-Americans, he described in detail not only the formal structure of the university, but also the informal rules of student life – its etiquette, its slang, and the accommodations made with the demands of the university authorities. Work and play, sports and examinations, discipline and drink: Bristed provides a mixture of analysis, criticism and narrative which brings the Cambridge student world of the 1840s vividly to life.[2]

---

[1] Note in Trevelyan's copy of the second (one-volume) edition of 1852, now in Trinity College Library, Adv. C. 25. 24, p. 5. He had read the book at least once before, in 1895: see his annotation on Paley mnemonics on p. 91 below. Trevelyan was Macaulay's nephew; his copy had once belonged to his uncle's friend Thomas Flower Ellis. His assessment was echoed by Peter Searby, who called the book 'the most detailed and the most thoughtful account of Cambridge undergraduate life ever penned': P. Searby, *A History of the University of Cambridge: Vol. III: 1750–1870* (Cambridge, 1997), p. 585.

[2] His account is drawn on extensively by Searby, *History*, pp. 585–612. Cf. P. Searby, 'A New Yorker in early Victorian Cambridge', *Cambridge* 33 (Winter 1993–4), pp. 58–63.

Charles Bristed: playboy, scholar and litterateur

Charles Astor Bristed was born in 1820, the son of the Revd John Bristed, an Englishman who had emigrated to the USA, where he made a reputation as a writer on economic and political subjects.[3] John Bristed had married the daughter of John Jacob Astor, an immigrant from Waldorf in Germany who was building up a commercial empire in fur trading and later moved into property; at his death in 1848 Astor was the richest man in the USA. His name survives in that of the Waldorf Astoria, a famous late-nineteenth century grand hotel in New York; the Astor dynasty in England was founded by Charles Bristed's nephew William Waldorf Astor, the first Viscount Astor. The Anglo-American connection this suggests began much earlier: Bristed's mother died when he was twelve, and he was then brought up in John Jacob Astor's household at Hellgate, on the East River near New York.[4] Here he belonged to a bachelor household frequented by the poet Fitz-Greene Halleck and the Anglophile writer Washington Irving. At school in New York he was taught by an eccentric Cambridge graduate, Henry Herbert, who was later to pioneer the professional literature of sport and hunting in the USA under the pseudonym 'Frank Forester'. Young Bristed was sent to the nearby Columbia College,[5] but was soon withdrawn and entered at Yale in 1835, still aged only fifteen.

Bristed spent three years at Yale, where the curriculum as at Cambridge included both Classics and mathematics, graduating in 1839. He then stayed on for a fourth year as a 'resident graduate'; as he says himself in Chapter 2, this was a recipe for idleness, but he used it to begin his career as a writer. Articles in the *Yale Literary Magazine* were followed by pieces in New York newspapers and magazines.[6] His grandfather had thought of sending Bristed to a German university (Astor was of course himself German, but

[3] For biographical detail on Bristed, see S.G. Bowerman, 'Charles Astor Bristed', *Dictionary of American Biography* 3 (1929), pp. 53–4; C.A. Stray, 'Charles Astor Bristed, 1820–74', *Oxford Dictionary of National Biography* (online release, October 2004).

[4] So named for the dangerous cross-currents and treacherous reefs of this part of the river, which the house overlooked.

[5] Founded as King's College in 1754, but patriotically renamed Columbia College in 1784, this became Columbia University in 1896. 'Columbia College' survives as the name of the undergraduate division of the university.

[6] This was the beginning of a prolific career: the bibliography of Bristed's publications (pp. 390–412) includes well over 200 articles published between 1841 and his death in 1874.

the practice became increasingly common in the USA from the 1840s); but eventually it was decided to send him, at least initially, to Cambridge.[7] He arrived there in October 1840, planning to stay for a year. In the event, a serious illness prevented him from travelling back to the USA, and he did not return till the spring of 1846, a year after he had graduated. On his grandfather's death in 1848, Bristed inherited property and money which freed him from the need to earn a living. In the 1850s he travelled widely in Europe, spending months at a time in Rome, in John Jacob Astor's native Rhineland and in Paris (where he witnessed the usurpation of 1852). His life was in some ways that of a playboy – he was known for his love of fashionable clothes, fine food and wine, and the theatre – but he was also busy writing articles on literary and sporting topics. Bristed's output included articles for *Blackwood's* and *Fraser's Magazines* in Britain and the *American Review*, *Galaxy*, *Literary Review* and *Knickerbocker* in the USA. He was most comfortable writing short pieces: as he himself recalled (p. 194), 'When younger, I used generally to write an essay in fragments and piece them together as best I could'. The mode of construction is evident in the contents list of *Five Years*; and the three long chapters (11, 12, 15) in which he describes his second year, third year and repeated third year are in fact clusters of briefer pieces. On several occasions, however, he turned a series of articles into a book, and in 1852, two of these appeared. One was *The Upper Ten Thousand*, which reprinted a series of ten 'Sketches of American society' published in *Fraser's* between March 1850 and September 1851, in which he had depicted the world of the New York social elite for British readers. The other was *Five Years*, in which he described student life at Cambridge for readers in his own country. Bristed's original plan, conceived after his return to the US in 1846, had been to publish magazine articles which might then be collected in book form, on the same plan as *The Upper Ten Thousand*. As he explains in his Preface, however, the editors of his two chosen US outlets were unhappy with his criticism of American colleges, and so the project lay dormant till the summer of 1851, when he wrote most of the book.[8]

---

[7]   His original plan, as he tells us (p. 80), had been to spend a year at Cambridge and then move on to a German university. The first part of this plan perhaps reflected the preferences of his father, then still alive (he died in 1855).

[8]   An earlier version of Chapter 7 ('The boat race') had been published in the *Yale Literary Magazine* in 1841, and a revised and corrected version in the *American Review*, to which Bristed was a regular contributor: 'English University life. No. 1: The Boat Race', *American Review* 5 (April 1847), pp. 353–6. Chapter 8 appeared in the same

In the 1850s and 1860s Bristed became a well-known figure in New York social and literary circles, veiled only lightly under his favourite pseudonym, Carl Benson. He belonged to a circle of writers and artists who supported the claims of Gallic civilization – and sensuality – against the established puritan culture of the traditional Boston social elite.[9] The interest in horse-riding which is occasionally revealed in *Five Years* reflected a life-long passion: Bristed kept several horses and liked nothing better than to go 'trotting'. This sport, involving riding in a light carriage pulled by one or two horses, was a favourite in New York, where men of all classes trotted down Third Avenue, then raced each other the five miles to the Harlem Bridge.[10] Bristed also wrote frequently for sporting journals such as *Wilkes' Spirit of the Times*; when in France and Germany he sent them weekly letters about local races, commenting as well on current events, theatre and opera. Yet he was also a serious scholar who kept up his Latin and Greek and retained a keen interest in comparative philology. He published an edition of Catullus, albeit an elementary one,[11] and gave papers to the early meetings of the American Philological Association after its foundation in 1869.[12] In 1855 he contributed to the short-lived annual *Cambridge Essays* an article on American English which was later described by H.L. Mencken as 'to this day the most intelligent brief discussion of the subject ever printed.'[13]

In short, Charles Bristed was a man about town, but a learned and

---

journal, as 'English university life. No. II: A Trinity Supper': *American Review* 5 (June 1847), pp. 629–34. It was presumably the editorial reception of No. III in the series which prompted Bristed to abandon the project. By that time he had written what became Chapters 1–9 (see his Preface).

[9]   For an account of New York literary culture in this period, see E.G. Burrows and M. Wallace, *Gotham: A History of New York City to 1898* (New York, 1999), pp. 683–7.

[10]   See Bristed's account in Ch. 1 of *The Upper Ten Thousand*; cf. Burrows and Wallace, *Gotham*, pp. 720–1.

[11]   *Selections from Catullus: for the use of classical students* (New York, 1849). This was largely based on an edition published in England in 1845 by the Eton master W.G. Cookesley; Bristed added some notes of his own. At one time he planned an edition of Horace.

[12]   The first was published as 'Some Notes on Ellis's Early English Pronunciation', *Transactions of the American Philological Association* 2 (1871), pp. 114–137.

[13]   'The English Language in America', in *Cambridge Essays, Contributed by Members of the University: 1855* (London, 1855), pp. 57–78. H.L. Mencken, *The American Language* (New York, 1919), p. 79.

cultured one.[14] He both worked and played hard – rather like the high-achieving honours students in Cambridge whom he describes so well in *Five Years*. At least he did so while his health permitted: in the later 1850s, the medical condition which had kept Bristed in Cambridge in the previous decade returned, and for much of the rest of his life, until his death in 1874, he was a semi-invalid.[15] He married twice and had two sons, both educated in England. His first son, John, boarded at Cheltenham College; his second son, named Charles Henry Maine after Bristed's Cambridge friend (Sir) Henry Maine, having spent some time at Stonyhurst (the second Mrs Bristed had converted to Catholicism), followed his father's footsteps to Trinity College, Cambridge, whence he graduated in 1893. This ended the direct family connection with England, but it was continued less directly by the migration from the USA in 1890 of Bristed's nephew William Waldorf Astor, from 1917 the first Viscount Astor.

Reporting home: a transatlantic genre

Five Years belongs to two distinct genres: the university memoir and the travel memoir. In the first of these, his predecessors included John Wright, whose anonymous two-volume *Alma Mater, or Seven Years at Cambridge* (1827) had included examination papers and even music. Wright entered Trinity in 1814 and graduated in 1819; his account is less detailed and sophisticated than Bristed's, but gives valuable information on college and university life.[16] William Everett, son of the US minister in London, published a memoir of his time in Cambridge in 1865, benevolently reviewed by Bristed.[17] Everett's account, originally a series of lectures, is an accomplished work but does not match up to Bristed's in detail or depth of analysis. In 1890 Samuel

---

[14]   As a reviewer of *Five Years* put it, he was 'half a dandy and half a scholar by natural inclination': (Anon.) 'College education in England and America', *North American Review* 75 (1852), p. 47.

[15]   Hence the title of the collection of articles, reviews and poems he published in Baden in 1858–9: *Pieces of a Broken-Down Critic. Picked up by Himself.* The condition was rheumatic fever, which led to heart disease.

[16]   In his review of *Five Years*, Clark refers to Wright's memoir (though without naming it) as 'coarse, vulgar and unfaithful': 'Cambridge life according to C.A. Bristed', *Fraser's Magazine* 49 (1854), pp. 89–100, at p. 95.

[17]   W. Everett, *On the Cam* (Boston, 1865). The book was published in London in 1866 and went into several editions. Bristed reviewed it anonymously: *The Nation* 1 (10 Aug. 1865) 182–4. On Everett, see H.C. Porter, 'A Harvard Unitarian in Victorian Cambridge', *Journal of Ecclesiastical History* 53 (2002), pp. 527–44.

Satthianadhan published in Madras *Four years in an English University*, a brief account of contemporary Cambridge aimed at his fellow-Indians, and which included an appendix on the Indian Civil Service examinations.[18] Like Bristed, he was writing for his fellow-countrymen, but the severely practical aspect loomed much larger. This is understandable not only on account of the greater geographical and cultural distance, but also because those in charge of the ICS examinations discriminated against Indians.[19]

As for the travel memoir: in 1803 John Bristed had published an account of a tour in Scotland which included considerable detail on its universities.[20] After later travels in the USA, he published the work for which he is best known, *The Resources of the United States of America*.[21] Travel writing in the opposite direction included Frederick L. Olmsted's *Walks and Talks of an American Farmer in England* (1850). Olmsted, who became the leading landscape designer in the USA (his achievements include the University of California campus at Berkeley, and Prospect and Central Parks in New York) was inspired by the work of Joseph Paxton, designer of the Crystal Palace, in Birkenhead.[22] Olmsted's book, like *Five Years*, alternates narrative with sections of dramatised dialogue, and Bristed may have been influenced by it. Ralph Waldo Emerson, in his turn, who devotes the twelfth chapter of his *English Traits* (1857) to Oxford and Cambridge, draws on Bristed

---

[18]　S. Satthianadhan, *Four Years in an English University; With a Chapter on the Indian Civil Service Examination by A.C. Dutt* (Madras, 1890). A much enlarged 2ⁿᵈ edn appeared in 1893.

[19]　See P. Vasunia, 'Greek, Latin, and the Indian Civil Service', in J.P. Hallett and C.A. Stray (eds), *British Classics outside England* (Waco TX, 2008), pp. 61–93.

[20]　*Anthroplanomenos, or, a Pedestrian Tour through Part of the Highlands of Scotland, in 1801*, 2 vols (London, 1803). The main title is in Greek, and can be roughly translated, 'wandering man': hence perhaps the pseudonym 'Wanderer' which Charles Bristed used at one time (see Bibliography A2, 1856–7).

[21]　*The Resources of the United States of America, or, A View of the Agricultural, Commercial, Manufacturing, Financial, Political, Literary, Moral and Religious Capacity and Character of the American People* (London, 1818).

[22]　The mention of Olmsted's campus landscaping reminds us that an important aspect of the 19ᵗʰ-century exchange of ideas across the Atlantic was the recreation of a collegiate campus ideal in the USA. See A. Duke, *Importing Oxbridge: English Residential Colleges and American Universities* (New Haven, 1996). Bristed himself played a part in this transfer: Andrew White, founding president of Cornell, testified that 'my ideas on the [campus planning] were further developed' by reading *Five Years*. A.D. White, *Autobiography* (New York, 1905), vol. 1 p. 287.

for information.[23] *Five Years*, then, can be located in a nineteenth-century genre (or genres), and is one of several attempts to describe and analyse life on one side of the Atlantic for an audience on the other side. What makes Bristed unique is that he wrote both ways: in 1851, while the final chapters of *The Upper Ten Thousand* were appearing in *Fraser's Magazine*, he was preparing the text of *Five Years*.

Bristed's Cambridge

The account of Cambridge in *Five Years* follows for the most part a predictable course from arrival, through initial puzzlement, the curiosities of college and student customs, to the routine of undergraduate life – socialising, study, examinations, discipline, religion, town-gown relations – in the successive years of a young man's residence in the University.[24] All this, however, is enlivened by Bristed's curiosity, his determination to understand how and why the Cambridge system worked as it did and his concern to explain this to American readers. This concern helps to explain why he places Cambridge in perspective by visiting other institutions. In the spring of 1843 he spent three days at Oxford, interrogating dons and undergraduates (see Chapter 12). In 1845 he visited Eton, and also secured written accounts of the school from two friends: the Eton master William Johnson (later Cory), and William Clark of Trinity. These accounts are given in Chapter 23, and are interesting both in their detail and in their differences: Johnson was an Eton and King's man, Clark had been at Shrewsbury, a much less prestigious school but one whose products had been consistently out-performing the Etonians for some time.[25] A final comparative perspective is given by Bristed's discussion of American colleges in Chapters 32–5.

---

[23]   He also cites V.A. Huber's *The English Universities*, tr. and ed. F.W. Newman (London, 1843); it is surprising that Bristed himself nowhere engages with this account, by a German whose English translator is free with his comment and criticism.

[24]   The most useful account of Cambridge in the period remains D.A. Winstanley's *Early Victorian Cambridge* (Cambridge, 1940), a mandarin narrative account in the form a series of detailed and Trinity-centred thematic essays. If Winstanley (like Searby's, *History* though in a different way) is introspective, then M.McK. Garland's *Cambridge before Darwin: The Ideal of a Liberal Education, 1800–1860* (Cambridge, 1980), though a useful survey, at time feels not quite at home in its subject.

[25]   See the account of Eton in the 1840s in H.C. Maxwell-Lyte, *History of Eton College* (London, 1875), pp. 405–13, which emphasises (p. 409) the embarrassment caused by the appointment of assistant masters who had been at Shrewsbury and knew Greek

These are, however, not the only features which make *Five Years* such a striking mixture of insider's observation and outsider's insight. Bristed's student career at Cambridge was unusual in ways which enabled him to gain additional insight into the workings of the colleges and University. He arrived as a graduate, rather than from school, and a foreign graduate at that. It was not uncommon for men who had reached degree level at University College or King's College, London, at Trinity College Dublin, or at one of the five Scottish universities, to enrol at Oxford or Cambridge; much less so for students from abroad. Bristed enrolled at Trinity as a Fellow-Commoner, but at the beginning of his third year, he downgraded himself to an ordinary undergraduate (pensioner). In the 1840s Oxford and Cambridge still had a small number of students who claimed special privileges and exemptions on grounds of birth or money. Noblemen and their sons were able to proceed to examinations and degrees over lower hurdles than others, and in college had better rooms and dined at high table with the fellows (hence 'Fellow Commoner'). It was this last privilege, and the mature literary discussion he hoped would follow, which Bristed aimed at in enrolling as a Fellow Commoner in 1840. By occupying this special status and then giving it up, he was able to observe college life from a variety of positions. His career was also unusual in that the illness which struck him in 1841 (described in Chapter 10) forced him to suspend his studies; he thus graduated in 1845, rather than in 1844 as originally planned. Not only did this give him two third years (Chapters 12 and 15), and so more time to study the workings of college and university, it brought him into contact with additional year-groups and gave him the added perspective of a man whose location in his second third year (1843–4) was anomalous. Most undergraduates came and went; a few stayed on as fellows, and were often prone to a concern that they would become 'donnish'. Bristed was neither one nor the other; a superannuated undergraduate who almost went in for a fellowship examination but finally decided against it.

What struck Bristed most about Cambridge was the high intellectual standard of the honours men, their combination of mental and physical fitness, and the intensely competitive spirit which pervaded the university.[26] This needs to be put in perspective: less than half the undergraduates in Cambridge in the 1840s proceeded to degrees, and many of those who

---

better than their senior colleagues. The account is anonymous, but was written by Bristed's friend and informant William Johnson.

[26] See A. Warwick, *Masters of Theory: Cambridge and the Rise of Mathematical Physics* (Chicago, 2003), pp. 56–8.

did so were content to work for a pass degree (the Poll men or *Polloi*: 'the masses'). Bristed's circle of friends and acquaintances consisted largely of the student elite, together with some of the dons.[27] Though he did not belong to what is now the best-known of the undergraduate societies, the Apostles, he was close to several of its members, and his book is a useful source for the history of the society in the 1840s.[28] The hothouse atmosphere of competition and rigorous study was largely focused on the Mathematical Tripos, Cambridge's oldest university examination and, until the Classical Tripos was first examined in 1824, its only one. Like many others, Bristed had come to Cambridge trained in Classics and determined to pursue it; like them, he was obliged to work for the Mathematical Tripos and to pass it with honours before being allowed to enter the classical examination. This restriction, partially relaxed in 1849, was finally abolished only in 1854.[29] As Bristed found when he visited Oxford, the situation there was the exact opposite, Classics being compulsory and mathematics optional.[30] As a tripos examination drew near, intense speculation took place about the leading candidates for the first class of honours (in mathematics, the Wranglers). The competition took place between individuals, but college pride was very much at issue, and in particular, that of the two great rivals

---

[27] Within this elite, indeed within a large college like Trinity, there were subgroups based on proximity of rooms, schooling, religion and friendship. We might guess that Charles James Monk, who wrote home to his father (formerly Regius Professor of Greek and now Bishop of Gloucester) in 1843 that 'wine is now little drunk in Cambridge', probably did not attend supper parties of the kind Bristed describes in ch. 8. (Monk papers, Trinity College Library, C1/59, letter of 10 December 1843.)

[28] The Apostles were founded as the Cambridge Conversazione Society in 1820, when undergraduate discussion of moral and political topics was still viewed with alarm by many dons. Until the 1850s, however, the Apostles seem to have made no attempt at secrecy; at that point they went underground, having become 'too popular for their own good': Peter Allen, *The Cambridge Apostles: The Early Years* (Cambridge, 1978), pp. 9–10. Allen calls *Five Years* 'One of the most valuable accounts of student life in Victorian Britain' (*Apostles*, 182). William Lubenow's *The Cambridge Apostles 1820–1914* (Cambridge, 1997), which makes extensive use of contemporary sources, curiously makes no mention of Bristed.

[29] The restriction came into effect three years later, in 1857. See C.A. Stray, 'The first century of the Classical Tripos', in Stray (ed.), *Classics in Cambridge (Proceedings of the Cambridge Philological Society*, Supp. vol. 24), 1999, pp. 1–14.

[30] Until 1864, the only route to an honours degree in Oxford lay through Honour Moderations in Classics. This examination, taken after 5 terms, was followed, for the classical student, by the Greats (Literae Humaniores) course of 7 terms.

and the largest colleges, Trinity and St John's. Bristed conjures up the atmosphere vividly, and his extended stay in the University enables us to see how much variation there might be between years. The make-up of the honours list depended on the talent available in the relevant peer-group, on work habits, but also on the questions set by examiners and their decisions on 'drawing the line' (between degree classes). In one year, the first class might be relatively inclusive, in another, severely restricted. In 1845, when Bristed sat the Classical Tripos examination, the second class (including himself, who came second) consisted entirely of men who had reasonable hopes of a First. One of the examiners, indeed, wanted to include them in the first class, but was over-ruled by his colleagues.[31] In 1841 there had been a 'slaughter'[32] in the mathematical (Senate House) examination which had a knock-on effect on the classical examination which followed it: many men predicted to gain Firsts were downgraded, and some left for Oxford to recover; the first class contained only five men, less than half its usual size, and for the first time since their institution in 1751, the Chancellor's Medals for classical composition were not awarded.[33] The atmosphere in Oxford was rather different. Examinations there retained a much larger oral element, and examinees were not in direct competition with one another – in theory a single class could contain all or none of the candidates. University life was also even more centred on the colleges than at Cambridge, and the social status of undergraduates counted for more. The contrast was striking with the intellectual austerity and intense competition which Bristed witnessed among the 'high men' in Cambridge.[34]

The pressures of preparation for the Tripos made themselves felt in the later stages of an undergraduate's career. From the first, however, college examinations presented hurdles which not all students surmounted. By the time Bristed reached Cambridge, all the colleges held internal examinations, and Trinity men were subjected to them every year.[35] The first-year examinations were largely classical, reflecting the fact that many students

[31]   See Ch. 24.

[32]   Bristed's word: see p. 128.

[33]   See below, p. 63.

[34]   On these contrasts of ethos see C.A. Stray, 'Curriculum and style in the collegiate university: Classics in nineteenth-century Oxbridge', *History of Universities* 16 (2001), pp. 183–218.

[35]   On college examinations, pioneered by St John's in 1765, followed by Trinity in 1790, see the chapters by J. Smith and M. Underwood in Smith and Stray (eds), *Teaching and Learning in 19th-century Cambridge* (Woodbridge, 2003), pp. 107–38.

came up from schools where no mathematics was taught – as was the case in the public schools. In the following year, however, mathematics loomed large, and men who aimed at entering the Classical Tripos, which was examined in their tenth term immediately after the Mathematical Tripos, began to prepare for low honours in mathematics: just enough to enable them to enter the classical examination. At this point, men had to plan their reading and decide which topics to concentrate on. Those who aimed at any kind of honours also began to plan their private tuition, regarded as essential in the run-up to the tripos examinations.[36] The growth of a fiercely competitive examination system had not been accompanied by any effective teaching provision in Cambridge. Professors were not compelled to give lectures, and some did not even reside.[37] Trinity men were lucky to have some effective lecturers, notably William Hepworth Thompson, whose lectures on Plato drew large and admiring audiences; men in small colleges were seriously disadvantaged in this respect. This was where the choice of a good private tutor (coach) could make all the difference; and Bristed gives a richly detailed account of how this teaching was done. His first coach was Tom Taylor ('Tom Travis') whose informal and vigorous style is captured in Chapter 13.[38] Later on, Bristed took on Henry (later Sir Henry) Maine, who despite his youth (he was two years his pupil's junior) turned out to be an excellent coach, and who became a close friend.[39]

---

[36] See Warwick, *Masters of Theory*, pp. 49–113.

[37] In Ch. 12 Bristed gives some telling details on the (low) attendance at professorial lectures.

[38] Taylor had a colourful career. He was elected to a Trinity fellowship in 1842. Having moved to London, in the mid-1840s he was both Professor of English and a successful comic playwright. His increasingly numerous contributions to *Punch* led eventually to its editorship (1874–80). Taylor also managed to fit in a legal career and work as a civil servant. As a dramatist he was remarkably prolific and several of his plays were performed in the US: Abraham Lincoln was watching his *Our American Cousin* when he was assassinated in 1865. In his third edition (p. 75), Bristed comments, 'He is one of the most prominent playwrights of the period, 1872'.

[39] As we have seen, Bristed named his second son after Maine; and it may be significant that Maine's first son was named Charles (neither Maine's father nor his father-in-law was so named). Henry Sumner Maine was Senior Classic in 1844, and was Regius Professor of Civil Law 1847–54. After moving to London and giving lectures on jurisprudence, in 1861 he produced his most famous book, *Ancient Law*, in which he argued for the development of ideas of social identity from status to contract. The book's success led to his appointment as a legal member of the governing council of India; on his return in 1869 he was elected Corpus Professor of Civil Law at

Towards the end of his book, Bristed turns to his home country, comparing American colleges with English universities and concluding that they are sadly deficient in their teaching and scholarship (Chapters 32–3). On the other hand – and this is one of the most effective and surprising aspects of *Five Years* – a parallel comparison of the moral state of English and American universities constitutes in effect a denunciation of the state of affairs in Cambridge (Chapter 30).[40] Bristed was horrified by the casual acceptance of sexual and other kinds of vice by his fellow-undergraduates. Soon after his arrival at Trinity, another Fellow-Commoner casually suggested to him after dinner that they should go together to Barnwell – the village near Cambridge notorious for its prostitutes. Other examples Bristed gives we might think relatively trivial (for example, applying a moustache to a sleeping man's face with burnt cork), but his indictment is detailed and he is clearly trying to be fair. His account is the more impressive because of the candour with which he admits his own immorality. At his graduation ceremony in 1845 he was meant to kiss the Bible, but he was unhappy about the religious commitment this symbolised and did not let his lips touch the book (p. 227). As he tells us, this did not go unnoticed, and he lost much of his previous moral authority as a result. But it is clear that it was the moral failure itself that entered into his soul, a failure that he never forgot, and which he was honest enough to share with his readers.

Perhaps the most fundamental contrast between Cambridge and American universities identified by Bristed was that between the intense intellectual competition in the former and the emphasis on rhetorical training in speaking and writing at the latter. As his friend 'Tom Travis' explained to

---

Oxford. Maine was knighted in 1871, and became Master of Trinity Hall in 1877; in 1887 he was appointed to the chair of International Law. See G. Feaver, *From Status to Contract: A Biography of Sir Henry Maine, 1822–1888* (London, 1969).

[40] This account was heavily drawn on by Gordon Haight in his essay on Victorian male chastity: G.S. Haight, *George Eliot's Originals and Contemporaries* (Macmillan, 1991), pp. 210–8. Bristed's denunciation, whose truth was simply denied in some quarters, is difficult to evaluate. But another visiting American, Benjamin Moran, had found Cambridge to contain 'more lewd females than any other place of equal size in Great Britain': *The Footpath and Highway; or Wanderings of an American* (Philadelphia, 1853) p. 351. W.G. Clark, in his review in *Fraser's Magazine*, suggested that 'The black sheep are always the most conspicuous of the flock', i.e. Bristed's examples might be accurately drawn but unrepresentative ('Cambridge life according to C.A. Bristed', *Fraser's Magazine* 49 (January 1854), pp. 89–100, at p. 96). For a useful recent study, see P. Howell, 'A private Contagious Diseases Act; prostitution and public space in Victorian Cambridge', *J. Historical Geography* 26 (2000), pp. 376–402.

a puzzled Englishman to whom Bristed had been trying to describe how American colleges functioned, 'It is there just as if we were to consider the President of the Union a greater man than the Senior Wrangler' (p. 109). Bristed himself, when he first appeared at the Cambridge Union, made a considerable impression with his fluent oratory (no doubt helped by his dress – clothes of a foreign cut, a waistcoat emblazoned with the Stars and Stripes, and the lace-encrusted gown of a Trinity Fellow-Commoner).[41]

American and British reception

Bristed's book has had a history which is worth telling in its own right (and to which, indeed, the present edition belongs). We have seen that his earlier articles had raised American hackles; reviewers of *Five Years*, though most of them praised its shrewd analysis and rich detail, had criticised Bristed's egotism, as well as his denigration of American universities. One American reviewer of the first edition commented that

> Although disfigured with a great deal of vanity and egotism, this is a decidedly clever book. It gives the most perfect insight into English university life, both mental and physical, that we have yet had, and is valuable as demonstrating the deficiencies of our own collegiate system.[42]

The same mixture of admiration and derision appears in another American review, which begins:

> Mr Bristed's book contains an intolerable amount of flippancy, slang, and self-conceit. But it also affords much information upon a very interesting topic – information which would be sought in vain elsewhere.[43]

The reviewer is not alone in the US in objecting to Bristed's praise of Cambridge and denigration of American higher education. He points out that Bristed's experience of the latter is almost entirely confined to Yale, and that the American colleges are much poorer than Trinity College Cambridge. A Southern reviewer, whom one might expect to resent the

---

[41] See [Clark], 'Cambridge life', p. 99.
[42] *American Review* 15 (Mar. 1852), p. 283.
[43] 'College education in England and America', *North American Review* 75 (July 1852), pp. 47–83, at p. 47.

Yankee author, was noticeably less judgmental.[44] A more severe note is
sounded in the *Boston Review*, probably by a puritanical Harvard don. Bristed
is praised for his overall achievement: '[The book] gives probably the most
complete view of the interior and daily workings of one of those great
English universities that has ever been given to the public.' As for Bristed's
critique of undergraduate morality, however, 'The author ... has presented
a picture so black and revolting of their vice, that we could hardly dare
to exhibit it at full length in these pages'. But the reviewer is a fair judge,
if severe: 'in his second volume ... he talks like a man and a Christian.'[45]
Another New England reviewer is dismissive on another count:

> It is well that so few of our young men can afford the three or four
> thousand dollars per annum necessary to the support of a Fellow
> Commoner, and well it is that still fewer have the taste to wade
> through so much pedantic drudgery. We do not need this aristocracy
> of scholarship; there is too much real work to be done in our young
> Republic – problems better than Euclid's, worth the solving, presented
> by the advent of every destitute immigrant upon our shores, by every
> cry for want, that is still heard even in our land of plenty.

The same reviewer, however, offers a balanced view of Bristed as stylist
and as egotist:

> Elegant and correct diction is the first excellence of the book; a sort of
> self-glorification, not arising from conceit, but rather from the delight
> of his heart in recollection of what was, perhaps, the pleasantest part
> of his life, makes the first defect.[46]

The range of opinions is a useful reminder that Bristed's criticism of
American institutions and praise of Cambridge varied between North and
South, and within the North might depend on institutional and religious
affiliation.

What of England? It was surely unwise of Bristed to place on his title page
a line from Aristophanes declaring that 'wise men learn much even from

---

[44] 'English Universities', *Southern Quarterly Review* 22 (Oct. 1852), pp. 414–43.

[45] *Boston Review* 2 (March 1862), pp. 134–56: 'English and American university life',
at pp. 140, 147. *Five Years* was reviewed along with Thomas Hughes' *Tom Brown's
Schooldays* and *Tom Brown in Oxford*.

[46] *Sartain's Union Magazine* 10 (Apr. 1852), p. 356.

their enemies', and his friend W.G. Clark of Trinity, for one, was angry at its inclusion.[47] The immediate cause may lie in an unfortunate encounter in New York in 1850, when Bristed lent a large sum ($1000 in all) to a young British officer who subsequently absconded. The officer's father Charles Edward Law, who ironically enough was MP for Cambridge University, refused to honour his son's debt.[48] The incident was the more wounding because it arose from Bristed's making himself a 'proxenos' (ambassador) in New York for visiting Englishmen, at a time when relations between the two countries were often uneasy. A major cause of tension had been the US financial panic of 1837, which had led to bank collapses and the repudiation of debts. Bristed's arrival in Cambridge in 1840 thus came at a difficult time to be an American in Britain. Two of his friends at Trinity had suffered from the bank collapses: we learn in Chapter 7 that Dunbar Heath had lost around £1000, in Chapter 8 that Horatio Mansfield's father had lost £20,000. The wider context of *Five Years* thus includes political and cultural tensions, as well as reciprocal literary accounts.

Bristed's Cambridge readers

The first English readers of Bristed's book included several of his contemporaries at Cambridge, whose comments have been preserved in

---

[47] See the interesting and largely jovial review, 'Cambridge life according to C.A. Bristed. With notes by P. Jenkinson', *Fraser's Magazine* 49 (1854), pp. 89–100, at p. 91. 'Philemon Jenkinson' was identified by the Cambridge antiquarian John Willis Clark as W.G. Clark (no relation): see A.T. Bartholomew, *Catalogue of the Books and Papers … relating to … Cambridge … bequeathed … by John Willis Clark* (Cambridge, 1912), p. 59. W.G. Clark is known to have contributed several articles to *Fraser's*: see p. 157; he is one of Bristed's informants on life in the English public schools (Ch. 23). The author's complaint, on pp. 90–1, that Bristed calls him 'Onesimus Tomkinson' and describes him as red-haired, is a blind: Bristed nowhere writes anything of the kind. Onesimus was the runaway slave whom St Paul sent back to his master Philemon, with a letter (the *Letter to Philemon*). Red hair was commonly associated with immorality in Victorian England, and this was reinforced by the belief that Judas had been red-haired: see R. Altick, *The Presence of the Present: Topical Realism in the Victorian Novel* (Columbus OH, 1991), p. 326. According to a note in T.F. Ellis's copy of *Five Years*, Macaulay was also incensed by Bristed's epigraph.

[48] The tale is told in a brief pamphlet by Bristed entitled *American Hospitality and English Repudiation*, in which his correspondence with Charles Law is reprinted. In Bristed's *The Upper Ten Thousand* (1852), the hero (modelled on Bristed himself) is similarly defrauded by 'Ensign Lawless'.

three marked copies of the second edition.[49] A copy now in Trinity College Library (Adv c.25.24) belonged to George Otto Trevelyan (Trinity 1857), who annotated it extensively, and whose verdict on the book was quoted above. It had previously been owned by Macaulay's friend Thomas Flower Ellis (Trinity 1814); Trevelyan thought it possible that Ellis was responsible for some earlier annotations, though they showed detailed knowledge of Cambridge in the 1840s, well after his time there. If Ellis was indeed the annotator, he may have been drawn on information from his son Francis (Trinity 1842, BA 1846); unless Francis Ellis was himself the annotator. Also in Trinity College Library (LL 696.B.6) is a copy belonging to and annotated, alas only lightly, by William Whewell (Trinity 1812, Master 1841–66). Cambridge University Library holds a copy (Cam.d.852.12) annotated by Frederick Bowring (Trinity 1840); this copy, later owned by the university Registrary and antiquarian John Willis Clark, also contains a few annotations by Henry Hodgson (Trinity 1834). There are also copies of the third edition of 1873 annotated by Frederick Whitting (King's 1856: King's College Library, NW.CU.T.Bri) and by the historian John Saltmarsh (King's 1926: Cambridge City Library, C.36.9).

Through the comments these men wrote in their copies of *Five Years* we gain a detailed picture of the response of several generations of Bristed's Cambridge readers. This is especially interesting in the case of his contemporary Bowring and of Hodgson, who though older than Bristed was a fellow of Trinity while he was there (1840–5). The later annotators, including Whitting and Trevelyan, at times report on changes which had occurred since Bristed first wrote (as he himself did in his third edition); but they also draw on a powerful corpus of local and institutional memory. Many comments are brief, usually identifying the individuals veiled by Bristed under pseudonyms, but occasionally direct or reported memories are recorded, throwing a light on the text which would otherwise be lost. At times the annotators disagree with one another, for example about the identity of an individual. At other times they disagree, sometimes violently, with Bristed himself; most strikingly, with his denigration of George Denman in Chapter 8: 'The Barnwell girls [i.e., prostitutes] know him well, and the Dons look askew at him' (p. 55). On reading this, Trevelyan was moved to write, 'A lie Charles Bristed. I am proud of having known Denman well. A more preposterous characterisation never was written'.

---

[49] All three editions were published by Putnam in New York; very few copies of the first edition (half of which was destroyed by fire) seem to have reached Britain. The third edition of 1873 was also published by Sampson Low in London.

The annotations are thus of interest in several ways. They have a historical interest in enabling us to identify, almost without exception, all those to whom Bristed refers. But they also reveal a local tradition, focused on a shared institutional loyalty to college and university, of reading a richly detailed text which is both descriptive and critical of Cambridge.

The annotations are identified in the footnotes to this edition as follows: B = Bowring; E = (?) Ellis; H = Hodgson; S = Saltmarsh; T = Trevelyan; W = Whitting. All other footnotes are Bristed's, except for my own, which are distinguished by [square brackets]. Individuals are usually identified by the annotators simply by surname. I have where possible supplied their colleges and dates of matriculation (e.g. Trinity 1840), assuming that readers interested in pursuing them further will do so via the *Oxford Dictionary of National Biography* in some cases, and in almost every case in J. and J. A. Venn's *Alumni Cantabrigienses, Part II: 1752–1900* (Cambridge, 1940–54).

Note on the text

The charge of 'vanity and egotism' levelled in the *American Review* may have been prompted by Bristed's account of his own education at Yale in Chapter 2 – for which he himself apologises, though arguing that the reader needs to know about it. Another target, however, may well have been the enormous appendix, amounting to a third of the whole book, in which Bristed reprinted in full not only several Cambridge examination papers, but also nine of his own prize-winning student essays and declamations.[50] These swelled the two-volume first edition to a total of nearly 900 pages. In the one-volume second edition, the Appendix was abandoned, but this was still a substantial book of 441 closely-printed pages; the third and final edition of 1873 included both excisions and additional matter and ran to 572 pages.[51] The present edition is based on the text of the first edition of 1852. The lengthy Appendix has been omitted, but Bristed's additions to his third edition have been included. Other, smaller, omissions are noted as they occur in the text. Bristed's expansive view of his book, his interest in classical scholarship and, it must be said, his vanity, led him to include

---

[50] In his *Fraser's* review, W. G. Clark kindly ascribes this to a charming naivety, adding 'I got some prize essays and poems in my time, but I would not reprint them for a good deal' ('Cambridge life', p. 96).

[51] Bristed's preface is dated July 1872, and the Library of Congress registration is dated the same year; but the title pages of copies known to me are dated either 1873 or 1874.

lengthy passages of his own and others' student writing, in English and in Greek, which for most readers are likely to be uninteresting or inaccessible. Others may turn to copies of the original. Greek passages have been translated, transliterated or omitted. The additional matter included in this edition consists of the introduction, annotation and an index – badly needed, and lacking in all the original editions – and a bibliography of Bristed's published work which will, I hope, make it easier to pursue future assessments of an unduly neglected figure. It makes no claim to be comprehensive – an almost impossible aim in the case of such a prolific occasional writer – but does, I believe, give a representative account of his output.

Acknowledgements

In Cambridge, my alma mater as it was Bristed's, I have benefited from the help and local knowledge of John Pickles and Jonathan Smith. For the scanning of the original text I am obliged to Beatrix Bown and John Dawson. The award of a Jackson Brothers visiting fellowship enabled me to work on Bristed's papers at the Beinecke Library, Yale University, in October 2005: my thanks in particular to Una Belau, Christina Kraus and Frank Turner. Help and encouragement of various kinds have been given by Eileen Curran, Daniel Hartwig, Ian Jackson, Bob Kaster, William R. Massa jr and David Southern. The decisive advice of Patrick Leary, Sheldon Rothblatt and Gill Sutherland was much valued (and acted on). The late John Betts (characteristically) took a chance in agreeing to publish this book; Simon Baker and Anna Henderson have been supportive in taking it through the process of production.

Bibliography

A listing of all secondary works referred to in the Introduction and in the editor's footnotes to Bristed's text.

Abraham, C.J., *The Unity of History; or Outlines of Lectures on Ancient and Modern History, Considered on the Principles of the Church of England* (Eton, 1845).

Allen, P., *The Cambridge Apostles: The Early Years* (Cambridge, 1978).

Altick, R., *The Presence of the Present: Topical Realism in the Victorian Novel* (Columbus OH, 1991).

Annan, N.G., *Leslie Stephen: His Thought and Character in Relation to his Time* (London, 1951).

Anon., 'A bit of our boyhood', *Fraser's Magazine* 43 (1851), pp. 631–42.

Arnold, R., *The Whiston Matter. The Rev. Robert Whiston versus the Dean and Chapter of Rochester* (London, 1961).

Barham, R.H., *The Ingoldsby Legends* (London, 1840).

Bartholomew, A.T., *Catalogue of the Books and Papers … relating to … Cambridge … bequeathed … by John Willis Clark* (Cambridge, 1912).

Beverley, R.M., *A Letter to His Highness the Duke of Gloucester, Chancellor, on the Present Corrupt State of the University of Cambridge* (London, 1833).

Bieri, S.J., *Percy Bysshe Shelley … Youth's Unextinguished Fire, 1792–1816* (Newark DE, 2005).

Bowerman, S.G., 'Charles Astor Bristed', *Dictionary of American Biography* 3 (1929), pp. 53–4.

Briggs, W.W. (ed.), *Biographical Dictionary of North American Classicists* (New York, 1994).

Brock, M.G., and M.C. Curthoys (eds), *The History of the University of Oxford, Vol. VI: Nineteenth-Century Oxford, Part 1* (Oxford, 1997).

Burrows, E.G., and M. Wallace, *Gotham: A History of New York City to 1898* (Oxford, 1999).

Bury, M.E., and J.D. Pickles, *Romilly's Cambridge Diary 1842–1847* (Cambridge, 1994).

Cayley, C.B., *The Vision of St Brahamus touching the Restoration of Monasteries* (Cambridge, 1843).

[Clark, W.G.], 'Cambridge life according to C.A. Bristed, with notes by P. Jenkinson', *Fraser's Magazine* 49 (January 1854), pp. 89–100.

Diamond, A. (ed.), *The Victorian Achievement of Sir Henry Maine* (Cambridge, 1991).

Drury, H. (ed.), *Arundines Cami, sive musarum Cantabrigiensium lusus canori* (Cambridge, 1841; 6th edn. 1865).

Duke, A.D., *Importing Oxbridge: English Residential Colleges and American Universities* (New Haven, 1996).

Empson, W., Review of A.P. Stanley's *Life and Correspondence of Dr. Arnold*, *Edinburgh Review* 81 (Jan. 1845), pp. 190–234.

Evans, J.H., *The First Three Sections of Newton's* Principia (Cambridge, 1834).

Everett, E., 'Biographical memoir', *Works of Daniel Webster*, vol. I (Boston, 1851).

Everett, W., *On the Cam* (Cambridge, MA, 1865).

Farrow, S., 'Debating and its discontents', *Language and Communication* 26 (2006), pp. 117–28.

Feaver, G.S., *From Status to Contract: A Biography of Sir Henry Maine, 1822–1888* (London, 1969).

Fidler, I., *Observations on Professions, Literature, Manners and Emigration in the United States and Canada in 1832* (London and New York, 1833).

Galton, F., *On Hereditary Genius: An Inquiry into its Laws and Consequences* (London, 1869).

Garland, M.McM., *Cambridge before Darwin: The Ideal of a Liberal Education, 1800–1860* (Cambridge, 1980).

Greeley, H., *Hints Towards Reforms, in Lectures, Addresses, and Other Writings* (New York, 1850).

Grote, G., *History of Greece*, 12 vols (London, 1846–1856).

Haight, G.S., *George Eliot's Originals and Contemporaries* (London, 1991).

Hall, B.H., *A Collection of College Words and Phrases* (Cambridge MA, 1851).

Huber, V.A., *The English Universities*, 3 vols, tr. F.W. Newman (London, 1843).

Irving, W. ['D. Knickerbocker'], *History of New York from the Beginning of the World to the End of the Dutch Dynasty. A New Edition* (New York and Philadelphia, 1809).

Kolb, G.J., 'Charles Astor Bristed, Henry Hallam and Tennyson's "Timbuctoo"', *Tennyson Research Bulletin* 4 (1986), pp. 197–210.

Lewis, G.C., *An Essay on the Influence of Authority in Matters of Opinion* (London, 1849).

Lewis, T., *Plato Against the Atheists, or the Tenth Book of the Dialogue on Laws* (New York, 1845).

Lubenow, W.C., *The Cambridge Apostles, 1820–1914* (Cambridge, 1997).

Maffit, J.N., *Rev. John N. Maffit, and his Late Unfortunate Marriage, a Narrative of All the Facts Relative to his Marriage with Miss Frances Smith of Brooklyn, N.Y. – Their Private Correspondence and the Cause of her Death, as Published in the Police Gazette* (New York, 1848).

Mahony, F., *The Reliques of Father Prout* (London, 1836).

Maxwell-Lyte, H.C., *History of Eton College* (London, 1875).

Mencken, H.L., *The American Language* (New York, 1919).

Mitford, W., *History of Greece*, 10 vols (London, 1784–1818).

Neale, J.M., and B. Webb, *The Symbolism of Churches and Church Ornaments* (Leeds, 1843).

Newsome, D., *Two Classes of Men: Platonism and English Romantic Thought* (London, 1974).

[Paley, W.], *Gradus ad Cantabrigiam* (London, 1803).

Porter, H.C., 'A Harvard Unitarian in Victorian Cambridge', *Journal of Ecclesiastical History* 53 (2002) pp. 527–44.

Rogers, H., 'Recent developments of Puseyism', *Edinburgh Review* 80 (Oct. 1844), pp. 309–75.

Roget, J.L., *A Cambridge Scrap-Book. Containing in a Pictorial Form a Report of the Manners, Customs, Humours and Pastimes of the University of Cambridge ... By a Special Commissioner, Appointed by Himself. With an Appendix of Papers on Applied Mathematics* (Cambridge, 1859).

Satthianadhan, S., *Four Years in an English University; With a Chapter on the Indian Civil Service Examination by A.C. Dutt* (Madras, 1890).

Searby, P., 'A New Yorker in early Victorian Cambridge', *Cambridge* 33 (Winter 1993–4), pp. 58–63.

————, *History of the University of Cambridge, III: 1750–1870* (Cambridge, 1997).

Sewell, W., *An Introduction to the Dialogues of Plato* (London, 1841).

Shepard, C.U., *Treatise on Mineralogy* (New Haven, 1832–5).

Sheppard, C.A., 'Benjamin Dann Walsh: pioneer entomologist and proponent of Darwinian theory', *Annual Review of Entomology* 49 (2004), pp. 1–25.

Shipley, A.E., *'J': A Memoir of John Willis Clark* (London, 1913).

Smith, J., and C.A. Stray (eds), *Cambridge in the 1830s: The Letters of Alexander Chisholm Gooden, 1831–1841* (Woodbridge, 2003).

Smith, S., 'Public schools of England', *Edinburgh Review* 16 (1810), pp. 326–34.

Stewart, D., *Outlines of Moral Philosophy* (Edinburgh and London, 1793).

Stray, C.A., 'The first century of the Classical Tripos', in id. (ed.), *Classics in Cambridge* (*Proceedings of the Cambridge Philological Society*, Supplementary Vol. 24), 1999, pp. 1–14.

————, 'Curriculum and style in the collegiate university: Classics in nineteenth-century Oxbridge', *History of Universities* 16 (2001), pp. 183–218.

————, 'Charles Astor Bristed, 1820–74', *Oxford Dictionary of National Biography* (online release, October 2004).

————, 'From oral to written examination: Oxford, Cambridge and Dublin 1700–1914', *History of Universities* 20 (2005), pp. 76–130.

Thirlwall, J.C., *History of Greece*, 8 vols (London, 1835–44).

Thompson, S.P., *Life of William Thomson, Lord Kelvin* (London, 1910).

Turner, F.M., *The Greek Heritage in Victorian Britain* (New Haven, 1981).

Venn, J. and J.A., *Alumni Cantabrigienses, Part II: 1752–1900* (Cambridge, 1940–54).

Waite, J. (ed.), *Latin and Greek Verse* [by T.S. Evans] (Cambridge, 1893).

Warwick, A., *Masters of Theory: Cambridge and the Rise of Mathematical Physics* (Chicago, 2003).

Whately, R., *Elements of Rhetoric* (London, 1828).

Whewell, W., *Of a Liberal Education in General: and with Particular Reference to the Leading Studies of the University of Cambridge, Part 1* (London, 1845).

Whibley, C., *In Cap and Gown: Three Centuries of Cambridge Wit*, 2nd edn (London, 1890).

White, A.D., *Autobiography* (New York, 1905).

Winstanley, D.A., *Early Victorian Cambridge* (Cambridge, 1940).

To Theodore D. Woolsey,
President of Yale College, &c., &c.

Dear Sir:

It is now fourteen years since I fell under your notice, and
you did me the honor to take an interest in my welfare,
which subsequent occurrences authorize me to regard as still
subsisting. I know of no one to whom I can dedicate this
book with more propriety than yourself, or by whose perusal
of it I shall feel more honored. If *you* read it, the trouble it has
cost me will not have been thrown away.

Very truly yours,

C. A. BRISTED.

Preface

I write this book for three reasons:

First, very little is accurately known in this country about the English Universities.

Secondly, most of what we hear respecting those institutions, comes through the medium of popular novels and other light literature, frequently written by non-University men, and almost always conveying an erroneous and unfavorable idea of the Universities.

Thirdly and principally, there are points in an English education which may be studied with profit, and from which we may draw valuable hints.

Few Americans have the opportunity of growing up into manhood among half a generation of the most highly educated class in England; nor is it indeed altogether desirable that many should have. I myself owed it to an accident. There are few persons among us qualified by their knowledge of the subject to do it justice. Had I ever seen even a decent review article on English University education, this book would not have been written.

It has been my object to give a picture of English University life just as it is; to do which correctly, I have been obliged to mingle gaieties and gravities. Should the reader not assent to my conclusions, he will at any rate have a tolerable idea of the facts. The same motive – a desire to depict accurately what I saw and experienced, and the impressions which such a life makes on an American – has obliged me to speak of myself more frequently than is altogether pleasant for either reader or author.

Of the bad arrangement and want of system displayed in the book, I am as conscious as the severest critic can be. These faults must be attributed to want of ability, not want of care. To deal with the minutiae of a system so complicated as that of several independent Colleges combined in one University – rejecting what is unimportant, and lucidly setting forth what is worthy of remark – becomes an extremely difficult task where everything is so different from the corresponding arrangements among ourselves. My original intention was to present merely a series of sketches, without any attempt at filling up the connecting links throughout. I began the sketches, and two different Magazines at different times began to publish them, but were very soon afraid to go on, because I did not pretend to conceal our inferiority to the English in certain branches of liberal education. I then resolved to refrain, not merely from publishing, but from writing any more, until as many years as I passed in England had elapsed since my return thence. With the exception, therefore, of the first nine chapters, the whole of this work has been written during the past summer, and I can truly say that my opinions on all the matters discussed in it have undergone no important change for the last five years; all my observation has tended to confirm them.

Should this book fall into the hands of any Cambridge man, he may condemn it as abounding in petty and uninteresting details. If so, I would commend to his attention a brief apologue:

An Arab traveller had occasion to visit London. On arriving there his attention was attracted by a great crowd in the street. He drew near, and found to his surprise and disappointment that the object of Cockney curiosity was a *camel*, belonging to the caravan of some Barnum of the day. He wrote home to his friends, 'the frivolity and childishness of these English are intense. Yesterday I beheld a large concourse of people staring at an ordinary camel, that one of our boys would not have turned his head to look at.'

Horneshook, Hellgate, Sept. 1, 1851.

1

First Impressions
of Cambridge [1840]

The Building with a Tower is the "Freshman's Church". There are offices there daily. It abounds in good works, and occasionally casts out a (printer's) devil.

The sage council not being able to determine upon any plan for the building of their City, the cows, in a laudable fit of patriotism, took it under their peculiar charge; and, as they went to and fro from pasture, established paths through the bushes, on each side of which the good folks built their houses.

Knickerbocker's New York.[1]

And round the cool green courts there ran a row
Of cloisters, branched like mighty woods,
    Echoing all night to that sonorous flow
    Of spouted fountain floods.

Tennyson, Palace of Art

Imagine the most irregular town that can be imagined, streets of the

---

[1] [The *History of New York* published in 1809 by Washington Irving under the pseudonym of Diedrich Knickerbocker.] (**Editor's note**: All footnotes in square brackets are the editor's; see the Introduction, p. xxix.)

very crookedest kind, twisting about like those in a nightmare, and not unfrequently bringing you back to the same point you started from. Some of these tortuous lanes are without trottoirs, like the streets of old Continental towns; but it is more common to find a passage or short street all *sidewalk* – as we call what the English call causeway – without any carriage road.[2] The houses are low and antique; sometimes their upper stories project out into, and over the narrow pathway, making it still narrower; and their lower stories are usually occupied as shops – tailors and booksellers being the predominant varieties. Every now and then your road passes over a muddy little river, not larger than a tolerable canal, which rambles through and about the town in all sorts of ways, so that in *whatever* direction you walk from *any* point, you are pretty sure to come to a bridge before long. Such is the town of Cambridge – the *bridge* over the *Cam*.

Among these narrow, ugly, and dirty streets, are tumbled in, as it were at random (for the whole place looks as if it had been dancing to Amphion's music,[3] and he had left off in the middle of a very complicated figure) some of the most beautiful academical buildings in the world. However their style of architecture may vary, according to the period at which they were built or rebuilt, they agree in one essential feature – all the colleges are constructed in quadrangles or courts; and, as in course of years the population of every college, except one,[4] has outgrown the original quadrangle, new courts have been added, so that the larger foundations have three, and one (St. John's) has four courts. Sometimes the 'old court', or primitive part of the building, presents a handsome front to the largest street near it; but frequently, as if to show its independence of, and contempt for, the town, it retires from the street altogether, showing the passer-by only its ugliest wall, and smallest, shabbiest gate. This is particularly the case with the very largest and most distinguished colleges.

You enter, then, by a portal neither particularly large nor very striking in its appearance, but rather the reverse, into a spacious and elegant square.

---

[2]   [The oldest English word for a raised firm surface across soft ground is *causey*; this became *causeyway* and then *causeway*. The modern term *pavement* was in use when Bristed wrote, and it is not clear why he did not use it.]

[3]   [Amphion, son of Zeus by the Queen of Thebes, was commissioned to build the city walls. Hermes gave him a golden lyre, which when played made the stones move into place.]

[4]   Downing College, which only went into operation in 1800, and may be considered still in its infancy. (**Editor's note:** All footnotes without brackets are Bristed's except for those qualified by an initial (B), (E) etc. See the Introduction, p. xxix.)

There are neat grass-plots and walks, a fountain in the centre; on one side stands a well proportioned chapel, in one corner you catch a glimpse through a tantalizing grating of a beautiful garden, appropriated to the delectation of the authorities. In a second court you find sounding and venerable cloisters, perhaps a veritable structure of monkish times, if not, a satisfactory imitation of that period. And as you look on the walls, here rich with sculptured ornament, there covered with trailing and festooning ivy, the theory and idea of the college edifice begin to strike you – its front is inside for its own benefits; it turns its back upon the vulgar outside. But you have not yet fathomed and sounded its spirit of seclusion. The entries are narrow and low; the staircases narrow and tortuous; the iron-bound doors, closed by some mysterious spring, or open only to show another door within, look like the portals of a feudal dungeon. But up those break-neck stair-cases, and inside those formidable doors (sometimes with the additional preliminary of a small, dark passage), are luxurious suites of rooms, not exactly like those of a Parisian hotel or a 'double-house' in the Fifth Avenue,[5] but quite as beautiful and much more comfortable. The apartments and the entrance seem made in inverse proportion to each other; a mere hole in the wall sometimes leads you to half a house of rooms; and most cosy rooms they are, with their prodigiously thick walls that keep out the cold in winter and heat (when there is any) in summer, their impregnable *sporting-doors* that defy alike the hostile dun and the too friendly 'fast man', and all their quaint appurtenances, such as book-cases of the true scholastic sort, sunk into and forming part of the wall, so that it would not be easy to appropriate them or the space they occupy to any other purpose – queer little nooks of studios, just large enough to hold a man in an arm-chair and a big dictionary; unexpected garrets, which the very occupant of the rooms never goes into without an air of enterprise and mystery, and which the old priests used for oratories – perhaps; the modern Cantabs keep their wine in them.

Late in October, 1840, a young New Yorker was losing himself among the impracticable streets, and admiring the remarkable edifices of Cambridge. He was surprised at the number and variety of the academical buildings and their distance from one another; for, though knowing that the different colleges were separate and independent foundations, connected only by a few general ties, he had expected something like contiguity of location,

---

[5] [One of the ways of measuring social status on Fifth Avenue in New York – where Bristed himself had a house at one point – was the width of frontage on the street.]

and was not prepared to find them scattered over an area of some miles. Nor was it without some degree of curiosity that he inspected such of the population as he met, a curiosity which they were not slow to retaliate with abundance of eye-glasses. Dressed in the last Gothamite[6] fashion (then, as now, a reproduction of the preceding year's Parisian), with the usual accessories of gold chain and diamond pin, the whole surmounted by a blue cloth cloak, he certainly bore no resemblance, in point of costume, to any of the academical public whom he encountered. The Cantab's garb generally consists of a not too new black coat (frock or cutaway), trousers of some substantial stuff, grey or plaid, and a stout waistcoat, frequently of the same pattern as the trousers. Straps[7] are unknown to him, and instead of boots he wears easy low-heeled shoes, for greater convenience in fence and ditch jumping, and other feats of extempore gymnastics which diversify his 'constitutionals'. The only showy part of his attire is the cravat, which is apt to be blue or some other decided color,[8] and fastened in front with a large gold-headed pin. During the middle of the day this outfit is completed by a hat of the average ugliness of English hats, but before 12 a.m., and after 4 p.m., you must superadd the academical costume. This consists of a gown, varying in color and ornament according to the wearer's college and rank but generally black, not unlike an ordinary clerical gown, and a square-topped cap, which fits close to the head like a truncated helmet, while the covered board which forms the crown measures about a foot diagonally across. It is not by any means a *sine qua non* that the cap and gown should be in good order and condition; the latter is often sadly torn and faded, while the former retains but few traces of its original form after the rough usage it has undergone. To steal caps and gowns is no more an offence against the eighth commandment in Cambridge, than to steal umbrellas

---

[6] [That is, New York fashion. 'Gotham' was a name applied to New York by Washington Irving, a frequent guest at the nearby house of Bristed's grandfather John Jacob Astor; since 1941, it has become well known as the home city of Batman.]

[7] [Loops attached to the bottom of trouser-legs, which passed under the waist of boots.]

[8] Words of this class I spell without the u, because the practice of good writers varies sufficiently to leave their orthography an open question and allow any person to adopt whichever form he prefers; not because Webster, who is no authority at all among scholars, spells them thus. [The American lexicographer Noah Webster, who had previously advocated spelling 'onur' and then 'honour', ending up with a patriotic desire to make American different from British English: hence 'honor'. See E.J. Monaghan, *A Common Language: Noah Webster's Blue-Back Speller* (Hamden CT, 1983), pp. 109–30.]

is with us – an additional reason for their appearance being little thought of. In one thing only is the Cantab particular – the one nicety of every English gentleman, however clumsy or shabby the rest of his dress may be – his linen is always faultless. A dirty shirt, or even a badly got up one, is a phenomenon in the University. Peculiar as the academic costume is, its effect is by no means unbecoming; on the contrary, it adds, in a majority of cases, to the dignity and style of the wearer.

Nor must it be supposed that the gownsmen are thin, study-worn, consumptive-looking individuals. The stranger's first impression was, that he had never seen so fine a body of young men together. Almost every man looked able and ready to row eight miles, walk twelve, or ride twenty 'across country', at the shortest notice, and to eat half a leg of mutton and drink a quart of ale after it. One would hardly suspect them to be students at all, did not the number of glasses hint that those who carried them had impaired their sight by late reading.

The young American who noted these particulars felt somewhat bashful among a crowd of strangers, even as he does now on making his appearance before you, reader. Yet it is necessary that he should go on, however painful it may be to his modesty, to tell how he came there, and for what purpose, which he will do as briefly as possible in the next chapter.

2

Some Preliminaries,
Rather Egotistical but
Very Necessary [1835–9]

I was fifteen years old when I went to New Haven to enter the Freshman class,[1] at Yale College. In the school where I prepared, one of the masters was an Englishman,[2] and the instruction given partly on the English model. I had been fitted for Columbia College, the standard for the Freshman class in which institution was then nearly equal to that for the Sophomore[3] at *Yale*. (I never met a New Englander who knew this, or could be made to believe it, but it is perfectly true notwithstanding.) The start which I had thus obtained confirmed me in the habits of idleness to which a boy just emancipated from school is prone, when he has nothing immediately before him to excite his ambition. During the first year I did little but read novels

---

[1] Or Donking class. (B) (**Editor's note**: All footnotes followed by (B), (E), (H), (S), (T) or (W) are the editor's transcriptions of other annotations; see the Introduction, p. xxix.)

[2] [Henry Herbert (Caius 1825), scion of an aristocratic family and possibly a remittance man, taught at Revd Huddart's Classical School 1831–9. He went on to be a pioneering professional author (on field sports and hunting).]

[3] 2nd year class. (B) [Bristed's opinion of the relative merits of Columbia and Yale is also aired in his discussion of American colleges: see ch. 32.]

and attend debating societies; and the comparison of my experience with that of others leads me to conclude that this is the case with most boys who enter well prepared at a New England College; they go backwards rather than forwards the first year. In the second year came on a great deal of mathematics, laborious rather than difficult; much of it consisted in mere mechanical working of examples in trigonometry and mensuration, which were nearly as great a bore to the best mathematicians in the class as to the worst. I never had any love for or skill in pure science, and my health, moreover, being none of the best, I very early in the Sophomore year gave up all thoughts of obtaining high honors, and settled down contentedly among the twelve or fifteen who are bracketed,[4] after the first two or three, as 'English Orations'. There were four prizes, one in each year, which could be obtained by classics alone, and of these I was fortunate enough to gain three. But they were very imperfect tests; indeed there was at that time no direct means of determining who was the best, or second, or third, classical scholar in any class.

Most of our young countrymen are eager to rush into their destined profession immediately on leaving college, at the age of eighteen or nineteen. Several of my contemporaries did not wait for Commencement day to begin, nominally at least, their professional studies; but I was by no means in a hurry to finish my education, thinking that a long start is often the safest, especially as I was looking forward to a profession which, above all others, should be entered on after much deliberation and mature judgment. Meaning, then, with God's help, to be a clergyman, I wished first to make myself a scholar, and for this purpose resolved to spend some time at a European University. But when it came to starting, my courage failed me; I was afraid to expose my ignorance abroad, and determined to stay at home another year. This year I would willingly have spent in my native city, as affording more advantages for study; but those who had the disposal of me thought it best that I should remain at New Haven, where accordingly I took up my quarters again as a resident graduate – a very rare animal in those parts. Poor Mason,[5] who was to have been our

---

4   [That is, regarded as being roughly equal. Bracketing of candidates, as we shall see, was a vital and often contested part of the Cambridge marking system.]

5   [Ebenezer Porter Mason, born in 1819, like Bristed entered Yale in 1835; he died in 1840. According to *Memorials of Eminent Yale Men* (1914) II, pp. 87–8, he was a 'youthful genius' who created an astonishing impression among his contemporaries. Beginning in the summer of 1838, he and some of his classmates built a 12-inch telescope with a focal length of 14 feet, at the time the largest telescope in the U.S.

great American astronomer, was my only companion in that position. The experience of that year fully justifies me in asserting, that if I wished to unmake a partially formed scholar, and to divert the attention of a young man who had a taste that way from such studies, I would send him to reside in no place sooner than in a New England college town. There was no one able to instruct me or inclined to sympathize with me, except two or three gentlemen whose professional duties in the college rendered it impossible for them to give me any regular assistance; but there were plenty of debating societies all about, and no end of young debaters. Without being considered much of a 'speaker' or 'writer' as an under-graduate, I had figured to some extent in the *Yale Literary*,[6] and had just attained that *beau jour de la vie* when a young man gets his first 'piece' into a city magazine. All this fostered the habits of semi-literary idleness which the (so-called) studies of the senior year, appear purposely framed to encourage. Moreover, I formed rather an intimate acquaintance with a Mississippian (it was before the days of repudiation) who was always anxious to talk politics, and we used to read about a dozen newspapers a day, and throw the contents of them at each other. When it is stated that I was an ultra abolition Whig and he a slaveholding Democrat, the quantity of belligerent nonsense we interchanged, and the valuable result of our discussions may be easily imagined. The only tangible residuum that I ever realized from our debates was a pretty large bill for cakes, ice-cream, and sherry-cobblers.[7] Indeed, so put to it was I for some daily work to balance me, as it were, and give me regular habits of study, that for the last three months of the year I joined the Law School, and then finding what I ought to have known before, that I should never make any progress in scholarship by myself at New Haven, I packed my trunks for England. Still it would be unjust to myself to say that I had absolutely wasted the twelve months. They were only comparatively lost. I did about as much in them as I ought to have done in three or four. I had broken ground in Juvenal, Thucydides, Aristophanes, and Pindar,

---

He won special admiration from Sir John Herschel for a paper of 'Observations on Nebulae'. Mason was commemorated by his professor, Denison Olmsted (see p. 339), in *Life and Writings of Ebenezer Porter Mason; Interspersed with Hints to Parents and Instructors on the Training and Education of a Child of Genius* (1842).]

[6]   [See Bibliography 2, 1838–41.]

[7]   [A drink combining sherry, soda, lemon and crushed ice, which Bristed proudly claimed to have introduced to Cambridge – see his account on pp. 148–50. In France *un sherry-cobbler* was 'much consumed in the early novels of Jean-Paul Sartre': P. Thody and H. Evans, *Faux-Amis and Key Words* (London, 1985), p. 180.]

authors who then seldom entered into the reading of an American college student: on the whole, it may fairly be said that I was a favorable specimen of a graduate from a New England College, and rather above the average than below it. Of mathematics I *knew* only a little Euclid and algebra, having gone through the college course of Mechanics, Conic sections, &c., to as much purpose as some travellers go through various countries. As to the rest of my education and accomplishments, they were the usual ones of an American student; that is to say, I could talk a little French and Spanish, and read a little German, had a boarding-school girl's knowledge of the names and rudimentary formulae of two or three sciences, could write newspaper articles in prose or verse, had a strong tendency to talk politics, and never saw a crowd of people together without feeling as if I should like to get up and make them a speech about things in general. I had read abundance of novels, poetry, and reviews, a fair share of English history, and a great deal of what the school books and the newspaper reporters call 'specimens of eloquence'. I had a supreme opinion of my country (except in matters of scholarship), and a pretty good opinion of myself. To complete the list, it should be added, that I could black my own boots, and, on a pinch, wash my own handkerchiefs. In short, with the exception of easiness of manner and presence of mind (two qualities in which I have always been deficient), I made a very tolerable representative for the reading section of Young America to send among English scholars.[8] It is very awkward to write these things about one's self, but it seems impossible to dispense with them. In the course of this book, different standards of education, and the comparative knowledge of instructors, as well as pupils, in different places, will be very freely spoken of; and the reader who comes to these comparisons will naturally ask, what were my qualifications for forming

---

[8] [Trevelyan comments, 'That was not Macaulay's impression on the only occasion that he met Bristed.' In his journal for 19 June 1850, Macaulay wrote: 'Breakfast party Prescott, Mahon, Lord Carlisle – Young Hallam, Milnes – a raffish Yankee named Bristed intruded himself – he had been introduced to me years ago by young Campbell and must, I think, have got scent of this breakfast. For otherwise he would hardly, ill bred and impertinent as he is, have come at such a time in the morning, and have forced himself on me when he knew that I had guests. It was all I could do to be civil – though educated here at Cambridge he had the vilest nasal twang and all the manners of a thorough Jonathan.' ('Jonathan', or 'Brother Jonathan', a common term for Americans in 19th-century England.) My thanks to William Thomas, whose edition of Macaulay's Journal was published by Pickering and Chatto in 2008.]

any opinion on these subjects at all. And unless I tell him, it would not be easy for him to find out; for though the internal evidence of this book may sufficiently expose my fitness or unfitness for the task at present, still in order to estimate my progress or profit at the University he must know something of the foundation I had to build upon, which such indirect internal evidence would not supply.[9]

---

[9] A most interesting account to those who have known Americans for half a century. He may have been conceited; but he had real self-knowledge. (T)

3

Introduction to College Life

Having laid in a stock of necessaries (according to the suggestions of your tradesmen) it will save you trouble to hand them over at once to the custody of your Bedmaker & Gyp.

Disciplinis bonis operam dato.
Cambridge statutes.

The first thing that the American reader has to impress on his mind is, that the several Colleges are distinct and independent corporations. They are on different foundations, that is to say, the funds which support them are derived from different sources; their officers are distinct, their lecture-room subjects different, though with a general resemblance; their very gowns vary. The confederation of these independent corporations constitutes the University, which may, in its relation to the colleges composing it, be compared to our Federal Government in its relation to the separate States with this important historical difference, however, that the Colleges sprang into existence *subsequent* to the founding of the University. Indeed, the only practical connexion that the Under-graduate usually has with the University in its corporate capacity (unless he should be of a riotous turn, so as to bring himself under the Proctor's notice) consists in his previous examination, alias the 'Little Go',[1] and his final examination for a degree, with or without honors. Robinson, of Trinity, may be three years in the University with Brown, of Corpus, and never come in contact with him, or be aware of his existence, till in the last Long Vacation, when he is putting on all steam and 'coaching' violently for the Classical Tripos, he hears suddenly one day at a wine party that 'Bennedy has a Corpus man reading with him, who is likely to be among the first five'. Then, for the first time, has Brown an existence for him.[2]

When, therefore, a boy, or, as we should call him, a young man, leaves his school, public or private, at the age of eighteen or nineteen, and 'goes up' to the University, he necessarily goes up to some particular College, and the first academical authority he makes acquaintance with in the order of things is the College Tutor. This gentleman has usually taken high honors either in Classics or Mathematics, and one of his duties is naturally to lecture – only you may be sure that if he has a turn for Classics he is not set to lecture on Mathematics, or *vice versa*, as used to be the case at Yale.[3] But this by no means constitutes the whole or forms the most important part of his functions. He is the medium of all the students' pecuniary relations with the College. He sends in their accounts every term, and receives the money through his banker; nay more, he takes in the bills of their tradesmen, and settles them also. Further, he has the disposal of the college rooms, and assigns them to their respective occupants. When I speak of the College Tutor, it must not be supposed that one man is equal to all this work in a large college – Trinity, for instance, which usually numbers four hundred under-graduates in residence. A large college has usually two Tutors – Trinity has three – and the students are equally divided among them – *on*

---

[1] [The Previous Examination (the official title – previous, that is, to the Senate House or degree examination) was a multi-subject test first examined in 1824. The Oxford equivalent was Responsions (1808).]

[2] [Brown and Robinson: with Jones, the standard names in the period for generic reference; as in G.C. Lewis's 1862 spoof *Inscriptio antiqua: in agro Bruttio nuper reperta edidit et interpretatus est Johannes Brownius*. Bennedy: George Kennedy of St John's, a leading classical coach. The pseudonym may also hint at his more famous brother Benjamin Kennedy, headmaster of Shrewsbury School and later (1867–89) Regius professor of Greek at Cambridge.]

[3] Except at King's. Shilleto who did not know the multiplication table was for some years their Maths lecturer. (B) [Richard Shilleto, Trinity 1828, 2nd Classic 1832, fellow of Peterhouse 1867; a leading classical coach. He had scraped through the Mathematical Tripos as 'Wooden Spoon', i.e. at the bottom of the honours list.]

their sides the phrase is – without distinction of year, or, as we should call it, of *class*. The jurisdiction of the rooms is divided in like manner. The Tutor is supposed to stand *in loco parentis* – but having sometimes more than a hundred young men under him, he cannot discharge his duties in this respect very thoroughly, nor is it generally expected that he should.

To the Tutor, then, you go in October. Your name has been on the books since July. Mine was not, as I was a regular stranger. But that is merely a form. Before you are fairly in your college, you must pass an examination. At many of the colleges this is little more than nominal, any Master of Arts being qualified to admit a candidate; but at Trinity there is a regular test, though it must be owned the standard is not very high. The candidates for admission are examined in the First Book of the Iliad, the First Book of the Aeneid, some easy Greek and Latin Prose, Arithmetic, the elements of Algebra, two Books of Euclid, and Paley's Natural Theology.[4] Any one fitted for the Sophomore Class at Yale could pass here without trouble. The candidates are generally well prepared, and the examiners lenient: out of one hundred and thirty or more who offer themselves there are seldom more than four or five rejected. The principle seems to be, 'Let in every one, and if they can't keep on, that is their look-out'. In this way, various initiation fees are secured which would otherwise be lost. On a rough estimate, out of one hundred and twenty who enter every year at Trinity, more than twenty drop off by the beginning of the second year. This is the only entrance examination, and however much you may know, there is no such thing as entering in advance of the Freshman year, save only for men migrating from Oxford, who are allowed their Oxford terms, and can take second or third year rank at once. The regular examiners are the Dean and the Head Lecturer. The latter functionary was busy about some other matters when I presented myself several days after the beginning of the term. Accordingly, I was told that my classical examination would be postponed to some convenient opportunity, and meanwhile the Senior Dean would admit me on passing the mathematical part of the examination privately to

---

[4]   Now omitted [i.e. Paley]. (T) [William Paley's *Principles of Moral and Political Philosophy* (1785), *A View of the Evidences of Christianity* (1794) formed part of the Cambridge curriculum well into the 19th century, and a 'Paley paper' was set till 1920. His *Natural Theology, or, Evidences of the Existence and Attributes of the Deity* (1802) was not so used, though Darwin, for one, read it with care. On Paley's ideas and their reception in Cambridge, see Searby, *History*, pp. 309–13; A. Fyfe, 'The reception of William Paley's *Natural Theology* in the University of Cambridge', *British Journal for the History of Science* 30 (1997), pp. 321–35.]

him. This was the very thing I did not want, for I had literally not opened
a mathematical book for two years. In a mixed examination I hoped that
my classics would carry me through, but now I was called on to put the
worst foot foremost at once. However, there was no help for it, so to the
Dean's rooms I went next morning, and scribbled away for three or four
hours, doing Quadratic Equations, and the *Pons Asinorum*,[5] by *anamnesis*,
as a Cantab says of doing anything which you learned so long ago that it
seems to have been in a different stage of your being. Paley, I had read
within a year, and worked out an elaborate picture of the human eye to
complete my performances. Somehow I nearly floored the paper, and came
out feeling much more comfortable than when I went in. I might have
been easy about it any way, for the Dons are always ready to smooth the
entrance for a Fellow-Commoner, and it was among this class of students
that I enrolled myself by the Dean's advice.

These Fellow-Commoners are 'young men of fortune', as the Cambridge
Calendar and Cambridge Guide have it, who, in consideration of their
paying twice as much for everything as anybody else, are allowed the
privilege of sitting at the Fellows' table in Hall[6] and in their seats at Chapel;
of wearing a gown with gold or silver lace, and a velvet cap with a metallic
tassel; of having the first choice of rooms; and as is generally believed, and
believed not without reason, of getting off with a less number of chapels
per week. Among them are included the Honorables not eldest sons – only
these wear a hat instead of the velvet cap, and are thence popularly known
as Hat Fellow-Commoners. The noblemen proper, or eldest sons (of whom
there are never many in Cambridge, Oxford presenting more attractions for
them), wear the plain black silk gown and hat of an M.A.,[7] except on feast
days and state occasions, when they come out in gowns still more gorgeous
than those of the Fellow-Commoners. A Fellow-Commoner of economical
habits (and it is not easy for one of them to be of such habits) requires

---

5   [The fifth proposition of Book I of Euclid's *The Elements*, which states that the
angles at the base of an isosceles triangle are equal; so called from the difficulty
which beginners find in getting through it.]

6   ['Commoners' not because they are common, but because they are 'commensales',
that is, they share a table with the fellows. Similarly, the Commoners at Winchester
College originally ate with the Scholars.]

7   The initials of English academical titles always correspond to the *English*, not to
the Latin of the titles, B.A., M.A., D.D., D.C.L., &c. [But 19th-century academic
title-pages often carried such Latinate abbreviations as S.T.P. (Sanctae Theologiae
Professor) = DD.]

£500 a-year, and for the generality of them £800 is not too much. I made the experiment with £400, partly from ignorance, partly from the dashing way an American has of going at anything and trusting to Providence to get through.[8]

The not surprising result was that at the end of seven months I found myself a thousand dollars in debt. Indeed, so great is the expense *necessarily* incurred by this class, to say nothing of their greater temptation to unnecessary expenses, that even eldest sons of peers sometimes come up as Pensioners, and younger sons continually do.

Pensioner is the name given to the main body of the students. *Sizars* answer to the beneficiaries of American colleges. They receive pecuniary assistance from the College, and dine gratis after the Fellows on the remains of their table.[9] In former times they waited on the Fellows at dinner, but this practice has long been abolished. A similar one still prevails in some of our institutions.

The Freshman, when once safe through his examination, is first inducted into his rooms by a gyp, usually recommended to him by his tutor. The gyp (from *gups*, a *vulture*, evidently a nickname at first, but now the only name applied to this class of persons) is a college servant, who attends upon a number of students, sometimes as many as twenty, calls them in the morning, brushes their clothes, carries for them parcels and the queerly twisted notes they are continually writing to one other, waits at their parties, and so on. Cleaning their boots is not in his branch of the profession; there is a regular brigade of college shoe-blacks. The new-comer generally finds his apartment ready prepared for him, it being the custom for him to take the former tenant's furniture at a valuation by the college upholsterer, and make such subsequent additions to, or alterations in it, as his convenience requires or his fancy suggests.[10] Thus the movables and fittings of a room are not generally renewed all at once, but piecemeal, from time to time. The appearance of a student's apartment, though by no means splendid, is decidedly comfortable; it is well cushioned and sofaed, with a proper proportion of armchairs, and a general air of respectability – much better

---

[8] I was recommended to enter as Fellow-Commoner, because it would open to me the society of the Fellows and older men, which indeed is the only real advantage of the position.

[9] Those 'remains' are very liberally construed, the Sizars always having fresh vegetables, and frequently fresh tarts and puddings.

[10] [This process is several times discussed in the letters of Alexander Gooden of Trinity, Senior Classic 1840: Smith and Stray, *Cambridge in the 1830s*.]

on the whole than our students' rooms ever are. Fifty pounds would not be a high estimate for the usual value of the furniture. But the new occupant finds one deficiency. All the glass, china, and crockery of the man going out become, by immemorial usage, the bed-maker's property; accordingly our Freshman's first business is to provide himself, usually under the gyp's guidance, with a tea-set, and other like necessaries, among which decanters and wine-glasses figure conspicuously. An American student is somewhat surprised at having these articles recommended to him, as it were, by the college authorities. This is only the beginning of what he has to learn.

The *bed-makers* are the women who take care of the rooms; there is about one to each staircase, that is to say, to every eight rooms. For obvious reasons they are selected from such of the fair sex as have long passed the age at which they might have had any personal attractions. The first intimation which your bed-maker gives you is that she is bound to report you to the tutor if ever you stay out of your rooms all night.

And now having fairly installed the Freshman in his quarters, let us begin the day with him. Morning chapel goes in at seven, and as the English student does not pretend to the railroad speed of the American in making his toilet, the gyp is directed to call him at half-past six, or a little earlier. The bell tolls slowly for five minutes and strikes rapidly for five more before seven. Our Freshman is sure to be early, and does not require the three or five minutes' grace allowed after the clock strikes before the gates are shut.

However much the chapels of the various colleges may differ in size and architectural beauty, they agree in their arrangement. On entering that of Trinity, you find yourself in the ante-chapel, surrounded by monuments of distinguished scholars and divines, eminent among which stands out a fine statue of Newton. Passing through an oaken screen you walk down the long marble floor, between rows of movable benches, upon which the Pensioners sit, without distinction of year or person.[11] The Scholars, Bachelor or Undergraduate, sit on seats behind and above the Pensioners, and above them again, along the walls, are the seats of Noblemen, Fellow-Commoners, and Fellows, and the desks of the Dean and college officers. The students, as they enter, are marked with pins on long alphabetical lists, by two college servants, who are so experienced and clever at their business that they never have to ask the name of a new comer more than once.

It is in the chapel that the tyro generally begins to get definite ideas of

---

[11] Not exactly. All the freshmen sit on the left hand, a convenient arrangement for other people. (B)

the powers that be in the college, and this is accordingly the fittest place for introducing them. The college authorities (in University slang-phrase the *Dons*) are designated in the most general terms as *the Master and Fellows*. The Master of the College, or 'Head of the House', is a D.D., who has been a Fellow. He is the supreme ruler within the college walls, and moves about like an Undergraduate's deity, keeping at an awful distance from the students, not letting himself be seen too frequently even at chapel. Besides his fat salary and house (technically known as *the Lodge*), he enjoys many perquisites and privileges, not the least of which is that of committing matrimony.[12]

The *Fellows*, who form the general body from which the other college officers are chosen, consist of those four or five Bachelor Scholars in each year who pass the best examination in Classics, Mathematics, and Metaphysics. This examination being a severe one, and only the last of many trials which they have gone through, the inference is allowable that they are the most learned of the College graduates. They have a handsome income, whether resident or not; but if resident, enjoy the additional advantages of a well-spread table for nothing, and good rooms at a very low price. The only conditions of retaining their Fellowships are that they take orders after a certain time and remain unmarried. Of those who do not fill college offices, some occupy themselves with private pupils; others, who have property of their own, prefer to live a life of literary leisure, like some of their predecessors, the monks of old. The eight oldest[13] Fellows at any time in residence, together with the Master, have the government of the college vested in them.

The *Dean* is the presiding officer in chapel, and the only one whose

---

[12] [The Master during most of Bristed's stay in Cambridge was William Whewell, Master 1841–6. Master of Trinity from 1841 till his death in 1866, and the most powerful single figure in the university in that period. A reformer of mathematical teaching in his youth, Whewell became fiercely conservative in his middle age, resisting attempts at curricular and institutional change. As Master he was notoriously autocratic – insisting, for example, that undergraduates stand throughout his receptions. Later on, Bristed calls him 'thunderous Whewell' (p. 57). He was twice Vice-Chancellor, in 1842 and 1855, and his tall, burly figure was a familiar sight at ceremonial gatherings. Trevelyan rightly called him 'the biggest man … in the university' (p. 86). For his intellectual activities, which famously approached 'omniscience', see M. Fisch and S. Schaffer (eds), *William Whewell: A Composite Portrait* (Oxford, 1991). Whewell was memorialised in the 1870s and 1880s, but a modern biography is badly needed.]

[13] [In fact, those with seniority of election.]

presence there is indispensable. He oversees the markers' lists, pulls up the absentees and receives their excuses. This office is no sinecure in a large college; at Trinity they have been forced to divide the work, and appoint a Junior Dean. It is rather surprising that there should be so much shirking of chapel, when the very moderate amount of attendance required is considered. The Undergraduate is expected to go to chapel eight times, – or in academic parlance, to *keep eight chapels* a-week, two on Sunday, and one on every week-day, attending morning or evening chapel on week-days at his option. Nor is even this indulgent standard rigidly enforced.[14] I believe if a Pensioner keeps six chapels,[15] or a Fellow-Commoner four, *and is quite regular in all other respects*, he will never be troubled by the Dean. It certainly is an argument in favor of severe discipline, that there is more grumbling and hanging back, and unwillingness to conform to these extremely moderate requisitions, than is exhibited by the sufferers at a New England college, who have to keep sixteen chapels a-week, seven of them at unreasonable hours. Even the Scholars, who are literally paid for going, every chapel being directly worth two shillings sterling to them,[16] are by no means invariable in attending the proper number of times.

Other officers are, the *Vice Master*, the *Bursar*, i.e. the College *Purse-bearer* or *Treasurer*, and his assistant; Lecturers, assistant Lecturers, and assistant Tutors to the number of nearly twenty (some of these, however, are non-residents, and only appear at examinations); four *Chaplains*, and the *Librarian*. These last five are the only officers not Fellows. They are usually selected from the Bachelor Scholars who have just missed Fellowships.[17]

The Chapel service occupies, as nearly as may be, half an hour. After this, it is the custom to take a fifteen minutes' walk in the college grounds, for the purpose of affording the bed-maker time to get the rooms in good order, and of giving the student an appetite for his breakfast. By eight, he is seated before his comfortably blazing coal fire (how different from

---

[14]   [Christopher Wordsworth, master 1820–41, had attempted to impose a rigid discipline in 1838. In response, some of the junior members of Trinity formed the Society for the Protection of Undergraduates, printing league tables of chapel attendance by the fellows – some of whom scored very low marks. See Winstanley, *Early Victorian Cambridge*, pp. 391–3.

[15]   Five at Trinity. (T)

[16]   I <u>never</u> got my Scholarship money. (T)

[17]   On one occasion in the Long Vacation, all the other fellows being absent, I had for one night the custody of all the College keys, Masters Deans Tutors etc. (B)

our scorching, smouldering anthracite!),[18] with his kettle boiling merrily, and the materials for his morning meal on a diminutive table near him. These are of the simplest description – rolls, butter, and tea: an excellent preparation for a morning's reading. The mention of breakfast conveys to a Cantab no ideas of ham and beef-steaks; and if reminiscences of cold game pie and hot cutlets are ever called up by it, it is on account of those occasional breakfast parties, which from their late hour (eleven) bear more resemblance to a luncheon.

At nine, Lectures begin, and continue till twelve. There are some ten or eleven going on at once. The established length of each lecture is one hour. For the Freshmen there are two, a classical and a mathematical, both which they are required to attend; the Second and Third-year men have their choice of one lecture among three or four. The lecturer stands, and the lectured sit, even when construing, as the Freshmen are sometimes asked to do; the other Years are only called on to listen. The practice of taking notes is very general; there is plenty of stationery ready provided on the desks, but the students usually bring their own note-books and pens.

Having mentioned *Second and Third-year men*, it may be well for me to state at once that there are no such beings as *Sophomores*[19] at an English University.[20] The undergraduate course is three years and a third, and the students who have completed their first year are called successively *Junior Sophs* (abbreviated for *Sophisters*), *Senior Sophs*, and *Questionists*; or, more popularly, *Second-year men*, *Third-year men*, and *Men who are just going out*.

It is generally some time before one, when the student resorts to his private tutor. This gentleman, being a most important personage is to have justice done him hereafter at length. Suffice it to say, for the present, that he is by no means an 'aristocratic appendage', as a wise professor on this side the water once imagined, but an ordinary and almost absolutely necessary feature in the college life of every student, rich or poor. With this tutor, who is either a Fellow, or a Bachelor trying for a Fellowship, our Freshman reads a portion of some author he has prepared, or undergoes an examination (by pen, ink, and paper, as all examinations here are) on something he has *not* prepared for the purpose. With a mathematical tutor,

---

[18] [Anthracite was a dense and smooth variety of coal. Mined in Pennsylvania from early in the 19th century, it was the major heating fuel in the northern USA until the middle of the 20th.]

[19] 2nd year men or 'advanced donkies'. (B)

[20] At Trinity College Dublin, there are four classes of Undergraduates: the first two are called *Junior Freshman* and *Senior Freshman*.

the hour of tuition is a sort of familiar examination, working out examples, deductions, &c.

From two to four is the traditional time of exercise, two hours hard exercise a-day being considered (as it is) little enough for a man who wishes to keep his body in proper vigor. The ignorance of the popular mind has often represented academicians riding, travelling, &c., in cap and gown. Any one who has had experience of the academic costume can tell that a sharp walk on a windy day in it is no easy matter, and a ride or a row would be pretty near an impossibility. Indeed, during these two hours it is as rare to see a student in a gown as it is at other times to find him beyond the college walks without one. The most usual mode of exercise is walking – *constitutionalizing* is the Cantab for it. The country for miles around is very flat, and the roads are very good, two circumstances highly encouraging to pedestrianism. After walking comes rowing, which may indeed be called the distinguishing amusement of English University students. Cricketing, and all games of ball, are much practised in their respective seasons.

During the quarter of an hour preceding four p.m., the students come flocking into their colleges and rooms to prepare for dinner. The academic cap and gown are resumed, and the hall crowded with hungry Undergraduates, who are not, however, admitted within the screen until the Fellows and Fellow Commoners have assembled. Then a Latin grace is read by two of the Dons, and forthwith the demolition of eatables proceeds. The tables of the Undergraduates, arranged according to their respective years, are supplied with abundance of plain joints, and vegetables, and beer and ale *ad libitum*, besides which, soup, pastry, and cheese can be 'sized for', that is, brought in portions to individuals at an extra charge; so that on the whole a very comfortable meal might be effected but for the crowd and confusion, in which respect the hall dinner much resembles our steamboat meals. The attendance also is very deficient and of the roughest sort. But some of the company are better off. At a raised dais at one end of the hall the Fellows, Noblemen, and Fellow-commoners are banqueting on a dinner of three courses, with port and sherry, in addition to the malt liquor, and abundance of orderly and well-dressed waiters. Along the wall you see two tables, which, though less carefully provided than the Fellows', are still served with tolerable decency and go through a regular second course instead of the 'sizings'. The occupants of the upper dinner table are men apparently from twenty-two to twenty-six years of age, and wear black gowns with two strings hanging loose in front. If this table[21] has less state

---

[21]   Left hand in the Hall. (B)

than the adjoining one of the Fellows, it has more mirth and brilliancy; many a good joke seems to be going the rounds. These are the Bachelors, most of them Scholars reading for Fellowships, and nearly all of them private tutors. Although Bachelors in Arts, they are considered, both as respects the College and the University, to be *in statu pupillari* until they become M.A.'s. They pay a small sum in fees nominally for tuition, and are liable to the authority of that mighty man, the Proctor. The table nearer the door[22] is filled by students in the ordinary Undergraduate blue gown; but from the better service of their table, and perhaps some little consequential air of their own, it is plain that they have something peculiar to boast of. They are the Foundation Scholars, from whom the future Fellows are to be chosen, in the proportion of about one out of three. Their Scholarships are gained by examination in the second or third year, and entitle them to a pecuniary allowance from the college, and also to their commons gratis (these latter subject to certain attendance at and services in chapel), a first choice of rooms, and some other little privileges, of which they are somewhat proud, and occasionally they look as if conscious that some Don may be saying to a chance visitor at the high table 'those over yonder are the Scholars, the best men of their year'.[23]

Hall lasts about three quarters of an hour. Two Scholars conclude performances by reading a long Latin grace. The Dons are too full after dinner to read their own grace – such at least is the jesting traditionary explanation of the custom, and certainly on one or two occasions, when the officiating Scholars happened to be *non inventi*, I have heard the presiding dignitary return thanks in just two words, to wit, *Benedicto benedicatur.*[24]

After Hall is emphatically lounging time, it being the wise practice of Englishmen to attempt no hard exercise, physical or mental, immediately after a hearty meal. Some stroll in the grounds if the weather is fine, many betake themselves to the Union Society Reading-room to glance over the newspapers and periodicals, and many assemble at wine parties to chat over a frugal dessert of oranges, biscuits, and cake, and sip a few glasses of not remarkably good wine. These *wine parties* are the most common entertainments, being rather the cheapest and very much the most

---

[22] Also on the left. (B)
[23] I remember saying that to Herbert Mathis to please him. (T) [Perhaps Herbert Mather, Trinity 1893.]
[24] Sedgwick used to say more shortly Laus Deo. (B) [Adam Sedgwick, Trinity 1804, 5th Wrangler 1810, fellow of Trinity 1810, vice-master 1844–62; Woodwardian Professor of Geology 1818–73; a popular figure with both senior and junior members.]

convenient, for the preparations required for them are so slight as not to disturb the studies of the hardest reading man, and they take place at a time when no one pretends to do any work.

At six p.m., the chapel bell rings again. The attendance is more numerous now than it was in the morning. On Saturday evenings, Sundays, and Saints' days the students wear surplices instead of their gowns, and very innocent and exemplary they look in them. It must be owned that their conduct in chapel is very orderly and proper, considering the great opportunities afforded for subdued conversation by the way in which they are crowded together when kneeling. After chapel the evening reading begins in earnest.[25] Most of the Cantabs are late readers, so that supposing one of them to begin at seven, he will not leave off before half-past eleven, thus clearing more than four hours' consecutive work, his only intermission being to take a cup or two of tea, sometimes, but not often, accompanied by a slice of bread-and-butter. One solid meal a-day is the rule; even when they go out to sup, as a reading-man does perhaps once a term and a rowing-man[26] twice a week, they eat very moderately though their potations are sometimes of the deepest. Some students go to their private tutors in the evening; not unfrequently two or three meet in one another's rooms alternately to read some classical author or talk problems together – a very sociable way of acquiring learning.

Such is the reading-man's day; as to how the rowing-man passes his I say nothing for the present. He is the abnormal development of the type, and the consideration of his pursuits need not now be dwelt upon.

---

25   I suppose I <u>never</u> read in the evening while I was at Cambridge. (T)

26   [To rhyme with 'cowing', not 'going': see the next chapter.]

4

The Cantab Language

Proctorizing.

A quoy Pantagruel dist; Que diable de languaige est cecy? Par Dieu, tu es quelque hereticque. 'Seignor, non,' dist l'escholier, 'car libentissement des ce qu'il illucesce quelque minutule lesche du jour je demigre en quelqu'ung de ces tant bien architectez monstiers'.

Rabelais, Liv. II. Ch. 6.

One of the first and most necessary things to be acquired by a resident in a new country is some knowledge of its language. Even in the few pages we have thus far gone through, terms have frequently occurred which required explanation; and without some insight into the Cambridge vocabulary, it would be impossible to describe Cambridge life intelligibly, or to understand a true description of it. I therefore subjoin a list of the principal cant terms and Phrases in use, translating them, when possible, into equivalent slang of our own.[1]

Gownsman   A student of the University.

Snob   A townsman as opposed to a student, or a blackguard as opposed to a gentleman; a loafer generally.[2]

Cad   A low fellow, nearly = snob.

Reading   Studying.

A reading man   A hard student.

A rowing man (*ow* as in *cow*)   A hard case, a spreër.[3]

Shipwreck   A total failure.

Mild, Shady, Slow   Epithets of depreciation, answering nearly to the phrases, 'no great shakes', and 'small potatoes'.

Fast   Nearly the French *expansif*. A *fast* man is not necessarily (like the London fast man) a *rowing* man, though the two attributes are often combined in the same person; he is one who dresses flashily, talks big, and spends, or affects to spend, money very freely.

Seedy   Not well, out of sorts, done up; the sort of feeling that a reading man has after an examination, or a rowing man after a dinner with the Beefsteak Club.

Bumptious   Conceited, forward, pushing.

Brick   A good fellow; what Americans sometimes call a *clever* fellow.

To keep in such a place   To live or have rooms there.

---

[1]   [The first collection of Cantab words and phrases was the *Gradus ad Cantabrigiam* of 1803, probably compiled by William Paley (son of the famous William Paley) of Pembroke, 3rd Wrangler 1802. A revised, enlarged and illustrated edition was published in 1824. See J. Coleman, *A History of Cant and Slang Dictionaries, II: 1785–1858* (Oxford, 2004), pp. 801, 293–4; C.A. Stray, *Slang in 19th-century England*, 5 vols, (Bristol, 2002), vol.1, pp. v–xviii.]

[2]   A Philister in German student phrase. (B)

[3]   [Cf. A.E. Shipley, *'J': A Memoir of John Willis Clark* (London, 1913), p. 27: 'fast men, or, as they were sometimes called, rowing men, that is to say, those who frequently got into rows'.]

Hang-out   To treat, to live, to have or possess (a verb of all-work.) [4]

Like bricks, Like a brick or a bean, Like a house on fire, To the nth, To the n + 1th.   Intensives to express the most energetic way of doing anything. These phrases are sometimes in very odd contexts. You hear men talk of a balloon going up *like bricks*, and rain coming down *like a house on fire*.

No end of   Another intensive of obvious import. *They had no end of tin*, i.e. a great deal of money. *He is no end of a fool*, i.e. the greatest fool possible.

Pill   Twaddle, platitude. [5]

Rot   Ditto.

Bosh   Nonsense, trash, Greek *phluaria*.

Lounge   A treat, a comfort (an Etonian importation). [6]

Coach   A private tutor. [7]

Team   The private tutor's pupils.

Subject   A particular author, or part of an author, set for examination; or a particular branch of Mathematics, such as Optics, Hydrostatics, &c.

Getting up a subject   Making one's self thoroughly master of it.

Flooring a paper   Answering correctly and fully every question in it.

Book-work   All mathematics that can be learnt verbatim from books – all that are not problems.

Cram   All miscellaneous information about Ancient History, Geography, Antiquities, Law, &c.; all Classical matter not included under the heads of Translation and Composition.

---

[4]   'Where do you hang out'. (B)

[5]   Out of date 1857. (T)

[6]   [Bowring identifies 'pill' and 'lounge' as public-school phrases. On 'pill', he writes, 'Very little used'. On 'lounge', he comments, 'Dizzy makes his hero Coningsby say "breakfast is my lounge"'.]

[7]   [An importation from Oxford (a major centre for coaches of the horse-drawn variety), where the word in the sense Bristed gives first appeared in the 3rd edn. of Edward Caswall's *Pluck Examination Papers* ... (1836), p. 28.]

Composition   Translating English into Greek or Latin.

Original Composition   Writing a Latin Theme, or original Latin verses.

Spirting   Making an extraordinary effort of mind or body for a short time. A boat's crew make a spirt, when they pull fifty yards with all the strength they have left. A reading man makes a spirt,[8] when he crams twelve hours daily the week before examination.

Commons   The students' daily ration, either of meat in hall, or bread and butter for breakfast and tea.

Sizings   Extra orders in hall.

Don   A Fellow, or any College authority.

Little-Go   The University Examination in the second year.

Tripos   Any University Examination for Honors of Questionists or men who have just taken their B.A. (The University Scholarship Examinations are *not* called Triposes.)

'The names of the Bachelors who were highest in the list (Wranglers and Senior Optimés, *Baccalaurei quibus sua reservatur senioritas Comitiis prioribus*, and Junior Optimes, *Comitiis posterioribus*) were written on slips of paper; and on the back of these papers, probably with a view of making them less fugitive and more entertaining, was given a copy of Latin verses. These verses were written by one of the new Bachelors – and the exuberant spirits and enlarged freedom arising from the termination of the Under-graduate restrictions, often gave to these effusions a character of buffoonery and satire. The writer was termed Terrae Filius, or Tripos,[9] probably from some circumstance in the mode of his making his appearance and delivering his verses; and took considerable liberties. On some occasions we find that these went so far as to incur the censure of the authorities. Even now, the Tripos' verses often aim at satire and humor. [It is customary to have one serious and one humorous copy of verses.] The writer does not now appear

---

[8]   And a fool of himself. (T)
[9]   ['Terrae Filius' was the Oxford term. See K. Haugen, 'Imagined Universities: Public Insult and the *Terrae Filius* in Early Modern Oxford', *History of Universities* 16:2 (2000), pp. 1–31; For 'Mr Tripos', see C. Wordsworth, *Scholae Academicae* (Cambridge, 1877), pp. 17–21.]

in person, but the Tripos paper, the list of honors with its verses, still comes forth at its due season, and the list itself has now taken the name of the *Tripos*. This being the case with the list of Mathematical honors, the same name has been extended to the list of Classical honors, though unaccompanied by its classical verses.' Whewell on *Cambridge Education*, preface to Part 2.

Posted   Rejected in a College Examination.

Plucked   Rejected in a University Examination.

Proctors   The Police Officers of the University.

Bull-dogs   Their Lictors, or servants who attend them when on duty.

Wrangler, Senior Optimé, Junior Optimé   The First, Second, and Third Classes of the Mathematical Tripos.

Senior Wrangler   The head of the First Class in Mathematics.[10]

Add to these some words previously explained, as *gyp*, *sporting-door*, *questionist*, &c., and a number of London slang words with which Punch has made us familiar, e.g. lush and grub, for meat and drink; weed, for cigar; tin, for money; governor, for father; sold, for exceedingly disappointed or deceived; and a few pure Greek words, of which the most generally used are, *nous* (sense) and *kudos* (credit, reputation), and you have a tolerable idea of the Cambridge vocabulary – chiefly confined to the Undergraduates (except in the technicals like proctor, wrangler, &c.), but understood and acknowledged by the stiffest Dons.[11] Nor must it by any means be supposed the peculiar property of the rowing-men; on the contrary, the jargon of the reading-men is less intelligible to the uninitiated than that of any other class – for they piece out their conversation with Greek words, just as some would-be fashionables do theirs with French, until the 'Babylonish dialect' becomes nearly as bad as that of the student in Rabelais, and it takes a pretty good Greek scholar to understand their English. Thus I have heard

---

[10]   [The term is attested from 1791. The classical equivalent, 'Senior Classic', was in principle usable from the first Classical Tripos examination (1824), but I have found no examples earlier than 1839.]

[11]   The Romans used Greek words in the same way. Those named in the text were obsolete in my time; but we had plenty in use: parergon, epideictic, etc. When an undergraduate tried to get a friend to accept a bet he would ask him not to send him away 'aprakton'. (T)

propemp familiarly used for escort, and seen in a letter *ackmaze* for to be at the highest point. And this is not altogether affectation; to many of these men the strange words they use have become more familiar and convenient than the corresponding English ones, especially technical terms of the Greek philosophical writers (such as *idiotes, episteme, idea*), just as those who have lived much in France often find it more convenient to express certain ideas by French words than English ones.

5

An American Student's First Impressions at Cambridge and on Cambridge

A Fellow Commoner and a Commoner Fellow.

There are not a few persons in this community of ours, some of them not deficient in intelligence nor entirely destitute of the spirit of benevolence, who think it a most desirable and praiseworthy thing to stir up all the mischief they can between England and America. These well-disposed individuals doubtless have their reward, which I never felt inclined to envy them, my own ideas always urging me to a directly opposite course, either from some mental blindness which kept me behind the progressive democracy of this advancing age, or because I never intended to put myself in a position which would oblige me to propitiate or toady Irishmen[1] or slaveholders.[2] Ever since my early boyhood it had been a leading idea with me that the great branches of the Anglo-Saxon family, distinguished by their language, by their ethical principles, by their judiciously liberal political institutions, from the rest of the world, ought to work harmoniously together; that a great deal of the bad feeling between them arose from ignorance, and was therefore removable by mere contact and information; and that a citizen of either country who had the opportunity was doing his duty much better by endeavoring to promote a mutual knowledge of each other between the two peoples, and thus dispel many antipathies having more a hypothetical than a real foundation, than by laboring to revive and foster old germs of animosity which time and the natural course of events were already doing so much to kill. In wishing therefore to stand well and make a good impression at Cambridge from my first entry, I was actuated not merely by a desire after the promotion of my own *kudos* (to speak Cantabrigically), but by an honest wish to represent my country well and make the name of American respectable to many young Englishmen who had no personal experience of it. Indeed it was partly on this account, that I had put myself in a position so disproportionate to my financial resources as that of a Trinity Fellow Commoner.

I was well aware that in this endeavor there was considerable up-hill work to do, and sufficient discouragement to enter; that as the American admirer of England is sure to get some hard knocks at home, so the American in England is apt to be looked at in a false light by the individuals of a nation to which he is well disposed.

Mere mistakes of ignorance I was always prepared for, and it is but justice to my English acquaintances to say that they were generally as glad to have such mistakes corrected as I was eager to correct them. This charge of ignorance is, as we all know, sometimes denied and sometimes slighted by Englishmen; but it is rather understating the case to say that the majority of English gentlemen know less than they should about the condition and institutions of a people so nearly related to them, and whose political and social movements they might study to so much advantage in reference to their own country. In our past history, short as it is, we would hardly

---

[1] [Bristed was consistently prejudiced against the Irish. In his last letter, however, written a few days before he died in January 1874, he wrote, 'My servants have been like angels to me. Were I to live I should write a palinode on the Irish.']

[2] Interesting when we recall fashionable English feeling 1861–1865. (T) [This feeling was very much in favour of the South during the Civil War.]

expect them to be well up, coming into rivalry as it does with the more universally exciting events that took place in Europe contemporaneously, and other reasons may combine with national pride for making Waterloo a more familiar name to them than New Orleans; but surely an English gentleman who has attained his majority, might be expected to know that we have two Houses of Congress and that New York is not a slave State.

The old joke of presuming that a New Yorker or New Englander knows any man who may have gone out to Canada, St. Louis, or Texas, is really no joke at all, but a very common occurrence, which every American who has travelled or resided much in England must have verified for himself. Sometimes I have remarked instances where it might well be suspected that much of this ignorance was put on, and that – just as our public men assent to the romancings of Irish 'sympathizers', and wonder how England can be so blind and unjust as not to grant repeal, knowing better all the time – the Tory journalist when he asserted that bread was actually dearer at times in American than in English cities, *because* he had seen a New York shilling loaf which was not larger than a London tenpenny one, perfectly understood the relative value of the New York and English shillings. But in many cases no such explanation was admissible. The Liberals whom I met did not seem very much better acquainted with us than the Tories, but they were more anxious for information and better disposed towards us. The general bearing of such Tories, and that not merely young men or Dons at Cambridge, but Londoners, was very civil to me personally, but mingled with a sort of implied pity for my belonging to a country where a gentleman was out of place, could not get his deserts, and must necessarily be *kakonous to demo* [hostile to the common people]. For with the English Tory I found it a fixed idea that all our 'Upper Ten' are bullied and plundered by the mob, just as it is with the American Radical that all the mass of the English people are miserable serfs, and all the landed aristocracy bloated tyrants. With men of this sort I took a very summary course, neither more nor less than the ordinary American dodge of stoutly asserting and imperturbably maintaining our national superiority in morals and intelligence. Take the following as a specimen.

B. at the Dean's table, enjoying the beneficial provender thereon.   Enter (rather late) Strafford Pope, a young aristocrat with £30,000 a-year, and a large assortment of the most antediluvian politics.[3] P. has heard that B. is

---

[3]   [Probably Frederick Peel, son of Sir Robert Peel; Trinity 1841. See Searby, *History*, p. 589.]

an American and takes a seat alongside him half intentionally; B. knows P. by reputation as one of the few reading Fellow-Commoners. They strike up a conversation in the pauses of the dinner; by and by the discourse takes a political turn.

P.   A republic may be very well, when we can make all men angels, but till then it can't answer.

B.   Why, we make one answer very well, though our men don't pretend to be angels, and only some of our women.

P.   Answer very well! You have no law – or, at least, no means of enforcing the law, you know. (An Englishman always appends 'you know' to the very thing you *don't* know, and won't admit.)

B.   Oh, that's altogether a mistake on your part. I can see how it arises very naturally. You look around on your own lower orders and think how unfit they would be for political power; and so they are now no doubt. But wait till virtue and intelligence are diffused among your people as generally as they are among ours, and then you will be ripe for a republic and will have it too.

Whether I believed in this magnificent formula of our superiority in virtue and intelligence to the rest of the world or not, it answered its purpose at the time completely, utterly putting down the Englishman, who was so upset with indignation at my quiet assumption that he could not deliver himself of an articulate reply.

Some of the Fast men among the Fellow-Commoners and their toadies, whose love of deviltry was much greater than their wit, as soon as they heard of my nationality, determined to have some fun out of me, and accordingly invited me to various entertainments with the laudable intention of making me drunk and otherwise putting me through my paces. But these fellows gave me very little trouble; I may say it without vanity, for getting the better of them in anything which required the smallest exertion of *nous* was like being first in a donkey-race. In all repartees and wordy warfare I gave them quite as much as they could manage. As to the fluids, I had the fortunate or unfortunate natural gift, not unimproved by practice, of a rather strong head, and could imbibe a pretty good share, even of the villainously doctored Cambridge wines, without disturbing my bodily or mental equilibrium; so that the men who had promised themselves the treat of seeing a drunken Yankee, only made themselves very comfortably tipsy in their attempts to intoxicate me, especially as I was too prudent to rely entirely on my natural capacities without having recourse to an occasional artifice. On one special occasion, I recollect there was a dead set made at me, almost every one present out of fourteen diners challenged me to drink repeatedly. I stuck to the Hock – or, more critically speaking, to something in a green bottle – the bottle and glass were colored, that was the main point; the colored glass enabled me to fill and empty, in appearance, many times, while in reality I only poured out and tasted a few drops; the result of which stratagem was that two or three of the party put themselves completely *hors de combat*, and were deeply impressed with a sense of my capacity.

Never but once did I even come near getting into any difficulty on account of my country. One night after a dinner party, a Fellow-Commoner of older standing, who was leaving at the same time, carried me off to 'show me another set'. This other set consisted chiefly of the Beefsteak Club, some six or eight men who used to dine together once a week for the purpose of consuming incredible quantities of an extraordinary liquor called Cambridge Port, and having performed their usual duties, were then in what the Irish call a very high state of civilization. Among their guests was, to my horror and disgust, a Fellow of the college, just about to take orders. Before I could find a decent pretext for evaporating, one of the most 'civilized' undertook to banter me on my non-appearance in the classic regions of Barnwell.[4] It is not very difficult to quiz a drunken man, and I showed this one up so completely before his friends, that he became quite furious, and proceeded to make some very personal remarks upon 'Yankees', which provoked me to give him a rather dogmatic extempore lecture on the requisites of a gentleman and the duties of hospitality and courtesy. He of the Beefsteak, comprehending dimly what I said, and being at a loss for words, made, by way of answer, a belligerent demonstration, to which, in self-defence, I was compelled to make signs of responding. But before hostilities were actually interchanged, several men seized hold of each of us, and the scene which ensued was sufficiently ludicrous. I had from the first been more amused at than angry with the obstreperous individual, and had not the slightest idea of fighting him unless he actually struck me, besides I was perfectly sober, which could not be said of any other person in the room except the old stager who brought me, so that I could observe quite coolly what was going on. One very well disposed and very tipsy man, who was great upon boats but very slow at books, endeavored to pacify me by relating the results of his own experience with moral deductions, but in four several attempts could get no farther than to inform me that he had been 'f-five years in this u-university'. Another, who evidently gave

---

4   [The village near Cambridge notorious for its prostitutes.]

me credit for the most belligerent propensities, was expounding to me the laws of the University, which forbade duelling under penalty of expulsion for all concerned, and insisting that therefore it was impossible to call a man out &c. Meanwhile the other party was surrounded by his group of friends, who at length succeeded in persuading him that he had been guilty of a great breach of decorum, so that in the end he began apologizing to me and continued his excuses till they were almost as great a bore as the original offence. This incident did not fail to be repeated, and partly from the muddled condition of those who witnessed and assisted at it, partly from the inaccuracy of gossip, from which even Englishmen are not entirely exempt, it was repeated with various exaggerations, and finally settled into the form that I had drawn a knife on the asperser of my countrymen, and threatened him with instant annihilation.

Some trifling New York accomplishments, from which no one in my position could have expected much a priori, now came into play, and tended to give me consequence. It may seem ridiculous that a knowledge of particular meats and drinks, or the possession of a stock of well-cut trowsers, should have any effect on a man's position in a community professedly literary; but it was these trifles more than anything else that tended to raise the opinion which the younger portion of my new associates formed of me, and through me of the country.

One of the first things which surprises a young man from our Atlantic cities on visiting England, is the inferiority of the English in certain refinements of civilization – in which he was prepared to find them infinitely superior. It is with no small astonishment that the New Yorker, or Philadelphian, or Bostonian finds it almost impossible to get clothes made to fit in England;[5] nor, while doing justice to the mutton and ale of the country, is he less disappointed to find that there is no variety – the eternal steak, chops and potatoes, and big joints everywhere; and that the national taste in wine is of the most barbarous description, most of the fluid consumed under that honorable appellation being half brandy. Moreover, having usually mixed more with Frenchmen, Spaniards, and Germans, and speaking what he knows of their languages more fluently than the Englishman of the same age, he has a decided advantage when any native of the Continent happens to be present, or when Continental matters are under discussion. After recovering from the first surprise of these facts, I cherished them *as* great facts, which enabled me to show my superiority

---

[5]   30 years afterward G.W. Smalley told me that all Americans who dressed well, got their country and tourist clothes in London. (T)

to the 'benighted British', when they least expected it; and more than one youth who thought to astonish the American savage by a display of the mysteries of civilization, was rather astonished in his turn at my summary condemnation of English tailors and cooks, and my ostentatious learning in French wines and dishes. It may be supposed that the Fellows were not moved by any vanities of habiliment, but their epicurean and convivial tendencies led them to respect any hints in the matter of edibles and potables. A more intellectual way of becoming known was in the University debating society. I had, more by practice than natural ability or inclination, acquired that knack of speech-making which about every third graduate of an American college possesses, and accordingly, at the first meeting of the *Union* after our admission, extemporized an argument on the Chinese war. In this way, however, it was not possible to gain much renown, the debating society being a very third-rate affair: mere oratory is about as much viewed with the English as mere scholarship is with us. But in the legitimate business of the place I was not without resources. In accordance with the impulse first given by Newton, strengthened by other great scientific names, and only partially counteracted by such scholars as Bentley and Porson, Mathematics are made a necessary foundation for everything at Cambridge; and the only road to Classical honors and their accompanying emoluments in the University, and virtually in all the Colleges, except Trinity, is through Mathematical, all candidates for the Classical Tripos being obliged as a preliminary to obtain a place in that Mathematical list which is headed by the Senior Wrangler and tailed by the Wooden Spoon.[6] This preliminary passing in science being a terrible bore to the Classical men, and failure in it sometimes shipwrecking them for life, they consider themselves, and claim to be considered by others, victims and martyrs. Now I hated Mathematics as cordially as any Cantab of my contemporaries, and with more experience, if not more knowledge of the subject, while I really was fond of Classics; so as naturally to fall into the ranks of the aggrieved and complaining minority (there are about three Mathematical students for one Classical), and this helped to give me a position among those with whom I sympathized. In composition and cram I was yet untried, and the translations in lecture-room were not difficult to acquit one's-self on respectably. Finally, whatever I did, derived additional lustre from the blue

---

[6] See the chapter [27] on Recent Changes for an alteration in this respect. [The Wooden Spoon was the lowest scorer among the junior optimes – the last of the honours men. The title, first used in the 1790s, became redundant, along with that of Senior Wrangler, after changes in the tripos list in 1909.]

and silver gown, the Fellow-Commoners generally being more disposed to rowing than reading, and not particularly distinguished in any way for their intellectual performances. Indeed, they are popularly denominated 'empty bottles', the first word of the appellation being an adjective, though were it taken as a verb there would be no untruth in it.

And now, what impression did my new associates make upon me? With those of my own standing, and nearly my own age, I was much disappointed and somewhat disgusted. These youths of eighteen or nineteen seemed precocious enough in vice, but the veriest schoolboys in everything else – making a noise and throwing about pens and paper in the lecture-room, waxing uproarious at night over the worst liquors, working like schoolboys when they did work, translating with awkward literalness, and shifting most of the burden on the Lecturer when it came to Mathematics. In everything but physical development and vicious tendency they seemed years behind American students considerably their juniors, except that some – and only some of them – executed beautiful Latin verses with great facility.

In some respects, my generalization was very imperfect and incorrect. It had been my mishap, partly from my position as Fellow-Commoner, partly from local accidents, to fall among a bad set of Undergraduates. Had I, in the situation of my rooms, or of my seat at lectures, lighted among some of the best Eton, or Rugby, or Shrewsbury men, my first impressions would have been considerably modified. But in one important point they were correct. The English student of eighteen is more a boy than the American of the same age, in manners, in self-possession, in world-knowledge, in general knowledge of literature even. How far this precocity on our part is an advantage, is a question of which we shall have more to say hereafter. At that time, deeming it an unmixed benefit, I was not a little proud of it, individually and nationally.

But while not particularly pleased with those of my own immediate standing, I took great delight in the society of another class – the Bachelor Scholars. These men, averaging about twenty-three years of age, the best Classics and Mathematicians of their years, were reading for Fellowships – that is they were putting themselves through the best existing course of intellectual training and polish. Most of them well grounded in the grammar, and copiously learned in the vocabularies of the Ancient tongues, so that they read Latin and Greek more readily than one usually does French, were working over their Classics to the utmost pitch of accuracy, branching them out into philological discussions, then with historic lore, and illustrating them from the literature of other languages. Some were carrying up the results of their mathematical drilling, to the highest walks of pure science; and all were imbuing themselves with the sufficiently wide course of reading inclined within the limits of the metaphysical, or, as it is also and more correctly called, the *general* paper – a course which embraces Logic, Political Economy, Historical and Transcendental Metaphysics, and Ethics. Unsuccessful candidates, and others who wanted to laugh at the papers, used to call them *examinations on Whewell's books*; which, had it been strictly true, was saying a good deal for them, since the professor of Casuistry[7] has written no small quantity about various subjects.

The classical sympathies and mental symmetry of these men could be fully perceived only by a student like themselves, but any person not grossly illiterate must have been struck by their acquaintance with the literature of their own tongue – not the ephemeral and superficial part of it, but the classics of the language. For their relaxation, instead of cheap novels, political diatribes, or newspaper scandals, they read the old Dramatists, and the standard Essayists of byegone days. They formed Shakspeare clubs, to read and study *the* Dramatist – not exactly like those 'Shakspearian Readings', in which the actor or actress is the chief attraction. The criticism displayed in their conversation was much superior to the majority of what is lauded when read in print; and when they talked, it was not declamation, or pamphleteering, or sophistical exhibition, aiming only to gain the victory and produce an effect on the listeners, but a candid communication of knowledge and opinion, and a search after truth. The regular and hearty exercise they took every day, maintaining their bodies in vigorous health, kept their minds elastic, and at the same time drove out all moroseness and peevishness, rendering them eminently genial. And, while generally in moderate circumstances, and living on (for England) a very moderate income, they had a taste for some of the enjoyments of art, which they gratified in their temperate, honest way. Without the means of luxury, they preserved a gentlemanly aestheticism. Their dress was simple, not to say economical, but its cleanliness and freedom from pretension dispelled any disposition to criticise it. They could not afford valuable paintings, but their rooms were hung with choice engravings, the accumulations of their undergraduate years, a few pounds' worth at a time. They lived habitually on plain and substantial provender, but on festive days, when an old friend turned up unexpectedly, or an examination resulted triumphantly, or on any other occasion that provoked revelry, they enjoyed a *recherché* dinner,

---

[7] [William Whewell, Knightbridge Professor of Moral Philosophy 1838–55. The chair had been founded in 1683 as a professorship of 'Moral Theology or Casuisticall Divinity'.]

and a bottle or two of good wine as much as the most scientific epicure. They had not the command of an opera, or indeed any place of public amusement, and for a great part of the year were confined to the somewhat monotonous country about Cambridge, but for a month or six weeks in the 'Long' they rambled off to see the sights of Paris, or the galleries of Belgium, or the natural beauties of the Rhine and Switzerland, and came back far more delighted with their brief expedition than can be conceived by those who make it their business to worry from place to place in pursuit of diversion and excitement.[8]

The great change and improvement effected by a few years of collegiate life was to me one of the first problems connected with the English Universities. Home experience had not led me to expect such a start between the ages of twenty-two and twenty-five. My own pursuit of classical study had been founded more on predilection for it than on a very strong conviction of its general utility; but now I began to consider whether there might not be in it more of this practical quality than I had ever yet given it credit for.

As for the Fellows, some of the younger men displayed much the same characteristics with the Bachelors; others of the older stock seemed to have grown somewhat rusty in their retirement; which led me to suspect what indeed is a common opinion among the Fellows themselves, that the University is an excellent place for the regular seven years, or perhaps a few more, but after that time it is better for a man to leave it, unless he is strictly devoted to some purely scientific pursuit. And in this lies the value of the Trinity Fellowships, that being tenable (in the case of laymen) for seven years more (not involving residence) they afford a young man support until he can get fairly started in his profession, while the three years he has spent in reading for the Fellowship, themselves directly contribute to his getting the start by the regular and powerful mental training they put him through. But unfortunately many not otherwise so inclined are tempted into orders to keep their Fellowships.

---

[8] Excellent and perceptive account. I never read anything so good about Americans by an Englishman. (T)

6

Freshman Temptations
and Experiences

Natis in usum laetitiae scyphis
Pugnare Thracum est.

Horace.

English boys remain at school until the term boy is hardly applicable to them
(according to our notions, at least), and the academy-prospectus designation
of 'young gentlemen' becomes more appropriate; that is to say till eighteen
or nineteen years of age. It is impossible that for youths of that stature
(and they grow faster in England than in our Northern States) the school
discipline should not be relaxed a little from its extreme strictness; still
even for them it is pretty severe. From this state of close restraint they are
suddenly thrown into a condition of almost entire freedom, in which they
can go where they like, order what they please, and do almost anything
they please, only about two hours and a half of their daily time being
demanded by the college authorities, and from midnight till seven in the
morning the only period when they must be in their rooms or lodging-
houses. Tradesmen of all sorts give them unlimited tick; they can fill their
wardrobes with clothes and their cellars with wines; they may gratify the
'small vice' of smoking, and any greater vices they are so unfortunate as to
have, provided they do not openly outrage public decorum.

Having had a little more worldly experience than most Cambridge Freshmen, and being moreover fortified by a somewhat more refined taste (occasionally a valuable auxiliary to a man's principles) I kept clear without difficulty of all such boyish excesses. But there were seductions and dangers in the life I was leading, all the more perilous for not being appreciated by myself or others, and while passing for a terribly hard reading man, and a 'Sim'[1] of the straitest kind with the 'empty bottles', and enjoying a very exemplary character with most of the Dons, I was fast lapsing into a state of literary sensualism. The life about me was in many respects my ideal of worldly enjoyment. The studies which I preferred in just sufficient quantity, to amuse and excite without fatiguing me, abundance of good cheer for the body, pleasant literary companions, some reputation for talent obtained by very little exertion, and a reputation for goodness obtained by no exertion – everything combined to put me on good terms with myself. I became lazy, and addicted to sleeping over morning chapels, and consuming much claret after dinner; I also wasted many hours at billiards, indulging myself in this fascinating game as a compensation for having denied myself a horse on economical grounds. When a young main becomes fairly engaged at billiards, he seldom does anything else very regularly.

The life of a Freshman, after he has become fairly settled in his quarters, is not a very diversified one. The chief incidents of a University man's life are his examinations, and of these the Freshman has none worth mentioning until the end of his third term (unless he be a clergyman's son, and thereby entitled to go in for the Bell scholarship). One or two matters occurred during my first winter, that were of interest as giving me an insight into the political feeling of the University. Towards the end of our first term there was an election for High Steward, the officer who represents the University in the House of Lords. Lord Lyndhurst was the Tory candidate; his abilities and reputation, and the conservative majority among the members of the University, afforded little prospect of any successful opposition being offered to him. It happened, however, that a few years before, a young Whig nobleman (Lord Lyttelton) had come out head of the Classical Tripos, and being, though a Whig, a strong High-Churchman, and of unimpeachable character, it was thought that the High Church, Whig, and moral interests

---

[1]   I.e., Simeonite, a nickname given by rowing men to Evangelicals, to all religious men, or even quiet men generally. [Charles Simeon, King's 1779, Vicar of Holy Trinity church 1783–1836, was the leading Evangelical in Cambridge. His followers were known as 'Sims'.]

together might enable him to beat Lyndhurst.[2] But the Tories stood by their man – High Church, Low Church or no church, moral or no moral – and elected him by a vote of all but two to one.[3] The voters in these elections are all the M.A.'s who *keep their names on the Boards* (of their respective colleges) by paying an annual sum. While the voting went on in the body of the Senate House, the galleries were filled with undergraduates, who gave cheers and groans for a great many things and people, and hissed unmercifully the prominent voters for Lyttelton. About this time I first had full personal experience of the uncharitableness shown by these youthful Tories towards their liberal countrymen. Many of them, who seemed to have taken up the Romish idea that a blind devotion to their church establishment would atone for any irregularity in their lives, looked upon a Liberal as no better than a Dissenter, and a Dissenter as only one step above an Atheist. A professed Radical was regarded as a strange monster, always to be suspected. Though not generally prone to gossip, they could not help inventing and repeating absurd calumnies about him. It was told me of a man whom I knew slightly, that he had once said, when the subject of Church extension was under discussion, 'he would as soon subscribe for a brothel in every parish as a church'. I very much doubted his even having uttered so atrocious a sentiment, and was not surprised to learn accidentally, some time after, that this was a standing bit of scandal which had been attributed to all the presidents of the Liberal club successively for many years.

Toryism of the young men, and ideas suggested by it

I could not help contrasting the Jacobitism (Toryism is not a strong enough term for it) then prevalent among the students, not only with the political character of the University in other days, but with the general republican tendencies of young men of fashion under the Tory premier, William Pitt.[4] I was also led to compare it with the strong conservative spirit of our own collegians, and the Democratic longings of the German students; and was led

---

[2] [John Copley, Lord Lyndhurst, Trinity 1790, 2nd Wrangler 1794, fellow of Trinity 1795–1804; later Solicitor-General, Attorney-General and Master of the Rolls; MP for the University 1826; created Baron Lyndhurst 1827. George Lyttelton, 4th Lord Lyttelton, Trinity 1835, Senior Classic 1838; member of the Clarendon (1861) and Taunton (1864) royal commissions on secondary education.]

[3] This was the only fair competition of intellect for high office I can remember. Lyndhurst was one of the most prominent public men. (B)

[4] [William Pitt (the younger) was prime minister 1783–1801 and 1804–6.]

to the somewhat hasty generalization that the majority of highly educated young men under any government are opposed to the spirit in which that government is administered. Hasty and imperfect as the conclusion is, it certainly does hold good of many countries, and is a fact worthy consideration. Perhaps we may thus account for the phenomenon. Barbarous and ignorant nations magnify themselves and their country above all the rest of the world, and regard foreigners with contempt or aversion. So do, though in a less degree, the ignorant classes of all countries. The first effect of education is to open a man's eyes, and let him see his nakedness. He sees the defects in the government of his country; he exaggerates them with the ardor of youth, and takes that side which promises to remedy them, without reflecting at what cost the remedy may have to be purchased. Be the reason of the thing what it may, I am not disposed to view the thing itself as altogether worthy of lamentation; nor whatever harm it may sometimes do the individual, do I regard it as mischievous to the community, but rather the contrary. The position has been well maintained by at least two able philosophical writers of the present day,[5] that complete consistency is not to be desired in a state; that for the sake of counteracting the inherent evils of every form of government the *prestige* is often in favor of arrangements which do not follow from the general principle of the government. And it is clear that such counterbalancing measures will never be proposed by those who carry out to extremes the fundamental principles of the government, whether democratic or aristocratic. The existence of a minority holding certain opinions may be very desirable when the conversion of that minority into a majority would be a thing especially to be deprecated. Nor does it even follow that such a minority will carry out their ideas so seriously as to aim at a radical change in the government. The founders and supporters of the Edinburgh Review were theoretical admirers of a republic, but when the English Whigs get into office they do not endeavor to subvert the monarchy.

To return from this digression, the next thing that particularly struck me was what may be called to an outside observer or non-studious resident the great feature of English University life – the boat races, which begin towards the close of the second term, and continue all through the third. Boating is the University amusement *par excellence*. The expense of it is small, and the Cam so convenient – just behind the Colleges. At all times

---

[5] Mill *apud* Lewis, *Influence of Authority in Matters of Opinion*, p. 237. [J.S. Mill; G.C. Lewis, *An Essay on the Influence of Authority in Matters of Opinion* (London, 1849).]

of the year you may see solitary men in wherries, taking their shilling's or two shillings' worth of sculling up and down; while the boat-clubs for the formal Spring races are a convenient outlet for College emulation, the top of the river being an honor contended for nearly as strenuously as the Senior Wranglership or the head of the Classical Tripos – and not always by a very different set of persons. Will the reader accompany me to my first race, and see it just as I saw it.

7

The Boat Race[1] [1841]

Grafty Corner.

'Row, brothers, row!' *Lady of the Lake.*

'Go it, ye cripples!' H. Walker, Esq.

'Dear B. – To-day the first race of the season comes off. Be at my room not later than two, and I will show you the way. D.I.H.'[2]

---

[1] This chapter was originally published as an article in the Yale Literary Magazine, during the year 1841. ['A university boat race', *Yale Literary Magazine* 7 (Nov. 1841), pp. 36–40.] In 1847, it was republished in a city magazine; on which occasion, one of our wise newspaper critics discovered that it was copied from an article in Blackwood, written about two years after mine was in print. [The republication was under Bristed's favourite pseudonym of 'Carl Benson': 'English University life. No. 1: The Boat Race', *The American Review* 5 (April 1847), p. 353–6.]

[2] Dunbar Isidore Heath. (T, B) [Trinity 1834, 5th Wrangler 1838; fellow of Trinity 1840–7, Vicar of Brading, Isle of Wight, 1846–62. Heath was deprived of his living

44

Such were the contents of a curiously twisted note which I found upon my breakfast table one morning on returning from lectures. The writer was a Bachelor Fellow of Trinity, who knew more about America and Americans than any other Cantab then resident. Poor fellow! he had rather too much intercourse with us for his own profit: when the U.S. Bank[3] blew up, 'Dunny H.' was in for some £1000, or it may have been more – he never would own how much.

But I am digressing. There was not much time to lose, for it wanted but a quarter of two, and 'Dunny' was a punctual man. So, arming myself with an umbrella (it has a habit of raining *at least* once a day in England), I sallied forth to witness for the first time that exciting spectacle, a University boat-race.

There is one great point where the English have the advantage over us: they understand how to take care of their health. Not that the Cantabs are either 'tee-totallers' or 'Grahamites'.[4] There is indeed a tradition that a 'total abstinence' society was once established in Cambridge, and that in three years it increased to two members; whether it be still in existence, however, I have not been able to learn. But every Cantab takes his two hours' exercise *per diem*, by walking, riding, rowing, fencing, gymnastics, &c. How many colleges are there here where the students average one hour a day real exercise? Our Columbia boys roll ten-pins and play billiards, which is better than nothing, but very inferior to out-door amusements. In New England (at least it was so ten years ago at Yale), the last thing thought of is exercise – even the mild walks which are dignified with the name of exercise there, how unlike the Cantab's constitutional of eight miles in less than two hours! If there is a fifteen days' prayer-meeting, or a thousand-and-first new debating-society, or a lecture on some *specialité* which may be of use to half-a-dozen out of the hundred or two who attend it, over goes exercise at once. And the consequence is what? There is not a finer-looking set of young men in the world than the Cantabs, and as to their health – why, one hundred and thirty Freshmen enter at Trinity every year, and it is no infrequent occurrence that whatever loss they sustain from other causes (accidents will happen in the best regulated *colleges*), death takes away none of them during the three years and a half which comprise

---

after publishing sermons influenced by F.D. Maurice which an ecclesiastical court found to have been derogatory to the 39 Articles.]
[3]   [The Second Bank of the USA, situated in Philadelphia. A financial panic had begun in 1837; the Bank closed down in 1841.]
[4]   [Vegetarians, named after the food reformer Sylvester Graham.]

their undergraduate course. Whose memory can match this at Yale? If our youngsters exercised their legs and arms just four times as much as they do, and their tongues ten times as little, it would be the better for them every way. But I am not now reading a lecture on dietetics, so let us come back to the shores of the Cam.

Classic Camus being a very narrow stream, scarcely wider than a canal, it is impossible for the boats to race side by side. The following expedient has therefore been adopted: they are drawn up in a line, two lengths between each, and the contest consists in each boat endeavoring to touch with its bow the stern of the one before it, which operation is called *bumping*; and at the next race the *bumper* takes the place of the *bumped*. The distance rowed is about one mile and three quarters. To be 'head of the river' is a distinction much coveted and hard fought for. Each college has at least one boat club; in Trinity there are three, with three or four crews in each. About nine races take place in the season; they are of great use in preparing the men for the annual match with Oxford, in which the Cantabs are generally victorious.[5] Indeed, they are the best smooth-water oars in England, if not in the world.

The Caius[6] boat at this time was head of the river, the First Trinity second, the Third Trinity the third. Some hard pulling was expected among the leading boats. The Third Trinity were confident of bumping the first.

While you have been reading the above, you may suppose H—— and myself viewing the scene of action, distant about two miles from the town. The time of starting is at hand, and gownsmen (not in their gowns) are hurrying by us on all sides, some mounted, but the greater part on foot; some following the beaten track, others taking a shorter cut over fields and fences. Here comes a sporting character, riding his own 'hanimal'. See with what a knowing look man and horse approach the fence. Hip! he is over, and six inches to spare. And here is another, who, though not very well mounted, must needs show his dexterity at the same place. Not quite, stranger! The horse has his fore feet clean over, but it by no means follows that he will do the same with the hind ones. Crack! he has hit the

---

[5]   But once the Oxonians beat our eight oars with *seven*, which is rightly judged equal to half-a-dozen ordinary defeats. (One of the famous 7 (five I think) was Brewster afterwards Colonel of the Inns of Court Volunteers: B).

[6]   Familiarly pronounced Keys. There is an old joke about a man named Bunch having belonged to this college, and being called accordingly, 'Bunch of Keys'.

top bar and carried it off several yards. Not so bad after all. He might not do it again so neatly.

Bang! there goes the first gun! In three minutes there will be another, in two more a third, and then for it! What are those men laughing at? Ah! I see; no wonder. An ambitious character on a sorry hack has driven his Rozinante at a ditch. No you don't, mister! The horse, wiser than his rider, refuses the leap, with a sagacious shake of the head. He is hauled back for a fresh start, and the whip applied abundantly. Same result as before. The tittering of the passers-by reaches our hero's ears: he waxes wrathful, and discharges on the reluctant steed a perfect hurricane of blows!

Spla-ash! with the utmost composure imaginable the old horse has stepped into the ditch, say three feet deep, casting his rider headlong by the abrupt descent. Serves you right, my friend. We can't stop to see what becomes of you, for there goes the second gun, and we must make haste to secure a good place. Well, here we are, at the upper end of 'the Long Reach'. We can just spy the head of the first boat below yonder corner. As the hardest pulling always begins here we shall have a good view of it. Ha! do you see that pull? The eight stalwart Caius men bent to their oars the moment the last gun flashed, and its report reaches our ears as they are stooping to the second stroke. Here they come at a rapid rate, and with them the whole cortège of horse and foot, running along the bank and cheering the boats. Take care of yourselves! A young colt, frightened by the uproar, is exhibiting some very decided capers, to the manifest discomposure of those around him, and finishes by jumping into the river, fortunately not near enough to the boats to disturb them. His rider maintains his seat throughout, and they emerge somewhat wet, but otherwise apparently uninjured.

And whether they were or not, no one cared, for the leading boats were now rounding the upper corner of the Reach. On they come at a good rate, the Caius men taking it quite easy, and pulling leisurely, as much as to say, 'what's the use of hurrying ourselves for *them*?' Indeed the First Trinity had lost half a length, and were therefore in some danger themselves.

Caius passed me, for I was far from a good runner, so did the two Trinity boats and 'Maudlin' (Magdalene), when suddenly there uprose a mighty shout, 'Trinity! Trinity! Go it, Trinity!' and there was First Trinity shooting forward with a magical impulse, away, away from the threatening Third Trinity, and up, up, up to the head boat. The poor Caius crew looked like men in a nightmare: they pulled without making any headway, while the others kept fast overhauling them at every stroke. The partisans of the respective boats filled the air with their shouts. 'Now Keys!' 'Now Trinity!' 'Why don't you pull, Keys?' 'Now you have 'em, Trinity!' 'Keys!'

'Trinity! Trinity!' 'Now's your chance, Keys !' 'Save yourself, Keys!' And it did really appear as if the Caius men would save themselves, for, with a sudden, mighty effort, they made a great addition to their boat's velocity in a very short time. I began to fear they had been 'playing possum' all the while, and could walk away from us after all.

The uproar and confusion of the scene were now at their height. Men and horses ran promiscuously along the bank, occasionally interfering with each other. A dozen persons might have been trampled under foot, or sent into the Cam, and no one would have stopped to render them assistance. The coxswain of the Caius boat looked the very personification of excitement; he bent over at every pull till his nose almost touched the stroke's arm, cheering his men meantime at the top of his voice. The shouts rose louder and louder. 'Pull, Trinity!' 'Pull, Keys!' 'Go it, Trinity!' 'Keep on, Keys!' 'Pull, stroke!' 'Now, No. 3!' 'Lay out, Greenwell!' – for the friends of the different rowers began to appeal to them individually. 'That's it, Trinity!' 'Where are you, Keys?' 'Hurrah, Trinity! inity!! inity!!' and the outcries of the Trinitarians waxed more and more boisterous and triumphant, as our men, with their long slashing strokes, urged their boat closer and closer upon the enemy.

Not more than half a foot now intervened between the bow of the pursuer and the stern of the pursued, still the Caius crew pulled with all their might. They were determined to die game at least, or perhaps they still entertained some hope of making their escape. Boats have occasionally run a mile almost touching. But there is no more chance for them. One tremendous pull from the First Trinity, and half that distance has disappeared. They all but touch. Another such stroke, and you are aboard of them. Hurrah! a bump! a bump!

Not so! The Caius' steersman is on the look-out, and with a skilful inclination of the rudder he has made his boat fall off – just the least bit in the world – but enough to prevent their contact. The First Trinity overlapped, but did not touch.

Exulting shouts from the shore hailed the success of the dexterous evasion. Enraged at being thus baffled, the pursuers threw all their strength into a couple of strokes. The Caius men, knowing that this was their last chance, were doing their best to get away, but the other boat was upon them in a moment. Again the skill of the cockswain was brought into play, and again the pursuing boat overlapped without touching. But it was now clear that they were only delaying their fate, not averting it, for the Trinity men, going four feet for their three, were running them into the further bank in a way that left no room for change of course. 'Hurrah for Trinity!' shouted I, in the fulness of my exultation, and at that moment a horse walked against me and nearly threw me off the bank.

When I regained my feet, it was all over. Both boats had hauled off on one side, and ours had hoisted her flag. Trinity was the head of the river once more, and great was the joy of her inmates. Alas for human expectations! When the season ended, Caius was first and the First Trinity – No. 4.

8

A Trinity Supper Party [1840]

A Wine

Qui plenos hausit cyathos madidusque quiescit,
Ille bonam degit vitam moriturque facetus.

Ignotus Quidam

The social entertainments of a community are always an object of interest to the stranger, and many things may be learned from them. It certainly gave me a new idea or two when, on the Commemoration Day in November, I attended a Supper of the Dons in *Combination Room* (an apartment over the hall, devoted to the suppers and desserts of those in authority), after which meal, we, that is such of the Fellow Commoners as preferred grave society, sat with these college dignitaries round the fire playing whist for shilling points, and drinking bishop (mulled port), and a very enticing mixture appropriately called silky, the component parts of which, so far as I could judge from internal evidence, appeared to be made of rum and madeira.

Of ordinary undergraduate wine-parties there is no need to say much. Thackeray has summed them up according to their deserts: 'thirty lads round a table covered with bad sweet meats, drinking bad wines, telling bad stories, singing bad songs over and over again'.[1] The younger Fellows, Bachelor Scholars, and some of the more knowing among the older Under-graduates, understood the thing better; had good wine, with the simplest accompaniments, such as biscuits and oranges; and when they extemporized a supper, did it with equal simplicity. At such regales, one met with the three conditions of a perfect symposium: good dishes and wine, an entire absence of display and pretension, and the genial conversation of clever men. Some exquisites may be disposed to turn up their noses at people who never used claret jugs or sugar tongs,[2] but the richest plate and china seldom witness the enjoyment which those primitive and yet dainty repasts afforded.

Occasionally, when the *sunetoi* [intelligent] mix in with the ordinary run of men, if their viands do not become less choice, their conversation may; and their fun at times verges on the fast and furious, as the reader shall judge for himself.

'Shady rather this composition: you never know where to put your *an's*. I think we *may* get you a First though, by a triumph of art, that is − How are you off for Mathematics?'

'Very mild.'

'Ever read Euclid?'

'Rather. Say eight years ago. Can get that up in two days.'

'And Algebra?'

'When I was a boy, but never very brilliant in it.'

'If you can get ten marks out of five hundred, it is better than nothing. Better go to Dunny (Dunbar) first and see what he can do with you. Don't try too much at once. I cut the Algebra and Trigonometry papers dead my first year, and came out seventh.'

'*Verremos. apiteon* [Off we go].'

'Nay, stop the revolving axles of your feet a minute. Have you anything to do after tea? No? then come up and you'll find a few men at supper.'

---

[1]   [The quotation is from Ch. 15 ('Of university snobs') of Thackeray's *Book of Snobs* (London, 1855), p. 55.]

[2]   How the custom of taking sugar with the fingers should prevail at the University and nowhere else in England, is somewhat singular, especially as almost every man owns a sugar-tongs when he comes up; but such is the case.

I went back to Letter E, New Court,[3] read 80 lines of Aristophanes, and did a few more bits of illustration, such as noting down the relative resources of Athens and Sparta when the Peloponnesian war broke out, and the sources of the Athenian revenue (we had a book of Thucydides for one of our subjects), all which occupied me till half past nine.

'There will be some quiet Bachelors there, I suppose,' thought I, 'and a Junior Fellow or two, some of those I have met in combination,' and so thinking, I substituted a dress coat and boots for the loose slippers and George-Sandish half frock-coat, half dressing-gown, which figured prominently in my ordinary evening costume. It was about six steps across New Court, and three to Travis's staircase in the cloisters.[4] He kept in the third story, but long ere this ascent was completed the sound of voices and clatter of knives and forks gave token that the grub was under discussion. The outer, or 'sporting' door was of course wide open: passing through an interior one of green baize, I blundered up a narrow and totally unilluminated passage, and rapped instinctively at where the third door ought to be; then, scarcely waiting for the emphatic 'come in', plunged into the jovial assembly. Dead sell for the Nugee[5] and patent leathers! *Abandon* reigned throughout. One man was in a blouse, another in his shirt-sleeves, the amphitryon himself in a shooting-coat. There were not a dozen of them, but they made noise enough for thirty. As quietly as possible I slipped into the chair reserved for me at the host's right hand.

'Ah, B——!' and Travis squeezed my hand with a solemn and business-like affection. 'Just in time. What will you take? Ducks – grilled fowls – lobster *grating*, as our cook calls it – Lawson,[6] here's a young gentleman will trouble you for some duck. Try some champagne – not so good as you get in America, I'm afraid; we're waiting for free trade.'

The duck and champagne went to their appropriate place, and then, as every one was fully occupied, I had time to look about me and study the company. At the head of the table sits our worthy 'coach', Tom Travis. His fine person is not displayed to full advantage in a loose plaid shooting-coat, and his very intellectual but decidedly ugly features are far from being

---

[3] [Bristed kept in E1 New Court from Michaelmas 1840 to Easter 1841; he moved to A4 in the same court in Michaelmas 1841 and remained there until Easter 1845.]

[4] Tom Taylor. (T)

[5] ['Dead sell', a complete disappointment. Francis James Nugee was a fashionable Pall Mall tailor who specialised in coats.]

[6] [Effingham Lawrence: see p. 54.]

improved by a black wool smoking cap of surpassing hideousness. Take him as he is, he is a rare fellow – with American versatility and English thoroughness. He knows nearly a dozen ancient and modern languages, more or less correctly, and when you bring him out on Greek he would astonish a room-full of Yankee Professors. His mathematics are decidedly minus, but the use for them is past long ago. Two years ago he got up enough of his low subjects to go out among the Junior Ops, and then the way was easy to a high First Class in the Tripos; and, as he is well up in metaphysics, you may count on him for a Fellowship, probably his second trial. And after that what will he do? He is gay; a puritan might call him dissipated, but it is not wickedness aforethought, but an incurable passion for seeing *character* which drags him into all sorts of society – once he went off among the gipsies, Borrow-fashion, and stayed there long enough to learn their lingo.[7] He is independent in politics and *juste milieu* (by his own account) in church matters, very fond of law and equally so of theology – fonder of the theatre than either. Perhaps he will be a nominal barrister and an actual writer for Punch and the Magazines. Perhaps he will go quite mad and write a tragedy. Perhaps some of his liberal friends at the University we've got in town, profanely called Stinkomalee[8] by Oxonians and Cantabs, will make him Professor of Greek, or English or Zincali, it's all the same to him – in that great institution.[9] Or perhaps (here the reader, if a New-Englander, is requested to pull out his handkerchief, and borrow a *flaçon* of salts) he will stay here for three or four years as an M.A. pupillizing constantly, and his clothes will gradually grow blacker and his cravat whiter, till some day there will be stuck up on the Hall screen a small notice to the effect that 'Mr Travis requests the testimonials for orders'.[10] And after all there are worse parsons than he would make – yea, even in old Connecticut – for there is great earnestness in the man and benevolence extraordinary; he takes much interest in the poor and is very generous to them – too generous indeed, for he sometimes gives them his tradesmen's money – and he always minds his own business, but to be sure that is not so rare and Phoenix-like a virtue in England as with us. Any of these things

---

[7]   I doubt this. (B) [Taylor wrote of his time with the gypsies in the *Illustrated London News* in November and December 1851: see Searby, *History of the University of Cambridge*, p. 607.]

[8]   [The University of London, so called by its detractors from its being built near a stagnant pond.]

[9]   He was professor of English. (B)

[10]   Taylor really did think at one time of taking orders. (B)

Tom Travis may be (I ought not to omit the opinion of his gyp, who holds him in absolute veneration, that 'Mr. Travis will leave the college a Fellow, and come back a Judge'), at present he is a Bachelor Scholar and a 'coach' of rising reputation, in which last capacity it is that B—— has the most intimate connexions with him, that young man being in a violent state of cram for the May examination, and very nervous about the result.

The Vice is Effingham Lawson,[11] who puts you in mind of Bob Sawyer, 'a dissipated Robinson Crusoe', generally dispensing with gloves and wearing a *red* P-coat, and an enormous stick.[12] But under that unpromising exterior there is much learning, more common sense, and even considerable warmth of feeling. Break in upon him during the day, his deportment will be brusque and his replies monosyllabic; but give him a cigar and some whiskey-toddy on a winter night and after the third tumbler he will 'discourse most exquisite' politics, literature, or theology, till morning chapel. He is older than Tom by a few years, say three, which will make him twenty-six, and has only one more chance for a Fellowship, which, however, he is pretty safe for, as he will do very well all round, his classics being good enough to let his mathematics in, and his metaphysics brilliant.

On his right, diagonally opposite me, is a handsome little man with a predominating aquiline nose. Quite a youth, to look at, is Horace Spedding,[13] but he is considerably older than you would take him to be – older in every way – and a very hard customer you would find him, not at all easy to sell or come over. He was an Etonian, and of course is an elegant Latin versifier, and captivatingly innocent of mathematics, which does not in the least prevent him from being an acute and dexterous logician. The most remarkable thing about him is his *eironeia* [irony]. This is a peculiarly Cantab quality, inexpressible in English save by a periphrasis; you may call it the *opposite vice to hypocrisy*. Thus to bear Spedding talk in a mixed company (particularly if there are any freshmen or country clergymen to astonish) you would think him a monster of depravity, just fit for one of Eugene Sue's heroes; whereas he is in private life a very quiet and temperate man of high principles and steady practice. The Rugby men can't abide him, taking this

---

[11]   Lawrence Whigham? (E); Lawrence(?) (B); E.J. Lawrence (S). [Effingham John Lawrence, Trinity 1835, 29th Wrangler 1839, fellow of Trinity 1841.]

[12]   [Bob Sawyer is a minor character in Dickens' *Pickwick Papers*, issued serially in 1836–7; Bristed is quoting from his first appearance, in Ch. 2. The 'P-coat' was a hip-length coat made of pilot cloth (P-cloth), a heavy twill.]

[13]   Horace Mansfield. (T, B) [Horatio Mansfield, Trinity 1838, BA 1842, fellow of Trinity 1843.]

eironeia for natural wickedness; he in return laughs at them, and calls them *Arnold and water*.[14] There is American blood in Horace, but you will not easily find a man with a more thorough abhorrence of democratic institutions.[15] N.B. His father lost £20,000 by the US Bank.[16] To-morrow he is going in for a Scholarship, and is sure to get one; for, much as the Dons dislike him, they always elect the best man. No one ever dared charge them with unfairness. And his Fellowship will follow in time. Then he will probably invest his small income judiciously, for he has a great talent for statistics and finance, and in some four or five years you may find him in town, coming home from 'Change to read Plato. After a while his connexion, which is a good one, will procure him some attaché or legationship, and then woe to the foreign diplomat who comes in his way, for a *leerier* man than Horace is not on this side sundown.

That escaped-convict looking man, next Spedding, is the Hon. G. Dutton, Captain of the First Trinity.[17] Though a peer's son, he has come up as a pensioner, not an unusual step now, the expenses of a Fellow-Commoner being so great. He is an Eironiast, like Horace, but with him it takes a more practical turn. There never is a gay boating supper party without George Dutton. The Barnwell girls know him well, and the Dons look askew at him. But the man is always walking through the fire and never getting burnt. Immovably capacious of liquor, cold and passionless as Pitt or Paracelsus, he is the wonder and the admiration of his weaker companions.

---

[14] [Undergraduates coming up from Rugby during Thomas Arnold's reign as headmaster (1828–42) were noted for their moral seriousness; some said, priggishness.]

[15] Horatio Mansfield's mother was Mary Buchanan, d. of General Samuel Smith, of Baltimore. (S)

[16] [See the note on p. 45. Mansfield's father's US investments were probably made because he had married an American, the daughter of Gen. Samuel Smith of Baltimore.]

[17] George Denman. (T) [Hon. George Denman, Trinity 1838; Senior Classic 1842; a noted rower and walker; University Counsel 1857–72. As the son of a nobleman, he was able to sit the Classical Tripos without having gained mathematical honours; he was 'Captain of the Poll', i.e. top of the ordinary degree list.] Bowring comments, 'Capital! He has the look intensified now'. Trevelyan, however, disagrees violently with Bristed's account of Denman, especially with respect to the Barnwell girls ('Untrue. A lie Charles Bristed') and the dons' attitude to him ('Not at all like. Nobody more popular with the Dons as a whole, and rightly so'). He adds, 'I am proud of having known Denman well. A more preposterous characterisation never was written'.]

To hear him talk now, you would think his only object on earth was the Boat; working his men up the Long Reach at the top of their speed; running round the hall after dinner to see that none of them take sizings (pastry is bad for the wind, say the knowing ones); prowling about in all sorts of places, by night, and pulling them out of all sorts of places to send them off to bed at a proper hour. Yet that rowdy,[18] reckless boat-captain[19] manages to clear his seven-hours' reading every day, and no one stands a chance for Senior Classic alongside of him, except one steady, well-trained Shrewsbury man. (Marsden[20] and Dutton are sworn friends, by the way, each worshipping the other; so much for the evil effects of emulation, &c.) In more thorough bodily and mental training you cannot conceive a man to be; and there is no doubt of it that he will take a high stand at the bar – probably be, as was his father before him, a law-lord, some day – if there are any lords at all by that time – which there will be, Democratic Review[21] to the contrary notwithstanding.[22]

And who is next Dutton? Who but the redoubted Romano?[23] Is that man an Englishman, or an Anglo-Saxon at all? Short, dark, and much bewhiskered; his name too – Romano. Yes, he is very foreign, but an Englishman for all that, though he has lived much on the Continent, where he learned to speak three or four languages, play an instrument or two passably, and not only *tell* French dishes but absolutely cook them. Clever enough is Romano, but his university course has been a shipwreck, and he will probably end by going out unnoticed among the *polloi*. He stood well his first year, chose to be vexed his second, because he did not get a Scholarship at the first trial; migrated to a Small College; couldn't stand that, and came back again – just too late for a Trinity Scholarship. The only tangible result of his migration and re-migration was a joke from Spedding.

---

[18] Absurd. (T)

[19] I have heard excellent boating men say that Denman was the best captain and the best oar that ever came up to Cambridge. (B)

[20] Munro. (T, B) [H.A.J. Munro, Trinity 1838, 2nd Classic 1842, fellow of Trinity 1843–85; author of a famous edition of Lucretius (1864) and first holder of the Cambridge chair of Latin (1869–72).]

[21] [Perhaps the *Democratic Review of British and Foreign Politics, History, and Literature* (vols. 1–2, 1849–50).]

[22] Lord Denman. Not a bad prophecy. (B)

[23] Novelli (T, B), Romanis (W, S). Bowring adds, 'He looked half like an Italian and half Jew, the third half gipsy'. [William Romanis was not at Trinity; this is Augustus Henry Novelli, Trinity 1836, who migrated to Pembroke in 1839 and returned to Trinity in 1840: see below.]

B—— had unthinkingly asked, one day, 'What could have made Romano migrate to Pembroke?'

'Why,' quo' Horace, 'when Rum'un obtained the dignity of a Junior Soph, he suddenly became religious; so much so, indeed, that he thought of going as a missionary to the South Sea Islands, when it was suggested to him that there existed an extensive field nearer home, in the Small Colleges.'

Finally, on Travis's left sits Wilkinson, another shipwreck, so far as University distinctions are concerned.[24] He came from Eton capitally prepared. Even now the classic poets are at the tip of his tongue, and when the fit is on him he will reply to you in extempore verse. For instance, I once met him in our beautiful grounds, just before four, our early dinner hour.

'Well, Wilkinson, are you going to devour beef in the hall, or shall we take a stroll here in the sun?'

'Suave vorare bovem, sed suavius apricari', replied the unhesitating manufacturer of longs and shorts. Could there be a prettier spondaic line?[25] But alas! Wilkinson has little ability and less taste for mathematics. He will never get up enough of his low subjects to pass the Senate-house; so the Tripos is a sealed book to him. Still he must get his Scholarship, and may get his Fellowship; for in Trinity mathematics are not a *sine qua non*, though thunderous Whewell is doing his worst to make them so. But it is more probable that he will take a disgust at the whole business, and do something very mad; learn the flute, fall in love, or turn Romanist.

And now who is there on my side of the table? A stray Freshman or two like myself; a fat, beer-drinking captain of one of the second crews – Marsden; a quiet Scotchman,[26] irreproachable as a classic and a whist-player, but not very brilliant in any other department; and – yes! that man asleep on the other end of the sofa is Fowler the Australian.[27] He has just got out

---

[24] [Not identified in any copy; this may suggest that he did not last long at Trinity.]

[25] [A good example of the migratory anecdote. Exactly the same story was told of Thomas Saunders Evans, St. John's 1835, BA 1839, Professor of Greek, University of Durham 1862–89. Evans was an accomplished classical scholar, but graduated with a pass degree because of his inability to pass the Mathematical Tripos: J. Waite (ed.), *Latin and Greek Verse* [by Evans] (Cambridge, 1893), p. vii.]

[26] Huart? (B) [Huart is otherwise unknown; this is in fact H.A.J. Munro, identified above.]

[27] ?Langhorn (T), Forbes (B). [David Forbes, son of the Chief Justice of New South Wales; Trinity 1838, 28th Junior Optime 1841.]

in a bye-term after being plucked once, and has been getting – something that begins with D or I, on the strength of it. The effects of the first spree he is sleeping off; by and by we may perhaps see him in his Glory.

While my survey was going on the substantials have been consumed, the last morsel of the indispensable cheese demolished, the last stoup of beer emptied. The decks are cleared: Porcher, Tom's faithful gyp, appears with a mighty bowl.[28] That *otrire tamia* [nimble steward], Mrs. Porcher, produces the lemons and other punchifying appurtenances, and Travis himself hauls out from a 'wee sly neuk' two potent bottles.

'Do they make punch in America?' says my fellow-pupil, Menzies (pron. Ming-ees), opening his mouth for the first time.[29] 'Oh, yes; and other drinks manifold. Egg-nogg – sangaree.'

'What is sangaree?'

'What you call negus.'[30]

'Negus is *ne gustandum*', broke in Wilkinson.

'Do open the window, Horace, and let that pun out.'

'Sherry cobbler, mint julep, and –'

'Do tell us how mint julep is made'; and Travis in his curiosity actually looked up from the bowl, with whose contents he had been busy for the last five minutes; the third lemon remained uncut in his hand, and the knife fell vacantly on the table.

'You don't know!' I took confidence and drew myself up in conscious superiority of knowledge. 'It's the drink of Elysium. The gods combined their energies to concoct it. Bacchus gave his most potent spirit. Venus sweetened it with her most precious kiss. Pomona contributed her most piquant fruit, Flora her most aromatic herb, and Jove shook a handful of hail over all.' As I concluded this prose version of Charles Hoffman,[31] a burst of applause went round the table.

'Bravo!' quoth my coach. 'Fancy Flora walking up with both hands full of mint like Demeter in the Thalusia[32] –

---

[28] [Mr and Mrs Porcher also feature, as landlord and landlady, in the letters of a slightly earlier Trinity man, the ill-fated Alexander Gooden (Trinity 1836, Senior Classic 1840, d.1841): see Smith and Stray, *Cambridge in the 1830s*.]

[29] ? T. Markby (T), Dalzell (B). [Robert Dalyell, Trinity 1840, BA 1844.]

[30] [A drink made of wine, hot water, lemon juice and sugar, spiced with nutmeg.]

[31] [Charles Hoffman was the author of *Wild Scenes in the Forest and Prairie* (1839) and *Greyslaer: A Romance of the Mohawk* (1840), both published in London.]

[32] [The Thalusia was the festival of the first-fruits of Demeter, described in

dragmata kai makonas en amphotereisin hechoisa
[holding corn and poppies in both hands]

'B——, what does *dragmata kai makonas* mean?'

I gave the proper answer, and Travis stirred up the beverage for the last time.

A growl from the vice interrupted us. Lawson had been for the last ten minutes ornamenting the fine features of the sleeping Australian with a huge pair of burnt cork moustaches. He now looked up from giving his victim the last touch, and muttered, 'Don't talk shop! Let's have a song!' 'Very well!' responded Travis, to whom nothing ever came amiss, 'Romano has just got a new one by letter from Oxford. Come, Rum'un!' And Rum'un did as he was bid. Be it premised, for the benefit of the uninitiated, that Oxonians call the sporting door 'the oak'.

> Here's a song to my oak, my brave old oak,
> > That was never yet left ajar;
> > And still stands he a stout bit of tree,
> > All duns and intruders to bar !
> > There's strength in his frown when the sun goes down,
> > And duns at his portals shout;
> > And he showeth his might in the broad daylight
> > By selling the tutor's scout.
>
> CHORUS
> Then here's to my oak, my brave old oak!
> > That no heels, sticks, or pokers can mar;
> > And still may he last as in days long past,
> > All duns and intruders to bar.
>
> When I came up to Queen's I knew I was green,
> > But I swore I would ne'er be gay,
> > So I sported my oak and read for a joke
> > Full sixteen hours in the day:
> > But care comes to all, being plucked for my Small,
> > And finding but grief for my pains,
> > I next like a brick ran up all sorts of tick,
> > So sported my door remains.
> > > Then here's to my oak, &c.

Theocritus's seventh Idyll, from which 'Travis' quotes.]

I once knew the times, when the silvery chimes
   Of a well-plenished purse met my ear,
When 'your small account, sir', and 'very large amount, sir,
   To make up', for me had no fear.
Now duns rule the roast, as I find to my cost,
   And a merciless set are they;
But they ne'er shall get in to ask for their tin
   While my door can keep them at bay.
Then here's to my oak, my brave old oak!
   That keeps me all safe alone,
And still may he last, as in days long past,
   Till a hundred duns are gone!'[33]

After some applause and a moderate pause, Dutton was called on to volunteer (to speak Hibernicé), and promptly came forth with 'Vilkins and Dinah',[34] a rich Cockney ditty, one version of which may be found in Bentley's Miscellany for '43 or '44. It goes off very musically, even like a chime of bells, somehow thus:

It vas a licker-marchant in Londing did dwell,
Who had one only darter, a beautiful young gal –

'I observe the accuracy of the rhyme', says Travis.

Her name it vas Dinay, 'bout sixteen years old,
Who had a fine fortune of sillivere and gold;

and then proceeds to relate, with much humor and pathos, how 'Villikins' wooed the lovely Dinah; how the governor (as governors always do) had another 'lovyere' waiting for her; how he mildly expostulated with his refractory offspring in these moving terms:

O Dinay, my daughter, I pray you don' vex me,
For if you do, 'tis ten to one, I die of the apoplexy;

---

[33] [A parody of 'The brave old oak', by Henry F. Chorley, a prolific writer for the *Athenaeum*, published c.1834. The original text was much reprinted, e.g. in 1837 in *Knickerbocker's Magazine*, a journal to which Bristed himself contributed.]

[34] [A popular early-Victorian comic song, usually sung with a Cockney accent. It was apparently based on a street ballad, 'William and Dinah'.]

how

> Villikins, vile vollcocking (walking) her garding around;

discovered the 'cold corpus' of his true love, and thereupon drank up the 'pison' always provided in such cases; and then the melancholy conclusion was speedily relieved by a *choeur foudroyant*, so long, so loud, that it actually woke the Australian. Being waked up, Fowler was satisfactorily put through his paces, talked an indefinite amount of nonsense, rubbed his face in happy unconsciousness of its extraordinary appendages, and thereby blacked it all over, to the inexpressible delight of the Freshmen; sang a Parhyponoean[35] song which will hardly bear transportation, and finally extemporized a vigorous hornpipe, doubtless to the great comfort of the small, precise Don, keeping immediately underneath, whom Tom had dubbed 'Bloody Politeful', and was in the habit of paying various delicate attentions to, such as stealing his bread and drowning mice in his milk jug.[36] This concluded the evening's entertainments, and the company broke up at half past twelve, except Lawson and the American, who stayed with Travis till three, talking theology. Fortunately no one in Cambridge need go to morning chapel unless he chooses. Who shall say, after this, that England is not a land of liberty?

---

[35] [A nonce-word: 'out of his mind'.]

[36] ?John Brown, ?Mathison (T). [A.E. Shipley, *J: A Memoir of John Willis Clark* (London, 1913), 86, thought it was Mathison. Bowring, however, identifies the don as 'Cope, the dean'. William Mathison, Trinity 1835, fellow 1840; Edward Cope, Trinity 1837, fellow 1842. Cope was never Dean of Trinity; there is perhaps a confusion with John Cooper, Junior Dean 1838–44. In 1841 the rooms below Taylor's were occupied by Mathison.]

9

The May Examination [1841]

The Screens:- where college notices are posted.

Paper, paper everywhere,
And all our hearts did shrink,
Paper, paper everywhere,
Paper, and pens, and ink.
Rhyme of the Oxford Bachelere

It may have been observed from some allusions in the preceding chapter that, although still occasionally attendant at a jollification, I had partly shaken off my habits of idleness and set to work, and that this beneficial change was brought about by pressure of an approaching examination. In Cantab phrase I was suffering *examination funk*. This was my first chance of distinction. True, we had undergone occasional examinations in Euclid and Greek, but these were entirely at the option of our individual College tutors, and without any public result. Knowing but little as yet of the complicated system, I had paid but little attention to its workings in Triposes and University Scholarship examinations, though some knowledge of them was forced upon me by conversations in hall. When the great degree examination for mathematical honors came off in January and a 'Small-College' man[1] was Senior Wrangler, the announcement of this unusual occurrence did not particularly interest me; nor, just returned as I was from a winter expedition into Dorsetshire, did I even go to see the ceremony of degree-taking and behold the lion of the day. The Classical Tripos next month I knew and cared something more about, partly because it was a subject that more concerned me, and partly from the very uncommon circumstance of there being no Chancellor's Medals[2] adjudged that year.

All candidates for Classical Honors are first obliged to obtain a place among the *Junior Optimes*, that is to say in the third class of the three into which the Mathematical Tripos is divided. But besides this, two golden medals are given annually for classical proficiency to Bachelors, who are at least *Senior Optimes* or Second Class men in mathematics. It generally happens that one of the best two classical men in the year has this preliminary requisite, but an interval of three or four frequently occurs on the Tripos between him and the second Medallist. These Medallists then are the best scholars among the men who have taken a certain mathematical standing; but as out of the University these niceties of discrimination are apt to be dropped, they usually pass at home for absolutely the first and second scholars of the year; and sometimes they are so. Now, it happened that this year the mathematical examination was very difficult and made great havoc among the classics. Three Trinity men, and four from other colleges, all likely candidates for the First Class, were utterly plucked,[3] and several more 'gulfed', that is to say, they did just well enough to save their degree, but not well enough to be placed on the list of Mathematical Honors; so that *their* chance, also, for the Classical Examination was forfeited. As the First

---

[1] Stokes (B), Stokes no less (T). [Sir George Stokes, Pembroke 1837; Lucasian Professor of Mathematics 1849–1903, President of the Royal Society 1885–90; among the most prominent scientists of the age.]

[2] [Two medals for proficiency in Latin and Greek composition had been awarded annually by examination since 1752. The contest was until 1869 open only to those who had passed the Senate House Examination as Wranglers (1st class) or Senior Optimes (2nd class). A single medal for English composition was first awarded in 1813. In 1841, uniquely, no classical medals were awarded, for reasons which Bristed sets out below.]

[3] [Failed: see the list of Cantabrigian terms in Ch. 4.]

Class of the Classical Tripos seldom exceeds twelve, to knock out seven probable men considerably reduces its fair proportions; in fact, on the present occasion, it numbered only five. Moreover, of these five, the first three were *Junior Optimes*, and could not go in for the medals. There remained but two, bracketed at the foot of the Class, and these acquitted themselves so moderately, that the first two of the Second Class, who had been tempted into the Medal Examination by the scarcity of candidates, did just about as well. No one was good enough, according to the usual standard, for the First Medal; they could not give a Second, or two Second, without a First, and so none were adjudged. This caused a new outcry against the injustice to which Classical men were exposed, and frightened one Third-year man away to Oxford, while several declared that they would go out in 'in the Poll' (among the *Polloi*, those not candidates for Honors).[4]

In March, about the same time as the Medal Examination, took place that for the *Bell* (University) *Scholarships*, which concerned several men of my year, but not me. These Scholarships are open to Freshmen, who are sons of clergymen, and in moderate circumstances. The papers are chiefly Classical, a little Mathematics, as high as easy Mechanics, entering into it, chiefly for the sake of determining between the best candidates whose Classical merits are nearly equal. The Classical papers, being for Freshmen, do not include the more difficult authors, Thucydides, Pindar, Aristophanes, Plautus, &c., or Composition in Greek; but there is always enough Latin Composition, both in prose and verse, to frighten the uninitiated. A good deal of Homer is set, and generally a fair allowance of Cicero. There is also a paper in Scripture History and Greek Testament. Two of these Scholarships are vacant every year. Trinity generally gets the first, and frequently both. This year, the first man was a Johnian.[5]

The examination which was now approaching, and which particularly interested me, was the College Easter Term Examination, familiarly spoken of as 'the May'. The *Easter* is the third Collegiate Term, the other two

---

[4]   ['Polloi': literally, the masses as opposed to the elite. Alexander Gooden, who had graduated as Senior Classic the previous year, wrote to his father on 7 February 1841: 'Our plucked men this year are going to Oxford to retrieve [recover]. I fear we shall frighten classical scholars away from Cambridge'. Smith and Stray, *Cambridge in the 1830s*, p. 196. The unexpected results also led to a flurry of correspondence both locally (the *Cambridge Chronicle* and the *Cambridge Independent Press*) and nationally (*The Times*).]

[5]   Field. Kean of Trinity was 2nd (Kean is now dead). (B) [Thomas Field, St John's 1840; John Keane, Trinity 1835.]

being respectively called the Michaelmas and Lent. The nominal vacations are very long, and the actual ones still longer, so that there are not more than twenty-two weeks of real term time in the year[6] – that is, lectures are delivered and residence required for that period only, and a gownsman not disposed to study has the rest of the year to himself. For the reading men, the vacations are the busiest time, there being so much less temptation to idleness when all the idle men are away. The terms are still further divided, each into two parts, and after 'division' in the Michaelmas and Lent terms, a student, who can assign a good plea for absence to the *College* authorities, may go down and take holiday for the rest of the time, having already kept enough of the term to answer the *University* requisition. So, also, a student who is prevented by any accident from coming up at the beginning of either of these terms, may appear just before division, and keep the latter half. But with the division of the Easter term, the Collegiate year virtually ceases; for, though the statute term does not end till the Commencement in July, the Commencement practically takes place in the Long Vacation, all lectures having concluded with 'the May', and most of the men gone down.

The 'May' is one of the features which distinguishes Cambridge from Oxford; at the latter there are no public College examinations.[7] The Freshman is examined on the Classical authors which have been his lecture-room subjects for the year, and on First-year Mathematics, i.e. Euclid, Algebra, and Trigonometry. The higher Years are similarly examined, only with this difference, that, whereas in the Freshman examination Classics count twice as much as Mathematics, for the Junior and Senior Sophs Mathematics preponderate in an equal or greater ratio. There are slight differences in the details at different Colleges. Some divide the Classical and Mathematical Examinations, putting them a month apart; some have no examination for the Senior Sophs; some include in the Freshman Mathematical papers some Second-year subjects, such as Conic Sections; the Johnians give the most marks to Mathematics from the start: but the general scheme is nearly the same in all. So much by way of preliminary.

'What a paper this has been for Menzies! By Jove! how he must have walked into that Athenian navy! He's safe now – that is, if they can read his writing. Who set this?'

---

6 Five months out of twelve! (B)

7 [A confusing statement. In Oxford and Cambridge, 'public' referred to university as opposed to college institutions – thus the University Library was usually called the 'Public Library'. Bristed may simply mean that in Cambridge the college examinations were a university-wide phenomenon; as they had been since about 1830.]

'Goulburn.'[8]

'Ah! He's been studying Arabic lately, and may be warranted equal to any kind of hieroglyphics. I'm afraid this wasn't in your line altogether. How is it? Have you been performing with credit to yourself and satisfaction to your coach. What did *you* do with the navy?'

'Not much – it quite swamped me, except the Trierarchy[9] business.'

'Did you tell them the Attic Tribes and the Attic and Spartan Months?'

'On the contrary.'

'Did you draw that map of *ta epi Thraikes* and Brasidas' campaign?'

'Still less.'

'What *did* you do? Did you explain the *eisphora*, and the other sources of revenue?'

'Three pages of Böckh bodily.'

'And gave them a nice little life of Thucydides, of course.'

'Like bricks.'

'And no end of Aristophanes?'

'Any quantity.'

'Come, that's not so bad after all. If you did that, and the Constitution, *and* Aegina, *and* Nicias, *and* explained these passages, you *may* have got two-fifths' marks.' It was the third day of our May examination. Travis and myself were in the identical room that had witnessed the festivities recently recorded. The subject of our discussion was a printed sheet, all four sides of which were closely filled. I can't give you a better idea of it than by copying the first page *verbatim et literatim*.[10]

Thucydides Lib IV

I (1) What do we learn of the life, station and character of Thucydides from his own writings? (2) What is assigned as the date of his birth? (3) What account is given of his first vocation to write history, and with what probability? (4) Is it probable that he survived the end of the war? (5) What opportunities had he of acquiring information? (6) What period of time is embraced by his history? (7) By whom was it continued; and from what writers do we derive

---

8 [Henry Goulburn, Trinity 1831, Senior Classic and 2nd Wrangler 1835.]

9 [A system in which rich Athenian citizens covered the costs of maintaining a trireme.]

10 [The modern reader may be surprised at the number of detailed questions; but this paper is typical of 19th-century examinations in its demand for a number of very short answers.]

our knowledge of the history of Greece down to the time when it became a Roman province? (8) How far do you concur in the opinion expressed of Thucydides in the words *dokei polla charizesthai men Lakedaimoniois kategorein de Athenaion*? Quote from this book instances of the *enargeia*, the *lexeis poietikai* and the *paranomoioseis, parisoseis, antitheseis,* and *paronomasiai* attributed by Dionysius of Halicarnassus to the style of Thucydides? (10) What writers have imitated Thucydides? Quote instances of imitation.

II (1) Give an account of the Athenian constitution as it existed at the period of the Peloponnesian war. (2) How did it differ from that established by Solon? (3) What were the principal political measures introduced by Pericles and what was their effect upon the Athenian character and polity? (4) What were the principal parties at this time at Athens, and by whom respectively led? (5) What is meant by *he demagogia*? Whom do we hear of as filling that station?

III (1) What is the date of Aristophanes' play of the *Hippeis*? Give a brief account of its plot. Translate the following lines and refer to the passages in this book which illustrate them. [(2)–(3): Greek quotations from Aristophanes.] (4) Quote any other passages from Aristophanes which have reference to or illustrate events recorded in this book. (5) Mention any instances in the tragedians of such allusions to the political events of the day. (6) Quote the lines in Euripides supposed to have reference to Cleon, and the passage in Plato relating to the battle of Delium.

IV [Greek passage from Thucydides]
(1) What was the situation of *Nisiai* and *Pegai*? Explain their importance to the contending parties, and refer to any passages of Thucydides which illustrate it. (2) What was the political condition of Troizen and Achaia? (3) What is meant by *he protera ksumbasis*? Give its date and the circumstances which led to it. What was its effect upon the Athenian empire?

There, reader mine! Is that last page grave and solid enough for you? If not, I only wish you had to cram for these 'Thucydides Questions', as I did, and to write out forty pages save one of *scribbling paper* (a trifle larger than foolscap)[11] about them in four hours.

---

[11] [A characteristic element in the writing-based teaching, learning and examining in which Cambridge was a pioneer, especially in mathematics. It had been defined by the *Gradus ad Cantabrigiam* (1803) as 'An inferior sort used by mathematicians, and in the lecture room'.]

Examinations in our Colleges are seldom considered very important affairs to either party concerned in them. But at Cambridge the College and University Examinations are the staple and life of the whole system. They are the only recognised standards of merit, except a few prizes for essays and poems; their results are published in all the London papers, as regularly as the English Queen's last drive, or the Spanish Queen's last revolution; their rewards are not only honorary but pecuniary, coming to the successful candidates in the shape of books, plate, or hard cash, from the value of five dollars to that of five hundred or more; and in extent of reading requisite, accuracy of execution demanded, and shortness of time allotted, they are surpassed by no examinations on record. At the detail of the requisites which they exact, and the performances which they elicit, I have seen grave divines and professors on this side the water shake their heads doubtingly; so I do not startle you too much at first, but begin gently with the first year's one, ranking as you might suppose among the easier examinations, for it is limited in its range and you have a general idea of the work before you, whereas in a Tripos the only thing you can be certain of is that there is nothing which you may not be asked.

During the three terms of your collegiate year, extending from the twentieth of October, or thereabout, nearly to the end of May, you have been lectured on three Classical subjects, a Greek Tragedy, a book or speech of a Greek historian or orator, and a ditto of a Latin ditto. Of course you are able to translate them anywhere, and explain all the different readings and interpretations. But this is not half the battle – scarcely a third of it. You require a vast heap of collateral and illustrative reading after this fashion.

Our play was the Agamemnon of Aeschylus. Now for the question paper, or, as it is often called, the 'cram'[12] paper, you must first make yourself master of everything connected with the Greek stage arrangements, and the history of the Greek drama, for which you make large draughts upon *Donaldson's Greek Theatre, Müller on the Eumenides* (translated), and *Müller's History of Greek Literature*. Next, you get up all you can find relating to the history of the *dramatis personae*; then all the parallel passages collectable wherein Greeks, Romans, or English may be supposed to have imitated old Aeschylus.[13] Then you fortify your Greek geography, make maps of the signal-fires' route from Troy, &c. Finally, you ought to have read the other

---

[12]　[See the list of Cantab terms in Ch. 4. Here, 'cram' is anything other than knowledge of the linguistic aspects of the text itself.]

[13]　This year we were required to illustrate the chorus of Iphigeneia by the parallel passage in Lucretius. Many men I believe gave the whole, as I did. (B)

two plays of the Trilogy, for you are likely to be asked something about them; perhaps there may be a nice little bit of the Eumenides set, which is not to be understood by the light of nature. Similarly for the fourth book of Thucydides, you cram up everything you can about everybody mentioned in Thucydides generally, and this book particularly, taking in much Thirlwall, and Böckh, and Müller's Dorians, and the like.[14] And for the Tenth and Eleventh Books of Cicero to Atticus, (that was our Latin subject), all your knowledge of the great men of that period, and of the legal matters incidentally brought in (e.g. marriage, inheritance, *Comitia*), will be put into requisition. One little bagatelle I had almost forgotten. You will have to turn English prose into Greek and Latin prose, English verse into Greek Iambic Trimeters, and part of some chorus in the Agamemnon into Latin, and possibly also into English verse. This is the 'composition', and is to be done, remember, without the help of books or any other assistance.

Now either of the three subjects opens a pretty wide field before you, quite wide enough to bewilder a tyro, and here it is that the genius of your private tutor comes into play. Private tuition is nowhere alluded to in the university or College statutes; it is entirely a personal and individual matter; yet it is, after the examinations, the great feature of the university instruction, and the public lectures have come to be entirely subordinate to it. The English private tutors in many points take the place of the German professors; true, they have not the same explicit university sanction, but an equivalent for this is found in the final examination for degrees which they have all passed, and no man who has not taken a good degree, expects or pretends to take good men into his team. Of course inferior coaches will do for inferior men – *polloi* for *polloi*. Of late there has been some outcry against private tuition; but if not absolutely a *vital*, it is certainly an *important* element in the whole system, nor should it be suffered as a necessary evil, but admitted as a positive good. One effect of doing away with it would be to throw all classical honors into the hands of the public-school men. Your 'Eton boy' is a *young man* of nineteen, at least two years in advance of a Yale or Harvard Valedictorian in all classical knowledge, and in all classical *elegancies* immeasurably ahead of him. The only way in which you can bring up an inadequately prepared man to 'hold a candle' to such competitors is by diligent personal attention to him. Travis certainly put more into me in seven months than I could have acquired by my own unassisted labors in

---

[14] [Connop Thirlwall's *History of Greece* (1835–47); August Boeckh's *The Public Economy of Athens* (Eng. tr. 1842); Karl Otfried Müller's *The History and Antiquities of the Doric Race* (Eng. tr. 1839): all standard authorities.

two years; and of his exertions in my behalf, I shall always retain a grateful memory. But even with the best tutor – and it is not every man who can get a Travis to coach him – you must make up your mind to read six times as much as you can make use of on the papers, since you can only calculate the general run of the questions in them without being able to make sure of any individual one.[15]

All this time not a word of mathematics. The question has often been put to me, 'Why did you, with your classical tastes, go to Cambridge rather than Oxford?' To which I always reply that there is more classical learning to be picked up at Cambridge than I could ever hope to acquire. The truth is that the Cantabs are just as good scholars as the Oxonians, the former excelling in Greek, the latter in Latin; only at Cambridge you are dosed with mathematics into the bargain. But the College lectures and examinations for the first year embrace, as has been said, only Euclid, Algebra, and Trigonometry.[16] The mathematical men have read these before they came up, and the classical men don't wish to read them till just before they go out. So between too much knowledge and too little inclination to know, the mathematical lectures are but carelessly attended, and as the three mathematical papers count little more than half as much as the six classical, this part of the examination is comparatively disregarded. A classical man may cut all the mathematics but Euclid, while the prospective Senior Wrangler dare not take such a liberty with the classical papers. In the upper years all this is reversed.

I had not opened a mathematical book for more than two years, and certainly never intended to trouble the exact sciences again, but as the 'May' approached I began to feel nervous, and in accordance with Travis's suggestion put on a mathematical tutor for the last month. But 'Dunny' soon found there was not much to be got out of me on so short notice. My analysis was just sufficient to make it probable I had at some period of my life seen the inside of *Wood* and *Peacock*.[17] So I had to fall back upon

---

[15]   All examination papers are printed at the Pitt Press in the most mysterious way, and only leave the printer's hands about five minutes before they are submitted to the students, when they are sent to the examiner in a sealed packet, by a trusty messenger.

[16]   J.M. Heath's lectures on Euclid were the most exhaustive and exhausting I ever heard. (B) [John Moore Heath, Trinity 1826, fellow 1831, assistant tutor then tutor, 1833–44.]

[17]   The two principal text-books in Algebra. [James Wood's *Principles of Mathematics and Natural Philosophy* (4 vols, 1790–9); G.Peacock, *Examples Illustrative of the Use of*

the Euclid. A great godsend is Euclid to the classical men, not only here, but in the Scholarship and the awful, accursed Mathematical Tripos, does he stand them in good stead. Our troubles were to begin on Wednesday; I devoted the two days immediately preceding to getting up the first four books and the sixth, and by eight on Tuesday evening had them ready for immediate use.

At nine next morning, the Hall doors were thrown open to us. The narrow passage between the screens and the buttery was as full as it usually is just before 4 p.m., but the Trinitarians were thronging to a different sort of banquet. The tables were decked with green baize instead of white linen, and the goodly joints of beef and mutton and dishes of smoking potatoes were replaced by a profusion of stationery. Even the dais shared the general fate. At that high table where I had recently been feasting on spring soup and salmon, ducklings and peas, rhubarb tart and custard,[18] with old sherry, *quantum suff*, to imbibe, and the learned wit of the Dons for seasoning, I was now doomed – such is the mutability of human affairs – to write against time for four mortal hours. In those days it was not easy to throw me off my balance, for if a boy has any modesty in him, the training of a large American college, speaking continually to largeish audiences, writing about everything, and reading your writings in public, &c., is pretty sure to knock it out of him; yet I did feel rather nervous that Wednesday morning, and could not for five minutes begin composedly to write out the *Pons Asinorum* which headed our paper, though it had been familiar to me ever since my school days. The pen-and-ink system of examination has been adopted partially at Oxford and almost entirely at Cambridge,[19] in preference to the *viva voce*, on the ground, among others, that it is fairer to timid and diffident men. The advantage in this respect is

---

the Differential and Integral Calculus (1820).] It must be borne in mind that Algebra, Trigonometry, &c., as taught and examined upon at Cambridge are very different from the things that go by the same name in our colleges. Thus, for instance, from one third to one half of the Algebra paper (to which five hours are allotted), is composed of such questions as they call *problems* at Yale, and give specific prizes for. So too, out of the 22 propositions in the Euclid paper, five or six are original ones – 'deductions' they call them.

[18]   The English eat tart and custard together, pouring the latter over the former. If we did this they would call it a dirty habit.

[19]   We had a little viva voce in this examination, perhaps equivalent to a twentieth or twenty-fifth part of it. [For the contrast between the two universities, see C.A. Stray, 'From oral to written examination: Oxford, Cambridge and Dublin 1700–1914', *History of Universities* 20 (2005), pp. 76–130.]

somewhat exaggerated: the excitement, though not so great for the moment, is more constant, and the scratching of some hundred pens all about you makes one fearfully nervous. Then too, any little slips you make in a *viva voce* may be allowed for, or may even escape observation, but *litera scripta manet*; everything that you put down here will be criticized deliberately and in cold blood. Awful idea!

At one, 'close your papers, gentlemen' says the examiner who has been solemnly pacing up and down all the time. (This examiner is never your college lecturer or tutor, and of course never your private tutor.)[20] At two the hall assumes its more legitimate and welcome guise, dinner being thrown back two hours; at four[21] the grinding begins again, and lasts till eight; at night there is a supper put on specially for the occasion. How that supper is demolished! what loads of cold beef and lobster vanish before the examinees! Young ladies sometimes picture to themselves students as delicate, pale youths who live on toast and tea. Never was there a greater mistake. Men who study in earnest eat in earnest. A senior wrangler[22] sat opposite me one summer at the Scholars' table, and to see that man perform upon a round of beef was a curiosity.

Thus passed four days; eight hours a-day thinking and writing together at full speed; two or three hours of cramming in the intervals (for though the principle and theory is never to look at a book during an examination, or indeed two or three days before, that your mind may be fresh and vigorous, few men are cool enough to put this into practice); and long lounges at night, very different from the ordinary constitutional. Thus far I had rather exceeded my expectations, but there was still impending Monday's Algebra paper, and the thought of that left me very little rest on Sunday. A friend who had obligingly backed me to the extent of ten shillings, endeavored to comfort me with the assurance that if I had done my Classics properly, I must be safe without the Algebra, and if I had not, all I could do on Monday would not make much difference. But this satisfactory assurance did not afford me full consolation. Far more refreshing was our stroll through the Trinity grounds, where Travis and I spent the greater part of the day. Would that I could borrow D'Israeli's pencil for five minutes – or I could even be content with Poe's – to describe these grounds as they really are.

---

[20]   This year (1841) the Examiner in Euclid was Archibald Smith, Senior Wrangler and a famous mathematician according to our juvenile notions. (B)

[21]   Since altered. (B)

[22]   Cayley. (B) [Arthur Cayley, Trinity 1838, Senior Wrangler 1842; Sadlerian Professor of Mathematics 1862–95.]

The north and south walks are natural arcades, thickly canopied with the boughs of glorious horse chestnuts that fling their arms out fifteen feet, clear across the path, and down almost to the rails of the low paddocks in the midst. The west walk is protected from the high road by a broad ditch and a double row of limes,[23] and the east walk lies along the green sloping banks of the little Cam, which is *so* little here, and so regular even in its irregularities, that it looks more like an artificial stream in a pleasure ground than a real river. Come upon this bridge; it is before Whewell's reign, so you need not fear that that very worthy but somewhat dictatorial man will ride up to you with the information that 'a bridge is a place of transit and not of lounge'. Eastward you have just in front of you the Gothic gateway of the New Court; and north of it the College Library, a simple and chaste structure, built of fancifully-tinted orange and yellow stone, unequalled for beauty and durability. Look still further north, and over a bend of the Cam, on a spreading, sloping lawn, you see a large castellated building of the same yellow stone, with turrets and pinnacles in abundance. That is the 'New Building' of St. John's. Southward are two more antique bridges and a profusion of green, with the majestic towers of King's looming above it. Turning westward, you look up the central path through an arching avenue of lime trees. It is not long, perhaps the eighth of a mile, but as you look up it from the bridge it seems to join with the Fellows' Garden beyond the road,[24] and continue in a straight line to the very steeple of Coton Church, which terminates your view several miles off.[25] The picture is not complete without the 'men', all in their academicals, as it is Sunday. The blue gown of Trinity has not exclusive possession of its own walks: various others are to be discerned, the Pembroke looped at the sleeve, the Christ's and Catherine curiously crimped in front, and the Johnian with its unmistakable 'crackling'.[26] There is also here and there a

---

[23] This is the avenue of which Tennyson sings:

> Up that long walk of limes and past
> To see the rooms in which he dwelt (kept: less poetical?)
>
> *In memoriam* LXXXVI (T)

[24] Our fellows rejoiced in *two* gardens, one within, the other without the college grounds. ('Also a bowling green': T.)

[25] [It was this view which the Greek scholar Richard Porson (d.1808) had compared to the progression from a fellowship to a college living: 'A long dreary road, with a church in the distance'. See E.H. Barker, *Literary Anecdotes and Contemporary Reminiscences of Professor Porson and Others* (1852), vol. 2 p. 21.]

[26] All the different Collegians used to have slang names, derived from various

town snob to be seen and a fair sprinkling of servant-maids and children. Here it was we walked, adding marks, and calculating the chance of my First; and thus we made our calculations.

All the papers together are worth 3000, but no one gets full marks. This is owing partly to the great extent of the 'cram' papers, which are purposely made to cover as much ground as possible, that every one may find something in them he can do; and partly to the fact that the same man is seldom (I may say never indeed) first both in classics and mathematics.[27] The best man of the year has from 2000 to 2400. The ordinary limit of the First Class is 1200, but this standard is sometimes raised, for one feature of Cambridge examinations is, that they go by *breaks* rather than by actual number of marks, that is, by relative rather than positive merit; and it is this which makes it so difficult to predict your place with anything like certainty.[28] As the greatest accuracy is required, by all the examiners, and the greatest elegance by most of them, you must not only be solicitous for how much you have done, but for how you have done it. A little well polished up is worth more than a great deal turned off carelessly; and you often find in the fourth or fifth class, unfortunates who have covered as much paper as the head man. There are, say 130 Freshmen, who are arranged in nine classes, the First Class varying from twenty to thirty.[29] Fifty marks will prevent one from being 'posted',[30] but there are always two or three too stupid as well as idle to save their 'Post'. These drones are *posted* separately as 'not worthy to be classed', and privately slanged afterwards by the Master and Seniors. Should a man be posted twice in succession, he is generally recommended to try the air of some Small College, or devote his energies to some other walk of life.

'You will get full marks or very nearly, for your translations', said Travis,

---

animals; none of these have stuck except the 'Johnian pigs'. Their new bridge is popularly called *the Isthmus of Suez*. ('Also the Bridge of Grunts': T) [Trinity men were called 'bulldogs'.]

[27] Goulburn was. (B) [Not quite: as we have seen, he was Senior Classic and 2nd Wrangler in 1835.]

[28] [In fact, the marking system combined the two methods – what would now be called norm and criterion referencing. Marks were allotted to questions and totalled; but discretion was exercised in 'bracketing' and in drawing lines between classes.]

[29] 24 in our year. (B)

[30] [As the glossary in Ch. 4 shows, to be posted is to be failed in a college examination. The next sentence shows the origin of the usage: failed candidates are listed as unworthy on a public notice.]

'I hope. Put that down, 600. And it is safe to say half marks for the cram-papers − 450. About your composition I don't know. Did you do any Latin Verse?'

'There wasn't time.'

'Just as well there wasn't; and your Greek Iambics won't come to much. Then your Greek prose will count something − not a great deal, and your Latin prose is pretty fair: you might get two-thirds for it. Altogether, taking in your English verse, which will bring you some *kudos* from Bunbury,[31] − you may have quarter marks on the whole − 75 out of 300. Put in forty for the four *viva voces*. How much is that altogether?'

'1165.'

'How much Euclid did you do? Fifteen?'

'No, fourteen; one of them was a deduction.'

'Suppose one wrong: there are twenty-one on the paper, and the six deductions count half. Perhaps you have half marks and I should think not so much − say 170 out of 400.'

'Then I did three whole questions in Trigonometry.'

'Throw them in in case of accidents. This gives you 1300. You ought to be safe. Take my advice and don't fret about the Algebra.'

But this very good advice the young man couldn't take, and did fret himself about the Algebra, so much that he slept not a wink all night; for if the paper was an easy one it might be possible to pile up a hundred marks or more on it, which would make the First safe beyond a doubt. Of course the paper was not an easy one, and I did perhaps four questions in it after staying in as many hours, then came out in a fit of disgust, and threw it into the fire; but my labors were over, at any rate, which was a great consolation. That day I eat dinner for two, went to bed before nine that night, and slept *fifteen hours and a half.* Some of my friends say I have never been fairly awake since. Next day I took a long gallop; ditto ditto on the days succeeding, and when not in the saddle read the new magazines, for May had passed into June, while we were in full scribble.[32] By these relaxations I brought myself to a tolerably comfortable state of mind and body by Friday, so as to be prepared for the result. Meanwhile reports began to spread. Mistranslations leaked out, how one man had rendered *novas tabulas* 'new furniture', and another *ouk edras akme* 'there is no top to

---

[31] [Edward Herbert Bunbury, Senior Classic 1833, fellow of Trinity since 1835, college lecturer in Latin; one of the examiners.]

[32] The Examination ended remarkably late this year (1841), I think on June 8th.

(B)

the seat'. Discussions were raised about the first man of the year,[33] whether it would be Parsons, the Captain of Shrewsbury,[34] or Rothermann, the Newcastle scholar from Eton, or Henslowe of King's College, London, or Macintosh, from Glasgow (for there comes up a first rate Scotchman occasionally).[35] At length, late on Friday evening, as I was preparing a solitary cup of tea, one of my friends came tumbling into the room with the gratifying intelligence that 'we were all right'. So I was paraded in all the Cambridge and London papers with twenty-three more, as First-Class men in the Trinity Freshman Examination, which honor moreover entitled us to a prize of books at the Commemoration, next November, towards which the college gave us nineteen shillings and sixpence sterling, and we added as much as we liked, for this kind of humbug is common to English and American Colleges.

---

[33] The names are placed alphabetically in the class-lists, but the first eight or ten individual places are generally known.

[34] The head boy of a public school is called the *captain* of it.

[35] 'It was Clark of Shrewsbury School', comments Bowring, who identifies 'Parsons' as Clark, 'Rothermann' as Hotham, and 'Macintosh' tentatively as Stewart. [The college examinations book lists the candidates in alphabetic order but gives their marks: in mark order, they include Clark, W.G. 1991, Stewart 1892, Hedley 1863, Hotham 1863. 'Henslowe' is presumably Hedley. William George Clark, 1840, 2nd Classic 1844, fellow 1844–78, Public Orator 1857–69; Spencer Stewart, 1839; Henry Hotham, 1840, fellow 1845; Thomas Hedley, 1840, fellow 1844–56.]

10

The First Long Vacation [1841]

A friend in need is a friend indeed.

Virgil

Conticuere omnes.
They all went on tick together.

Free Translation.

A Bad Start

Thoroughly recruited by a week's rest, and additionally inspirited by the favorable result of the examination, I went down to London for a fortnight to deliver various letters of introduction and see a little of the Great Metropolis. It was the pleasantest and liveliest time of the year, the beginning of June, when even London boasts of a little sun, and the subterranean-looking wilderness of houses and interminable mazes of muddy streets are kindled up with a few stray beams. But I did not know people enough 'in town' to dine out every day, and the stranger in London who does not is apt to find the time hang heavy on his hands – even if there is a general election[1] going on as there then was; so before fifteen days had elapsed I was back again at Cambridge studying.

---

[1] [The election brought Peel and the Conservatives into power with a substantial majority.]

Studying in a vacation! Even so; for you may almost take it as a general rule that College regulations and customs in England are just the reverse of what they are in America. In America you rise and 'recite' to your instructor who is seated; in England you sit and construe to him as he stands at his desk.[2] In America you go sixteen times a week to chapel or woe be to you; but then you may stay out of your room all night for a week together and nobody will know or care. In England you have about seven chapels to keep and may choose your own time of day, morning or evening, to keep them; but you cannot get out of College after ten at night, and if being out, you stay till after twelve, you are very likely to hear of it next morning. In America you may go about in any dress that does not outrage decency, and it is not uncommon for youths to attend chapel and 'recitation room' in their ragged dressing gowns, with perhaps the pretext of a cloak; in England you must scrupulously observe the academical garb while within the College walls, and not be too often seen wearing white great coats or other eccentric garments under it. In America the manufacture of coffee in your room will subject you to suspicion, and should that bugbear, the tutor, find a bottle of wine on your premises, he sets you down for a hardened reprobate; in England you may take your bottle or two or six with as many friends as you please, and unless you disturb the whole court by your exuberant revelry, you need fear no annoyance from your tutor; nay, expand your supper into a stately dinner and he will come himself (public tutor or private) like a brick as he is, and consume his share of the generous potables, yea, take a hand in your rubber afterwards. In America you may not marry, but your tutor can; in England you may marry and he can't.[3] In America you never think of opening a book in vacation; in England the vacations are the very times when you read most. Indeed, since the vacations occupy more than half the year, he who keeps them idle, will not do much work

---

[2] [The recitation, or rehearsal of lessons, was the central pedagogical event in US colleges. A 'construe' (usually pronounced 'conster') involved the analysis and interpretation of a passage of Latin or Greek. The whole paragraph is a fine example of Bristed's ability to deploy comparative evidence.]

[3] The married men at Cambridge are usually such as take Orders late in life; they are men of some property and become Fellow Commoners of a Small College. A father and son were undergraduates together at Peterhouse in my time. There are some traditional jokes about this class of students, such as that one of them failed repeatedly in his endeavors to obtain a degree, and his son used to come running into the house with 'Ma, Pa's plucked again!' A married student is obliged to dine in Hall like the rest, and only freed from 'gate' rules.

during his College course. Then in the vacations, particularly the Long, there is every facility for reading, that is, no temptation not to read or interruption to your reading – no large dinners or wine or supper parties, no rowing men making a noise about the courts, no exciting boat-races, no lectures (owing to the private-tutorial system, the public lectures are, with some happy exceptions, rather in the way of than any help to the best men), the chapel rules looser than ever, the town utterly dull and lifeless. When I was ill at Cambridge during the greater part of two Longs, and could only read a few hours each day, I thought it the most lonely and desolate of places. It seemed a town without inhabitants. All the tradesmen who can, leave Cambridge, and of the 1800 students not 200 remain. Those that are left in each College (from half a dozen to forty as the size of the College may be) are all bound by the common tie of their studies; their very lightest talk has some *shop* in it, and if not personally acquainted at first they generally become so before the three months are over. Indeed, so attractive is the Vacation-College-life that the great trouble of the Dons is to keep the men from staying up during the Long. In the Small Colleges it makes a serious difference, for the few dignitaries of one of these lesser institutions often want to take a tour *en masse* and shut up the College, 'like a boarding-school', say the Trinitarians and Johnians in ridicule. But at Trinity the Scholars and Sizars have a *right* to remain in residence just as much as the Fellows themselves, being equally 'on the foundation'; and here the Undergraduate ranks are augmented by the Bachelors reading for Fellowships. But as the College authorities are in small force, sometimes not more than two or three Fellows being left, all students except Scholars and Sizars are warned off, save some few who obtain permission to stay by particular favor, and among these are always some Freshmen who have done well in the May. So assiduously does the reading-man set himself to his work from the very beginning.

I spent some six weeks in this way, reading Aeschylus and Euripides and taking copious notes thereon. I had few acquaintances of my own standing; they were nearly all Bachelor Scholars; my private tutor was one of them, and we lived very quietly and pleasantly, knee-deep in books all the morning till two, and then strolling about the beautiful grounds in the environs of the town. What little approach to out-door amusements one ever sees among the lower orders here is to be found at this season in the outskirts of Cambridge. About the end of June and beginning of July was a fair,[4]

---

[4] Not *Sturbridge Fair* founded by King John, and formerly very celebrated, but a smaller one called *Midsummer* or *Pot Fair*. [Both fairs date from the 13th century.

and we mingled among the people and went through the popular sports, rode in swings, attended the sixpenny itinerary theatres, and laughed at the tragic performance of 'Ennery, King of Hingland', and Fair Rosamond. I remember the date from the Fourth of July occurring just afterwards, when I celebrated by a 'hang-out',[5] and my English guests drank claret with as much liberality as if they had had a personal or patriotic interest in the reminiscence. Our after-dinner meetings two or three times a week were very moderate, never exceeding a couple of hours, after which we fell to work again. It was a quiet and virtuous existence, plenty of occupation without fatigue or excitement, and enough relaxation to keep us in the best condition. The only drawback to our felicity was that during the Long, the Cambridge confectioners, like those of Little Pedlington,[6] made no ice-cream unless it was ordered the day before; and this was not such a deprivation as it would be in New York, the English summers being not *quite* so warm as ours. I recollect being obliged to build a fire one day in this very July.

This kind of life had grown upon me so, that I resolved, though somewhat older than I could have wished, and a year above the average age of those in my standing, to go through the whole course, and consequently give up my original project of spending but one year at Cambridge and then proceeding to a German University. A very good resolution so far as the intention to make myself a scholar was concerned; unfortunately, immediately after it was taken, I went to work so as to destroy most of the benefits of it, by suddenly taking a trip homeward over the Atlantic, under the excuse of having to attend to my affairs. At my departure, I was in perfect health, stronger and nimbler than I ever was before or have been since, having practised vaulting over gates and leaping ditches, and other extempore gymnastics in vogue at Cambridge, till my performances actually astonished myself. But I left the thermometer at 70° in Liverpool and found it 90° at Boston, nor did it fall much below that for the two months I was in America. Finally, the confined air of a small state-room completed what the change of temperature had begun, and deranged my system so as to bring on a severe illness which manifested itself just as I was fairly settled at Trinity again in my new quarters, a very nice suite of

---

Stourbridge Fair declined in the 18th century and was finally abolished in 1934; Midsummer Fair still exists, but only as a funfair.]

[5] [A party.]

[6] [A fictional village, home of cant and egotism, depicted by John Poole in his *Little Pedlington and the Pedlingtonians* (1839).]

Fellow-Commoner's rooms[7] (for having come up late the first year, I was then obliged to take whatever I could get).

For seven months I lay in a precarious state, and for more than two years was exceedingly feeble, and unable to return home or to travel any distance from my place of residence. A palpitation of the heart, brought on by derangement of the liver and stomach, made it impossible for me to undergo any physical or mental exertion, and hardly allowed me to eat enough to support life. Having, as the first resource in this deprivation of ordinary employment, attacked all the miscellaneous reading I could lay hands on, my eyes began to fail and I was totally helpless. In this strait an opportunity was afforded me to test the value of English friendship, and obtain an insight into the best side of English character which otherwise I might not have done. Time was of great value to all my acquaintances that were Undergraduates or Bachelors (the idle men whom I had known in my first year were now absent, having been eliminated by the usual process), and the Fellows, though more at leisure, had still their routine of study and amusement which had not fitted them for, and was not agreeably varied by, the task of amusing an invalid who could do nothing to amuse himself and was even forbidden to talk. But these men sacrificed hours to me night after night, doing all in their power to divert and alleviate my unpleasant situation. Pecuniary embarrassments were added to my other troubles at this time. It was just after the failure of the U.S. Bank of Pennsylvania,[8] when a distrust of American securities and American debtors was beginning to spread in England, and my College tutor, to whom I was indebted, had no certain knowledge of my ultimate solvency, yet he acted towards me with the utmost delicacy. Great as the accommodation was, it never struck me so much as the kindness of those who used to visit me, six or seven in an evening, and whose interesting and cheering conversation made the tedious hours of my illness move lightly by. It would make too long a list to enumerate, them all, but there was one so particularly kind to me that I cannot help making mention of his name here. If JOHN GROTE ever sees this page, will he accept this public acknowledgment of my obligations to him, and this testimony to his kindness towards a sick and helpless stranger? The goodness and amiability associated in all private relations with the name

---

[7]   There is always a great demand for the rooms in College. Those at lodging-houses are not so good, while the rules are equally strict, the owners being solemnly bound to report all their lodgers, who stay out at night, under pain of being 'discommonsed', a species of College excommunication.

[8]   [See note on p. 45.]

of GROTE, rival the talent and learning which have long been publicly connected with it. More cannot be said; and had I said less, I should have to tax myself with ingratitude.[9]

While thus unable to take part in the studies and occupations that were going on about me, I nevertheless observed and heard not a little respecting them. 'Shop', or as it is sometimes here called '*Calendar*',[10] necessarily enters to a large extent into the conversation of the Cantabs, and it was one of my weaknesses to be amused by it. Of all kinds of personal gossip it is certainly the most harmless – what degree such a man took in such a year, who are likely to be the next Scholars and so forth. But, besides, I looked beyond this, to the light which such matters threw on the general system; indeed, the only way I had of improving my time, was to pick up all the particulars I could about the various colleges, and the most distinguished private tutors, and the modifications of study pursued at and under each. But before proceeding to detail any of these, a recent remark requires some explanation. I have spoken of being in debt to my tutor.

The Cambridge Credit System

It is pretty generally known that young men at the English Universities often contract debts as Undergraduates which seriously impoverish their families, or cripple themselves in after life. The University authorities have often been blamed for this, but it is easier to blame them than to state what they ought to do and can do to prevent it. The parties most in fault are the tradesmen, who without taking any pains to ascertain beforehand a Freshman's means and wants, tempt, solicit, and worry him into making purchases. The academical powers have made a rule that all bills shall pass through the college tutors; for the students' further protection they have enacted that any tradesman bringing a suit against an Undergraduate shall be 'discommonsed', i.e. all the Undergraduates are forbidden to deal with him. Many suspicious or doubtful characters are similarly treated, so as to warn the students that if they will hold any communication with them, it

---

[9] He was <u>very</u> kind to me 20 years afterwards. (T) [John Grote, Trinity 1831, fellow 1837–66, Knightbridge Professor of Moral Philosophy 1855–66. A liberal reformer who often annoyed the autocratic William Whewell, Grote founded a philosophical debating society known as the Grote Club. See J.R. Gibbins, *John Grote, Cambridge University and the Development of Victorian Thought* (Exeter, 2007).]

[10] Because the *Cambridge Calendar* contains all the list of triposes, Prizemen, &c. [The *Calendar* was first published in 1796, and had appeared annually since 1799.]

must be at their own risk. It is indeed said that the Dons set a bad example, by living extravagantly themselves. If all the loose exaggerations are pared away from this charge so as to bring it down to its nucleus of truth, the amount of it is that the Fellows eat and drink rather more luxuriously than is necessary. But this does not justify the Undergraduates in doing the same, any more than a son has a right to spend as much money as his father does.

It must not be supposed, however, that extravagant and impudent young men are the only ones who get into debt. There is another and less mischievous development of the credit system. When a young man of scanty means shows good talents and disposition it is common for his college tutor to trust him for a portion (half or more) of his college bills (frequently including the sent-in tradesmen's bills), during his second and third years, so that he may be free to avail himself of private tuition and other advantages, and in no respect crippled during his competition for honors. When the student takes his degree, he obtains by pupilizing enough to render further assistance unnecessary, and soon begins to pay off his debt, and when he gets his Fellowship he clears himself very speedily. It is in fact pledging his labor and time two or three years ahead, and though such a mortgage may in some cases prove an awkward incumbrance, the general result is good: it enables many first-rate men to get a first-rate education, which they could not otherwise have obtained. Sometimes a young man in this position falls ill or acquires bad habits, and his tutor loses the whole.

The tradesmen are in the habit of complaining that the tutors receive from their pupils money to pay them, and then keep it back for months or years, thus defrauding them of large sums in interest. Hearing this charge repeated beyond the University limits, I took the trouble to investigate it myself. The result of my inquiries was that the tutors' bills are paid on an average one term before the tradesmen's and that the tutor on the average of his pupils has to wait five terms, so the tradesman must wait six, or two years, and the tutor gains from two to four months' interest, which makes at English rates about 1¼ per cent. commission on all the money that goes through his hands – little enough for his trouble, even putting his occasional losses out of the question.

11

The Second Year [1841–2]

After the trial heat of the first May examination, the field of candidates for Honors begins to assume something like a calculable form. The *ruck* falls off rapidly, and the good men settle down to their pace. Many of them are now for the first time under crack private tutors – for it frequently, indeed usually happens, that a 'coach' of reputation declines taking men into his team before they have made time in public. When the Freshman[1] has not a public-school reputation, and sometimes even when he has, the result of the May decides whether he will go out in Honors or not – that is, whether he will be a reading or a non-reading man (for with all but the very badly prepared, going out in Poll is equivalent to doing nothing – so far as University studies are concerned – for at least half the course). If his success be such as to encourage him, he begins his work again, as has been observed, early in the Long vacation, towards the close of which, however, he takes a real vacation of a month or so (generally provided for in all engagements with private tutors, or for reading-parties), so as to come to his work fresh at the beginning of the college term. Though not so decisive in its results as the third year, this second year is the turning point for not a few. Some who have done very well in low mathematics,

---

[1] Hopkins took no freshmen till long after our day. (B) [William Hopkins, Peterhouse 1823, 7th Wrangler 1827; the leading mathematical coach of his day, numbering 17 Senior Wranglers among his pupils.]

break down after passing the Differential Calculus.[2] Some grow indolent and fall off from depending too much on their first year's success. Some Trinity men are disgusted by not getting a Scholarship at the first trial, and strike work in consequence.

A Foundation Scholarship being the requisite stepping stone to a Fellowship,[3] is naturally one of the first objects of our reading man's aim. At several of the colleges these scholarships are given to the students who acquit themselves best in the first May. At Trinity there is a special examination, held about the beginning of the Easter term, in which all Second and Third-year men are eligible candidates. To an American Collegian who has no motive for anticipating the routine of a fixed course, such a competition must seem singular. *Sophomores* and *Juniors* he would consider a very unfair match; and he would be still more surprised to hear that in those contests for Scholarships, the successful Second-year men beat all the Third year – it is a *sine qua non* that they should – those who have not another chance being naturally favored above those who have, *ceteris paribus*. But this is partly[4] accounted for by the fact that five or six of the best men in the third year are out of the way, having themselves been chosen scholars in their second year. The whole number of men making up the two years is about one hundred and seventy, and some seventy of these usually present themselves for the vacant Scholarships, which are from twelve to twenty in number, but generally less than fifteen. The successful candidates of the second year are usually to those of the third in the proportion of five to eight. This examination does not differ from the May merely in being optional; another very important distinction consists in the absence of subjects fixed beforehand; the candidates go in trusting to their general knowledge. At the same time there is not an *unlimited* selection from the Classics, as in the Tripos and the University Scholarships; the candidate need not expect to find any Pindar, Aristophanes, or Aristotle, any Persius, or Lucretius, on the papers; and seldom will there be any Plato, Aeschylus

---

[2]   The Differential is considered the first step in a really mathematical education; the next is to attack Geometry of Three Dimensions. One of our mathematical coaches used to divide mankind into two classes, those who had read Geometry of Three Dimensions and those who had not. [Bowring identifies the coach as Walton: i.e. William Walton (Trinity), 8th Wrangler 1836. Walton was a well-known mathematical coach, and published a collection of Tripos problems in 1842.]

[3]   Except in rare cases, as when a member of another college is chosen Fellow. ['This never happens at Trinity': B.]

[4]   Entirely. (T)

or Theocritus, Plautus or Juvenal. In Greek, Homer, Hesiod, Sophocles, Euripides, Herodotus, Thucydides, Xenophon, and Demosthenes; in Latin, Virgil and Horace, Cicero, Livy, and Tacitus, are the authors usually selected from; and this still leaves a pretty wide range, some of these authors being sufficiently voluminous. The Mathematical papers do not go higher than may be supposed to fall within the ordinary reading of a Third-year aspirant to Mathematical Honors. They are only half as many in number as the Classical papers, and probably do not count more than half as much; at any rate the examination is more favorable to Classical than to Mathematical men; a good Classic may get a Scholarship with the least possible quantity of Mathematics – say twenty marks out of four hundred – a Mathematician equally deficient in Classics must be first-rate indeed in his branch to succeed. In the present year (1842) it looked as if these proportions were to be somewhat more equalized, owing to a change in the head of affairs. Our master, Dr. Christopher Wordsworth (brother of the poet), had resigned and was succeeded by Dr. Whewell.

A Change of Dynasty

Dr. Whewell's accession to the Mastership of Trinity might well have been an era in the history of that 'royal and religious foundation'. The new Head was a gentleman of most commanding personal appearance, and the very sound of his powerful voice betokened no ordinary man.[5] He was a remarkably good rider even in a country of horsemen, and the anecdote was often told, and not altogether repudiated by him, how in his younger days, about the time of his ordination, a pugilist in whose company he accidentally was travelling, audibly lamented that such lusty thews and sinews should be thrown away on a parson. With these physical advantages was combined a knowledge almost literally universal. Some people are said to know a little of everything; he might be truly said to know a great deal of everything. Second Wrangler of his year, Professor of Mineralogy, and afterwards of Moral Philosophy,[6] author of a Bridgewater Treatise, and writer on a diversity of subjects, scientific and ethical, he kept up his Classics to an extent unusual for a scientific man, and did not neglect the lighter walks of literature. His name is on the list of the Cambridge Prize Poets, and is

[5]   He was the biggest man I think in the University. (B) [William Whewell, Trinity 1812, 2nd Wrangler 1816, fellow of Trinity 1817; Professor of Mineralogy 1828–32, Knightbridge Professor of Moral Philosophy 1838–55; Master of Trinity 1841–66.]

[6]   Technically called *Casuistry* in the University, and sometimes *Moral Theology*.

also known in connexion with several translations from the German. In conversation it was scarcely possible to start a subject without finding him at home in it. A story is current about him, not absolutely authenticated, but certainly of the *se non vero ben trovato* sort – that some of the Dons who were tired of hearing him explain everything, and enlighten everybody in Combination room, laid a trap to catch him in this wise. They determined to get themselves up thoroughly in some very out-of-the-way topic, and introduce it as if by accident on the first convenient occasion. Accordingly they pitched upon something connected with China, either – for there are two versions of the story – Chinese musical instruments or the Chinese game of Chess. Various odd books, and particularly a certain volume of a certain Cyclopaedia, were dragged out of their dusty repose and carefully perused. Next Sunday when the College dignitaries and some stranger guests were marshalled over their port and biscuit, the conspirators thoroughly primed, and with their parts artistically distributed, watched their time and adroitly introduced the prepared topic. One after the other they let drop most naturally a quantity of strange erudition, marvellously astounding, no doubt, to the Small-College Dons present, and apparently puzzling to the object of attack, for he actually remained silent for a full quarter of an hour, till just as the parties were congratulating themselves on their complete success, he turned to the principal speaker, and remarked, 'Oh, I see you've been reading the article I wrote for such a Cyclopaedia in such a year'. They gave it up after that. A man that knows so many things cannot know them all perfectly, and is scarce likely to know any one of them with the accuracy attainable by a man who has made that particular branch his *specialité*; and in England where the division of mental, like that of mechanical labor, is carried out to a degree which must be witnessed and experienced to be conceived, it easily happened that Dr. Whewell was looked down upon in each of his pursuits by the man who had no other pursuit but that one. In this respect he has been compared to Lord Brougham,[7] the extent of whose knowledge has destroyed all chance of his accuracy and polish in any one branch of it; but there is this important difference in Brougham's favor, that in one thing – oratory – he stands among the first of his age, while it could not be said of Whewell that he had attained a similar

---

7 [Henry Brougham, 1ˢᵗ Baron Brougham and Vaux, had been Lord Chancellor 1830–4. A leading Whig politician and intellectual, he was a moving spirit behind the *Edinburgh Review* (1802) and the University of London (1826). Brougham was a powerful orator and had also published a translation of Demosthenes' *De Corona* (1840).]

pre-eminence in any one branch. The mass of his general knowledge taken together, constituted his strength. There were few men of like pretensions to weigh or appreciate the strength of this; he was judged piecemeal, and part of him taken for the whole, by men whose whole development and training was partial. Sydney Smith's saying of him, 'that omniscience was his forte, and science his foible,' was very generally circulated and applauded.[8] But this ridiculed omniscience well fitted him for the head of a great College, numbering among its members and pupils men of so many different pursuits. In liberality and reach of study, and acquaintance with general and foreign literature, Cambridge is always before Oxford, and the Trinity men considerably in advance of the other Cambridge collegians. It might have been supposed that Whewell's accession to the Mastership was the very thing they wanted. Yet this event was anything but welcome to the majority of both Fellows and Undergraduates, who, if their wishes and votes could have influenced the matter,[9] would certainly have chosen either Dean Peacock or Professor Sedgwick to rule over them.[10] This repugnance towards a gentleman so distinguished arose from some unfortunate propensities of his, which had been conspicuous enough during his Tutorship, and which it was correctly supposed would be rather intensified than diminished by his elevation. The Professor of Casuistry was an intolerably *fussy* man – a rigid martinet, weakly punctilious about trifles. Such a man, however great his learning, or talents, or merit of any sort, may perhaps make a great Schoolmaster, but can never be a good presiding officer over students of mature years. By treating like schoolboys those nearly or quite arrived at the age and dignity of men, he chafes and worries them to no purpose, and some portion of the annoyance must at times react upon himself. While leaving untouched actual abuses (of which Trinity, like most old institutions, could boast a few fat ones), our new master enforced petty and

---

[8] [Alas, Bristed has transposed the two terms – it was omniscience which was allegedly Whewell's foible: 'what a fatal foible' (E or T). Also corrected by B.]

[9] Most of the College Headships are at the disposal of the Crown. [Not so, as Bristed acknowledged in an errata note at the end of his second edition; in fact, none except Trinity's.]

[10] [Adam Sedgwick, Vice-Master of Trinity 1844–62, Woodwardian Professor of Geology 1818–73; George Peacock, tutor 1823–39, Lowndean Professor of Astronomy 1837–58, Dean of Ely 1839–58. Sedgwick was conservative, Peacock a liberal, but both men were very popular with undergraduates. Christopher Wordsworth had been ailing, but hung on as Master till the Tories under Peel were returned in the 1841 election, thus making Whewell the most likely candidate.]

long neglected regulations about walking over grass-plots, and crossing the court without a cap and gown at certain hours; he revived obsolete laws against the domestic variety of tiger, which interdicted the possession of that useful animal to any but Noblemen or Fellow Commoners;[11] he exacted the most rigorous personal etiquette, causing it to be openly promulgated or secretly circulated by the tutors that when Undergraduates were invited to the *conversaziones* at the Lodge, they were expected never to sit down in the Master's presence.[12] By these and similar proceedings he made himself very unpopular with the mass of the students, and the Classical men were particularly annoyed at an avowed intention of changing the plan on which Scholarships had been given. It was semi-officially announced through the various tutors and other College officers (the Master is not supposed to hold any *personal* communication with the Undergraduates in his official capacity), that a certain modicum of Mathematics – I forget how many marks, but certainly more than many of the Classical men had been in the habit of aspiring to – would be absolutely insisted on, and the Classical papers of those who did not come up to this standard would not be looked at. The discontent that ensued was not of much importance in itself, but has some interest as illustrating the antagonism of Classics and Mathematics, and the absolute detestation in which a majority of Classical men hold purely scientific studies. Even in our Colleges this is easy to remark, but in a foreign University where both branches are carried out much further and more thoroughly, the line is very strongly drawn. 'Double men', as proficients in both Classics and Mathematics are termed, are very rare; to make one, not only diversity of talent, but a strong constitution is required. The work demanded of a man reading for high Honors in both Triposes is *tremendous*, and every year increasing; and the Calendar does not show an average of *two* 'Double Firsts' annually for the last ten years out of one hundred and thirty-eight graduates in Honors and more than twice that number of graduates altogether.[13]

The Classical men found the University Tripos regulations which required them to go out in Mathematical Honors before they could sit for Classical, exceedingly oppressive, but they endured them as sturdily as their elders

---

[11] There were but few Pensioners who 'hung out' servants of their own, which gave a worse air to the rule, as it seemed like a privilegium against those few. Fellow-Commoners used to be an exception to all laws, human and divine, at all the Colleges. I am not sure but they are so still at some of the small ones.

[12] The parties hence got the name of 'stand ups'. (B)

[13] There were *fourteen* Double Firsts between 1840 and 1850.

do the taxes; it was some compensation and consolation to be able to do without the much disliked study at Trinity, and get Scholarships and Fellowships by dint of Classics alone. For Trinity scholars had been so utterly unmathematical as to go out among the *polloi* and yet were elected Fellows after it.[14] The cases were not very common to be sure, but they were numerous enough for a precedent. To introduce into the College examinations any restrictions like those which embarrassed the University ones, was invading the votaries of Classic lore in their very citadel. What particularly annoyed them was the threatened loss of time − having to get up a certain quantity of mathematics twice or three times instead of once; since whatever they imbibed would be lost again in the intervals from the middle of the second to the middle of the third year, and thence to the last Long, or the term before the Degree; the intermediate presence of Classical work being sufficient to drive it out, even if it had interest enough in itself to stand any chance of being retained − which was not the case. They were willing to undergo the unpleasant dose once for all at the end of three years, but to take it once a year for three years in succession, was unendurable. Even the Mathematicians did not all agree with the Master, their College pride getting the better of their professional and scientific *amour propre*. Not believing that Trinity could be brought up to the Mathematical point of Johns, they feared he would only endanger its Classical superiority by his experiments. Ultimately this requisition of a stated amount of Mathematics in the Scholarship, after being enforced for a year or two, came to be practically a dead letter.[15]

The Little Go

But there is another interruption to which all students whether Classical or Mathematical, and whatever college they belong to, are subject in the middle of their second year; and which is noteworthy as showing the mutual independence of, or in fact conflict between the public and private instruction often to be observed at Cambridge. This interruption is the Previous Examination commonly called the *Little Go* (at Oxford *the Smalls*), being the former of the only two examinations required by the University for the B.A. degree. It is held near the end of the Lent (Second) Term. The

---

[14]　Mansfield, Gibbs, etc. (B) [Mansfield first appeared in Chapter 8 as 'Horace Spedding'; Frederick Gibbs, 1839, fellow 1845−53, tutor to the Prince of Wales 1852−8; CB 1858.]

[15]　Horrid tyranny. (T)

subjects are partly constant and partly variable; the variable ones, of which notice is given a year in advance, are a Greek author, a Latin author, and one of the four Gospels; the only constant subject at this time was Paley's *Evidences*. *Author* in the last sentence must be taken in a limited sense, as denoting one Book of Homer, Herodotus, Livy, or Tacitus, two short dialogues of Plato, one Greek Tragedy, or the like. The examination involves a little *viva voce*, and it was said that if a man did his *viva voce* well, none of his papers were looked at but the Paley. As it is only a pass examination, the examinees are arranged alphabetically, except a comparatively few, perhaps a fourth or fifth of the whole number, who have only just passed, and for whose special benefit a Second Class is provided.

It will be seen from the above statement that there is nothing in the *Little Go* to occupy a good schoolboy of fifteen more than three or four months; and for a Second-year Cantab of good standing, there is really nothing to prepare except the Paley; he might without danger trust to the light of nature for his Classics, or if scrupulous to run no risk, read them up sufficiently for practical purposes in three days, and the same time properly applied would make him master of his Evidences.[16] Nevertheless the Classical men do grumble a little, chiefly I imagine on account of the two or three days consumed in the examination, which some of them can ill spare at that juncture, and because they can gain no credit in a pass examination and may get disgraced by dropping into the second class through some carelessness in Paley. On the Mathematical men it comes rather harder; some of them, especially in the Small Colleges, are much behindhand in their Classics, and require some time to get up their subjects. But I believe no one of any mathematical eminence ever was plucked for the Little Go, though some have been placed in the second class; and it is so obvious that a Second-year collegian ought to know Classics enough to pass such an examination, that no attempt has ever been made to alter it in the way of *diminution*. But within the last three years, as one of a system of changes tending to equalize the requirements from Mathematics and Classics, two books of Euclid and ordinary Arithmetic were added;

---

[16]   Some of the technical memory artifices for getting up Paley were not unamusing, for instance the eleven proofs of New Testament authenticity were abbreviated into two barbarous Hexameters, thus:

> Quoted, *sui generis*, distinct tit., publicly, comment.
> Both sides, gospel, epist., adversa., catalogue, apocry.

[Trevelyan comments, 'They now, 1895, end 'adverse, catalogue, apocryphal'.]

and about the same time a knowledge of Old Testament History was made a requisite. There is a Third Examination during the Lent Term, in which Second-year men may be candidates, though the number who avail themselves of the opportunity is not large – the University Scholarship. I say *Scholarship*, for though there are several on different foundations, it has been so arranged that one is vacant every year and seldom more than one;[17] the examiners and style of examination are the same for them all, and they may be practically considered as one and the same. The examination is open to all Undergraduates, but the competition lies chiefly among those of the Third year. It includes more Latin composition than the Tripos, and even a wider range of authors, embracing Athenaeus, the Comic fragments, and such out-of-the-way subjects which enter into no other examination. Yet it sometimes happens that a Second-year man is the successful candidate, and there are rare instances of a Freshman gaining the prize. A large proportion of the candidates are from that year; the Freshman, not being definitely settled to his work, or having his relative place at all assigned him, tries more experiments than the Junior Soph, who having more definite and immediate objects in view, is unwilling to be drawn aside by a useless competition with better men. It might be supposed that the exercise and practice afforded by the examination would attract many in all the years, and so no doubt they would, if the individual results could be got at; but as only the best ten or twelve have any means of hearing even in the most indirect way how they have acquitted themselves, the great end of an examination – to correct errors and ascertain progress – is not attainable. Where but one man's standing is to be decided out of some eighty, of course the first object is to eliminate the candidates who have no chance, and whom a few of the Composition papers may effectually dispose of. Probably there are never more than a dozen or fifteen whose papers are carefully collected, and whose comparative standing the examiners themselves could tell with accuracy. This year (1842), a Johnian[18] gained the Scholarship, which usually falls to a Trinity, or King's man.

All the examinations above mentioned take place after the first term. But the Johnians have split their May, throwing back the easier subjects into an examination at the end of the Michaelmas term. In the third year of

---

[17]   There have been two vacancies together three times in the last ten years. The Foundations are four, the *Craven*, *Battie*, *Davies*, and *Pitt*, to which a new one, the *Porson*, has just been added. [This was set up in 1848, and the first scholarship awarded in 1855.] The annual emolument varies from £30 to £75.

[18]   Gifford. (B) [Edwin Gifford, St John's 1839, Senior Classic 1843.]

Whewell's administration he introduced a somewhat similar examination into Trinity, but only for the Junior Sophs. These *half examinations*, from being partial and not very difficult, have only a moderate importance attached to them. They make their First Class rather smaller than that of the Freshman May. When it is stated in addition that some of the Small Colleges also split their Second-year examination as well as their Freshman, and that some of them have a voluntary Classical examination, we have completed our enumeration of the tests, College and University, voluntary and compulsory, to which the Second-year man or Junior Soph is liable, and in which he is personally interested up to the end of his Lent Term. But these do not usually occupy his attention so entirely as to prevent him from taking a lively interest in the great University examinations, the Mathematical Tripos in January, and the Classical Tripos in February. For he now begins to understand more of the working of these, and to know, by reputation at least, the prominent candidates for Honors from his own College, and to be anxious about this Mathematical friend who hopes to be among the first Ten, and that Classical acquaintance who is in danger of the gulf.

It has been mentioned that the University Scholarship was this year borne off by a Johnian. *En revanche* we triumphed in both Triposes, having in Mathematics the Senior Wrangler[19] (who is almost always as a matter of course a Johnian), and in Classics the Senior Classic and Senior Medalist, as usual.[20] Some circumstances worth mentioning attended these examinations. Our Trinity Senior Wrangler (we have one so seldom that he is prone to be an object of curiosity and a pet) was a crooked little man, in no respect a beauty, and not in the least a beau. On the day of his triumph, when he was to receive his hard-earned honors in the Senate House, some of his friends combined their energies to dress him, and put him to rights properly, so that his appearance might not be altogether unworthy of his exploits and his College. He had generally the reputation of being a mere Mathematician, which did him great injustice, for he was really a man of much varied information, and that on some subjects the very opposite of scientific – for instance he was well up in all the current novels, an uncommon thing at Cambridge, where novel reading is not one of the popular weaknesses. His Johnian competitor,[21] who was a fearfully hard reader, and had once worked *twenty hours a-day* for a week together at a College examination,

---

[19]   Cayley. (B)
[20]   Munro and Denman. (B)
[21]   Simpson. (W, B) [Charles Simpson, St John's 1838, 2nd Wrangler 1842.]

almost broke down from over exertion just as the time of trial was coming on, and found himself actually obliged to carry a supply of ether and other stimulants into the examination, in case of accidents. Nevertheless he made a good fight of it, and having great pace as well as style in addition to his knowledge, beat the Trinity man a little on the bookwork, but was beaten two hundred marks in problems, which decided the contest. One of the low bookwork papers to which three hours were allotted happening to be rather shorter than usual, the Johnian, either as a bit of bravado to frighten his opponent, or because having done all that could be done he had no reason for waiting longer, came out at the expiration of two hours, having floored the paper in that time. His early exit did not escape notice, and the same evening a Trinity Senior Soph rushed up in great fear to the room of his friend, on whom the hopes of our College depended. 'C——! C——! they tell me S—— floored the paper this afternoon in two hours.[22] Is it so?' The Mathematician, who was refreshing himself after the fatigues of the day with the innocent and economical luxury of a footbath, looked up at the querist from his tub with the equanimity of a Diogenes, and replied: 'Likely enough he did. I floored it myself in two hours and a half'. The examination for the *Smith's Prizes*,[23] which takes place immediately after the result of the Mathematical Tripos is declared, and which serves to rectify or confirm the arrangement of the first three or four Wranglers, had a similar result; our man beat his opponent, but with nothing to spare.

The Senior Classic was a nobleman's son, also distinguished as one of the best oars on the river.[24] He had moreover been Captain (Head) of the Poll, for it is a privilege of noblemen's sons that they go out in Classics by first passing the *ordinary* degree examination instead of the *Mathematical*. This, and obtaining a degree by seven terms residence instead of ten (making just a year's difference),[25] are the only unfair privileges they enjoy. The reason assigned for both is the same – that they may be wanted in public life at an earlier age than the other students; and the intention evidently was, that those going out in Classics through the Poll should do so after a residence of two years and a half. But as this, though the spirit, is not the

---

[22]   C is Cayley, S is Simpson. (T)

[23]   [Two prizes for mathematics awarded by examination each year; first awarded in 1769. The Smith's prizes often confirmed the results of the mathematical Tripos, but on occasion enabled a naturally gifted mathematician to triumph over one proficient in examination technique.]

[24]   Geo. Denman. (T, B)

[25]   This also involves their exemption from Little Go.

letter of the law, some of them take advantage of the double chance, and enjoy the same length of time for Classical preparation as the other students, without being hampered by the Mathematical examination. On the other hand there are instances of young men who have chivalrously refused to avail themselves of this advantage, and have gone out in the Mathematical Tripos along with the mass of Classical students. The privilege holds good, even if the nobleman has entered as a Pensioner, but it does not extend to the Chancellor's Medals, all candidates for which are required to be Senior Optimes. The great damage done to the Classical men the year before, and the outcry it occasioned, made the Mathematical examiners very lenient this time.[26] No Classic was plucked, and the Senior Optime list stretched down to include as many as possible. But some of our Scholars had already gone out among the *polloi* through fear of the result. Both the Medalists[27] were Trinity men; the Second was only sixth on the Tripos.

When the examination for the Trinity Scholarships arrived, it may be supposed I was in no condition to present myself. Indeed I had a double disqualification exclusive of illness. First, as a Fellow Commoner, for they, being considered men of fortune, are not eligible to a Scholarship or Fellowship involving a stipendiary emolument. (This is not the case everywhere; Fellow Commoners can be scholars at some of the Small Colleges.) Secondly, as *a bye-term man* or one between two years. Although I had entered into residence at the same time with those men who were to go out in 1844, my name had not been placed on the College Books, like theirs, previous to the commencement of 1840. I had therefore lost a term, and for most purposes was considered a Freshman, though I had been in residence as long as any of the Junior Sophs.[28] In fact I was *between two* years − a position rather advantageous to a man who comes to the University with little knowledge of it, for after measuring and testing his acquirements and capacity, he can choose whether he will go out in Honors a year earlier or later, and thus virtually degrade.[29] And if he becomes a

---

[26] [The dangers of examiners' discretion were thus highlighted: leniency in 1840 had prompted severity in 1841 (the 'slaughter'), and this in turn now led to leniency.]

[27] [The first Chancellor's medallist was H.A.J. Munro, 2nd Classic, the second medallist B. Shaw, 6th Classic.]

[28] Twelve terms are required to be kept by the Statutes, but that during which the name is entered, and that during which the degree is taken are included in the number, making only ten terms of actual residence.

[29] *Degrading*, or going back a year, is not allowed except in case of illness (proved

Scholar of Trinity, and wishes to go out along with the men with whom he entered into residence, he will have an additional year to read for his Fellowship, for though he may pass the Mathematical examination with them, his B.A. and consequently his M.A. come later than theirs.

At the time of the examination I was not in Cambridge at all. I had gone to Paris for medical advice, in company with my friend and former coach,[30] who having gained his Fellowship the October previous,[31] and not being quite decided as to his future plans, was not a very regular resident, and had not overburdened himself with pupils. He took care of me and bantered me alternately – a treatment which did me no harm in the end, and amused him greatly for the time. An invalid who cannot ascend two pair of stairs without feeling the worse for it, is not exactly in a condition to appreciate or enjoy the pleasures of the gay French capital; my stay was only long enough to consult (without benefit) the physician to whom I had been recommended.

I shall not easily forget the difference between this and my next visit to Paris. It was in the spring of 1845, when I was restored to almost perfect health, and had just been recruiting after my final examination (the Classical Tripos), by a month's idleness and generous living. For eight days I had been lionizing Belgium under the disadvantages of continual rain, and during those eight days had worn out more than one pair of boots over the pavements of Bruges, Ghent, and Antwerp. The rainiest day of all was that on which I left Brussels in the Diligence for Paris, and a weary trip I had, arriving somewhere about midnight at my destination. The next morning was Sunday. The sun shone out as brightly as if he had been undergoing repairs and decorations during his temporary retirement – warm but not sultry, as an April sun is wont to shine between the rains. My *entresol* looked out on the gardens of the Tuileries, which I could see were thronged with people in their holiday clothes. I began to have recollection of the time when I used to play exquisite in Broadway, and the thought occurred to me as I proceeded to overhaul my trunks, that a man who had hardly been out of his University for three years was likely to be somewhat behind the Parisian fashions – or any other. However I did the best I could with myself, and strolled into the crowd. It seemed as if all the inhabitants of Paris had poured into those gardens – men, women, and children, all equally well

---

by a Doctor's certificate). A man degrading for any other reason cannot go out afterwards in Honors.

[30]   Tom Taylor. (B)

[31]   1841. (B)

dressed, gay, happy, and as sparkling as the beautiful fountains that were flashing in the sunshine. Such a contrast to my English associations, and to the Belgic mud and rain I had just encountered! On, on I walked, through the Place de Concorde, and up the Champs Elysées, among the stalls, and the itinerant merchants, and the goat-omnibuses full of rejoicing children, and the children of a larger growth who looked so merry on every side; and it was only at the foot of the Arc d'Etoile that I began to feel the want of that necessary fortification for the day which consists in the matutinal repast. Certainly there is no city or place in the world like Paris for pure amusement, no such place to recruit after hard work, when you have a few weeks to devote to idle enjoyment, good dinners, and collecting apparel for the outer man, and trinkets for your friends. How far it is a place for a foreigner to reside in who has any rational and permanent object of life in this world, or any serious thoughts of the next, is another question.[32]

Conflict between the University and College Systems

The result of the Scholarship Examination had just been declared when I returned to Cambridge, and the Master's threat had been partially executed. Some Classical men of the third year, and one in particular of the second, had been thrown overboard for doing no Mathematics. Besides this, there was the usual number of disappointments. One of the unsuccessful candidates *migrated* – a common event on these occasions. A migration is generally tantamount to a confession of inferiority, an acknowledgement that the migrator is not likely to become a Fellow of his own College, and therefore takes refuge in another where a more moderate Degree will insure him a Fellowship. A great deal of this migration goes on from John's to the Small Colleges; Sidney is almost a colony of second-rate Johnians; at Christ's for three years successively while I was an Undergraduate, the first man was an emigrant from John's. Sometimes the migrating man turns out a dark horse, and stands very high at last; it proved so in the present case.[33] More rarely it happens that a good man from the start migrates out of John's or Trinity to save himself trouble, because at another College he

---

[32] [Bristed and his wife moved to Paris in 1851, the year in which much of *Five Years* was written. He witnessed the coup d'état of that year, and described it, and Parisian social life, in a series of articles for *The Literary World*. See Bibliography A2, 1852]

[33] Wratislaw, 3rd in 1844. (B) [Albert Wratislaw, Trinity 1840, fellow of Christ's 1844–53.]

will be given a Fellowship merely for his Degree – that is, for his place in the Mathematical or Classical Tripos, without having to undergo the additional subsequent examination.[34] Sometimes also, a Bachelor migrates for the same reason. The Small College Scholarships and Fellowships, it may be remarked, are not inferior to those of Trinity in pecuniary value; on the contrary they are generally more lucrative. It is a question of profit against honor.[35]

The five or six Second-year men who gain Scholarships at their first trial are considered to have won some honor thereby, and to have a fair prospect of being among the best men of their year in the University.[36] But this does not invariably follow. It frequently happens that some of them take a lower degree than those who are chosen Scholars at their second trial. Clever and industrious men who have come up not too well prepared sometimes take nearly two years before the effect of their 'coaching' shows itself, and then take a great start and develop rapidly in the third year; while those who begin on an excellent preparation are not unfrequently rendered lazy by their second year's triumph. The cases which have occurred of a man who missed his Scholarships altogether beating in the Senate House one who gained his at the first trial, may be in a great measure attributed to this, want of success having piqued the former to exertion during the important 'last Long', while success, perhaps unlooked for, at an early period has made the other careless and indolent. Something, however, is due to the difference of the examinations in some essential particulars. The narrower range of authors in the College Scholarship has been already noticed. But besides this, it contains no Greek composition, and Greek composition in the Tripos counts more than Latin, and is indeed one fifth of the whole examination. Then the time is allotted on a much more liberal scale. You are allowed four hours for a less amount of work than that to which the University assigns three. In the Classical Tripos pace is of the greatest consequence; a slow man stands a bad chance. In the Trinity Scholarship there is plenty of

---

[34]   Changed now, 1857. (E)

[35]   There are some *Bye-Fellowships* however in the small colleges, whose value is merely nominal – some £5 or £6 a-year. These are in no great demand and are usually given to inferior men. Sometimes they serve to keep good men from being *superannuated* (in Colleges where a man cannot he made Fellow after he has attained a certain age), since a Bye-Fellow can be elected to one of the regular Fellowships when a vacancy occurs.

[36]   There were 6 in our (2nd) year & they were afterwards the only Fellows of our year. Clark, Hedley, Hotham, Walker, Kean and myself Bowring. (B)

time to polish up. Sometimes it happens that a Second-year Scholar does badly in the University examinations, and then acquits himself well for the Trinity Fellowship. Three out of the six successful candidates in the present year thus fell and recovered themselves, owing to the combined influence of both causes.[37]

When the new Scholars are declared, but a few weeks remain before the May examination. The printed lists of this show the telling of the pace in more ways than one. In the first place the whole number of men in the year is sensibly diminished, about one fifth having fallen off. While from a hundred to a hundred and twenty go in at the first year's examination, only from eighty to a hundred present themselves at that of the second.[38] Then the first class is cut down to half or less than half its original dimensions, averaging about eleven. This, however, is not altogether owing to the hard work having its effect, and men giving up or breaking down in the second year who were industrious and successful in their first. The examination this year is principally Mathematical. The only strictly Classical paper is one on some dialogue of Plato. There is another on the Diatessaron (the Four Gospels) chiefly 'cram', and three short papers in 'morals' – Paley's *Natural Theology*, Stewart's *Outlines*, and Butler's three *Sermons on Human Nature*. These three, with the Eleventh Book of Euclid, are put into one long session of five hours. The other six papers are Mathematical, Statics, Dynamics, Theory of Equations, Conic Sections, Spherical Trigonometry, Differential and Integral Calculus, and one paper of Problems on all the subjects. Now it is quite possible for a Classical man, by polishing up carefully the Morals and Greek Testament and Plato (with the aid of the Euclid which is given him as a sort of sop), to get marks enough for a First Class, especially as the standard is two hundred marks lower than it was the first year. But the prize is not generally considered worth the expenditure of time. The votary of Classics is now beginning to keep a single eye on the Tripos, and is not easily drawn aside from his pursuit of a high place in that, and no one thinks the worse of him for being as low even as the Sixth Class in the May examination. Indeed, so far from success now insuring it to him hereafter, to stand high in the second May is rather against his chance of a good position on the Tripos, as the time

---

[37] Three out of 6: Hotham Walker and myself. (B) [Edward Walker, 1840, fellow 1845; Frederick Bowring, 1840, fellow 1844.]

[38] The number of *posts* [men who have been 'posted', i.e. failures], *aegrotats*, men absent on leave, &c., no more than seven or eight in any case, is about the same for both years.

which has been devoted to the particular 'cram', is so much taken from his general practice in translation and composition. On the whole there is not very hard working for this May as compared with the first, except among the best two or three in Mathematics, who are beginning to struggle for their places, and with them it is rather the result of their contemporary reading with their private tutors than of special study for the examination. If he who has been decidedly the best Mathematician in his first year comes out as decidedly superior in this, he may be considered pretty safe for the highest Wranglership out of Trinity; but if one or two others who were then close behind him are now a second time not far in his rear, there is a very good chance that their places may be changed next year, or at any rate in the Degree examination. Some men drop out of a good place this year by temporary misdirection and want of concentration of their powers, and not having their Mathematical abilities as yet fully developed by steady and exclusive application, these come up again in the third year, and are ultimately among the high Wranglers. From a variety of causes, the principal of which have been enumerated, the standard of marks is comparatively low; frequently the first man has not more than fifteen hundred.

Once or twice during the winter, as fallacious symptoms of recovery showed themselves, I had vague thoughts of reading for this examination; but I never was well enough to master even the Classical subject, and after reading a few pages of the Phaedo, and attending three or four lectures on it, was obliged to give up from sheer weakness and inability to sit an hour in a crowded room. It was a great deprivation to me, for our Plato lecturer[39] was a remarkable man, and though his readings had not at that time the University celebrity which they afterwards acquired, for it was only the third year of his course, they had already deservedly attracted a large attendance. I was compelled to remain in the busy place an idle looker-on. The dancer with a sprained ancle, the horseman with his bridle-hand disabled, the rower with a broken oar, the epicure condemned by his physician to diet – are all to be pitied for their tantalizing plight; but none of them are so deserving commiseration as a young man eager for the acquisition of knowledge, with everything around tempting him to it, and every one about him engaged in the pursuit, yet forced by the instinct of self-preservation to be systematically idle, and lie like a boat aground, seeing others float by him. Something of this has been my lot ever since; I cannot

---

[39] Thompson the tutor. (B) [William Hepworth Thompson, Trinity 1828, Regius Professor of Greek 1853–66, Master of Trinity 1866–86; famous for his good looks, dignified bearing and sarcastic quips.]

even now write or study eight hours a-day for six days consecutively (even with the most simple and abstemious regimen), without being quite worn out and obliged to strike work at the end of the week.

The examination was over and the students dispersing. One who has continued to be a reading man up to the end of the second year is generally pretty safe to go on as such, but it not unfrequently happens that he now drops the intention of being a 'double man', and concentrates himself upon Mathematics. I was left for a while almost alone. Some were going on reading parties, some taking a holiday before settling down to their work in the 'Long'. About this time I did one wise thing, which was to 'throw physic to the dogs', and thenceforward I began slowly to improve. Recovery being evidently a work of time, I resolved to stay quietly where I was, and some mental occupation being necessary, began to read a little again merely for diversion. First I attacked Aristophanes, as the most amusing author, and working a couple of hours every morning went through seven plays, which, added to my former knowledge, enabled me to say that I had read the old Comedian all through, and though from the circumstances of the case my reading was not very thorough, still it laid a foundation for future revision, and I had mastered the author's vocabulary, no small part of his difficulty. My work was done at a standing desk; I was not able to stoop or bend over a table. Very many of the students, even these in the best health, have, as a means of keeping so, adopted the plan of reading on the feet, which I believe is also very common in Germany. It is certainly the healthiest way, and after a few trials not at all fatiguing even to an invalid, though one is apt to think it must be before trying it. In the evening I used to take Horace and revive my old recollections of the Satires and Epistles, using an edition with copious notes, which I could look over while leaning back in my arm-chair, and seldom having occasion for a dictionary. This was light occupation, in which an hour or sometimes more passed away pleasantly. After finishing in this way the review of Horace, I took up the Tuscular Questions, the First Book of which I had read before (indeed had stood an examination at Yale on the whole five), but even in that First Book I had enough to learn. Still the verbal difficulties were not numerous; and to read Cicero leisurely, translating his elegant Latin into the choicest English you can find, is an interesting and not unprofitable occupation. After Aristophanes, I took up Thucydides, and read the Sixth and Seventh Books, but not in a way to know much about them – indeed, it is not until after having gone over it for the third time, and that very carefully, that you can feel at all sure of any difficult passage in that author. With the Hippolytus of Euripides I did more, getting it up well, and not merely in a philological, but also in a literary point of view, for the purpose of comparing it with Seneca's Hippolytus and Racine's Phèdre, which I read immediately after, and made a comparative synopsis of these three plays on the same subject.[40]

All such diversions would have been illegitimate for a regular reading man, but I read only for healthy mental occupation, and because I could not leave the place which I should have been too glad to abandon, could I by any possibility have reached home.

As my work, even in the dilettante manner in which it was carried on, had to be limited to less than four hours a day, some of the time during which I was forced to be idle on principle used to hang heavy on my hands. Miscellaneous novel reading I had been pretty well surfeited with in my younger days in New Haven. Exercise I could take none worth speaking of; I could not ride, nor run, nor row, nor even handle a billiard cue, and my walk was not more than a saunter. I used to stroll about the College grounds, thinking of my native city, which distance, and the impossibility of returning thither, had invested with a coloring of romance and sentiment for me. When I received a letter or newspaper from over the water, it was a white day in my calendar. The next greatest pleasure was the hebdomadal appearance of *Punch*, then in its very prime. I can recollect every article of Thackeray's, and the circumstances under which I read them – the hour of the day (it was just after my scanty dinner that the paper used to arrive), the green-curtained window looking out on the grounds, the big arm-chair I sat in, and the little compromise between a stand and a table in front of it. It happened that there were fewer men up this Long than usual, and of the Dons besides the Librarian, only one Fellow, who was supposed to be at work on an endless book always advertised by the University booksellers, but never likely to appear in actual type.[41] Even his company I could seldom enjoy, being scarcely even able to dine in the Hall.

Commencement

There was one event which broke in on the monotony of this vacation. The Commencement, usually little more than a form, was made a grand show by the Installation of a new Chancellor. The Chancellor is the nominal Executive of the University, but all his duties are performed by the Vice-Chancellor, one of the Heads chosen in rotation, so that the office is merely

---

[40]   [Bristed's five-page 'collation' of the plays is omitted.]
[41]   Edleston. It never did appear. (B) [Joseph Edleston, 1834, fellow 1840.]

an honor to compliment some nobleman with. The Commencement takes place during the first week in July, and is the nominal ending of the Easter Term, which has virtually concluded a mouth before. The real business done is conferring the M.A. degrees, and reading the prize compositions – that is to say, the Classical ones and the English poem, for the recitation of the Theological Essays would be rather a tedious affair, as they sometimes make a tolerably sized book. The Latin Essays are read a few days before Commencement. Almost the only parties in attendance are those personally interested. A few of the reading-men up for the Long may drop into the galleries, and some straggling townspeople be in the body of the house. But on this occasion the scene was changed. Cambridge was turned into a show place for that day only. Gold-embroidered crowns of noblemen mingled with the red gowns of Doctors of Divinity and Physic. Crowds of well-dressed strangers thronged the beautiful College grounds, looking as unamused as the great Anglo-Saxon race usually does when it gets together in a crowd. The Senate-House was thronged. All manner of big-wigs graced the scene and augmented the dignity of the Duke of Northumberland.[42] Some one of the royal family was there – I forget who, but recollect two officers pushing the people out of his way. Prince Albert came up to be made something or other, and put on some extraordinary dress. Illustrious foreigners were not wanted. Everett and Bunsen were created D.C.L's,[43] and had red gowns put over their diplomatic uniforms. The scandalous conduct of some members of the other University to our distinguished countryman when the same degree was conferred on him there some time later, is unhappily notorious, but it is not so generally known that a difficulty – though of a different sort, founded not on religious but on political grounds – was near occurring at Cambridge. Some precise member of the Senate started this objection: 'We give Honorary Degrees only to persons of

---

[42] [Hugh Percy, Duke of Northumberland, was Chancellor of the University from 1840 to 1847.]

[43] LL Ds. DCL is the Oxford equivalent. (T) [Edward Everett was US envoy extraordinary and minister plenipotentiary to the court of St James 1841–5; he also served at different times as US Secretary of State and president of Harvard University. His lengthy oration at the dedication of the Gettysburg cemetery in 1863 was overshadowed by that of Abraham Lincoln, who followed him. Christian (Baron) Bunsen, Prussian ambassador to the court of St James 1842–54. A pupil of Niebuhr, he was an important intellectual conduit for German scholarship in Britain; his friends included Thomas Arnold of Oxford, and Julius Hare and Connop Thirlwall of Cambridge]

royal blood, and Ambassadors are admissible to them merely in their quality of representatives of crowned heads. Now Mr. Everett does not represent a crowned head; how then can we give him a Degree?' Fortunately some one recollected that the American Minister was a D.C.L. of Trinity College, Dublin, members of which are admitted *ad eundem gradum*[44] at Cambridge, which solved the difficulty at once; indeed it was settled so quietly that not many people were aware of its existence.

The unusual throng made the winners of the Browne medals, the Porson, the Camden, and the Chancellor's English medal, extraordinary lions, as instead of an audience of half a dozen old Dons, and twice as many Undergraduates, they had a *crowded house* of beauty, nobility, and fashion to recite before. The Browne medals are three in number, for an ode in Latin Alcaics, an ode in Greek Sapphics, and a brace of epigrams in Greek and Latin. The Porson prize (of books) is for a translation from Shakspeare into Greek Iambics; the Camden medal for an exercise in Latin hexameters. The subjects of these exercises are announced at the end of the First Term, and the candidates have about three months to write them in. These prizes are sometimes taken by the best men in the year, sometimes by second-rate ones. The continually recurring reason that they make too much inroad into the preparation for the Tripos, prevents many of the first Classics in the year from trying for them, particularly in the case of the Greek ode, which is an altogether out of the way exercise, Greek Sapphics not being written in any of the examinations. On the whole I believe the Porson was considered the most honorable, and there was more competition for it among the good men. But there is a generally prevailing idea in the University that success in an extensive examination on general knowledge of language, not specially prepared for, is a fairer test of merit and ability than gaining a prize which has been elaborately worked up in private, and it not unfrequently happens that the Senior Classic has never written for a medal or Porson. The general run of the English poems may be guessed at. There are some good men among the Prize Poets – Praed, Macaulay, Tennyson.[45] The last was for a long time the only one who broke loose from the trammels of Heroic couplets. He wrote in blank verse with a *forged* motto from Chapman. It was said that he gained the prize by mistake.

---

[44] [Holders of degrees at Oxford, Cambridge and Trinity College Dublin had reciprocal rights to degrees at the other institutions.]

[45] [Macaulay won the Chancellor's medal for English verse in 1819 and 1821, W.M. Praed in 1823 and 1824, Tennyson in 1829 for 'Timbuctoo'.]

Smyth [46] the Professor of History, had been long looked up to by the other examiners, who were accustomed to be guided by his decision. Having lit on Tennyson's poem, and being much puzzled by it (it was something out of the common, and just the thing to astonish an ancient Don) he pencilled on the outside, '*Look at this!*' meaning thereby merely to call the attention of his brother examiners to it as a curiosity. But it happened that he was taken ill or called away from Cambridge on business, and the others were obliged to meet and decide in his absence. His note of admiration was mistaken for a sign of approval, and the palm adjudged to the future Laureate. Such is the legend; some say that the poet's *apostolic* friends invented it to palliate the discredit of his having gained a prize poem. Some years ago another bold youth wrote a poem in Spenserian stanzas, which took the prize. This broke the charm, and a variety of metres have since been attempted with success — the success that is of getting the Chancellor's medal.

On the present occasion the six prizes were divided among three men, and five of them between two of our year. The Greek ode and epigrams were carried off by the Trinity man [47] who had headed the first May, and was one of the three favorites (all from our College) for Senior Classic; the two Latin prizes, and the English poem by a Small Colleger, whom this triple success introduced to the University world in which he was destined to be a distinguished figure. [48]

As the Long vacation drew to a close, I gave a symptom of returning vitality by passing my Little-Go. There is a post-examination for this in the beginning of October — a sort of appendix to the regular one for the benefit of plucked men and aegrotats. As the former constitute the greater portion of the thirty or forty who present themselves, the few reading-men whom sickness or other accident has placed in their company, show particularly well by comparison. A man passed at this examination who had been plucked three times. One does not know whether such a person's want of capacity is more worthy of pity, or his fortitude and perseverance of admiration.

---

[46] [William Smyth (Peterhouse), Regius Professor of Modern History 1807–49.]

[47] Clark. (B) [W.G. Clark.]

[48] Maine. (B) [(Sir) Henry James Sumner Maine, Pembroke 1840; fellow and tutor of Trinity Hall, Master 1877–88; Corpus Professor of Jurisprudence at Oxford, 1869–77. Maine tutored Bristed and became a firm friend; Bristed named his second son after him, and Maine's first son Charles may have been named after Bristed.]

12

Third Year [1842–3]

A DEBATE at the UNION.

Abiit, evasit, excessit, eripuit.

Cicero.

They love the winner of the race, if only he who prospers,
looks at prizes with a simple grace.

Anon.

Quand on n'a pas ce que l'on aime,
Il faut aimer ce que l'on a.

We start, for soul is wanting there.

Byron.

A Change of Position

When the collegiate year recommenced once more, I threw off the blue and
silver, and turned Pensioner. It was rather an uncommon step, but there had
been a precedent for it not long before. A friend of mine after one year's

experience of Fellow-Commoner life, had changed his grade, partly from pecuniary motives, and partly to be eligible to a Scholarship.[1] I had both these inducements, and a third still more pressing – my health, which made it necessary for me to shun the luxurious dinners of the upper table. It was coming down a step in life, and a sort of confession of poverty on the face of it, but I had the satisfaction of finding that none of my old acquaintance among the Dons, to whose friendship I attached any value, changed their conduct and bearing towards me in the least. And I have generally observed this to be the case, that when a man freely confesses his pecuniary inability to maintain a certain position, he is not held at any discount for it, but his honest determination is rather applauded. It is your keeping up appearances, Spanish grandee shift and deceit, trying to be what one is not, that provoke sneer and coldness. My most intimate friends generally congratulated me on the step, as now having a better opportunity to profit by the advantages which the main body of the students enjoyed. Being now able to work a little in earnest, I started on the principle of shying for several things at once, in the hope of getting some of them; a proceeding which better suited my physical condition, more fitted to accomplish small separate pieces of work than to aim steadily at a remote end, and a task of indefinite amount. To a Trinity student in his third year, more opportunities of this sort are open than in his first two. He has a chance for all the University prizes open to the Freshmen and Junior Sophs, with additional training for them, and the Members' Prizes for Latin Essays besides; and in his own College, an English Declamation, a Latin Declamation, and an English Essay. I determined in the coming year to make shots for all these four, and also for a College Scholarship and a First Class in the May; and as I ultimately attained three out of the six objects, the speculation was not altogether a bad one.

The *Declamations* are, what in Yale College language would be termed *Disputes*. At the beginning of the Michaelmas Term a number of questions are giving out 'on subjects connected with the History of England', say the terms of the founder of this prize, but as the intervention of England in European affairs has taken a pretty wide range, so these questions take a pretty wide range in European history. Every third-year-man chooses his question, and writes on it, giving in his exercise at the end of the term; during the next term ten or twelve of the best are publicly recited in the chapel, and about the time of the Scholarship examination silver goblets are adjudged to the best three, the first worth £20, the others £10 each. To the best two Latin Declamations prizes of books are adjudged. The 'moral,

---

[1] Fussell. (B) [John Thomas Fussell, Trinity 1844 (as Curry), BA 1848.]

antiquarian, or literary' subject of the English Essay, is publicly notified at the beginning of the Collegiate year, when the prize for the former year's essay is adjudged, and the exercises need not be given in till next July, so there is no lack of time to the Senior Soph who makes a point of getting it. But he must take care not to attempt compassing his object by mere quantity and weight of paper. That would be fatal to his success, even were his production in other respects worthy of favor. It is distinctly required that the essay be not of greater length than can be conveniently read aloud in half an hour; and much shorter limits are assigned to the Declamations. Two cases came under my observation where very good men lost their chance because they had 'written a book', as one of the examiners expressed it. Questions referring to the History and Policy of the Stuarts, the Wars of William and Anne, the History and Benefits of Colonies, the Crusades, the Monastic institutions, the Social, Political, and Literary condition of the English people at different periods, distinguished characters in English History compared with one another or with illustrious foreigners; such were the ordinary subject-matter of the English declamations. The Latin ones were usually on some topic of Classical history. For the English Essay I recollect such subjects as *the Life of Erasmus, the Influence of Alexander the Great's Conquests on the Arts and the Literature of Europe, the Platonic Element in Cicero's Philosophy, the Abuse of Political Theories, the Military Orders of the Middle Ages, the Colonial Policy of the Ancients.* They generally lean to the historical or antiquarian, but are sometimes purely literary or philosophic. The prize, ten pounds, is generally converted (part of it at least) into books by the prizeman.

The competition for these English prizes is remarkably moderate; sometimes, indeed I may say generally, there are not more than three or four competitors for the essay. Even the Latin Declamations are not always taken by the best Classics of the year.

The *Members' Prizes* of fifteen guineas each, given by the representatives of the University in Parliament, are four in number, two open to all Bachelors, two to all Senior Sophs, or all men *who have resided seven terms,* even though Bye-term men like myself. The subjects are on all possible topics – historical, moral, theological, literary, philosophical. The preparation of these exercises, coming as they did successively, and not all at once, did not hinder me from going on with my more regular classical work to a certain extent. I put myself under my old friend and coach Travis (I suppose, I may as well continue to call him by that name), and worked up two plays of Aeschylus, besides reading Juvenal, not too thoroughly, as I afterwards found by sad experience in the Tripos, and by myself I ran over some Cicero and Livy, to get up my Latin style for the Declamation and Members' Prize. Still, being as yet able to average only about four hours' work daily, and compelled to abstain from all study at night, I had to cast about for ways of passing my evenings amusingly, and not altogether unprofitably. And first I took up the 'Union' again, for I was not only able to talk, but to make myself heard, and the moderate excitement of making a speech proved rather a beneficial exercise.

Literary Friends – 'The Apostles'

Any American Collegian who may chance to read this book, will have wondered long ago why I have said nothing about the 'speakers' and 'writers'.[2] Equal if not greater would be the surprise of an Englishman, when told of the important position which these two classes of students – or as he would deem them non-students, non-reading men – occupy at an American College. 'Only think' said Travis once to an acquaintance after I had been trying to explain to him the state of things at Yale College, 'it is there just as if we were to consider the President of the Union a greater man than the Senior Wrangler'. 'How strange!' replied the other. Writing English as a means of acquiring reputation or honor is almost unknown among the Undergraduates. The only incentives to it are Declamation Prizes in a few of the Colleges, for the University prizes for Moral and Theological Dissertations go by learning, more than style. To tell a Cantab that such an Undergraduate had a fine English style, would seem as irrelevant as the information that he knew a good deal of law or physic.[3] Even when a precocious politician contributes to the London papers (as one did about this time), it does not materially enhance his reputation. I was once talking to a friend about my exercises for the Trinity prizes, and how difficult I found it to practise one style for an oration and another for an essay; he was much surprised that I had had sufficient practice in English composition even to attempt such a variety. This same man understood perfectly the difference between Aristotelian and Thucydidean Greek prose, and could write either as occasion required. With public speaking the case was nearly similar. Conceive one general debating Society for the whole University, which has about twelve hundred Undergraduates in residence for two terms, and sixteen hundred for the third. What protracted debates our students would

---

[2]   [See ch. 33 for a discussion of these.]
[3]   It was an immense help in the Classical tripos. I knew a man who got 74 marks out of 75 for a Greek translation paper with a howling mistake in it. (T)

have in such a case, and what scrambling for the seven offices every term. But at Cambridge not half the Undergraduates are members, and many of these are attracted solely by the reading-room. The debates are sometimes adjourned in half an hour for want of speakers; the offices frequently go a begging, and at a contested election there are seldom more than three hundred and fifty votes polled and not often that number. Occasionally, however, on exciting public questions of the day an animated debate would be got up, and I have heard very good amateur speaking. The Union has its periodical fits of brief excitement and at this particular period its affairs were at a favorable crisis. The rooms had just been newly fitted up and enlarged, and there happened to be an influx of men in the new Freshman year who were just the very persons to give the thing a start. These were of no great numerical force, but a few men with a will can do a great deal in such matters. Poor Henry F. Hallam[4] was one of them, though he seldom spoke in the Union himself. But he was instrumental in getting up a small debating society of about forty members, called the Historical, at which tolerably lively debates were kept up, and the members of which attended the Union pretty regularly so as always to form the nucleus of an audience there. Another was a peer's son, now a member of Parliament, who had a love of public affairs and a precocious seriousness almost American. A third was a Dissenter,[5] somewhat above the average age of Freshmen (two peculiarities which made him a character at once), having a flow of speech and a faculty of thinking on his legs which an Englishman seldom possesses unless he is a professional talker – i.e. a barrister or an M.P. of long standing – and not always even then. There were other aspirants to the name of orator, ambitious Small-College men, and a hard-working Trinity Scholar or two carried away by the novel impulse. We got up stirring political debates – democracy against aristocracy, toleration against church exclusiveness, old common sense against Young England[6] – and soon had

---

[4] [Henry Fitzmaurice Hallam (Trinity 1842) was 9th Classic in 1846. He was the younger brother of Arthur Hallam, whose death in 1833 his friend Tennyson lamented in *In Memoriam*. Henry himself also died prematurely, in 1850. For his links with Bristed, who published an obituary of him (Bibliography A2, 1850), see G.J. Kolb, 'Charles Astor Bristed, Henry Hallam and Tennyson's "Timbuctoo"', *Tennyson Research Bulletin* 4 (1986), pp. 197–210.]

[5] Tooke. (B) [Thomas Tooke, Trinity 1842, BA 1849.]

[6] [The romantic Tory movement of the 1840s which reacted against industrialisation and intellectual radicalism, idealising a traditional order of feudal society and monarchy.]

crowded houses for nights in succession. A debate on such an evening was an animated and interesting sight. The doors were open to all University men, members or not, and the audience amounted at times to four or five hundred. The English style of speaking and of *hearing* is very different from ours. Expressions of approbation and disapprobation on the part of the audience being frequent, the speaker aims more at points than with us, and when he has said a good thing or what he means to be such, looks out for the *Hear! Hear!* as a matter of course. It is much more agreeable to him (except at the very beginning of his career) than our solemn silence. The applause cheers him, the disapprobation piques him; both rest him and give him time to take breath – or a glass of water – and arrange himself for a fresh start.

Whenever there was a contested election for the Presidency of the Union, it turned more on the personal popularity than on the actual services and reputation of the candidate, and generally came to be a contest between the reading and 'rowing' men.[7] When it came to a hard fight the former usually succeeded; the same industry and ability that aided them in their studies, generally enabling them to triumph in the canvas. There was but one exception to this rule. When the rowing men were lucky enough to get hold of a title who would run for them, they were safe to win. There is no resisting John Bull's lord-worship. Charles J. Vaughan,[8] one of Arnold's favorite pupils, a University Scholar and Senior Classic, at present Headmaster of Harrow, and altogether a gentleman of great abilities and merits, was put up for the Union presidency when an Undergraduate, and beaten by a Johnian nonentity who had Sir before his name;[9] and the exception was verified a second time at my own expense this very year.

But as the Union and Historical only took up two nights in the week, there was some other amusement to be looked out for, as my friends who used to hold what at one time we called 'Whig parliaments' in my rooms, now that I was able to take care of myself, had left me to myself. In some cases it was only transferring their trouble from one place to another, as I would lounge about into the rooms of those whom I knew for general

---

[7] [See the glossary in ch. 4.]

[8] [Vaughan was a pupil at Rugby from 1829 to 1834, and was very close to Thomas Arnold, who had become headmaster of the school in 1828. He was Senior Classic in 1838 and became headmaster of Harrow in 1844. For the blighting of his later career, see p. 204 n. 17.]

[9] Sir J. Lighton. (W) [Sir John Lighton, St John's 1836; President of the Union 1843.]

literary conversation – even to talk Calendar if there was nothing else to do.[10] Sometimes I would tumble in upon a reading set who were amusing themselves in their way, after a hard day's fagging at Composition or Mathematics, with Aristophanes or Ovid, in a knot of three or four together, making an extempore addition to their temporary club. But this was too much like work for me, and my style of reading and comment too desultory for them, so I did not practise it often. It was more in my way to find some one who had done his day's work entirely so far as Classics or Mathematics were concerned, and chat quietly over endless cups of tea – or even potations more generous. Now at Trinity there was more cultivation of general literature than at any other College, and there were an unusual number of Freshmen at this time who took an interest in rhetoric and public speaking as well as subjects of general literature, in which matters I had some reputation, on the strength of my country; so that there was not much difficulty in finding places to spend my evenings in.[11] Several of the men with whom I was most intimate, belonged either at this time or subsequently to a society which although a strictly private club, and in no way putting itself prominently forward, has exerted and does exert a very considerable influence on the literary train of thought in the University of Cambridge, and on the opinions of the English literary public – the Cambridge Apostles.

There is an association founded by the contemporaries of the late John Sterling, and called from him the *Sterling Club*.[12] It comprises among its members men distinguished in various and somewhat different walks of life: theologians, like Maurice of King's College, London, and Stanley, Arnold's biographer; poets like Tennyson and Milnes; novelists like Thackeray; some universal geniuses. They are mostly Cambridge men, Stanley and some few Oxonians, Thomas Carlyle, I believe, the only non-university man among them.[13] By way of school or nursery to this club, there was a club at Cambridge of Undergraduates, popularly called *the Apostles* (it was said because they had usually thirteen members in residence).[14] Some of them

---

[10]   Bristed was thought an awful bore at this time. (B)

[11]   The English now rather exaggerate our facility of speaking in public and believe that every American is born a debater.

[12]   [John Sterling, Trinity 1824, migrated to Trinity Hall 1826; president of the Union 1827; BA 1834. The Club was founded in 1838: see Allen, *Cambridge Apostles*, pp. 182–97.]

[13]   A list is given in Carlyle's life of Sterling. (B)

[14]   [On the relationship between the two bodies, see Allen, *Cambridge Apostles*,

took high Honors, more generally in Classics than in Mathematics; some of them did not compete for Honors at all; but they all had a certain fondness for literary and metaphysical pursuits in common, and none of them were *solely* reading men. They were always on the look-out for eligible members to supply the place of those who had left the University and stepped into the regular club,[15] and were very ingenious in making the acquaintance of men that were in any respect lions, and drawing them out to ascertain if they were of apostolic material. Sometimes they were very successful in catching celebrities just as they began to develope themselves. At one time, for four years in succession, the University Scholar was an apostle; but shrewd people remarked that in three cases the lucky man had been elected into the club after it was pretty certain that he would be University Scholar. These men did not make any parade of mystery, or aim at notoriety by any device to attract attention; they did not have special chambers for meeting, with skeletons in the corner[16] and assemble in them with the secresy of conspirators; nor did they wear breastpins with initials of bad Greek sentences or other symbolic nonsense on them, as our young Collegians do. They did not attempt to throw any awful veil of secresy over their proceedings; it was known that they met to read essays and hold discussions, with occasional interludes of supper. I have more than once seen the compositions which were prepared for these meetings: the authors did not seem to think that either the interests or dignity of their club suffered materially from letting an outsider so far behind the scenes.

Their immediate and tangible influence in the University amounted to just nothing. But imperceptibly they exercised much. Their association together had a great mutual effect on the formation of their minds and characters, and thus indirectly on the whole body of men, since an apostle was not cut off from his other friendships by belonging to this Society; and the parent club taken in connexion with its embryo,[17] formed a most innocent and effective *camaraderie*. It is just possible that some of my apostolic friends would not be over-flattered at the application of the term *innocent* to them, as they usually prided themselves on being *leery*, and having such

---

pp. 182–4. Allen comments, 'While Bristed was mistaken in his belief that there was a direct relationship ... his recognition of their combined influence was astute ...' (p. 184).]

[15] Nonsense. (T)

[16] [Bristed is presumably referring to the Skull and Bones Club at Yale.]

[17] ['Embryo' was the term used by the Apostles for prospective members, though it is not clear if it was in use when Bristed wrote.]

virtue as they possessed rather Platonically by than through original instinct
and want of experience like a child, or a woman. But what I mean by
calling the Sterling Club an innocent and effective *camaraderie*, is that its
members, controlling as they did among them many avenues of approach to
the public and means of influencing the public mind, were able to benefit
one another and help on one another's reputation very much, while at the
same time they did so with a fair and legitimate partisanship, not by blowing
up factitious renown with wholesale puffery, or in any way imposing on
the public and corrupting their taste and judgment. Thus when a member
of the club publishes, one of the fraternity has a footing in the Edinburgh,
another in the Quarterly, a third in Fraser, a fourth in Blackwood, and so
on – among them all there is a pretty good chance that his beauties will
not be hid, or the reading community allowed to overlook his merits. Nor
is it by such formal and systematic efforts only that they set forth his claims.
In ordinary casual conversation they have continual opportunities of putting
them forward. One man, I remember, who was a remarkably good reader
(for a small room), used to have a knack of bringing in Tennyson so as to
read portions of him, and the poet lost nothing in his mouth. Tennyson
and Thackeray[18] may be particularized as owing much to their comrades
for setting them prominently before the world. But in all this there is no
false pretence or deception. Let any, for instance, look at Sterling's review of
Tennyson in the *Quarterly*,[19] or the review in the *Edinburgh* also by a brother
apostle;[20] there is no daubing, or whitewashing in them, no putting on the
butter of adulation with the knife of profusion – none of the extravagant
and unmitigated praise with which the members of a Mutual Admiration
Society here would *criticize* one another's productions.

It is not possible for any clique, however excellent and liberal its individual
component members, to be without some *shop* and cant of its own. The
cant of these men was inveighing against cant. It must not be supposed
that they were mere imitators of Carlyle in this – the names of some of the
members are enough to show that they had plenty of original men among
them; but they all affected much *earnestness* and a hearty dislike of sham
and formula, which rendered them far from popular with the *High and Dry*
in literature, politics, or religion. The younger members at the University

---

18   He was not an Apostle. (T) [Bristed's mention of him follows from his belief in
a link between the Apostles and the Sterling Club, to which Thackeray belonged.]
19   ['*Poems* by Alfred Tennyson', *Quarterly Review* 70, Sept. 1842, pp. 385–416.]
20   [James Spedding, 'Tennyson's *Poems*', *Edinburgh Review* 77, April 1843,
pp. 373–91.]

were eyed with terror by grave, plodding Johnians as something foreign, German, radical, altogether monstrous – they hardly pretended to know what. About the Society proper – the Sterling Club – some immense mares' nests were discovered at different times, and I am sorry to say that some Evangelical newspapers let loose a great deal of trash on the subject once or twice – indeed they talked as much nonsense as the Puseyites.[21] The Society was represented as established for the promotion of infidelity on the German plan, the denial of Christ, Templar-fashion, and other things 'horrible and awful', but which the accusers did not deem it 'unlawful' to name at length. As many of the members were in Orders, and same of them indeed dignitaries of the Church, the charge became a pretty serious one. All the ground for it was that poor Sterling, who, though the eponymous hero of the club, does not seem to have been the leading man in it, was shaken in his religious faith towards the close of his life; therefore, the association must be an infidel one. If he had gone mad and cut his throat, it might with equal justice have been called a suicide club. What particular great and chief end the Society had I do not pretend to say – it is not exactly necessary that it should have had any. I suppose a number of literary men may club together in a quiet way without any other purpose than that of mutual amusement and improvement. At any rate whatever objects they had were literary, not religious or irreligious; religion only catered into their discussions as it must into those of all serious men and real *philosophers – lovers of wisdom*. Nor was their faith exposed to any peculiar danger beyond that which threatens all men engaged in high intellectual cultivation and living in a literary atmosphere – the danger of rating the intellectual too high in comparison with the moral.

The heresy which I found in these men was a purely intellectual one – an utter under-valuation of and almost contempt for rhetoric and oratory. My acquaintance was chiefly confined to the younger men, my contemporaries or juniors at the University, but the influence of the older men was visible in the younger – and it certainly was a general feature of them all that they looked down upon the art of public speaking as something necessarily shallow, insincere, and ignoble. They owned that the ideal orator was a great man, perhaps the greatest man conceivable; but the actual attempts at approximation to him they deemed mere charlatanism, and this dislike seemed to be accompanied (as is often the case with our dislikes, physical or intellectual) by an unfitness for success in that line – a turn of mind not

---

[21] [A popular name for the Tractarians, from Edward Pusey of Christ Church, Oxford, a leading figure in the movement.]

popular, more philosophical than oratorical. Besides Hallam I never knew but one[22] of the members who was really born and cut out for a public speaker, and that one was never an enthusiastic member of the Society, and seemed to have been taken into it when they were short of recruits, or in some other way to have got in by mistake. With Hallam the opposing influences were curious to observe. He was made for a debater, the very neatest and most elegant extempore speaker I ever heard. His unprepared speeches were more critically and tastefully worded than most men's written compositions; and this elegance of manner was based on great power of thought, the polish never impairing the strength, and supported by startling dexterity in argument. Most of his collegiate friends urged him forward in the career for which he seemed so signally marked out. But his co-apostles threw cold water on his taste, and I have little doubt it was their influence which so long held him back from speaking at the Union. They doubtless really believed it to be an inferior occupation for him. When I mentioned to some of them in no measured language my opinion of his talents for public speaking, they regarded it as little as if I had praised him for riding well, or getting up a supper with taste. I seemed to them to pick out one of his minor excellencies as a subject for praise. However, we debaters had the best of it for a time, and our great triumph was when an M.A. Fellow [of] Trinity, perhaps the most anti-rhetorical in his professions of all the apostles, actually came down to the Union, and made a long speech in which he showed much anxiety to acquit himself well.

Accidents of the Mathematical Tripos and of the University Scholarship

With the New Year came on the great University examinations, which excited the usual interest. The Senior Wrangler this time was Adams[23] of John's, since celebrated as *the other* discoverer of Le Verrier's planet. He won in a canter, so to speak, having three thousand marks to the Second

---

[22]   Sunderland? (T) [Thomas Sunderland, Trinity 1830 (having entered in 1825), BA 1830. See the chapter on 'Thomas Sunderland and the Cambridge Union' in Allen, *Cambridge Apostles*, pp. 40–55.]

[23]   [John Couch Adams, Senior Wrangler 1843; Lowndean Professor of Astronomy 1856–91. He sent evidence of the position of Neptune to the Astronomer Royal in 1845, but this was not acted on, and in 1846 U. Le Verrier independently located the planet.]

Wrangler's fourteen hundred, so that there was more numerical difference between them than between the Second Wrangler[24] and the spoon. A singular case of funk occurred at this examination. The man who would have been second (also a Johnian),[25] took fright when four of the six days were over, and fairly ran away – not only from the examination but out of Cambridge, and was not discovered by his friends or family till some time after. As it was, he came out ninth in the list of Wranglers, the high papers of the last two days affecting sensibly the places of only the first ten or fifteen. By getting the Second Smith's Prize he might have retrieved his prospects of a Fellowship – but here our best man from Trinity,[26] who was only Third Wrangler, and but for the accident would have been fourth, cut him out. We wanted some little consolation of the sort, being in a terrible minority this year. In the Classical Tripos where we generally looked for one or both Medalists as a matter of course, we had but one man in the First Class,[27] and he only eighth of the eleven composing it. People began to put the blame on our Master, unjustly enough, as the men of that year had not entered under his auspices. The fact was, that a few years before there had been a great scarcity of Trinity Fellowships,[28] so that men to whom the emoluments of learning were an object had become afraid to enter there until the supply of good candidates was thinned out a little. But in the University Scholarship where the Third-year men of crack reputation came into play, our College met with a worse, because more unexpected disappointment. There were four Trinity men expected to fill the first four places in the Classical Tripos of 1844, and three of these were now to fight for the Craven, with no danger except from one Kingsman.[29] King's College

---

[24] Bashforth, Joh. (T) [Francis Bashforth, St. John's 1839, 2nd Wrangler 1843, fellow of St John's 1843; achieved immortality as inventor of the Bashforth chronograph.]

[25] Goodeve. (T, B) [Thomas Goodeve, St John's 1840, 9th Wrangler 1843.]

[26] Gray. (T, B) [Benjamin Gray, Trinity 1839, fellow 1843.]

[27] Gell. (T, B) [Frederick Gell, Trinity 1839, 8th Classic 1843, fellow of Christ's 1843–61.]

[28] [In the 1840s, 6–8 elections were made each year; Bristed may be thinking of 1837, when there were only 3.]

[29] Johnson. (T) [William Johnson, later Cory, King's 1842; fellow 1845–72; the best-known Eton master of his day. Johnson inspired generations of pupils with his teaching of history and literature after his appointment at Eton in 1845, and achieved renown as a practitioner of verse composition, but resigned in 1872 after conflict with the headmaster, Thomas Hornby. The reasons remain unclear, but as with Hornby's dismissal of Oscar Browning in 1875, both independence of the school's official hierarchy and what was seen as undue familiarity with pupils were involved.

stands in an anomalous position with regard to the rest of the University. It is a mere prolongation of Eton School. Its half-dozen Undergraduates, who have been the best 'Collegers' at Eton, become Scholars and Fellows of the College as a matter of course, and also get their degree from the University without passing any examination for it.[30] As a necessary consequence they have no opportunity of distinguishing themselves in either Tripos. But the University Prizes and Scholarships are open to them, and here they prove formidable rivals of the Trinity men. As the dangerous Kingsman was in his Second year, it was calculated that besides the chance of three to one against him, the not unjust preference, ceteris paribus, shown to candidates who have no more opportunity left, would turn the scale against him. But now an outside competitor appeared in the person of the Pembroke Third-year man who had carried off three prizes at the last Commencement.[31] I was almost the only man in Trinity who knew him personally, and having very early in our acquaintance formed a high idea of his ability, and especially his quickness and pace (an important element of success),[32] ventured to talk of him as a likely candidate. The idea of a Small-Colleger beating all Trinity was deemed preposterous, and such a hint looked upon as a sort of treason to the College. Nevertheless it proved true; he came out the winner, with the Kingsman and one of our three close at his heels, and all the rest nowhere. Thereupon he became quite a lion. Still there was a strong party not prepared to admit that he would be Senior Classic, and the Trinity man[33] with whom his College had declared to win (he who had been next to the successful candidate for the Craven), was regularly booked and entered for the head of the Tripos against him. It bid fair to be a very pretty race. The Trinity man was the best in Greek, the other

---

Johnson retired to his family estate and changed his name to Cory; he later moved to Madeira, married and had a son, and taught young women without charge. See F. Compton Mackenzie, *William Johnson Cory: A Biography* (London, 1950).]

[30] [It was widely believed that by a compact made between the college and university in 1456, scholars of King's could proceed to the BA without examination. This had been conclusively disproved by George Peacock in his *Observations on the Statutes of the University* (1841), but the Provost of King's, George Thackeray, who died in 1850, ignored the evidence. His successor, Richard Okes, was more amenable, and the supposed right was given up in 1851.]

[31] Maine. (T, B)

[32] In this examination, we had thirteen lines of Milton for Latin Hexameters, fifteen lines of English prose to translate into Latin, and nine lines to translate into Greek, and but two hours and three quarters for the whole.

[33] W.G. Clark. (T, B)

in Latin; and Greek, especially Composition, counts more than Latin, in the Tripos. On the other hand, the Pembroke man had the *prestige* of the Scholarship, and superior rapidity of work, while his opponent had more accuracy and polish. Then again, he of Trinity was already well prepared in Mathematics, and the other had all his to get up, and as he must be a Senior Optime to contend for the Medal, this was a great dead weight upon him. But again, the Trinity man's knowledge of Mathematics might tempt him to read for a Double First, and thus distract his attention from the one object. Friends of the candidates made bets (not very large ones to be sure: I ultimately won seven pounds on my man) and the whole affair with its calculations and contingencies was like a race or an election – except that there was no foul play.

I went in to this examination in common with some sixty more outsiders, chiefly to find out by experiment if I was strong enough to sit through the Trinity Scholarship next term, and also to become used to the feel of an examination, as I had not passed one since my first May, with the exception of the short and easy Little-Go. Beginning thus with the most difficult examination in the University, I probably wrote a great deal of trash, but no one seeing it except the examiners, it was of little consequence. During the rest of the Lent term I was reading and writing for the Members' Prize, which besides the labor of Latin Composition required much Roman History 'cram'. Also I read with a friend some low Optics with a view to the May examination – a very foolish speculation as I had been over no Second-year Mathematics, and was not in a state to get up the subject in a reliable way. I moreover attended the Greek Professor's[34] Lectures on Pindar and the College lectures on Plato[35] to the Second year.

The small number of students attending Professors' Lectures has often been remarked upon, and the most unfavorable conclusions drawn thence as regards the character of the instruction given, and the diligence of the instructed. The Divinity Lectures are crowded, because attendance on them is necessary to insure testimonials for orders, but otherwise the Professor's rooms are apt to exhibit a beggarly account of empty benches. Dr. Whewell, notwithstanding his high reputation, had comparatively a small class when I attended his Lectures on Moral Philosophy, probably not more than fifty. Very possibly it has been much increased since the establishment of the *Moral Science* Tripos. Professor Sedgwick had an attendance of not more than thirty at his Geological Lectures in the year 1841. The Greek Professor's Class in

---

[34] [James Scholefield, Trinity 1809, Regius Professor of Greek 1825–53.]
[35] [Given by Scholefield's successor in the chair, W.H. Thompson.]

1843 was rather under than above thirty. In all this there was nothing so bad as Buckland's[36] lecturing on Geology to *three* hearers at Oxford; but I was actually myself one of a class of three who attended Professor Cumming's[37] supplementary course of Chemistry in the year 1841.

But there could be no greater error than to take the attendance at Professorial Lectures as any test or indication of the studious or non-studious propensities of English University men. It is *because* they are working so hard that the great body of reading-men do not come to the lectures – working with their private tutors (who correspond to German professors in some respects, as has been observed) for the Tripos, the Scholarships, or the College Mays. If the Greek Professor were really called on to teach the University Greek, he would be lost at once – he could not even attend to the hundred or hundred and twenty men of the three years who intend to go out in the Classical Tripos. There is no Latin Professorship in the University.[38] The number of men likely to take up and pursue any one of the single Natural Sciences, Botany, Chemistry, Geology, &c., for use or amusement in after life, is probably not greater than the proportion who really attend the lectures on these sciences. With regard to the College lectures delivered to the Junior and Senior Sophs, there is frequently, it must be owned, a very moderate attendance at them also. Sometimes this is owing to the limited nature of the subject. For instance, one of the best Mathematical Fellows at Trinity or John's is lecturing on some high branch of Mathematics – something of which the Differential Calculus is merely the alphabet; none but high men can take interest in, or derive profit from such lectures. Now as there are only on an average twelve Wranglers from John's, and nine from Trinity every year, the class is of necessity limited to a dozen, and the lecture takes very much the form of an examination. In Classics it depends chiefly on the lecturer whether he has a good class or not. The lectures, though mainly for the benefit of a particular Year which is to be examined at the May in the subject lectured upon, are open without extra fee to all the College, and a lecturer who has made one author his

---

[36] [W.W. Buckland, since 1825 reader in geology at Oxord; in 1845 he was appointed Dean of Westminster. Buckland deserved a large audience, as his lectures seem to have been both entertaining and instructive. He was famous for his omnivorosity – he vowed to 'eat his way through the animal kingdom'.]

[37] [James Cumming, Trinity 1796, Professor of Chemistry 1815–61.]

[38] [The Latin chair was founded in 1869 through a fund set up by pupils of Benjamin Kennedy, headmaster of Shrewsbury School 1836–66, Regius Professor of Greek 1867–89.]

spécialité, and can translate and explain him in an interesting manner, will be sure to have a large attendance. Our Plato lecturer at Trinity[39] furnished a striking example of this. His room was always crowded; his audience comprised not only the Junior Sophs for whom the lecture was specially intended, but Senior Sophs, Bachelors, and even Fellows. Nay, some men of other Colleges applied to be admitted; but this, if I remember rightly, was contrary to the College rules and usages. The lecturer was tall and handsome, of a commanding and dignified appearance; when he played bowls the grace of his attitudes reminded one of an ancient statue. His translations were exquisite; he would preserve the force of every Greek particle (except, of course, such as *mens* and *des*, which only served the Greeks for points) while using the most elegant English; but his illustrative comments were the great attraction. The knottiest philosophical theories were illumined by his dry jokes, which lavished equal satire on ancient and modern speculators.[40] I attended three of his courses for three successive years, with unabated pleasure. Of the Protagoras, which was the subject this year, I had been careful enough to provide myself with an interleaved copy, and the notes then taken are among my most cherished manuscripts. This term I was called on to recite both my Declamations, English and Latin, in the chapel. Every Senior Soph is nominally required to write an English and a Latin Declamation, but many beg off one or both; probably about fifty of each are sent in. The eight best of each had been selected for recitation, to five out of which sixteen, the five prizes were to be awarded. It was officially intimated in the Lecture-rooms that the Master would be pleased by a general attendance of the students, but in spite of this manifesto we had a very slim audience, not more than a dozen. I recollect poor Hallam posting himself right opposite the high desk or tribune, where I stood, keeping me under fire of his eye-glass the whole time; and when I came to a period of which I had given him a private rehearsal during a constitutional on the previous Sunday, going off into a quiet laugh that almost disconcerted my gravity even in the awful presence of Whewell.

The Union Debating Society, which had taken such a start at the beginning of the academic year, was now growing too lively, and evincing an Irish sort of vitality by a succession of rows. To keep up an interest in the debates, we had persuaded men of reputation to come forward as

---

[39] Hepworth Thompson. (T) He is now Master. (B)

[40] I recollect Thompson saying of the Oxford Platonical dunce Sewell, 'If any gentleman wishes to throw a shilling away he can buy Mr Sewell's book'. (B) [William Sewell, *An Introduction to the Dialogues of Plato* (London, 1841).]

candidates for the offices, and a Trinity Bachelor Scholar of high standing was put up for the presidency of the Lent Term.[41] He was carried after a hard contest, and the defeated party tried to console themselves by making a disturbance, and annoying the assembly, especially on business nights. I may say here that English young gentlemen at a public meeting are more ungentlemanly than any class of our people (for a meeting of Irish or other foreigners in New York is not to be considered an American meeting); they never look upon the occasion in a serious light, but seem to consider it the most natural one for a lark. Two of the members got into a dispute on the floor of the house, which was afterwards continued out of doors.[42] The whole affair at length would make a very pretty bit of Trollopania; but when gentlemen by birth and education do not behave as such, it is not pleasant to dwell on their disgrace, even for the pleasure of retaliating on Mr Dickens. Suffice it to say, that one of them promised to horsewhip the other, and the threatened man assaulted his threatener with a 'life-preserver', knocking him down and nearly killing him;[43] which coming to the ears of the College authorities (both parties were Trinity men), the wielder of the bludgeon was *dismissed* – not expelled – from the College, and subsequently took a degree at one of the Halls in Oxford. An attempt was made to turn him out of the Union also, which, after a noisy discussion of two or three nights, ended in our getting a large majority, but not the requisite two-thirds vote. This happened just at the end of the term, and immediately after the 'rowing men' put up for the next term's presidency a Freshman who had no qualification in the world but being an Honorable.[44] Our side had become so disgusted at the late turmoil that no prominent man would come forward; at last I volunteered to stand the fight, for the express purpose of keeping out the other. But the title was a talisman not to be overcome, and I was left in a minority. After this the debates fell off, and did not rally till late in the next year, when the Young England and Monastic questions brought them up again. About this time came the College Scholarship Examination, at which I presented myself, but having somewhat arrogantly underrated the Classical standard and scarcely attempted to prepare myself

---

[41] F.W. Gibbs, tutor to P. of Wales. (W) President, Lent Term 1843. (S) [Frederick Gibbs.]

[42] Craufurd and Peacocke. (T) [Edward Craufurd, Trinity 1838, President of the Union Society 1839; George Peacocke, Trinity 1841.]

[43] Pshaw! (B)

[44] Hon. F.S. Grimstone, Magd. (W) President, Easter term 1843. (S) [Hon. Francis Grimston, Magdalene 1842.]

in Mathematics, I cut no very distinguished figure. The Declamations also were now adjudged, and I missed both the Latin, but was consoled with the first English. It was my first success since returning to work, and about the showiest prize I could have taken. The best Mathematical man of the Second year[45] having failed to get a Scholarship for want of Classics, it was taken as an earnest of the Master's intention to require 'double men', and some Freshmen were frightened and migrated in consequence, whereby we lost a high Wrangler or two for 1846.

There was an amusing mistake made in this Scholarship examination. One of the extracts for translation began – 'In equo Trojano scis esse in extremo; sero sapiunt', which one man – and he was a clever fellow too, but liable to be muddle-headed at times like many clever people – translated 'You know it was on the tail of the Trojan horse,' &c.[46] These mistranslations are part of the by-play of and relief to an examination, and the accumulation of them forms a sort of University Joe Miller.[47] Travis is responsible for this one; I suspected him of inventing it, but he assured me that it was really made by a schoolmate of his younger brother. 'Caesar captivos sub corona vendidit.' 'Caesar sold his captives for less than five shillings.' And this one he credited to a pupil of his own – 'Est enim finitimus oratori poeta; numeris adstrictior paullo verborum autem licentia liberior.' 'For a poet lived next door to the orator, too licentious in his language, but more circumspect than numbers.'

In the Tripos of 1841, a beautiful passage from Theocritus was set. It is in the Thalusia (7th Idyll), where the poet and his friend, after a hot summer walk, sit down to repose in a sylvan retreat; trees over their heads, running

---

[45] [Walter Grant, Trinity 1839; did not graduate and entered the army.]

[46] [A good example of a difficulty which occasionally occurs in reading *Five Years*. Bristed is referring to what he may assume his readers will know: that the Latin cited comes from a letter of Cicero's (*ad familiares* 7.16), 'Toward the end of [Ennius's] 'Trojan Horse', you know, there's the phrase "wise too late".' The intertextual allusion to Cicero and through him to Ennius is an extreme case of the assumption of the reader's knowledge.]

[47] [Joe Miller was a popular London comedian of the early 18th century. After his death in 1738, a book of jokes was published with his name attached. It became a bestseller, and grew larger with successive editions; by 1865 it contained 1300 jokes. See Robert Hutchinson's introduction to the Dover Books facsimile reprint of 1962. The collection of examination 'howlers' was one of the results of the fiercely competitive spirit of Cambridge examinations. Such collections have occasionally been published; for example, A. Hendriksson, *Non Campus Mentis: World History According to College Students* (New York, 2001).]

water at their feet, birds singing above them, bees humming around, cicadas chirping, loads of fruit dropping into their very mouths; and then says the jolly bard –

Tetraenes de pithon apelueto kratos aleiphar.

'The cement of four years' old was loosed from the top of the jars', *nempe*, to have a merry drinking-bout of it, as the context goes on to show; but with this line the examiner had stopped his extract, leaving the matter somewhat obscure; and one man,[48] deceived by the zoological character of much that had gone before – the mention of various kinds of insects and birds – rendered the line thus: 'And the ape was removing from his head the dirt of four years' standing' – the beauty of which is that, so far as syntax and construction are concerned, the words might have this meaning: *apelueto* might be a deponent, and there is a form *pithon* for *pithekos*.

In the 'Moral Papers' very odd answers are sometimes given. Paley is an author quite capable of being turned into nonsense by a slight mistake, and he and some other 'moral' authors come much into play in the Poll and Little Go, where a large number of the examinees are likely to make more than slight mistakes in attempting to write out what they have attempted to get up. One unfortunate who had confounded together the opening paragraphs of the *Evidences* and the *Natural Theology*, having 'cut' a paper in despair, the examiner found at his desk, on one of the sheets which he had been vainly trying to fill, only this commencement of a sentence, 'If twelve men find a watch.'[49] Another luminary gave as Paley's *definition* of *virtue*, 'Man acts more from habit than reflection.'

During the short Easter term there is not much hard work done among the Senior Sophs, except by two or three of the best Mathematicians who are fighting for the head of the year. Those who have got their Scholarships are inclined to indulge themselves a little, those who have lost them usually get a fit of pique, and don't care where they are in the Examination. The Classical men generally are looking to their Tripos, up to which they now have a straight course of nine months before them, and are not willing to break in upon their routine by preparing 'Morals', Greek Testament, and Mathematical subjects ahead of their regular order, for the May. The

---

[48]   Cope. [Edward Cope.] Surely it was a joke of that excellent scholar, and a very good joke too. (T)

[49]   [Paley was famous for his comparison between a watch and the even more complex intricacy of the Creation.]

Mathematics at this, the last regular College examination, are pretty high – Astronomy, Integral Calculus, the most difficult Dynamics, and the latter part of the Principia, general Questions and Problems in all branches – nothing that can be done without Differential, except parts of the Optical and Hydrostatical papers. To give the *polloi* and Classical men something to do while the Astronomy, Problems, and High Dynamics are going on, they have two papers of translation from the subjects for the ordinary degree examination of next year, and one of low Mathematics, on which papers marks are given enough to keep a man from being 'posted', but not enough to influence perceptibly his standing in the classes. The papers not Mathematical correspond nearly to those of the Second-year examination – one on the Acts, two half papers on 'Morals' (Butler's *Analogy* and Paley's *Evidences*), and one on some portion of Aristotle. Our Aristotle lecturer[50] was a master of his subject, and his lectures were well attended. They came in very *apropos*, after those on Plato of the term before. Every man, it has been said, is either a Platonist or an Aristotelian;[51] and the Trinity students had a capital opportunity of making their choice, by hearing the distinctive merits of the two great philosophers set forth to the best advantage by their able and enthusiastic admirers. It has often surprised me, considering the very practical character of Aristotle's greatest extant works, and the perfection of common sense which they display, that no attempt has ever been made to introduce any part of them into our Academical course. A great many of the suggestions in his *Rhetoric* and *Politics* are perfectly true to the present day, and have never been improved upon; and his *Ethics*, however inferior to those of the Christian dispensation, may, whether regarded in an ethical or a metaphysical point of view, teach much to our new-light reformers. True he is a difficult author, but not more so than others that have a place in our course, Sophocles for instance. *Verb. sap. sat.* I hope I may live to see the experiment tried. The First Class in this year's May examination varies from five to eleven, the whole number of examinees being about eighty. Its usual number is eight. The standard for admission into it had fallen rather low about this time, for while the first man in it could, and sometimes did get twenty-four hundred marks, the last had on some occasions less than eight hundred and fifty. This emboldened me to work for a First Class, though I had but three papers out of nine to rely on, as all the Mathematics I could

---

[50]   Blakesley. (B) [Joseph Williams Blakesley, Christ's 1827, migrated to Trinity 1830, 21ˢᵗ Wrangler and 3ʳᵈ Classic 1831; fellow of Trinity 1831.]
[51]   Coleridge, Table Talk. (B) [Cf. D. Newsome, *Two Classes of Men: Platonism and English Romantic Thought* (London, 1974.]

hope to do were a few questions in Optics, some elementary propositions of the science and the description of an instrument or two, perhaps fifty marks in all. So I ground away, cramming Acts and 'Morals' and polishing up three Books of the Nicomachean Ethics as well as I could, and also writing Greek prose, which entered into the paper. The experiment was not successful. I had underrated the range of the New Testament paper and did not clear one half of it, and on the Morals I afterwards found that my answers, though correct, were not long and explicit enough. In the Aristotle paper I did better, standing third on it. It was the only paper of the last day, and as such had five hours assigned to it, and five hours hard work it took, comprising as it did translations of the most difficult passages, critical illustrations, questions on the history of Aristotle himself, the history of his works, the history of metaphysical and ethical schools, and to finish off with, a nice little bit of English to be translated into Greek. Our best Classic had not time to floor the paper. To destroy any chance I might have left, the standard of the First Class was run up; it contained only six men, the lowest of whom had above eleven hundred marks. Several candidates for Wranglerships kept me company in the Second Class, and I was given to understand that I ought to think myself very well off in not being lower.

A Visit to Oxford

While the result of this examination was pending, I went for a few days to Oxford, where the virtual term[52] ended rather later than ours. My stay being only three days, I had no great opportunities of personal observation, but by comparing what I did see with the result of my knowledge obtained at various times through others, I could note very considerable differences.

The general impression that we in this country have of the two Universities is that, Mathematics are studied at Cambridge, and Classics at Oxford. The reader has seen that there is no want of Classical Study at Cambridge. Cantabs are stronger in Greek, the Oxonians in Latin,[53] but

---

[52]   [Both universities had a full term and a (shorter) teaching term; Bristed presumably refers to the latter.]

[53]   It might also be said that the Oxford Scholarship was more elegant, the Cambridge more accurate. The mutual banter of the Universities well illustrates both these distinctions. The Oxonians used to say that the Cambridge men never could write good Latin prose; the latter retorted that there never was an Oxford man who knew the difference between *ou* and *me*. [Two kinds of negative in classical Greek, the object of much scholarly debate.]

they both read Classics; the Cambridge men however read Classics *and Mathematics*, the Oxford men Classics *and Logic*. This is the great pervading difference.

There is but one Undergraduate gown for all the Colleges at Oxford, and the gold-tufted cap which at Cambridge only designates a Johnian or Small-College Fellow-Commoner is here the mark of nobility. Instead of Pensioners and Fellow-Commoners, the students are called Commoners and Gentleman-Commoners.

The academical year is divided into four terms – Michaelmas, Hilary, Easter, and Trinity – instead of three as at Cambridge; but as they are proportionally shorter, the period of residence is about the same.

There are two annual periods of general admission for students, and correspondingly two great University Degree examinations, one at the end of the Michaelmas Term, the other at the end of the Easter. The Honor and Poll men are all examined together, as they used to be at Cambridge, and the candidates are arranged in five classes, the fifth and largest of which corresponds to the Cambridge Poll. The Aristotelian mental and moral philosophy, as found in the Ethics and Rhetoric, constitute the base of the necessary part of this examination. Next in importance come Herodotus and Thucydides. Beyond this the Classical part of the examination is in a great measure voluntary; a student sends in a list of the *books*, i.e. authors on which he will be examined – twelve I have understood to be a sufficient number for a First Class, though of course it is possible to take in more than this and only get a third – and the viva voce, which forms an important part of the examination, is confined to them. Composition there is of course, but more Latin than Greek, and some original Composition. 'Morals' also come in to a certain extent, as arising out of the Aristotle. The cram is tremendous, the authors being read for matter more than language, which constitutes another great difference between it and the Cambridge University examinations; the College Mays at Cambridge are more like the Schools at Oxford. The First Class averages six, which as the examination is half-yearly, makes it about equal to the average of the First Class at Cambridge. The examination in Mathematics takes place subsequently, being a voluntary after the Classical, just as at Cambridge the Classical is a voluntary after the Mathematical. The candidates are not numerous – about ten in each examination, or twenty in the year. The First Class does not average more than *three*. The standard of it, so far as I could learn, corresponded to that of a low Wrangler in Cambridge. The whole number of candidates for Honors is nearly the same at Oxford as at Cambridge; if there is any difference, the average at the former is a trifle less. Both in Classics and Mathematics the men of each class are alphabetically arranged, so that there is nothing corresponding to the Senior Wrangler or Senior Classic.

How the standard of a First Class in Classics at Oxford compares with one at Cambridge is a much disputed point. The Oxford men claim that theirs is much higher, and allege as one proof that several crack Classical men who were either absolutely plucked in the slaughter of 1841, or frightened away on the same occasion, migrated to Oxford, and after remaining there some time came out only in the Second Class. But as it was, though probable, by no means certain that these men would have been in the First Class at Cambridge, this argument does not go for a great deal. Even if such a thing were to happen as a Cambridge University Scholar migrating to Oxford and taking a Second Class, it would be no more than has happened to the Ireland University Scholar at Oxford, which shows that the Degree examination there has peculiarities of its own, independent of general Classical ability. I knew an Oxford Second-Class man who certainly was a first-rate scholar in several things. He could not be floored anywhere in Pindar, even if put on in the middle of a sentence; and it was told me that when called up to *viva voce* in the Latin poets, he knew by heart all the passages given him to construe, so that merely glancing at the first line he repeated the rest in the original, and then translated it without further reference to the book. He said he had been floored in the Logic and Morals. Now I do not think breaking down on one paper would keep a man out of the First Class in the Cambridge Tripos, if his performance in the others was first-rate. But on the other hand the range of authors for the Cambridge Tripos is wider – in fact is only limited by the limits of the Classical ages in Greek and Roman literature; while I have heard of an Oxford First Class man who had read no Plato, and another who had read no Demosthenes; and this I fancy could hardly happen at Cambridge.

Of the four classes which are considered Honors, the *Fourth*[54] is in popular estimation preferable to the *Third*, because it is customary when a student only goes in to pass, but does very well in some of his papers, to lift him up out of the Fifth Class into the Fourth. You cannot tell therefore, from a man's being in the Fourth Class whether he has broken down in Honors or done well in the Poll, while a Third Class is an unmitigated failure in Honors; those only being in it who have tried for Firsts and Seconds, and sent in their lists of authors accordingly. While on this point I may mention the fate of a personage somewhat notorious by name among us, *the Rev.*

---

[54]   At Oxford! (B) This was known as the 'Honorary Fourth'. (T)

Isaac Fidler, who once wrote a book about his experience in America.[55] On our side the water he is not unfrequently classed with Trollope and Dickens, but in his own country is a prophet altogether without honor and never mentioned in such good company. I fancy that abusing America only gives a man a sort of prestige in certain quarters in England, a kind of *prima facie* claim to be heard, like doing well at the University; but will not be sufficient of itself to make his reputation, unless he follows it up with something better; and Mr. Fidler having written his book of abuse, but not backed it up by any other fictitious productions, made no renown for himself. This gentleman, with all his pretence to learning, had never taken a University Degree at home, and when he attempted the experiment, rather late in life, and considerably the senior of his examiners,[56] he came out in the Third Class, and his name is there to this day on the list for the Easter Term, 1840, as any one may see who possesses a copy of the *Oxford Calendar.* The best of the joke is, that, according to the delightful geographical and political confusion of ideas which Europeans now and then exhibit in reference to things American, he was taken at the University for a countryman of ours! because he hailed last from Canada!! and I had some difficulty in persuading an Oxford man that this was not the case. In the minor examinations at Oxford the same general features are observable in distinction to those at Cambridge; the presence of *viva voce* as an important element, the absence of Mathematics, and the student's selection of the books on which he is to be examined. At the *Smalls,* as the previous Examination is here called, each examinee sends in his Greek and Latin *book*; but the term *book* must be taken in a larger sense than that of *author* at Cambridge – for instance three or four plays might be required at Oxford to make a *book.* It follows that the *Smalls* is a more formidable examination than the *Little-Go.* The rest of it consists of Logic, for which the student may, if he please, substitute two or three Books of Euclid. The College examinations, called *collections,* are strictly private. Each student chooses a Greek and a Latin book once a term, and is examined on them by his College tutor. No rewards are given for proficiency in these examinations. Prizes for essays, verses, &c., either at the particular Colleges or in the University at large, are much fewer than at Cambridge, indeed the great point at Oxford seems

---

[55] [Isaac Fidler, *Observations on Professions, Literature, Manners and Emigration in the United States and Canada in 1832* (1833). Fidler took his BA in 1840, aged 45.]

[56] At Oxford as at Cambridge, the Degree Examiners are all of the Young Don species. The Scholarships and Fellowships are examined for by older men.

to be to concentrate all the interest of the three years and a half upon the final examination.

Some particulars of separate Colleges are worth noticing. Christ Church, the great college of Oxford, answering to Trinity at Cambridge, which might be as populous as Trinity if it chose, confines itself to about a hundred and fifty Undergraduates, wishing to keep up a reputation for being aristocratic and exclusive. You cannot get into Christ Church without having good connexions and influence, so it is said. Trinity men also are wont to distinguish themselves in the University examinations, which is another difference between that college and Christ Church. All Souls has *no Undergraduates*; nor does this arise from any corruption or abuse: it was originally founded for Fellows only, who, according to the statutes, are to be '*bene nati, bene vestiti, et moderate docte in arte musica*'. It is in fact a pleasant club of well-born, gentlemanly men, with some literary or scholastic tastes, who reside or not, just as they please, and are paid £100 a-year for no particular merit or act, except the negative one of not partying. All the Colleges at Cambridge have equal privileges and rights, with the solitary exception of King's,[57] and though some of them are called Halls, the difference is merely one of name. But the Halls at Oxford, of which there are five, are not incorporated bodies, and have no vote in University matters, indeed are but a sort of boarding houses at which students may remain until it is time for them to take a degree. I dined at one of these establishments; it was very like an officers' mess. The men had their own wine, and did not wear their gowns, and the only Don belonging to the Hall was not present at table. There was a tradition of a chapel belonging to the concern, but no one present knew where it was. This Hall[58] seemed to be a small Botany Bay of both Universities, its members made up of all sorts of incapables and

---

[57] The peculiar position of King's has been alluded to. Besides the privilege mentioned of taking a degree without passing any examination, its members, when on their own premises, are not subject to the Proctor's authority. [The two proctors were the senior disciplinary officials of the University.] The government of the College is very pedantic and despotic, at least it was in my time. Exeats, or permission to go down during term, were never granted but in cases of life and death, and an unusual number of chapels were exacted.

[58] [St Alban's Hall, notorious for receiving men expelled from other colleges at both universities. See M.G. Brock and M.C. Curthoys (eds), *The History of the University of Oxford, Vol. VI: Nineteenth-Century Oxford, Part 1* (Oxford, 1997), p. xxiv, and the engraving on which this comments, by the leading early-Victorian satirical artist George Cruikshank (Plate 54).]

incorrigibles; one man had been dismissed from St. John's, Cambridge, for driving a tandem into the college grounds, and over a Don or two; another from Trinity College, Cambridge, for some equally gross offence; a third from an Oxford college for a third flagrant misdemeanor; and a fourth had been plucked an incalculable number of times, and stayed long enough at the University, he said himself, to be a Doctor of Divinity.

The Oxonians profess to be more of gentlemen than the Cantabs; they certainly have more wealthy and titled men among them, and therefore more luxury, and possibly more refinement of manners. On the other hand, I shall not be suspected of envy or accused of misrepresentation, when I assert a notorious fact, that they are, as compared with the members of the other University, unacquainted[59] with general literature, unpractical and very antediluvian in all matters of politics and world-knowledge. A Cambridge friend of mine who had migrated from Oxford, told me that he did so because there were only two sets of men there, one who fagged unremittingly for the Schools,[60] and another devoted to frivolity and dissipation;[61] that he could find nothing between the two – no literary men who knew something besides their cram-books and shop – no half reading half literary men of leisure, as at Cambridge. I have never met with persons who knew so little of what was going on out of doors as the Oxonians I had the fortune to encounter at my visit there. Even of the question which was then agitating their University – the Puseyite movement – they seemed to possess no certain knowledge. 'We leave all that to the M.A.'s', said one to whom I put some query respecting the state of feeling among the Undergraduates on the subject. The question was asked in a room full of Christ Church men, twelve at least, and I do not think the same number could have been brought together at Trinity who would have showed such incompetence to amuse or be amused by, to teach something to or learn something from, a stranger. There is an absurd, irritating, boarding-school-like system of petty rules prevailing at most of the Oxford Colleges, making a state affair of the merest trifles, such as getting half a cold fowl from the buttery, which must belittle the minds of all concerned either in enforcing or suffering it. Confectioners are not allowed to send ice-cream to a student's rooms; it has to be smuggled in. On asking the cause of this peculiar prohibition, I

---

[59] Not so now. (B)

[60] The place of examination, as the *Senate House* is at Cambridge.

[61] It is the character of the Oxford idle man to be less violently dissipated than the rowing Cantab, but more frivolous than the fast one. The exquisite in dress, a rare bird on the banks of the Cam, is not uncommon on those of the Isis.

was told in sober seriousness that the enactment was first made at the time
of the cholera in 1832, and that *as it was not the custom to alter any law at
Oxford that had once been passed*, it had remained in force ever since. Even
in their specialities of Classics and Logic, the Oxonians have given few
outward signs of vitality. Take away Scott and Liddell's *Greek Lexicon*,[62] a
valuable book certainly, and Linwood's *Lexicon of Aeschylus*,[63] and all the
rest is owing to men like Whately and Arnold, anti-Oxonian in feeling
and opinion, and quite out of place there.

A determined radical might attribute this backwardness of the Oxford
men to the old Tory character of the University and the greater number
of noblemen and rich men here than at Cambridge; nor is it improbable
that these causes have something to do with it. An admirer of science and
contemner of the dead languages might account for the different intellectual
condition of the two Universities by the compelled study of Mathematics at
Cambridge, and their almost entire absence at Oxford. But unfortunately
for this solution, it happens that at Cambridge the Classical men are usually
the ones most distinguished for general literary knowledge and enlightened
views. Trinity, the great Classical College, is the great Whig College also,
and St. John's, the nursery of Senior Wranglers, is equally the hot-bed of
bigotry. Indeed it was this that always puzzled me when speculating on
the subject; the general plan of the Oxford system seemed more liberal and
liberalizing than that of the Cambridge. No compulsory Mathematics; what
was compulsory the study of one of the most practical and acute authors,
not merely of his own age, but of any age,[64] sufficient *viva voce* to give
readiness and confidence, yet the actual result proved just the other way,
whether I relied on my own experience or trusted the testimony of others;
there was far less general knowledge and love of literature, and infinitely less
liberality of sentiment at Oxford than at Cambridge. Without pretending
to explain the discrepancy, I shall make bold to hint at one or two things
that may have something to do with it.[65]

There is one way in which the Mathematical element at Cambridge
may make that University more progressive than the other. The higher
branches of Mathematics certainly require and exercise *originality* more than
Classical studies, and accordingly, the good Mathematicians who come up
to Cambridge (for *making* a man a mathematician who is not so naturally

---

62   [H.G. Liddell and R. Scott, *A Greek-English Lexicon* (Oxford, 1843).]

63   [W. Linwood, *A Lexicon to Aeschylus* (London, 1843).]

64   Aristotle. (B)

65   [Trevelyan comments on this paragraph, 'Interesting and important'.]

I consider a very exceptional case, and we must therefore look rather at the influence which the Mathematicians have on the University than the influence which it has on them) may infuse more originality of thought and speculation into the whole body. Against this, however, must be set off the engrossing nature of the study of Mathematics, which demands the learner's whole concentrated attention, and gives him a perilous bias one way; but this does not apply to the Graduates and Fellows, who have leisure to turn their thoughts to other subjects. Again, there is an evident tendency at Oxford to read authors too much in reference to their matter only, so that with the exception of the Composition – and that depends in a great measure on early practice and drill – a memory of extraordinary capacity is the great reliance in the Schools. Now our feeling at Cambridge was rather against an extraordinary memory, unless it was accompanied by extraordinary talent: as standing instead of talent, it was looked down upon, and deemed an accomplishment for a boy rather than for a man. Such a one would do better, I often heard it said, if he had not so good a memory; he depends too much upon it, and does not think enough. I suspect, too, that the absence of College examinations at which honor can be gained, and the paucity of College and University prizes at Oxford, have an unfavorable effect. Moreover, the Scholarships and Fellowships are, with some noble exceptions,[66] usually close; they depend on favor or locality of birth-place or school. It must happen that many good men grow tired of reading three years for a single end, without any intermediate diversion or stimulus, and are tempted into the ranks of the idle and dissipated; while those who continue their reading become cramped and rusty from the fixed pursuit.

These remarks on Oxford are very imperfect and unsatisfactory, I am well aware. The incurious nature of most Oxford men, and the difficulty of getting any information out of them, must be my excuse.[67]

---

[66]   Such as the Balliol Fellowships, open to the whole University by examination.

[67]   I think he learned a great deal about Oxford in the time. (T)

13

Private Tuition

On returning from my short visit to Oxford, I set to work for the English Essay, and soon after finishing and sending in my exercise (name under seal as usual), was encouraged by taking solus the University Latin Essay Prize. Before this, however, I had started with the intention of going out next year in both Triposes, and had accordingly put on two coaches. My old friend Travis being no longer a resident,[1] I had recourse to a Johnian, one of the few Classical men of that College, as different a man from Travis as might be, but quite a character too in his way.[2] He was so large and dignified in person as to have acquired the soubriquet of Jupiter – in those miserable, drizzling, spitting days of which the English climate boasts an extra share, we used to appeal to him, by this name, to exercise his influence with the clerk of the weather – one of the best-natured and one of the laziest of mortals: his end and occupation and pleasure seemed to be to lie all day on a sofa, writing Greek and Latin verses, which he did beautifully, or reading English poetry. For Mathematics – having to begin from the beginning, the six months before me were not too long a time – I took shelter in a great refuge of Classical men, who had a wonderful reputation for putting through incapables, and worked some thirty or forty pupils regularly.[3] This

---

[1]   Tom Travis [i.e. Taylor] left college I think in 1843. (B)
[2]   Jupiter Thompson. (E, B) [Cf. P. Searby, *History*, p. 606. This is Henry Thompson, Trinity 1834, migrated to St. John's 1836, fellow 1841–97. 'Popularly known as "Jupiter" Thompson, from his fine presence' (Venn).]
[3]   Walton. (B) [William Walton, Trinity 1832; fellow of Trinity Hall 1868–85.]

'putting on two coaches for the last Long', is an ordinary practice; and there are few terms or vacations during which a student is not engaged with one tutor at least. Being so important a feature in the University system, private tuition demands a more particular examination and description than the occasional references to it hitherto incidentally made supply.

The private tutor at an English University corresponds, as has been already observed, in many respects to the Professor at a German. The German professor is not *necessarily* attached to any specific chair; he receives no fixed stipend, and has not public lecture rooms; he teaches at his own house, and the number of his pupils depends on his reputation. The Cambridge private tutor is also a Graduate, who takes pupils at his rooms in numbers proportionate to his reputation and ability. And although, while the German professor is regularly licensed as such by his University, and the existence of the private tutor as such is not even officially recognised by his, still this difference is more apparent than real; for the English University has virtually licensed the tutor to instruct in a particular branch by the standing she has given him in her Examinations. Thus a high Wrangler may be considered *ipso facto* a competent instructor in Mathematics, and so on. But the private tutor's office is somewhat peculiar in the details of instruction, owing to the causes which first called the system into being and now perpetuate it.

The publicity given to College and University Honors, and the importance assigned to them, have been already more than once alluded to. They exceed anything of which we have any conception in our academical institutions. True, the publicity does not come in the same way; there is no crowding of Commencements to hear the young men make speeches; but if a comparatively small number of the public come to gaze at the successful student, his name goes forth to all who read the papers – for in every newspaper not only the results of the Degree Examination and the University Prizes, but all the College Examinations and College Prizes are conspicuously reported. When I was elected Scholar of Trinity, Dr. Whewell thought it worth while to write express to Mr. Everett, announcing the fact in advance of the press, as if our Minister would be justified in regarding it as a sort of national matter. When an acquaintance of mine, who was related to a member of the Cabinet, wished for a start in the diplomatic line, the statesman's first advice to him was, 'be sure to get a Wranglership'. As to the first men of the year, they are no end of celebrities for the time being. A small biography of the Senior Wrangler is usually published in some local paper near his native place, thence transferred to the Cambridge papers, and from them copied widely into other journals; while the School which sent up the University

Scholar and Senior Classic generally takes care that something shall be said about him. But the honor is far from being the only point of the temptation. All these Examinations, except the two Triposes,[4] bring with them some solid testimonial in the shape of books, plate, or money – more generally the last, and sometimes to a very considerable amount. A Trinity Scholarship is worth £60 a-year, if the holder remains constantly in residence – £40[5] to most men, according to the extent to which they usually avail themselves of it. Some of the Small-College Scholarships are worth £100 *per annum*. A Fellowship gives an income of from £200 to £400.[6] A friend of mine[7] was, during his third year, between School 'Exhibitions', College Scholarships and Prizes, and the University Scholarship, in the receipt of more than *Seventeen Hundred* dollars; and as his expenses did not exceed half that sum, he was a gainer to the amount of the other half by receiving his education. Indeed, it is a common saying, and hardly an exaggerated one, that a poor student by taking a high degree supports not only himself, but his mother and sisters for life.

Now it is evident that students come up to the University with all degrees of preparation – some from the public schools already accomplished Classics, and requiring only to enlarge their sphere of reading, get more philosophical conceptions in syntax, and increase their pace in Composition but with very scanty knowledge of Mathematics[8] – some from private tutors, who have perhaps read two years ahead in Mathematics, but are rather *shady* in Greek and Latin – others from private schools or tutors, not too well prepared in anything. Moreover, while the public-school man has had a previous trainer for the Classical examinations of the University in those of his own school, many of his fellow-students are not in a position to apply their knowledge with the best effect to the system in which they find themselves. To make up for former deficiencies, and to direct study so that it may not be wasted, are two *desiderata* which probably led to the introduction of private tutors, once a partial, now a general appliance. Now, it is true, that the extent of ground to be gone over in Classics is too great for any one who enters *very* deficient in them to be worked up by any means so as to take a good degree, yet even here a great deal may be done, and a very inaccurate and superficial knowledge be filled in

---

4   And even these indirectly, as they lead to Small-College Fellowships.

5   £20. (B)

6   From 150 to 600 at Trinity. (E)

7   I think this was Maine. (B)

8   The ignorance of maths of the Eton boys is astounding. (B)

and polished up to a surprising extent; while in Mathematics, the student who comes up knowing only his First-year subjects, but with a very good capacity for science, has time enough, under proper direction, to get a place among the first twenty Wranglers, or even the first ten. And it is through his tutor's aid that many a Classical man, who could never have passed of himself, saves his distance in Mathematics, or is even pushed into the Senior Optimes, so as to be qualified for a Medal; and that many a Freshman takes a First Class in the May Examination, and is thereby encouraged to go on reading for Honors, instead of being disgusted and killed off at the outset. Moreover, even for the subjects in which a student enters well prepared, the coach is most useful to keep him at his work and prevent him from losing ground. The daily or ter-weekly attendance has a beneficial effect in making the pupil work regularly, nor is the tutor in most cases at all slow to blow up any of his team who give signs of laziness. Indeed this was an acknowledged requisite of a good coach. 'I am afraid of going to T——,'[9] you may hear it said, '*he don't slang his men enough*'.[10] In working up a clever man whose previous training has been neglected, in cramming a man of good memory but no great brilliancy, in putting the last polish to a crack man and quickening his pace, so as to give him a place or two among the highest in either Tripos – in such feats a skilful tutor will exhibit consummate jockeyship; he seems to throw a part of himself into his pupil and work through him.

The student reading with a Classical tutor translates to him from some (prepared) author, brings him Composition prepared at home, and writes out in the tutor's rooms, examination fashion, both translations and compositions, which, after being corrected, are compared with the tutor's models. As much of the pupil's reading must be done by himself, the great object of the tutor is the Composition, but he also serves as a general commentator and last resort in difficulties; it is also his business to make selections of hard passages from authors whom the student may not have

---

[9]   T is Shilleto. (E) I cannot read Shilleto's honest letters to this day without shame. I blush to think that I got the same degree as that admirable scholar. (T) [Another hand adds, 'Both Shilleto and GOT were 2nd classics in their respective years. GOT was coached by Shilleto'. Richard Shilleto, Trinity 1828, 2nd Classic 1832; the leading classical coach; fellow of Peterhouse 1867–76. His letters to Trevelyan have not been traced.]

[10]   Bowring, who evidently took 'T——' to refer to Tom Taylor, comments, 'Taylor was a very bad tutor & a most lazy dog'.

time or inclination to read the whole of, and to point out proper books for 'cram' and philological information.

In Mathematics, examinations – that is, working examples and problems – are the principal exercise, most 'book-work' difficulties being sufficiently explained in the books, though some tutors consider their own manuscripts better than any of the books, and make their pupils copy them. The men are continually writing out book-work, either at home or in their tutor's rooms; they practise it to get pace as well as accuracy.

An ordinary tutor takes five or six pupils a-day, giving an hour to each. One of great celebrity will have twice as many if a Classic, or four times as many if a Mathematician. A mathematical tutor can drive a much larger team than a classical; the latter cannot well have more than three men construing to him at a time, nor can he look over and correct the Compositions of more than ten in a day with the care and accuracy desirable; the former can be making explanations and setting examples to a squad of eight or ten together. The one to whom I now resorted [11] used to give his thirty pupils regular 'fights' as he called them; he would set ten or twelve of them to write out a paper on some subject, and give them marks for it just as in an examination; and the results of these *fights* papered the room during a whole term or vacation, till there was no place left on the walls for any more.

The men who have taken the very highest degrees do not always make the best tutors. The most celebrated coach for high Mathematical men was a seventh Wrangler; our friend of the *fights* an eighth Wrangler. [12]

To many of the *polloi* coaches are no less necessary, though the quality in demand is of an inferior kind. The chief requisite of a Poll coach is patience, as his pupils are likely to be very stupid or very lazy, and in either case very ignorant; a man of any ability and knowledge going out in the Poll is able to be his own tutor for the occasion.

The regular fee of a private tutor is £7 a term, if you go to him on alternate days, or £14 if every day. Noblemen and Fellow-Commoners pay more, and Sizars about one half. [13] The charges for the vacations are proportional.

The intercourse between the private tutor and his pupil varies of course according to the character and age of both parties, but it is usually of the most familiar kind, the former seldom attempting to come Don over the

---

[11]   Walton. (B)

[12]   Hopkins, Walton. (B)

[13]   The fees the same for all. (E)

latter. When they are personal friends, as is not unfrequently the case, it becomes very free and easy, sometimes blending amusement with instruction in a rather comical way. When I was recovering from illness sufficiently to 'put on' Travis again, he used to come to me, to save me the ascent of his three pair of stairs, and a man who had been my fellow pupil [14] with him from the beginning of our Freshmanship, would meet him there. We were reading Aeschylus, and something had possessed us to attack the *Supplices*, which we afterwards concluded was rather a waste of our time, the corruptions and difficulties of the play being so great that it is scarcely ever set except in University Scholarships, and the poetry not of a character to repay the trouble of making out its meaning. Here is the sort of scene we three used to have.

(A cosily furnished room about twelve feet square. Present Travis and his two pupils; also any number of lexicons, seven German commentators, and two English ones scattered about in various places. The owner of the apartment attired in a very old dressing-gown and slippers, half buried in an arm-chair, and looking what some young ladies call interesting, i.e., pale and seedy, and hardly able to support the two or three books which he is holding at once. Menzies, a little man with a very positive eye-glass, perched on a sofa, and just visible among a pile of learned tomes surrounding him. Travis standing up with a much interlined and dog's-eared Aeschylus in his hand, and occasionally walking about, or rather turning round, for the limits of the chamber do not admit more. The manner of instruction is this: – the pupils construe five or six lines alternately, the construer stopping himself or being pulled up short by Travis, at the end of every line, and a long discussion and annotation intervening between that line and the next, accompanied with consultations of some or all of the nine commentators. One of the sufferers has just been reading half-a-dozen lines of the almost unknown tongue, and takes a long breath before attacking the translation.) [15]

Travis: Now then, Bristed, go on!

B: 'But respect thy suppliants, O earth-holding, almighty Zeus, for the male race of Aegyptus, intolerable in their insolence;' *hubrin* an accusative, with *kata* understood, isn't it?

T: Don't say *kata* understood; call it *an accusative of reference.*

---

[14] Menzies (Dalzell). (B) [Dalyell.]

[15] Uncommonly well told and to the life. (B)

B: 'Pursuing me in a' – can you say *hurriedly* for *dromoisi*, as you would for *dromo*, in Herodotus?

T: Yes: what's the construction of *meta*?

B: Tmesis with *deomenoi*. 'Seek to take forcibly me a fugitive'; *biaia* adverbial, I suppose.

T: Of course; go on; *poluthrōoisi mataisi*.

B: *mataisi* is an *hapax legomenon*, isn't it?

T: No, I believe not.

(A hunt for *mate* among the commentators and lexicons. Menzies, who has the Linwood nearest him, announces that it occurs also in the Choephorae, meaning *a crime*, and here means *wanderings*.)

B: 'Noisy wanderings' – will that do?

T: *maten – mataios* – it *may* mean *crimes*, or *rashness* here, perhaps. I thought it did. (Scribbles down a memorandum for future reference on the margin of his book.) I'll think of it. Go on, Menzies.[16]

(Menzies reads seven or eight lines; the first two or three are not very difficult, and he charges them with great determination.)

M: 'The beam of thy balance is over all, and what without thee is accomplished to mortals? O! O! Ah! Ah!'

T: Never mind the interjections.

(Menzies makes a long pause.) *Hode marptis*, 'This snatcher', *naios* 'at sea', *gaios* 'on land.' I'm at sea altogether myself.

T: 'This snatcher from the ship is now on land.' Don't go to sleep, Bristed.

M: 'May you labor for these things.'

T: 'Before these things, snatcher, may you perish', that is, before you carry me off.

M: *Ioph om* is Egyptian, isn't it?

T: Probably; not Greek, at any rate. (Some one knocks at the door.)

B: I thought my sporting door was shut.

T: Never mind, don't answer; he'll go away

M: Here's some Egyptian, or something – *kakkas no duian*.

B: (looking up out of a German edition.) Haupt reads *kabbas*. A very good emendation. It is the herald, then, that speaks, *kabbas* 'come on down here', *boan amphaino*, 'I can tell you'.

M: And what about *no duian*?

T: *Duian* must have something to do with *due*, but *no* – *no*, no, I don't know what that means.

---

[16]   Dalzell. This was Dalyell [sic] now consul at Erzeroum. (B)

B: (Diving up from among three editors with an air of great exaltation.) They all give it up as hopeless.

T: Well then we'll give it up as hopeless.

(Outsider knocks at the door.) Our friend don't give it up as hopeless. 'Come down, I tell you.'

(The outsider probably hearing the last words imperfectly and construing them into an invitation to come in, enters without more ceremony.)

B: Ah, Dunbar, how are you?

(Dunbar,[17] a grave heavy Scotchman, walks into the middle of the room (which only requires one step), becomes aware of what is going on, says 'oh, you're busy', and is slowly turning to go out.)

T: Don't go. We'll soon be through. Sit down and take a book.

(B. hands Dunbar a Niebuhr's Rome, stuck full of ragged bits of paper, to mark places where cram is to be got up. Dunbar opens it at the largest of these marks, and sits down to a dissertation on the *nexus* and *addictus* – about as interesting as Fearne on Contingent Remainders. B. reads some more Greek and proceeds to translate.)

'I see these preludes are introductory of forcible miseries to me. Go in flight to the protection of the shrine' – that's what they say *alkan* means – 'Ferocious he revels' – *klida* active here?

T: No, no; take both your adjectives adverbially.

B: 'He revels ferociously of purpose, in a way intolerable both at sea and on land. O king, anticipate him by your orders' –

T: There you go again! What voice is *protassou* ?

B: Middle.

T: Well then, 'arrange yourself before us – stand before us.' Now, Menzies! *Oukoun oukoun.*

M: (Making a desperate dash at the passage and rendering it with a literalness that would have gladdened the heart of a New England tutor.) 'Won't there be, won't there be pullings, pullings, and stickings, very bloody, murderous cutting off of the head?'

(Dunbar shuts up his book, looks at Menzies as if he had some doubts of his sanity, and walks solemnly out of the room.)

M: Whom does she say that of, herself or the herald?

B: Which you please, my dear, as the man said of the puppet-show.

T: She says it of the herald – threaten him with the king's vengeance. That will do for you.

(B. reads a few lines and proceeds to translate.) 'Go, you cursed wretches

---

[17] [Not identified.]

to the cursed' – I say, Travis, *amis* means matella. It's very improper and besides doesn't agree with the context. (Another long turning over of commentators – ultimately it is decided on Dindorf's authority that *amida* has crept into the text *ridiculo errore* for *amada* which Hesychius explains to mean a ship *apo tou aman ten hala*, because it sweeps the brine.)

'Then along the briny path of many currents with a master's insolence, yea, all bloody from my studded staff will I put you' – pauses and looks up, suspecting something wrong because Travis has let him translate four lines without interrupting him.

T: (who has been looking out of the window for the last two minutes.) – O Menzies, there's *such* a pretty girl just gone by! Bristed, have you had your walk to-day? Put on your boots and let's go out and see her. (*Exeunt* Travis and Menzies.)

It should be observed in palliation of their haste, that a pretty face is a rare sight in Cambridge. You don't see one once in three months on an average.

Scenes like the above make coaching appear rather a farcical performance, and must not be taken as a general type of the operation. Yet even where the communication of knowledge takes this jocose turn, it is not the less true that much knowledge is communicated.

It would indeed be too much to say that every private tutor is a conscientious man; probably that could not be affirmed of *any* body of instructors amounting to several hundred. Some of the instances where men who have gone out in the Poll take Poll pupils, especially to go on a reading party, are the grossest cases of *governor-doing*,[18] being merely associations for the more convenient pursuit of idleness and dissipation on the part of all concerned, tutor as well as pupils. But such cases are happily exceptional. Nevertheless advantage has been taken of them by a College dignitary here and there, jealous of the lucrative and independent position enjoyed by some of the tutors who have married (either giving up their fellowships or not waiting to get them, or even having failed to get them, for the competition at Trinity and John's sometimes excludes very good men), and support a family on the proceeds of their teams. But there is little likelihood that the practice will be abolished or essentially modified unless the whole system of the University and College examinations should undergo a fundamental change. The present staff of College Lecturers could not, except in some few of the smallest Colleges, supply the demand for instruction; in the

---

18   [Cheating one's father.]

large Colleges their number would require to be multiplied by a very large factor. Nor, even were they thus increased, could any public lecturer have the intimate knowledge of his pupils' acquirements, deficiencies, capacities, and wants, that the private tutor has, nor would he be likely to take so strong a personal interest in each individual of them. The etiquette and official distance between the two parties go a great way to prevent this. Moreover any College arrangements would leave the vacations unprovided for, and it is in the vacations that the greater portion of a reading man's work is done. For my own part I am sensible of having derived the greatest advantage from the gentlemen with whom I read at different periods, and am convinced that, without them, I should have gained but very moderate benefit from the public instruction of the College; and I believe every man except those from the public schools would say the same thing. They, having undergone a similar drill previously, could better do without private Classical instruction, but even many of them would be hard put to it without a Mathematical coach. Nor would it be possible, even were it desirable, to put down private tuition in fact, though it might be done in name. It could not be made unlawful for two men to assist each other in Classics and Mathematics reciprocally. A little of this goes on as it is. A B.A. friend of mine reading for a Fellowship, coached me very successfully in Mathematics for one examination, and I paid him in kind by assisting him in Classics the next Long. Were the legitimate private tutors abolished, this sort of arrangement would become more frequent, and it would carry with it many of the alleged evils of private tuition as now existing – such as its being unauthorized, interfering with the public lectures, &c. – with the additional evil that the work would not be so well done.

It certainly must be annoying to a College Don that a man who has perhaps taken a lower degree than himself, and has no legal or formal place in the University, should yet enjoy a larger income and a greater local reputation in addition to the comforts of a family. But the latter is a penalty which the Don must pay for his official dignity and extra-local reputation; out of the University the private tutor is only B.A. or M.A. or at most 'late Fellow', the Dean or tutor of a College is always somebody on a title page, whether he edits a Classic or publishes a sermon. And as to the former, it has been already shown that a lecturer who wants a large class and a reputation for lecturing, and has the ability to deserve them, need never fail to have a crowded room. On the whole we may say that, *admitting the present examinations as fixed facts*, the private-tutorial is the best mode of preparing for them. It is dear – but England is a dear country,

and everything connected with an English University education is expensive
– and there is this peculiar compensation in the case of the expense of the
private tutor, that *it repays itself by its own operation.* The poor Undergraduate
who pays his £7 or £14 a term to his tutor, receives the same amount from
his pupil when himself a B.A.

14

Long Vacation Amusements
[1843]

A Breakfast Party.

Judicious drank.
Pope.

I had set to work in earnest to read for both Triposes. With my Classical
tutor I attacked the Oedipus Tyrannus of Sophocles, an author into whose
difficulties I was just beginning to have a little insight, and also wrote
Composition, not in his rooms like an examination, but leisurely at home,
as well as translations of the most difficult passages in the Third Book of
Thucydides. With my other coach I began Mathematics from the beginning
– that is to say from Algebra. It was a melancholy reflection that I had first
been set to work on the mystery of x and y eight years before. During
that space of time my advance in literature and general mental development
had been definite and appreciable; in Mathematics I seemed to have been
standing still. This was the fourth time I had begun Algebra, and essayed
with no weakness of purpose to get it up properly. But it was as slow and

disagreeable work as ever, and one day after I had been blundering along for a fortnight without getting into Trigonometry, I suddenly resolved to give up the idea of going out in Honors, for that year at any rate. Being a *bye-year* man I could choose the year below without formally degrading, and this would put me on an equality with other men by giving me a second chance for a Scholarship. So I threw Mathematics up, and having only Classics to devote myself to, read with my tutor five plays of Sophocles and some Demosthenes, and by myself, all Theocritus and all the twenty plays of Plautus – which was one of my weaknesses and considered a great loss of time, as Plautus is no help in Composition and few men read more than three or four plays to get a vocabulary. As my health gradually improved under the even temperature of an English summer, I also began to look about for some little amusement, not a very easy thing to find in a Cambridge Long. Discovering that I was strong enough to play billiards,[1] I entered into the exercise with much ardor, but it soon became so fascinating and took up so much time that I was obliged to wean myself of it.

It happened that there was this summer, beginning before the vacation and lasting to the end of it, an unusual influx of American visitors, no less than seven, at as many different times, some just landed on the shores of Europe, others on their way back from the East, and each of these visits was an incident in my tolerably monotonous life, and an occasion of festivity. But the most marked and important feature of this Long was my introduction to another stranger, which took place thus.

Among the men up this Long, who were all reading-men of course, I was especially intimate with two sets. One consisted of three or four Apostles, men who belonged to different Colleges but were united by the bond of their club, and most of whom I had known previous to their joining it, indeed I had introduced some of them to each other. For I had become at this time a *medium* – not exactly in the signification in which the term has become popular in our newspapers (yet somewhat in a spiritual sense too), but a man who knew and 'hung out to' clever and pleasant people, and introduced agreeable lions to one another. These men were all immediate aspirants for high Honors and consequently in a fearful state of work. The Pembroker[2] was booked to lead the Tripos, and at the same time had the pleasant prospect of getting up all his Mathematics for a place among the Senior Ops; the Kingsman was the favorite for the next University

---

[1] Billiard-rooms were not legal at that time, but their existence was generally winked at. They are now regularly licensed both at Cambridge and Oxford.

[2] Maine. (E)

Scholarship; and one of the Trinity men, tempted by an unusual number of vacancies,[3] was making a tremendous rush for a Fellowship, though it was not his last chance. I noticed these men's habits of reading, and it was curious to mark the difference. The Pembroker had not *physique* enough to work more than nine hours daily,[4] which indeed is one beyond the average time allotted by experience and tradition. He would have attempted more, but I used to haul him out by main force, and compel him to take an hour's walk every day, under the plea that I had money on him and was bound to look after his training, besides making him talk and be idle for an hour or so occasionally of evenings. He of King's,[5] a most regular and well-ordered man in mind and body, with a clear head, a good digestion, and a sound conscience, read straight on his ten hours a day, and assured me that he never felt better, and was ready to run and jump like a boy when he went out for his constitutional. The Trinitarian[6] had a peculiar style of his own. He differed from most reading men in keeping late hours. He rose at ten, read from eleven to half-past three, then took a short walk; after dinner, he lounged or read the papers till seven, when he fell to work and never stopped till two in the morning.[7] This man (he is the *Horace Spedding* of the supper party) might almost be said to know the Greek Drama by heart; if you gave him a line in any prologue, or soliloquy, or messenger's speech, he could go on with the next.

The Introduction of Sherry Cobbler

Of my other set of acquaintances I saw more from meeting them every day in hall. They were Trinity Senior and Junior Sophs, some Scholars, some candidates for Scholarships next time, were chiefly reading men without any pretence to literature, or metaphysics, or 'earnestness' of any sort except

---

[3] [Seven fellows were elected in 1843; there had been five vacancies in 1841 and seven in 1842.]

[4] Good God! (T)

[5] Johnson of Ionica afterwards Cory. (T) [Johnson's *Ionica*, a volume of poems, was issued in 1858.]

[6] Horace Mansfield. (T) [Bowring takes the 'Trinitarian' to be W.G. Clark, and comments, 'No! this is a blind. Wm Geo Clark was & is a stout well made man above the average height. He was Maine's rival. "Horace Spedding" (Mansfield) was a little acute-looking aquiline-nosed man, which agrees with the description of Spedding.']

[7] 9½ hours. (T)

in work; and all looked up to the Trinity candidate for head of the Tripos as their great man. They took their work more leisurely, though getting through a fair share of it; even the Coryphaeus, who had most at stake, was not inclined to give up his rubber when there was a chance of one in the evening; and they found time to get up continual breakfast, wine, and supper parties. One of the foremost in these agreeable variations of academic exercises, was a man considerably the senior of his year – probably close upon thirty.[8] He had entered his name on the books nearly ten years before, then turned Methodist, and actually become a Methodist preacher, after which he changed back again and entered the University, as a preliminary to taking Orders in the Church of England. In all ordinary topics whereon men are apt to disagree, he and I disagreed, for he was Young England in politics and Puseyite in Church matters, but we had a kindred bond of union in a love for, and a certain knowledge of that branch of the fine arts which relates to the aesthetics of the table. He was a connoisseur in venison and mutton, and a judge of old wine (one of the only three Englishmen I ever knew to have good Madeira), and possessing sufficient property of his own to indulge in these innocent tastes, bid fair to make a worthy member of the Church jovial. It was a very early weakness of mine to be curious in good dishes and drinks,[9] and I was just now dabbling in the science with all the zest of a man who has been for twenty months obliged to weigh and ponder over every morsel he eats and drop he drinks, and is at last beginning to be able to live a little like other people. At this very time the anti-American part of *Martin Chuzzlewit* was in course of publication, in which occurs, it will be remembered, a description of sherry cobbler.[10] This description struck F's fancy amazingly. After meditating upon it for

---

[8]   Fussell? Fussill? (T), Fussell (W). [James George Curry Fussell, admitted to Trinity 1832 as James Curry, readmitted and matriculated 1841; BA 1845 (Classical Tripos, 2nd class); HMI 1852–83. Elder brother of the Fussell mentioned in ch. 12; both changed their surname from Curry in the 1840s.]

[9]   According to Grahamite and tee-total rules I ought to have been a confirmed drunkard and glutton long ago, yet I never find any difficulty in living on vegetables and water for a week at a time, when I want to work hard in hot weather, or have any other reason for following a spare diet.

[10]   [Dickens' novel, published in book form in 1844 but previously serialised from Jan. 1843, told of its hero's being defrauded by an American land corporation and caused great offence in the USA. Dickens' hostility was largely based on American piracy of his work, in the days before international copyright. See S.P. Moss, *Charles Dickens' Quarrel with America* (Troy NY, 1984). The sherry cobbler, its assembly and Martin's ecstatic response to it is described in Ch. 17 of Dickens' book.]

some time, he broke out one day, when six of us were discussing in his rooms the luxuries of the season – strawberries, and raspberries, and various other sorts of berries, which in England flourish all together, and the whole summer through – and imbibing the eternal port and sherry – one fine summer afternoon I say, while we were thus occupied, he broke out with, 'Bristed, did you ever drink sherry cobbler?'

I confessed that I had. 'Can you make it?'

This was a question that took longer to answer. Though it was many years since I had last been engaged in the process (on which occasion a young lady from the neighboring nation of South Carolina had particularly insisted on my putting in *enough sherry*), I probably recollected enough of the theory to put it into practice again; but there was a difficulty in procuring some of the requisite materials – ice for instance. Here they looked astonished, *ice*, as it is commonly understood in England, that is *ice-cream*, being a very common article of consumption at Cambridge. But simple ice, sufficiently clear to be put into a beverage, was at that time unknown in England; they have become familiar with it since, thanks to Lake Wenham.[11] However the original mover of the matter thought he had sufficient influence with the confectioners, or, failing that, chemical knowledge enough of his own to obtain the rare luxury by artificial means; and two others of the party undertook to procure the necessary description of straws. So I invited the company to meet in my rooms three days from that time and *try sherry cobbler*.

It was not necessary to put a private laboratory at work for freezing the ice. The crack confectioner of the place undertook to supply it, though somewhat puzzled by the order, coupled as it was with one for soda-water glasses, or tumblers of the largest size; and equally puzzled were the milliners' girls at the application of our foraging party for straws. But all these preliminary difficulties being happily overcome, the six assembled on the appointed day, in my *summer* room (I was luxurious enough to have two) to test the transatlantic beverage. I was conscious of ten curious eyes watching my every movement, as I proceeded to concoct the cobbler. Having at length arranged it to suit my taste, I took an experimental suck, put in another straw and handed the glass over to our authority who, grave as a judge, proceeded to the trial. The eyes of the party were now directed to him with an anxiety in which I alone did not participate, the

---

[11]   [Lake Wenham near Boston, noted for the purity of its water. Thousands of tons of Wenham ice were imported to England via Liverpool from the mid-1840s onwards; it was claimed that newsprint could be read through a two-foot thickness.]

few drops imbibed having satisfied me that the national beverage was able to take care of itself. F—— laid hold of the straw and applied his lips to it for a few seconds without manifesting any emotion in his features. Then he paused a moment, took a longer draught and rolled up his eyes, making a great display of the whites – a trick he had learned during his excursion into the Methodist Church – then removing his lips reluctantly from the straw, he uttered his oracular decision, 'It will do'. Forthwith every man seized a knife and a lemon, and the manufacture of cobblers went on. I do not undertake to say that these were the first made in England, but they certainly were the first made at either University: it did not take long to naturalize them at Cambridge. As the beverage is a much weaker one than the Cantabs had been in the habit of drinking, besides that it requires to be imbibed more slowly than unmixed wine, I may congratulate myself on having done something to promote the cause of sobriety, as well as of table aesthetics. But republics are not the only communities that show themselves ungrateful to their benefactors. In less than three years the origin of the drink was forgotten. Before I left the University, an Eton Freshman at a wine party, asked me, *if we drank sherry-cobbler in America*!

15

A Second Edition
of Third Year [1843–4]

The Water Cure

Just at the end of the vacation every one feels it a duty to himself to go *somewhere* for a little while. I went to visit a friend residing near Cheltenham. Mesmerism, the Water Cure,[1] and some other German novelties, had just then possessed the good people in that part of the country, and I was induced to try the prevailing panacea, which I underwent five days – and never before did I fully appreciate the force of the metaphor, *to throw a wet blanket* on any thing. Even now it presents a sadly ludicrous spectacle to

---

[1] [The Water Cure (hydropathy) had been popularised in the 1820s by the German Vincent Priessnitz, whose spa at Gräfenberg in Silesia became very fashionable. The treatment usually combined drinking mineral water, being wrapped in wet sheets and taking showers. See the informative and entertaining account by E.S. Turner, *Taking the Cure* (London, 1967).]

my mind's eye, as I recall myself helplessly swaddled in seven blankets over a wet sheet, powerless to move hand, or foot; or squatted in a sitz bath, trying to keep myself warm by reading the fire in Schiller's Bell-Song.[2] At the end of the fifth day, the process had to be given up in self-defence, as, in addition to certain physical obstructions, it brought on a lowness of spirits which rendered life a burden to me.

I am aware how dangerous a thing it is for a layman, with necessarily limited knowledge, to meddle with professional subjects. In delivering any opinion upon them, he runs a great risk of stultifying himself. But it must be recollected that the Water Cure was essentially unprofessional in the outset; that it was invented – its differentia or specific features that is to say – by an illiterate peasant; and, though some of the faculty have been induced partially or entirely to countenance it, proclaimed itself from the first antagonistic to the ordinary treatment of regular physicians. In making, therefore, a very brief digression on the Water Cure, I do not consider myself intruding on any professional or scientific ground.

The idea of drawing bad humors out of the body, through the action of the skin, excited by the application of cold water, is a neat, simple, and plausible theory; but its disciples overlook one important counteracting fact, the tendency of continual external applications of cold to produce congestion and a stoppage of the animal functions. A person with a tendency to imperfect circulation, and the ordinary consequences of it – cold extremities, constipation, irregular action of the heart, &c., will find all these symptoms fearfully increased by any attempt at the Water Cure; indeed the operator upon me confessed, after I had thrown him up, that those in whom the last-mentioned symptom existed ought not to attempt undergoing the treatment, although he had admitted me as a patient, with full knowledge of what my chief difficulty was. No doubt, great benefit has been derived from the treatment in some cases. When a man with a naturally strong constitution has fallen into idle or sedentary habits, and by luxurious living and insufficient bodily exercise has clogged a machine originally good, the shock and irritation produced by the cold applications may give him a fresh start, which is aided by the altered regimen. Literary men with means enough to live well, and addicted to a profuse use of tobacco, are often in this plight. But the rough-washing which succeeded so admirably with the hidebound cow that was the first hydropathic patient, and answers for many a strong man who has *hide-bound* himself by working his stomach and brain too much and his legs too little, will be death to a

---

2   [*Das Lied von der Glocke* (1798) describes the casting of a bell.]

weak man or a delicate woman. And it may further be questioned whether these strong men grown rusty, do not derive most of the benefit they gain from the accessories of the system – from the regular hours, the long walks, the simple and unstimulating diet; and whether, if they adopted the same early rising, the same out-door exercise – enough to give a man a good sweat every day, which every man ought to have – the same temperate regimen, with such use of cold water as cleanliness and comfort prompt – they might not receive just as much benefit without going through the daily purgatory of wet sheets, sitz baths, and the like, and with less waste of the vital powers.[3] Certain it is that those who have been at a Water Cure Establishment, and profess and really appear to have received much temporary relief, are apt, after a few years, to re-apply to it, which can only arise from one of two things, or the combined influence of both. Either a great part of the benefit derived from the treatment is owing to the attendant regimen, and when that regimen ceases the original evil returns; or else the Water Cure gives, in some cases, a temporary excitement to the system, which, like other excitements, is followed by a corresponding reaction, and requires to be renewed.

A Crack Classical Coach

On returning to Cambridge, at the commencement of the Michaelmas Term, I was stimulated by gaining the English Essay Prize, and soon after set to work with one of the two crack Classical tutors. For as there were two Mathematical coaches of eminence, so were there two Classical; only the former had a reputation for different styles of men, while between the latter there was somewhat of a rivalry, especially this year, when each was coaching a candidate for the top of the Tripos. It was doubtful whether

---

[3]   A man's whole system is renewed (physiologists tell us) once in about seven years. One effect of Hydropathy seems to be to produce this change in a quicker period, and – as we may suppose every man good for so many changes, unless cut short by accident – to burn the candle faster. A literary friend once wrote to me about the great good he had derived from the Water Cure. It came out that at the same time he was in the habit of taking daily horse exercise, which I begged him to practise years before, as the only effectual remedy for constant biliousness. [Could this be Tennyson? The poet certainly took the water cure, though he told only a few friends about his experience of it. In his review of *The Princess* in the *American Review* (1848), Bristed suggests that some of the faults in the poem might be due to this experience. Cf. Kolb, 'Bristed, Hallam and Tennyson', p. 205.]

these professed trainers of 'men among the first five' were exactly suited for me, or whether I was likely to do credit to their mode of instruction; but a desire of seeing all I could of the different ways of teaching, and some little curiosity as to what stand I could possibly hope to take (which a tutor of such experience would probably be able to determine pretty nearly), induced me to read with the oracle of the Shrewsbury men,[4] who had in hand at that time nearly all the Trinity set mentioned in the last chapter. I must have puzzled this gentleman exceedingly, my reading ran in so different a line from that of most of his pupils, and my way of doing things was so different. When he gave me Elegiacs or Alcaics to write, I used to sit looking very desperate at them for a long time, and then produce something exceedingly lamentable, not exactly in the way of false quantities, but very unclassical and prosaic; and as he was not backward in slanging – one of the requisites of a good coach, as has been remarked – he would give it to my unfortunate Compositions right and left. Once I let some verses fall into the fire, and was going to pick them out. 'Let them go!' quoth he, 'That's the best place for them.' On the other hand, I used at times to hit off translations from Aristophanes, and other difficult authors, in a style that won commendation from him. I recollect once doing a long bit from the Amphitruo of Plautus into blank verse, and handing it up to him with an air that said, 'There! you must admire that whether or no'.

Our way of working with him, I should say, was this. There were three rooms on the first floor of the house, the upper part of which he and his family occupied: in one of these he used to hear sometimes one pupil construe, sometimes two or three in a class on Pindar or some other favorite author; and in the other two his pupils were writing Compositions and Translations, with nothing but the usual amount of stationery to assist them. Sometimes, however, we could not help asking one another for a word. Occasionally, but rarely, we took extra Composition to do at home. I read part of the one of Demosthenes' Orations that everybody reads;[5] and then he broke off in the middle, said I could do that well enough, and had better go on with Aristotle – which I did, taking up the Nicomachean Ethics where I had left them off in the Spring, and continuing with the Fourth and

---

[4]   Shilleto or Kennedy. (E) [Probably George Kennedy, since the coach is described as good at 'slanging' and teaches on the ground floor of his house. Shilleto, who taught in a converted loft at his home, was criticised for not 'slanging his men enough': see p. 137. The reference later in the present chapter to 'my Johnian coach' (p. 166) confirms the identification of Kennedy.]
[5]   [*De Corona* (On the Crown).]

Fifth Books. He had his little diversions, too, as well as Travis, and some times would break out in the middle of a long sentence with some question about Webster or Calhoun.[6] I read this term like a man with a sole eye to the Tripos; the only *parergon* I had was delivering my Commemoration Speech – not writing it; that I had done at Cheltenham – and attending an Epigram Club that some of us had started. The Speech is delivered by the author of the First Prize Declamation. He chooses his own subject. I took for mine *The Principle of Liberality*, chiefly for the pleasure of having a fling at the Antediluvians in Church and State. It *did* vex a few, and by way of losing none of the effect, I had it printed.[7] Of this Composition I felt a little proud – not for any particular merit that even myself could discern in it, but because it was the means of my making a valued acquaintance.

There was one of our Fellows whose reputation with the University at large was that he had been Senior Wrangler some years before; with his friends, under which term a very small body of men was comprehended, this was the least of his claims to regard.[8] He was of old family and good fortune, a liberal in politics, and had his physical strength and development at all kept pace with his mental, would probably at this moment be representing the City of Bath in Parliament. But his health had broken down from too much study and thought, even before he entered the University, and while an Undergraduate he read but three or four hours daily;[9] being, however, one of those Mathematical geniuses who are born to be Senior Wranglers, he carried off the prize to the particular discomfiture of the Johnians.[10] But whereas geniuses of this kind are frequently one-sided and very much abroad in other subjects, he had knowledge enough of other branches to have given him a reputation without his Mathematics. He was an excellent

---

[6] [Daniel Webster, a leading US politician of the antebellum era, made three unsuccessful attempts at the presidency before his death in 1852. John C. Calhoun, vice-president 1825–32, was later a leading defender of slavery.]

[7] [See Bibliography A1, 1843. The declamation was also included in the first edn. of *Five years*, vol. 2, pp. 208–16.]

[8] [Robert Leslie Ellis, Trinity 1836, Senior Wrangler 1840; fellow of Trinity 1840–9. Ellis, who was William Whewell's brother in law, died prematurely in 1859.]

[9] There you are! So did Lord Rayleigh. (T) [Hon. John William Strutt, Trinity 1861; Senior Wrangler 1865; fellow of Trinity 1866–71; Cavendish Professor of Experimental Physics 1879–84; Nobel Prize 1904. One of the great figures of Victorian physics.]

[10] Caius had the 2nd man, Dean Goodwin. (B) [Harvey Goodwin, Caius 1836, fellow 1841–5, Bishop of Carlisle 1869–91; a popular figure in Cambridge, where a road was named after him.]

Metaphysician, which caused him to be distinguished for his proficiency
in the Doctrine of Chances, where a mere Mathematician is almost sure
to fail; a very good Latin and Italian scholar, and not deficient in French,
while his acquaintance with the literature of his own language was wide
and varied. Still it was not so much the extent of his information – for
there were several men in the University, John Grote for instance, whose
range covered more ground – that struck one so much as the power he
had over it. His mind was the best arranged and most symmetrical I ever
encountered. Whatever he knew was in its place and ready for use. As to his
moral qualities he was a thorough gentleman, with a suavity and amiability
that no bodily suffering could disturb, the purest taste, the loftiest principle.
Though of moderate stature and so thin and fragile that it seemed as if a
violent gust of wind might blow him bodily away, his personal appearance
was dignified and commanding. His features were very regular and very
expressive (a rare combination), and a fancy he had of parting his long hair
down the middle, gave his head an exceedingly picturesque appearance.
Once an Oxonian dining at the Trinity Fellows' table, was impressed by
the intellectual and interesting countenance opposite him, and asked if it
did not belong to a poet; when informed that the object of his curiosity
was a Senior Wrangler, he could hardly conceal his disappointment. But
E—— *did* have a reputation for poetry, so far at least as writing verse
translations went.

It was a day or two after Commemoration (about the middle of
November), that on entering the College gate, after a post-prandial lounge
at the Union, I was informed by *moonshine* – such was the *sobriquet* of our
rubicund-nosed porter – that Mr. E—— had been at my rooms inquiring for
me.[11] How he knew, it was hard to say, as E—— lived two courts off and
I three; but these College servants, like some others, have a knack of finding
out all that is going on. Now in a place where intellect and acquirements
are the highest standard of nobility, such a call was like the summons of
a prince, or to take a comparison nearer home, I felt as the editor of the
—— might, if his Excellency the President of the United States had sent
him a special messenger to request his presence. I crowded sail immediately
for E——'s quarters, which were up in a turret, literally, for the entrance
was, and by a most break-neck staircase, too; though when you were fairly
inside the second door, about half a house opened upon you. There was the
usual amount of awkwardness and hesitation on both sides, while I stated

---

[11]   E is Ellis; the rubicund porter was Styles. (T) He died prematurely of ale, poor
fellow. (B)

the reason of my visit, and he informed me that his object in calling was to look at my Commemoration Discourse, if a copy was visible, as he had heard its delivery very imperfectly. (No wonder, for the pulpit had been placed in exactly the most inaudible situation, and the Hall, however well calculated for purposes of feeding, and holding examinations, was a most unacoustic place to speak in.) We gradually fell into conversation upon other matters, till lighting on old English Ballad Poetry which happened to be rather a hobby with both of us, we kept up an animated conversation to a late hour, and after that night frequently exchanged visits.

The Epigram Club was an idea started one evening by six or eight of us. The number was increased to *thirteen*, none of whom, I am happy to say, have gone to the 'land o' the leal' yet, notwithstanding the omen.[12] Some of us were very heavy men to all appearance, and our first attempts mild enough, but Cantabs have a thorough way of taking up and trying out anything they lay hold of, and we made rapid progress. It surprised me to see how much wit could be knocked out of materials so solid. Ultimately some of our productions were informally requested for *Punch*, and some for other publications. But with true English reserve the Society came to an agreement that all their transactions should remain in manuscript. Our rival candidates[13] for Senior Classic were both members of this club, as they are now both contributors to the same Magazine.[14] They were the best of friends, and both wrote very good verses; the Small Colleger was felicitous in imitating Macaulay and Coleridge, and the Trinitarian elaborated perfect burlesques of the Popian versification and the University Prize Poems.

---

[12]   There was a rich bull committed by one of this Society. The club having to meet in his rooms on a certain evening, he wrote twelve notices, and then wearied himself for half an hour trying to recollect *who the thirteenth member was.*

[13]   Maine and Clark. (B)

[14]   Fraser's. (B) [The *Wellesley Index to Victorian Periodicals* credits Clark with six articles in the magazine between 1849 and 1872, but lists none for Maine. Bristed had good reason to know of Maine's authorship, not only as a friend of his, but also as the author of ten 'Sketches of American Society' which appeared in *Fraser's* between March 1850 and September 1851 (later published as *The Upper Ten Thousand* in 1852). It seems likely, then, that Maine was the author of one or more of the unattributed articles in the magazine (there are fifty for 1851).]

I Bet on the Winning Man

They were very good friends; but their supporters and seconders sometimes clashed a little. The Trinity set, who had put me down as wanting in proper feeling for the honor of my College, still professed strong hopes that our man would lead the Tripos, and being much bantered by them I occasionally resorted to the true English argument 'What'll you bet?' The odds were certainly against me, as I backed my man to be not only Senior Classic, but First Chancellor's Medalist, and to be a Medalist at all he must be a *Senior Optime* in Mathematics. This part of the business he accomplished with that tight shave which is rather gratifying to a Classical man, as it shows that he has thrown away no more time on Mathematics than was absolutely necessary. The Trinity man, who might easily have been a Wrangler, was also among the *Senior Optimes*, but twenty-four places higher.

The Mathematical Tripos this winter was remarkable for the total *bouleversement* of all the results of all the College Examinations. The favorite was Senior Wrangler, but scarcely another man of the thirty-seven Wranglers occupied his presumed place, positively or relatively. Our best man from Trinity[15] was only sixth, but he beat two others of the College who were expected to be among the first five.[16]

It was about this time (the middle of January), that my tutor, having made up his mind about my chances for next year, took occasion to deliver his opinion upon them. 'You can get a First Class in the Tripos,'[17] said he, 'but you will have to work for it.' I told him that working hard was with me out of the question, that I could only read about five hours a day, and had to get up all my Mathematics which would take the whole last Long. He intimated that I ought to work at Composition five or six hours a day for six months to bring me up to the standard, 'and as you can't do that,' said he, '*actum est.*' Then he advised me to go out in the Poll. This is the course which many a man, Mathematical as well as Classical, takes out of

---

[15]   Warren. (B) [William Warren, Trinity 1840; 6th Wrangler 1844; fellow of Clare Hall 1848.]

[16]   Hedley and Walker. Warren's success was usually attributed to Ellis' exceedingly improper conduct – he being Examiner – in giving the papers he set to Walton to revise, Walton at this time taking private pupils, of whom Warren was one. (B) [Thomas Hedley appears in chh. 9 and 11 as 'Henslowe'; Edward Walker, Trinity 1840, fellow 1845.]

[17]   The *Classical* Tripos is generally spoken of as *the* Tripos, the Mathematical one as *the Degree Examination.*

pride, when he finds that from early idleness, ill-health, or any other cause, his Degree will not be equal to what he thinks his abilities deserve. The subject was discussed by us at intervals for several days, but my mind was pretty well made up. After the first two or three months of my illness, when it was evident that recovery would be a work of years, and probably never complete at that – from that time I gave up perforce ambitious desires, and contented myself with playing such second part as I could. I would not be ashamed of trying for the best of everything, and failing. So I told my tutor that I was willing to take my chance; at any rate I would have a shy at a College Scholarship, though that involved another dose of Mathematics. By way of taking a surfeit of Classics previous to beginning this disagreeable work, I went in to the University Scholarship examination, which was a hollow thing, as sporting men say. The Kingsman,[18] who had run last year's successful competitor so close, was the favorite, and won in a canter. He too was one of the lights of our Epigram Club, and afterwards became an Apostle. The examination was a very fair one; less cram and fewer out-of-the-way passages than are usual in a University Scholarship.[19]

Just after this came on the Classical Tripos, for the head of which our two friends were running, neck and neck. The Pembroke man, of an excitable disposition naturally, and rendered unusually nervous by indifferent health, scarcely gave himself sufficient food or rest,[20] ransacked all manner of note-books and collections of marked passages, and seized upon all the eligible English verse he could find to translate into Greek and Latin, till he had acquired a pace which was astounding to behold. His rival went on in the same quiet way as ever, doing his work beautifully, but just at the old rate, and never missing his Saturday night whist or breaking in on any of his old habits. It required some philosophy in a man to care so little whether he was first or second.

On the first day of the Examination, one of the thirty Candidates for classical Honors was frightened at the leading Paper and fairly ran off, not appearing at any of the subsequent ones. He was a sharp man enough, and had taken a very respectable Mathematical degree.

I was now undergoing for the third time since I entered the University, and the I-don't-know-how-many-eth time in my life, a course of low Mathematics. A Bachelor friend who felt an interest in my success, undertook

---

[18] Johnson; the Pembroke man is Maine. (T)

[19] [Bristed includes some university scholarship papers in the Appendix to his first edition: vol. 2 pp. 381–99.]

[20] Maine used (it was said) to drink tea 3 or 4 times a day. (B)

to coach me quite en ami, which kindness I partially repaid afterwards with Classics for his Fellowship. It really seemed as if the repeated efforts of years had made some impression on the repulsive subject. I knew more Algebra than I had ever done before – indeed I felt rather a proficient in it, and a little circumstance happened about this time to confirm such a half serious, half mock infatuation on my part. Our Kingsman, after having attained his University Scholarship, suddenly took it into his head to learn Mathematics, and to persuade the other four or five Undergraduates of his College to learn with him – for which purpose they were obliged to procure a new College Mathematical lecturer, the old one[21] being a Classical man, and, so far as his Mathematics were concerned, a fiction. As these Etonians had never read anything before in the way of science, except ordinary arithmetic, they were in the very infancy of Mathematical conceptions, and I used, in my evening wanderings, to drop into my friend's room now and then and give him a little assistance in the mystery of equations. When I repeated this to my coach, he burst out into an Homeric inextinguishable laughter at the idea of my being able to teach any Algebra – finding in the lowest deep a lower still. I may here mention, incidentally, that my occasional pupil, somewhere about this time, left off being a Puseyite, and adopted more liberal and Arnold-like views on Church matters. Any one who has great faith in the pure sciences, may attribute this important change to the Algebra if he chooses. After Algebra, I took up low Trigonometry, which I had never probably studied before, and crammed it into me as far as De Moivre's theorem, and some other pleasant little formulae of the same nature and magnitude, measuring half a page long a-piece; and all these I certainly understood – that is to say, could trace the working of them, and see how they were arrived at – but never could perceive any particular use or discern the least beauty in them. I thought of making an attempt on Conic Sections (which are read *analytically* in the Cambridge books), but never got further than copying sundry manuscripts of my former coach[22] (him of the large team), for my attention was required by the First Three Sections of Newton, which, with Euclid, were to be my great dependence. The Euclid I knew by experience was to be got up in two days, so I put it off for the last two; the Newton I polished up with great zeal – it was something new to me and not altogether uninteresting. The book, which for a long time existed only in the manuscripts of Johnian lecturers, contains a series of English demonstrations of the Lemmas of the *Principia*, which

21   Shilleto. (B)
22   Walton. (B)

are only *affirmed* in the original Latin.[23] I forget whether it was before or after this that I assailed low Statics, and, after getting up the Mechanical Powers, *Vis Viva*, and other formulae, mostly from Whewell's books, went so far as to attempt several problems, but I never remember doing a whole one. A very poor array of Mathematics this, to take in to an Examination, but it was only as a sort of pass to give my Classics a chance. On them I could bestow but little time; what I did assign to them proved to be very badly laid out for having only time to attempt getting up one kind of verse Composition, and calculating that Hexameters were likely to be set, I read straight through six Books of the Aeneid, and then wrote some hundred Hexameter lines for practice. Of course, Elegiacs were set.

These verses are hardly in the line of a man who has not been brought up on the English public-school system, but as they have great weight in the Examinations, one cannot afford to neglect them entirely. Their importance was particularly impressed upon me just then, by the result of the contest for Senior Classic, which was declared in favor of the Pembroke candidate, thus endorsing the decision of the University Scholarship examiners the year before. His success was chiefly owing to a very superior copy[24] of Elegiacs. As these verses, written in a limited time, under the eye of examiners, and with no means of assistance beyond the requisite stationery, afford a better example of what a crack versifier can do than any of the Prize Odes, which are carefully and leisurely composed at home, I make no apology for inserting them here.[25]

The making of Greek and Latin verse is one of the most showy manifestations of English scholarship, and certainly the most surprising one. To read an ordinary Classical author *ad aperturam libri*, certainly implies a good acquaintance with his tongue; but it is readily accounted for by practice and study, and is only more difficult than reading any book in a modern language by as much as the ancient language is the harder of the two to acquire. To write Latin and Greek prose with facility and elegance, though involving a further command of the two languages, has also its parallel in our experience with respect to modern tongues. But to write verse in any language, seems to imply such a familiarity with all its niceties as can only

---

[23] [J.H. Evans, *The First Three Sections of Newton's* Principia (Cambridge, 1834). In his preface, Evans acknowledges his use of manuscripts prepared by coaches.]

[24] 'Copy' is applied exclusively to papers of verse Composition. It is a public-school term transplanted to the University.

[25] [Nor does the editor for omitting them. Their author is identified by Bowring as H.S. Maine; he comments, 'I have read far better verses of [H.A.J.] Munro's'.]

be acquired by one who makes it as it were his second mother-tongue. Many a person who can converse freely in German, or read an Italian book with nearly the same ease as an English one, or write a correct letter in French, would shrink from the idea of attempting poetry or verse in either of these languages. And there are two additional features which increase the surprisingness of the performance. First, as the Classical languages are no longer habitually spoken in the English schools, the scholars lose one of the principal ordinary means of acquiring the knowledge of a strange tongue – conversation. Secondly, the standard of these verses, as specimens of metrical composition, is very high. In mere smoothness and elegance they absolutely surpass the majority of the ancient models. To end a Pentameter with a trisyllable, as Propertius does *passim*; to make caesuras which are common with Lucretius; to put the enclitic after a verb instead of the preceding substantive or adjective of a clause, as Ovid himself does – like *maestus adestque dies* – all these are inadmissible licenses. One thing the reader will be apt to infer, that such an accomplishment can only be the fruit of long and special training – which is emphatically the case. A public-school boy begins certainly as early as ten years of age, if not earlier, to grind at 'longs and shorts'. The first step is to make him do *nonsense verses*, that is to say, the scheme of a line is given him thus –

$$\_\,\smile\smile \quad \_\,\smile\smile \quad \_\_ \quad \_\_ \quad \_\,\smile\smile \quad \_\_$$

which he may fill up with any words that will scan without regard to their meaning or want of meaning, *Pergite praecipites quos pridem Jupiter inquit*, or even greater nonsense than this.[26] Then an exactly literal translation of a Latin line is given him in the precise order of the original, then a line with the words transposed, and so on through several intermediate steps, till he is fairly launched upon translating English verse into Hexameters and Pentameters, or 'Longs and shorts', as the Elegiac metre is commonly called. This is the stanza at which they are most practised, and at which they acquire the greatest facility. After this they are most worked at Alcaics. Hexameters are also written, but not so frequently (Eton is almost the only place where they do them well), and Sapphics very rarely. It is a sort of traditionary prejudice, that Hexameters and Sapphics are hardly ever good, and the theory verifies itself by causing them to be less cultivated. An Eton boy sends up a copy of Longs and Shorts once or twice a week for

---

26   [The scansion is correct in Bristed's first edition, but in the second edition, the first foot of the hexameter is misprinted $\smile\,\_$.]

seven years of his school life.[27] Probably three fourths of these boys never thought of writing a couplet of English verse, or could do it if set at it. But we have not yet done with the complications of this singularly artificial system. A false quantity is the unpardonable sin, *yet the actual pronunciation affords no clue whatever to the quantity of the penults of dissyllables*; căno *I sing*, and câno the ablative of cānus *hoary*, rēgis *of a king*, and rĕgis *thou rulest*, being pronounced exactly alike.[28] And lest the swing and intonation of the voice itself should give any assistance, it is the custom to read Classical verse *as much like prose as possible*. Having noticed this during the recitation of some of the Commencement Odes, which, as the successful candidates read them, could never have been taken for verse by a person without the printed book, I inquired about this peculiarity from men of three or four different schools, and they all certified to the generality of the practice, without, so far as I can recollect, giving any reason for, or defence of it. The consequence of all this is that Latin-verse writing becomes totally a

---

[27]   I should hope so. (T) [At about this time, the Eton master Thomas Balston told his pupil James Fitzjames Stephen, 'If you do not write good longs and shorts, how can you ever be a man of taste? If you are not a man of taste, how can you ever hope to be of use in the world?' N.G. Annan, *Leslie Stephen: His Thought and Character in Relation to his Time* (London, 1951), p. 20. Stephen was a pupil of Balston's from 1842 to 1845.]

[28]   As the subject of Pronunciation is one which excites some little interest with us, and about which I have often been asked questions, it may as well be stated briefly that students in England pronounce as they do in New England, with the exception that they do not make false quantities in the penults of tri-syllables, for instance they never say habēbam, or Caesāris, or Consūles, or Quirītes, all which were common at Yale, in my day. Neither do they pronounce fecerat *fesserat*, which was considered a point of such importance at New Haven, that one of the Professors wrote a Pamphlet to insist on the shortening of long vowels in the first syllable of Dactylic words. But they give the vowels their English power, and in dissyllables lengthen by accent, not by quantity, thus they say mānus do-mus, not mănus dŏmus. In Greek also the vowels have their English power, and the same exceptions prevail as in New England – the pronunciation of *ai* and *ei* like *i*, instead of *a*, and the preserving y hard throughout. Only they do not call *meta* and *kata metre* and *cater*, as the New Haven tutors used to. [In his third edition, Bristed comments (pp. 222–3) on recent moves to reform the pronunciation of Latin (to make it sound like Italian) and of Greek, to make it sound like modern Greek; the latter he thinks 'simply barbarous'. At Cambridge the former reform was led by H.A.J. Munro as Professor of Latin, 1869–72. R.C. Jebb, Public Orator 1869–76, in 1870 not only followed his lead, but introduced a Greek archbishop in Greek using the modern pronunciation.]

matter of *eye*, though some versifiers fancy from never having analysed their own mental perceptions and the growth of this acquired faculty, that *ear* has a great deal to do with it. An Eton Captain will write twenty Elegiacs in an hour, and twelve or fifteen Hexameters; while at the University this pace is seldom increased but the quality improves. From what has been said of this school drilling, it may be guessed that no man who begins to write Latin verses late in life can hope to make much hand of it. I used to take the line of laughing at the whole affair, and denying the sense or use of it. Sometimes I turned the tables on the over-critical ones, as to what was, or what was not *classical*. The reader may perhaps remember Captain Medwin's story about the Schoolmaster who heaped contempt on a line which Shelley sent up,

> Jamjam tacturos sidera celsa putes

not knowing that it was taken verbatim from Ovid.[29] A somewhat similar case fell under my own observation. I was showing to a very precise Etonian some Elegiacs by a Scotch friend of mine, which I rather liked – a translation of Herrick's beautiful lines

> Gather ye rosebuds while ye may,
> Old Time is still a-flying, &c.

The second line was

> Nam fugiunt, freno non remorante, dies.

The Verses were by a Scotchman, and, of *course*, must be bad. My Etonian objected to the phrase *freno non remorante*, as not authorized. I thought it good Latin, and said so, but not being able to find an instance, was obliged to give it up for the time. While going through Ovid's Fasti several months afterwards, I found in the Sixth Book this couplet:

> Tempora labuntur tacitisque senescimus annis,
> Et fugiunt freno non remorante dies.

The Caledonian being taken short for a Pentameter had bagged the whole line. At the first public opportunity I proclaimed my discovery to the Etonian. There is nothing like sticking to your principle. He held out that it was inelegant Latin, nevertheless – Ovid had been nodding on that occasion.

---

[29] [See S.J. Bieri, *Percy Bysshe Shelley … Youth's Unextinguished Fire, 1792–1816* (Newark DE, 2005), pp. 76–7. Medwin was Shelley's cousin.]

The above instance might induce a suspicion that there is a little *centoism* about this Latin-verse making. Such is indeed the case, and the more you read and write Latin verse, the more of this centoism do you discover. One of the great effects, objects, and merits of the seven years' more or less grinding at school is, that it stores the student's mind with common-places of verse, lines and half-lines and quarter-lines descriptive of such familiar objects and occurrences as the sun or a lark rising, the nightingale singing, the grass growing and trees budding at the approach of Spring, &c., &c.; and the faculty of utilizing this store of treasure is much increased by the character of the verses usually set to translate. There is a kind of English pastoral poetry – a school of which Shenstone is perhaps the most favorable specimen – which I never found out the use of till I was at Cambridge. It was made and invented expressly to be translated into Latin Elegiacs.

Even where phrases and half-lines are not copied bodily, there is often a resemblance in structure and form, the new line being built after the old one; thus

> Primaque ut aeriâ scandat alauda viâ

recalls Ovid's

> Protinus aetheriâ tollet in astra viâ

Just as in Bailey's 'Festus'[30] the line

> The mind hath phases as the body hath

is modelled upon Shakspeare's

> The earth hath bubbles as the water hath.

But it must be said, in fairness, that there is at the same time much original and elegant poetry to be met with among these compositions. Our Trinity man, who was second medallist this year, had taken a Porson and excelled in Greek Composition; but this January, as if anticipating his rival's excellence in Latin, he distinguished himself in the same way by an original copy of Elegiacs, written for the Tripos Paper[31] – a mythological account of the birth and progress of Love, and his reconciliation with the Muses, that would not have disgraced old Naso himself. One couplet was particularly admired:

---

30 [Philip Bailey's *Festus*, a version of Goethe's *Faust*, was published anonymously in 1839. An enlarged second edition (1845) was very popular in the US.]

31 [See note on the word *Tripos*, in the vocabulary of Cambridge terms (Ch. 4).]

> Flava calescentem male dissimulabat Amorem
> Luna – calescebat dissimulatus Amor.

As to the style of translation, it is of a very free order; in fact, should in many cases be called imitation rather than translation.[32]

About this freedom of translation there is one thing to be observed, that it is a freedom of *addition* and not of *retrenchment*. As a general rule, you are required to express all the ideas of the original, and may then add any ornaments to fill out the measure. The translations express all that is in the English, and a little more; I could not understand this for some time, and used to err by trying to translate too literally. Thus, when my Johnian coach, in the summer of 1843, set me for the first time to write Elegiacs, and gave me as the subject of the experiment Moore's *Last Rose of Summer*, I took one line of the Latin for every two of the short English lines, and began

> Ultimus, en, solus, calicum florescit ab aestu.
> Ah! comitum marcet tota venusta cohors!

In his copy, each of the short lines was expressed by a long line of Latin, thus

> Ultimus aestivâ tenerarum e gente rosarum
> Flos desolatis eminet ille comis;
> Lucida de toto circum vicinia prato
> Vanuit, et sociae deperiere rosae.

Only one case of packing the Latin into less space than the English by a good versifier ever came under my observation: it was where a Senior Classic translated three lines from Byron –

> Where the hues of the earth and the hues of the sky,
> Though different in color, in beauty may vie,
> And the purple of ocean is deepest in dye.[33]

by this couplet,

> Quâ coelo et terrae varius color, una venustas
> Et latices nigris subrubuere vadis.

---

[32]   [A section is omitted giving Kirke White's poem 'The night it was still, and the moon it shone', the original of the Latin verses omitted above; Bristed claims that the Latin is superior to the English]
[33]   [Byron, *The Bride of Abydos* 323–5. Bristed misquotes the first line, which begins 'The tints of the earth'.]

I have often fancied, in making comparisons of poetical translations from the German and other modern languages, that our countrymen succeed better than the English, and that the reason of this may be found in the fact of most English translators being taught by their school experience to aim at imitation rather than translation, and put in ornaments of their own. Certainly the most accurate and vigorous translator of German poetry in England is Carlyle[34] – a non-University man. Such a principle, however, must be laid down cautiously, and with allowed exceptions. Merivale's Schiller[35] is a most commendable specimen of accurate rendering.

Having given one superior specimen of Latin verse, I shall conclude what I have to say about it here with a sample from the other end of the piece. A few days before going in for the Tripos I wrote a translation from the opening of Byron's Parasina, of which my tutor said, 'If your verses were always as good as these, you might get *some* marks for them'. The following may, therefore, be taken as the lowest standard of what would pass muster in an Examination:

> It is the hour when from the boughs
> The nightingale's high note is heard, &c.

> Nunc, primâ in terras ducente crepuscula nocte,
> Clarior e ramis vox, Philomela, tua est;
> Nunc majore videtur amans dulcedine vota
> Dulce susurranti fundere saepe labro.
> Nunc ventique leves et aquae vicinia moestis
> Auribus intendunt suppeditare melos;
> Purpurei modico calices nunc rore madescunt
> Conveniunt coelo sidera clara suo;
> Et magis in fuscos jam jamque abiere colores
> Oceanoque latex, arboribusque comae.

Greek verse stands on a somewhat different footing from Latin. It is of later date as an element of school education. Probably it came in with Porson,[36] and the establishment of the Porson Prize by his executors did much to encourage it. King's College London men, and other Classics not

---

[34]   [Carlyle's first book was *Schiller and Goethe* (1823–5). This was followed by his *German Romance* (4v, 1827), a collection of translations which included Goethe's *Wilhem Meister*.]

[35]   [J.H. Merivale's *Minor poems of Schiller …* was published in 1844.]

[36]   [W.S. Landor and his Rugby schoolfellows had composed in Greek in the 1780s. The Porson Prize was first awarded in 1817.]

from the public-schools, evince a preference for Greek Iambics; they say this
sort of Composition is more dependent on, and more a test of Scholarship.
For my part I could never see much difference between the two in this
respect; there always seemed to me as much knack and centoism in the
one as in the other. Sometimes in the Porsons you will find a whole line,
bodily transplanted from a Greek Tragedian. Once in looking over one,
I met with

> *hoto charakter empephuke somati*
> [character is set by nature on anyone's body]

which I marked as a good line, and well might, for when I came to read
the Medea two years after, there it was:

> *oudeis charakter empephuke somati*
> [no character is set by nature on the body]

Nevertheless, it is certain that many begin to write Iambics after entering
the University, or but a short time before. A first-rate man, who was first
Bell Scholar in a very well contested year, and a candidate for Senior
Classic until he broke from ill health, told me he had never written any
Greek verse till a year before he came up. It was one of the instances
he was giving of his insufficient preparation on account of his invalid
state. The fact too of all having a fairer start, encourages more men to
practise Iambics. But it must be owned that the best – those which get
full marks at examinations, and are handed about and copied as models
– are the productions of men who have had abundant training. There is
one school famous for sending up writers of Iambics – Shrewsbury – which
indeed has a great reputation for Scholarship generally, and particularly
for grammatical accuracy.

The difficulties of Greek verse are of a higher kind than those of Latin,
and the sort of English set to be translated of a higher character. Shakspeare
and Milton, Ben Jonson, Henry Taylor, Shelley's *Cenci*, the best English
translations of *Faust* and *Wallenstein* – such are the books which usually
furnish passages. You will seldom find anything very seedy set for Iambics.
The reading and study of Shakspeare and the old English Dramatists
generally, has been much promoted at the University by the practice of
writing Greek verse – perhaps it is one of the best things that can be said
for it. The style of translation, like that used in writing Latin verse, is very
free, the main object being to show a knowledge of the Greek Dramas,
and adopt phrases from them corresponding to the English ones – as if
in translating Sophocles into English, one were to go out of the way to

introduce as many Shakspearian words and phrases as possible. Even with great license of paraphrase, it is often exceedingly difficult to express the English idea in Greek, and the very best men are put to some straits. Thus I have seen Ben Jonson's

> Temp'ring his greatness with his gravity,

rendered by (and the translator was a man of reputation in this way)

> *sebas te pantas emmelos epraksato*

literally translated 'and he exacted respect from all with good taste'.

The *pace* attained in writing Greek verses never equals that acquired in Latin, partly from the practice being begun later in life, partly because the work is intrinsically more difficult. Twelve an hour is considered very fast. About twenty-eight English lines are usually set in the Tripos, which in rendering into Greek would naturally be expanded into thirty-five, and very few of the candidates finish them in the allotted two hours and a half. Sometimes a First-Class man does not write more than fourteen. One year when the first four men on the Tripos all finished their copy and got very nearly full marks, was considered an extraordinary one.

I have spoken of Greek *Iambics* only, because they are the only Greek verses habitually written. Anapaests have occasionally been set in the Tripos, Anapaests and Long Trochees in the University Scholarships. Sapphics are never written except for the Greek Ode; Homeric Hexameters, very rarely in the College, and never I believe in the University examinations.[37]

And now, it may be asked, how far is this Latin and Greek verse-making really a test of scholarship, and is it, as such, worth the time spent on it? My own answer would be unfavorable, but I may be somewhat prejudiced by the detriment which the want of the accomplishment caused myself. Certainly it does not always follow that a good versifier in Greek and Latin is a good scholar. It befell me at the time of my final extinguishment in the Tripos, to be sandwiched between one of the best Latin versifiers and the best Greek versifier of the twenty-four candidates, and the best copy of Latin verses has been more than once sent up by a Second Class man – although in this examination the verse Composition papers count one fifth of the whole. And sometimes high First Class men get but few marks for their verses. In the former case, it may be supposed that the parties have

---

[37] [Omitted here is a set of Greek Alcaics written by A.C. Gooden, Senior Classic 1840.]

come up very well prepared, and been idle during part of their course;[38] the school knack of making verses has stuck by them, while their acquaintance with different authors has not been sufficiently kept up and extended. A Scholar of Trinity, some of whose Lyrics were thought sufficiently good to be included in the published collection of verses called the *Arundines Cami*,[39] was *last* in the Second Class; he had probably neglected his Classics to study Mathematics, since he stood well among the Wranglers.[40] As to the converse branch of the proposition, it will hardly be doubted with Germany in view, that a man may be a very good scholar without being able to write Latin and Greek verses elegantly and fluently. The effect of practice in such matters may be illustrated by the habit of conversing in Latin, which German students do much more readily than English, simply because the former practise it, and hold public disputes in Latin, while the latter have long left off 'keeping Acts', as the old public discussion required of candidates for a degree used to be called.[41]

Classical prose Composition is of course an important point in the training of a candidate for Classical Honors, and there are few men, even of those who ultimately go out in Mathematics alone, but have had some drilling in writing Latin. Greek prose is the hardest of all Composition, and marked highest in the Tripos; there are seldom more than five or six men in a year who write it well. The difficulty of accentuation – a subordinate art requiring no small practice in itself[42] – it shares with the

---

[38] Young Hope Edwards for example. (T) [William Hope, later Hope-Edwardes, Trinity 1835.]

[39] [*Arundines Cami*, edited by Henry Drury (Caius 1831), had first appeared in 1841. It went into several editions, the sixth and last being published in 1865, after Drury's death, by Henry Hodgson, one of Bristed's annotators – see the next note.]

[40] H. Hodgson, 1838. (B) [Henry Hodgson, Trinity 1834, fellow 1840; 24th Wrangler and last in the 2nd class of the Classical Tripos, 1838. Hodgson himself adds, 'The reason given me by George Kennedy who examined was that all the first and second class in 1838 were equal to the usual first class standard and that he wanted to put all there but was (no doubt properly) outvoted. He added that the first real break was after me.']

[41] [The Acts were discontinued in 1839; viva voce examinations were retained in the faculties of Divinity, Law and Physic until the introduction of new statutes in 1858. See Stray, 'From oral to written examinations', p. 88.]

[42] Where quantity is the guide to pronunciation, accentuation must be mere matter of eye and memory, and the general rules to which it is reduced are subject to numerous and arbitrary exceptions. [Trevelyan comments, 'The merest pedantry, as practised in England. Fox did not use accents as a rule'.]

composition of Iambics, so it would seem to do the difficulties arising from the abstruse syntax of the language; but these latter difficulties make themselves more felt in prose than in verse, perhaps because there is less opportunity for centoism in the former. In the mere matter of words, too, a serviceable poetic vocabulary is much easier to collect and retain than a prose one.

Though the method of translation is of course more literal than that adopted in rendering verse, there is still sufficient margin left for embellishment, and much importance is attached to displaying a knowledge of idiom. A man will frequently go a little, or more than a little out of his way to bring in a bit of what, in stage phraseology, would be called *business*. And among single words those most unlike the corresponding ones in English are preferred. Thus, you must not say *administrare rempublicam* for taking part in public affairs, but *capessere rempublicam*, though the former word is used by good Roman authors as much as the latter. When I was at my best for Latin prose, I had a collection of idiomatic phrases, six or eight of which I would have engaged to bring into the translation of any half-page of ordinary English that could be given me; and those who were better skilled in Greek prose than myself could do the same with that. The term Composition seems in itself to imply that the translation is something more than a translation.

Original Composition – that is, Composition in the true sense of the word – in the dead languages is not much practised. There is a Latin essay written in the University Scholarship Examination, and another in the Medal Examination; there are the Commencement Exercises and the College Declamations already mentioned, and there are verse prizes for Second and Third-year men in most of the Colleges. At Trinity there are three open to all the three Years. Composition in Greek there is none except the Browne Ode.

The present is not an unfit occasion for saying something more about the style of translation required from Greek and Latin into English. It might be supposed from the freeness which characterizes the Composition, that a like license of paraphrase and ornament was allowed in translating from the dead languages as well as into them. But such is not the case. The greatest accuracy is required, under pain of 'losing marks'; the meaning of the smallest particle must be expressed, the least shades of difference between nearly synonymous words strictly conveyed. This accuracy, however, not only does not require, but absolutely forbids *bad English*, which would be surely visited with the loss of a large percentage of marks 'for style'. Whenever a difficulty occurs of such a nature that it cannot be entirely set forth in the translation, explanation in a note is allowable – in some cases required.

A particular instance or two will give a more intelligible idea of the accuracy required than any general description. I had been translating for my private tutor a passage in the *Medea*, where she asks Jason,

> *Ti drosa? Mon gamousa kai prodousa se?*
> [In doing what? Surely not in marrying and betraying you?]

When he came to my translation of this line he said, 'But you haven't marked the peculiarity here. What's the difference between a man's marrying and a woman's?' I replied that in Greek the respective terms were *gamein* and *gameisthai*, and in Latin *duco* and *nubo*. 'Well, but you see Medea uses the active here; you should have explained in a note that this is because she puts herself in Jason's place, otherwise an examiner might think that you didn't know the distinction.'

In the Classical Tripos of our year occurred these lines from the *Andromache* of Euripides –

> *Ouk oun ekeinou tama takeinou t'ema?*
> *Dran heu. Kakos d'ou, med' apokteinein bia.*

which most men would translate offhand,

> And are not my things his, and his mine?
> Yes, to do them good, not ill, nor slay by violence.

And this would be right were *me* the negative employed, but the use of *ou* (in rather a singular position here) shows that the negation refers not to the infinitive in the second line, but to the indicative (*eisi* understood) in the first, so that the translation should run, 'To do them good they are, to do them ill or slay by violence they are not.' And the knowing ones, who were in this case the best men of our year, and the best scholars generally (for the last examination papers become objects of immediate interest to all the reading circle) declared at once that the whole passage – thirteen lines – had been set for this one catch.

These two cases fell within my own experience, a third was matter of tradition. In the Tripos of 1840, the Trinity man who was bracketed Senior Classic[43] translated, probably from inadvertence, *he eirene*, peace, in a passage from Thucydides, where the article was of importance. When the examiners came to compare notes, and he was found to be on an equality with his

---

43   Gooden. (B)

Johnian competitor, one of them, a Shrewsbury man,[44] held out a long while against the bracket, saying it was a shame to make a man Senior Classic who could translate *he eirene, peace*, without the article.[45]

---

[44]   Kennedy or Shilleto. (E) [It is perhaps significant that Gooden's main rival, France of St John's, was also a Shrewsbury man. So too were Kennedy and Shilleto, but as the former was a Johnian, he is probably the examiner referred to.]

[45]   Shilleto talked to me about this bracket. He said that another of the examiners favoured one of the two candidates because he 'could write a book', a plea which Shilleto ridiculed with intense contempt. (T)

16

The Scholarship Examination
[1844]

The result of the examination for the Chancellor's Medals is declared very soon after that of the Tripos. The two old competitors had a hard fight for it again, and again the Pembroke man came out first by a neck. It now wanted but a month of the College Scholarship, and I was in the agony of Newton and Statics, as before stated. The only diversions I had were the Plato Lectures, which I could not lose, happen what would, and occasionally attending a talk at the Union (where the Debates were beginning to look up), or at our little Historical. The latter was beautifully arranged as regarded different sets of opinions for keeping up lively discussions; it had been founded chiefly by Liberals, but there were Tories and Conservatives enough in it to defend their aide vigorously in a political question. The Union was very one-sided. Its majority professed a species of mixture of old Toryism and Young Englandism, a fusion more bigoted than either of its bigoted elements. Will it be believed that they actually passed, and by a considerable majority, a vote affirming that it would be expedient to re-establish monasteries in England! Such Liberals of us as there were, however, did not by any means let this or any other question go by default. We lifted up our voices pretty loudly, nor indeed did we confine ourselves entirely to the ordinary course of debate. A queer friend of mine[1] wrote a ballad ludicrously showing up the would-be monks; two of us had it printed, sent

---

[1] [Charles Bagot Cayley, Trinity 1841: *The vision of St Brahamus Touching the Restoration of Monasteries* was circulated in Cambridge in 1843; a copy survives in the Clark Collection in Cambridge University Library. The text was reprinted in

it round as a circular to the whole University, and wound up the joke by getting it attributed to Travis, to his utter disgust, both because he was just at that time dubitating whether he might not go into the Church after all, and because the doggrel was not quite equal to Ingoldsby, and popular prejudice pronounced it even worse than it really was.

And now, somewhere about the end of March or the beginning of April (for it was just after Easter, and according to the old saw

> Let Easter happen when it will,
> It's always in March or April),

the important time for us Senior Sophs of Trinity drew nigh. There are three or four different sets of men among the Third Year Candidates, with different interests and aspirations. First, those who are looking forward to Fellowships. It might be supposed that, as the Fellows are only in the proportion of one to three of the Scholars, any man with a reasonable prospect of a Fellowship ahead would be sure of the Scholarship introductory without much trouble. Yet it sometimes happens that men who have ultimately come out as high as second or third in the Classical Tripos, or among the first eight Wranglers in the Mathematical, and who therefore, it is reasonable to suppose, might have stood a good chance for Fellowships, miss their Scholarships from some accident, perhaps a feeling of security. This has even befallen men who afterwards took good *double* degrees – Senior Optimes in Mathematics, and First Class men in Classics. It is not, therefore, prudent in any man to take his Scholarship for granted, and the best men of the Third Year are generally the most nervous from the recollection of their disappointment the year before.

Next to these come another class whose final expectations are less lofty. They may be decent Wranglers, or high Second Class men, or Double Seconds; that is the limit of their university views, and the Scholarship the limit of their college ones. If they stay up at all as Bachelors, it will be only to enjoy the full benefit of their income from the Scholarship, and for greater convenience in taking pupils: or to attend Divinity Lectures. Others, again, are Classical men not yet decided whether they will go out in Honors, being doubtful if their probable place on the Classical Tripos can warrant the exertion and drudgery of getting through in Mathematics, and their success or failure in this examination will go far towards determining them. And yet others, Classical men also, are not anxious to go out in

C. Whibley, *In Cap and Gown: Three Centuries of Cambridge Wit*, ed.2 (London, 1890), pp. 189–92.]

Honors at all, but would like to get a Scholarship as a sort of compensation to their friends and themselves, and a handsome way of retiring from the other contest with flying colors.

We had a large opening this year – seventeen vacancies. To counter-balance this advantage, the lower year was a very strong one; it contained a Mathematician of great pace and endurance, who was afterwards Senior Wrangler,[2] and several capital Classics. Hallam was one of these, and so was the future Senior Medallist,[3] who was of a family of several brothers that all wrote Greek Iambics by instinct. Our year was weak enough. After taking out the five men who gained their Scholarships at the first trial, we had only one very good Mathematician left, and no very good Classic. The one in most repute was a son of the late Sir R. Peel, now M.P. for Leominster, and his father's *political* successor.[4] All these little personal matters, and many more, were as thoroughly canvassed as the history, merits, and chances of horses before a race, or office-seekers before an election.

Finally arrived *the* Wednesday. The Hall was opened at nine, and seventy or eighty men rushed in to scribble. Our first paper was Greek translation, and, to my surprise and joy, contained a long bit of Plato and a hard bit of Theocritus – authors not usually set in the Scholarship, and therefore likely not only utterly to confound the Mathematical men but to trouble some of the Classical ones, particularly of the Second year. The extra length of the paper, there being five selections instead of the usual four, was also of considerable benefit to me, for my pace, though not very good, was such as to leave a comfortable margin in four hours, and some of the others might be crowded by the additional extract. But in spite of these advantages a morbid feeling of disgust came over me soon after I sat down, and I was on the point of throwing up my papers and walking off. Luckily I thought better of it, and on gradually reflecting how favorable to me this first morning's examination was, I felt a fresh stimulus, and worked diligently the whole four hours, taking care not to throw away any chance by going out before the time, as I had done the previous year.

The bit of Plato set us was from the Tenth Book of the *Laws*. An

---

[2] Hensley. (T, W) [Lewis Hensley, Trinity 1841, Senior Wrangler and fellow of Trinity 1846.]

[3] Lushington. (T, W, B) [Franklin Lushington, Trinity 1843, Senior Wrangler 1846, fellow of Trinity 1847. Lushington was one of five talented brothers, including Edmund, Senior Classic 1832. The family was singled out by Francis Galton in his chapter on 'Senior Classics of Cambridge' in *On Hereditary Genius* (1869).]

[4] [Frederick Peel, who appeared in Ch. 5 as 'Strafford Pope.']

American Professor's *edition* of this Book contains by his own confession *two* mistakes of construction in the notes to this very passage.[5] I translated the whole extract, *which I had never seen before* (nor had any of us, for the Laws is seldom read even by Bachelors, on account of its many corruptions and the want of proper editors), correctly throughout, and as some of the Junior Sophs were marked higher than myself upon it, they must have done so too. I mention this because it illustrates what will be more fully treated of hereafter, the difference between the English and American way of *learning* things.[6] No doubt the Professor in question had read three times as much Plato as any of us three or four men who were best on this extract; perhaps it might be said, that in a rough and imperfect way he had more general knowledge of the Platonic philosophy; but it is long odds that any of us would have translated an ordinary selection from Plato – one where knowledge of language as well as matter came into play – much more correctly than he could.

The examination lasts but three days and a half, the number of papers being seven, two translation, two Latin composition, two Mathematics, and one general questions in Classical history and philology, &c – a paper which of late years had become somewhat unjustly slighted – we were therefore through our toils by Saturday noon. I had done quite as much Mathematics as I expected, but my performances on the Latin verse paper were very shady.

The candidates were now left to a week of suspense. This week I filled up with writing, not for, but rather *at* or *against* the University Latin Essay, for which as a sort of twice Third year man, I had a right to compete a second time. It has been mentioned that there prevailed in the University at this time a feeling of the most awful bigotry, combining all the worst parts

---

[5] [Tayler Lewis, Professor of Classics at Union College, New York, whose *Plato Against the Atheists, or the Tenth Book of the Dialogue on Laws,* was published by Harper Bros. in 1845. Two years later, Bristed and Lewis had crossed swords over an edition of Aeschylus: see Bristed's 'Classical Criticism', *Knickerbocker Magazine* 30 (Oct. 1847), pp. 325–30, which replied to Lewis's article, ibid., 30 (Sept. 1847), pp. 246–56.]

[6] Cambridge [way], if you please! It is easy to find a mistake on every page of Bohn's translation of Aristotle's Politics, done by a Balliol scholar. (T) [Edward Walford (1823–89), whose translation was published by Bohn in 1853. Walford was a prolific writer on classical and ecclesiastical subjects and the author of many biographies; from 1859 to 1865 he edited *Once a Week* … His theological opinions oscillated considerably: priest 1847, converted to Rome 1853, returned to Anglicanism 1860, back to Rome 1871. Cantabrigian carping at Oxonian inaccuracy was a common practice, Benjamin Jowett being a favourite target.]

of Young England Puseyism and old 'high and dry' Toryism. This feeling
was not confined to the Undergraduates, but was aided and abetted by many
of those in authority. One of its manifestations was a continual attempt at
reviving all manner of long-buried absurdities and obsolete rules. Many of
the University Statutes having been enacted when the Undergraduates were
boys of fourteen, had been tacitly thrown overboard with the new order of
things. Some of them it was attempted to revivify – always such as admitted
an *arrière pensée*. Thus there was a regulation *ne ad diversas ecclesias discipuli
vagentur* or something to that effect – a very proper one to prevent boys from
running about to different places of worship, and escaping the observation of
their tutors. But this was now sought to be restored with an aim at some of
the Parish Churches, particularly that of Trinity (not to be confounded with
Trinity College Chapel), Simeon's Parish Church, where Simeon's successor
and biographer Carus, the Senior Dean of Trinity College, always had a
number of Undergraduates among his congregation.[7] And it was maintained
that these did wrong in attending any other place of worship than the
University Church, Great St. Mary's. A sensible man on the other side quoted
another clause of the Statutes by which Undergraduates are forbidden to walk
in the town, unless accompanied by an MA, and showed conclusively that
the two regulations were called forth by the like state of things and stood
on the same footing. It was doubtless with reference to this contest that the
subject now given for the Undergraduates' Latin Essay was '*Quaenam beneficia
a legibus praescriptis diligenter observatis Academiae alumni percipient?*'

After four pages of grave introduction, I took a ridiculous view of the
whole question, and not content with showing up the purists in construction
of the Statutes, took the opportunity of letting off a little of my dislike
to Mathematics. So far as any chance of the prize was concerned, it was a
waste of time, unless the Vice-Chancellor or his deputy had been liberal
to excess; but it took just a week to compose, and filled up the period
before the result of the Examination was declared, after which I was to
recommence reading Classics with another new coach – my Pembroke
friend,[8] who, having just gone out with all the Honors, was to experiment
on me for his first pupil.

The decisive morning arrived. I had invited seven or eight friends to
breakfast – to rejoice or condole with me as the case might be – at ten,
the usual hour of a breakfast party, and after leaving morning chapel at

---

7 [Simeon's friend William Carus (Trinity 1823, dean 1832–50) carried on his
work after his death.]

8 Maine. (B)

seven, went pacing about the grounds in a great state of fidget, supported by my amateur Mathematical coach, and trying to fortify myself with a report I had heard two or three days before from a friend of one of the examiners, that my translation papers were ahead of the rest of the year. The examiners (the Master and the eight Senior Fellows, one or two of whom usually do their work by deputy) meet after chapel to compare results and elect the Scholars. About nine a.m., the new Scholars are announced from the chapel gates. On this occasion, it is not etiquette for the candidates themselves to be in waiting – it looks too 'bumptious'; but their personal friends are sure to be on hand, together with an humbler set concerned – the gyps, coal-men, boot-blacks, and other College servants – who take great interest in the success of their masters, and bet on them to the amount of five shillings and less. This time the conclave was prolonged rather later than usual; there was evidently a difficulty in deciding between some of the candidates. It usually happens that about two thirds are elected unanimously, while for the remaining vacancies there are many of nearly equal pretensions, among whom it is not so easy to decide. Just before nine, my coach went off to chapel to wait for the announcement of the result; and I returned to my rooms to superintend breakfast arrangements. My friend of the sherry-cobblers,[9] in a greater state of excitement than one would have deemed a man of his years capable of, popped in upon me while thus engaged. We began to sing, or make a noise dimly approximating to singing, to conceal our feelings. A long, very long fifteen or twenty minutes elapsed, and then my gyp, first to bring the tidings, rushed in at full trot to assure me that it was all right; and seeing my convivial friend, took occasion to congratulate him also on his election. Then appeared the special messenger, who had been delayed a few moments by taking down the names of the new Scholars. Soon after, our Plato lecturer,[10] my College tutor, stalked in direct from the scene of action (he had been one of the examiners) in his full academicals, like Tragedy in gorgeous pall, to tender me his congratulations in a majestic and Don-like manner; and after him Professor Sedgwick. By this time, too, the breakfasters had begun to assemble, and we made a merry party, three or four of us being among the new Scholars. Chicken salads and cutlets vanished right and left. The quondam Methodist parson[11] was in glorious condition, and before we broke up arranged a supper for that evening. When we strolled out into

---

9   Fussell. (T)
10   Thompson. (B)
11   Fussell afterwards a clergyman. (B)

the grounds, more than one group was lounging about and discussing the result of the examination. As generally happens, the best men in the lower year had beaten ours both in Classics and Mathematics. As also generally happens, some Senior Sophs, considered quite safe, were thrown out. Peel was one of these, and his failure strikingly proved the fairness with which these examinations are conducted; for, had the electors been disposed to favor his name, they might have done so without suspicion,[12] as he was considered a good scholar, and proved himself such in the end.

That night we reproduced the 'jolly revel' of Theocritus in a free practical translation. Our host, elated by a double triumph, for the College Declamations were just declared, and he had gained one of the Latin ones, had exhausted all his Amphitryonic resources to do justice to the party and the occasion. Turkey-legs devilled in wine, curried oysters, lobster *au gratin* (the Trinity cook used to call it *lobster grating*, just as he had converted *poulet grillé* into *pulled and grilled* fowl), and other appetizing condiments, graced the board, and that rare luxury in England, good Madeira, flowed abundantly. We were just enough to make two whist tables, and it must have been pretty well into the morning when we separated.

Indeed, my life for the next fortnight was somewhat sensual and luxurious. I lived well, played billiards frequently in the day time, and whist occasionally at night, and did not work much for my coach. I got up various aesthetic little dinner parties for my friends, both Fellows and Undergraduates, to celebrate my success. Our cook was really a good one, and could arrange almost any French *plat* in very respectable style, and there were some real English dishes which he achieved to perfection: I remember tench stewed in claret,[13] that would console a frequenter of the *Café Anglais* for the loss of his *turbot crême gratin*. I had gained such a reputation for dinner-giving, that men going to 'hang out' sometimes asked me to compose bills of fare for them. I boasted a good wine-merchant, *not* a Cambridge one of course.[14] Some of the duties of my new position actually favored this sybaritism. One of our privileges as Scholars, was a separate table in Hall. The meat and vegetables were supplied gratis; over the sizings, for which we paid, we had full control; and F——[15] and myself used to be studious

---

[12]   This is not generally thought. (E)

[13]   I revived a demand for this receipt, – to the intense interest of the Kitchens. They had to keep the tench in a stew for weeks, to take away the muddy taste. It was no better than a curiosity. (T)

[14]   The chief Trinity wine merchant was a haberdasher. (B)

[15]   J.G.C. Fussell? (W) Formerly Curry. (S)

in puddings and sauces (receipts for which he had picked up in Germany while on a reading-party) for the benefit of the whole table.

Yet let it not be supposed that this was all mere animal enjoyment. Some of the most intellectual conversation I ever listened to, or participated in, has accompanied and succeeded the claret at these little dinners. Like Homer's heroes who

> *Posios kai edetuos ex eron hento*
> [satisfied their hunger and thirst]

as a preparation for any important discussion, the cleverest and most brilliant men among my Cambridge friends were at the acme of their conversational power after a well arranged banquet; and not the least renowned for their care of the good things they took in and the good things they uttered, were the apostolic coterie. I have some of these after-dinner groups in my mind's eye now – Travis, a sort of small Borrow[16] all but the belligerency, knowing all manner of out-of-the-way languages and out-of-the-way places, ready to talk about any subject, all things by turns and nothing long; now making a pun, now telling a gipsy story, now joining in a grave critical and now in a graver theological discussion, always very brilliant and plausible, but not always very logical – the tall, grave statuesque Plato lecturer, half admiring, half ashamed of his apostolic *confrere*, dropping his magisterial decisions in polished sarcasms; E—— the poetic-looking Senior Wrangler[17] (who was an exquisite in his dinner costume, and always got himself up as carefully for a bachelor party as if he were to meet a roomful of ladies), conspicuous in his crimson waistcoat, speckled stockings, and very symmetrical white tie, occupying the most comfortable chair in the room, seeing through everything and everybody with his searching eyes, and occasionally with two or three of his close sentences tumbling down all that Travis had been saying for the last half hour – Henry Hallam, maintaining a modest silence as the youngest man present, but looking so eloquent that every one wanted him to talk, till at last he would talk wonderfully – the Pembroke man, also backward to speak before his elders (he had the rare merit of being either a talker or a listener as circumstances demanded), but, when he did speak, putting in keen and rapid remarks that told like knock-down blows[18]

---

[16] [In 1841 George Borrow had brought out *The Zincali, or, An Account of the Gypsies of Spain, with an Original Collection of their Songs and Poetry, and a Copious Dictionary of their Language.* On Taylor's interest in Gypsies, see p. 53, n. 7.]

[17] E is Ellis; the Pembroke man is Maine. (T)

[18] No great exaggeration. I had the immense privilege of a year of Maine at

– now and then a Rugby man, some pet pupil of Arnold's, a youth earnest
in his convictions, innocent without folly, learned without conceit, uttering
sentiments that from their simplicity might have come from a child, but
which a clever man would find it hard to gainsay or controvert. How those
men would converse! What fertility of illustration! What discriminating
subtlety! What original application of laboriously accumulated learning!
They made gospel of Walter Mapes' assertion –

> Poculis accenditur animi lucerna,
> Cor imbutum nectare volat ad superna.[19]

To recur to such men and such scenes with a fully appreciative recollection,
one must have had some winters' experience of a different sort of society,
where the frivolities of fashion and the malicious details of personal scandal
form the staples of conversation; where mind is frittered away in gossip or
prostituted in slander, and the best appliances of the table only draw forth
coarseness instead of wit; where sincerity is deemed a cloak for shabbiness
and any manifestation of the natural affections a mark of vulgarity – till at
last, talking to a horse-jockey about fast trotters becomes a decided relief
and a comparatively noble occupation.

All this time I was nominally going on with my new tutor, though not
fairly settled at work for the first fortnight. I went over the Theaetetus,
that most difficult dialogue of Plato, very slowly and carefully with him;
but my chief business was to prosecute Composition, in which I was very
much behindhand, a three months' cessation from any practice of the kind
in Greek having left me in a most forlorn state as to Iambics, and not very
well off for prose. In the evenings I read some of the harder Orations of
Cicero, to get up Roman law. Important as this short term was, since I
should soon be obliged to devote my best energies entirely to Mathematics,
I was tempted to give three or four hours a week to playing coach myself,
and superintending the Greek Testament of a friend whose ambition was
confined to passing among the *polloi*, and who was anxious to read with an
acquaintance in preference to a stranger. I always rather liked this sort of
work in moderation and could even now amuse myself any day after dinner

Calcutta. Delightful he then was. He was too much the collegian for London. Taylor
was very kind to me. (T)

[19]   ['The lamp of the soul is lit by drink/The heart imbued with nectar flies
aloft'. Walter Mapes (Map), a 12th-century British clerk and satirist, was a favourite
author of Bristed, who published several translations of his poems in the 1850s: see
Bibliography A2, 1850, 1851, 1856.]

with coaching a pupil, if he were not a very stupid one; and the habit of teaching, when it does not engross too much of a man's time, is of direct benefit to himself by helping him to learn better. There was the additional advantage that I made enough to pay my own coach.[20]

I had some curiosity to see how this tutor of mine, so young as he was, about two years my junior, and fresh from a team himself, would get on at first, and whether his known cleverness would help him or be in his way. The result removed all doubts and surpassed my most sanguine expectations. I could feel that I was being admirably jockeyed. He had the greatest dexterity in impressing his knowledge upon others, made explanations that came to the point at once and could not be misunderstood, corrected mistakes in a way that one was not apt to forget, supplied you with endless variety of happy expressions for Composition and dodges in translation – in short I was conscious of making progress with him every day, and only regretted that I could not continue with him through the Long.[21]

During this term I attended another course of Aristotle lectures – they were on the Rhetoric this year – but not with any express view to the May examination, which I had no intention of going in to, if it could be helped, and which I eventually escaped by an aegrotat from my physician.[22] He might be said to have done his best towards putting me in fit state for one, as not long before he had kept me *six hours* at table, on the occasion of a dinner which he gave to four or five of the new scholars as an appendix to and return for some of my 'hangings out'. The ostensible excuse for the certificate was a slight cold which I caught a few days previous to the examination, while showing two compatriots – a literary and a diplomatic lion – the curiosities of the place. It was a raw morning, and by way of doing the precise in costume I had put on a white tie, without which the academic dress is not strictly complete. Hence my *aegrotat*'s worth of cold.

---

[20] I do not think this if known would have been allowed. (B)

[21] It is quite true. At Calcutta Maine 'coached' me for the Competition Wallah, and was at last frightened at my having learned my lesson all too thoroughly. He was a wonderful instructor. (T) [The 'Competition Wallah' was an Indian Civil Service official who had entered by examination, first held in 1855. The term was popularised by Trevelyan's own book, *The Competition Wallah* (1864), based on a series of articles published in *Macmillan's Magazine* in 1863.]

[22] Fisher of Downing. (B) [Presumably this is 'our friend Dr F. of Downing, who would coolly dissect his neighbour's favourite cat', referred to by W.G. Clark in his review of *Five Years*: 'Cambridge life', p. 91).]

17

The Reading Party [1844]

A Reading Party.

Lucus a non lucendo.

A pleasant land of drowsyhead it was.
                                        Thomson.

After reading as well as I could by myself Plato's *Sophista*, which comes in natural order after the *Theaetetus*, and paying a brief visit to London, I started sometime about the end of June to join a reading-party in Brittany.

A too easy temper, or *ennui*, or mere wantonness, often makes men take a step with the perfect consciousness that they are doing a very foolish thing. It is notorious matter of tradition and experience that not one in a hundred of those who go on reading-parties makes a profitable use of his time – nay, that scapegraces who wish to 'do their governors' and delude them into the belief that they are 'reading' while doing anything but read, adopt this very plan as the most efficient – nevertheless it happens every year that some hardworking and well-disposed youths wander off in these parties. Perhaps the unfortunate has stayed two whole Longs at Cambridge already, and finds the prospect of a third summer there too dreary, or he thinks a change of air may do him good before the struggle of the last term, or some nice Bachelor friend of his is making up a nice party and wants to bring him into it; so, though he knows that the majority of men who join in such excursions do very little reading, he hopes to be one of the minority who form the exceptions. For it is not *impossible* to read on a reading-party; there is only a great chance against your being able to do so.[1] As a very general rule, a man works best in his accustomed place of business, where he has not only his ordinary appliances and helps, but his familiar associations about him. The time lost in settling down and making one's self comfortable and ready for work in a new place is not inconsiderable, and is all clear loss. Moreover the very idea of a reading-party involves a combination of two things incompatible – amusement and relaxation beyond the proper and necessary quantity of daily expense, and hard work at books. Any trip, excursion, or sojourn away from home (the University is the Undergraduate's home while he belongs to it) – either for the purpose of benefiting the health, refreshing the mind, or acquiring new ideas from contact with different people and scenes, presupposes as a necessary condition to its full enjoyment and profit the liberty of the *dolce far niente*. You must be able to ramble in woods, or ride along beaches, or climb hills, or lionize churches, or follow up casual acquaintances, or even lie on your back dreamily watching clouds sailing over head and ships gliding by on rivers, without being pulled up every half-hour by the thought of that chapter of Conic Sections to be read before dinner, or the melancholy reflection that this evening you have to undulate.[2]

Nevertheless men go on reading-parties in despite of this better judgment, and so did I on this occasion, though what made it an additional imprudence on my part was, that it being my business now to get through the Mathematical Tripos with the least expense of time and trouble, so as to save as much as possible of my energies for the Classical, I required very careful handling by an experienced coach, whereas the head and tutor of our party was a Bachelor of the present year, a high Wrangler himself, but with no practice as yet in the art of communicating information to others.[3]

---

[1]   I never read <u>except</u> on a reading party. (T)

[2]   This expression has no reference to unsteadiness of after-dinner movement, but merely to the *Undulatory Theory of Light*.

[3]   W. Budd, 3rd Wrangler 1844. (B) [Charles Budd, Pembroke 1840; Fellow of Pembroke 1848.]

Reading parties do not confine themselves to England or the Island of Great Britain. Sometimes they have been known to go as far as Dresden. We had decided to fix ourselves at some small town in France, and finally pitched up on Dinan in Brittany. Sometimes a party is of considerable size; when a crack tutor goes on one, which is not often, he takes his whole team with him, and not unfrequently a Classical and Mathematical Bachelor join their pupils. We were but a small lot; tutor and all only numbering five. A day was fixed for meeting at Dinan, the shortest route to which place was by Southampton, but having a desire to visit the picturesque old town of Rouen, I crossed at Folkestone, and traversed the whole width of Normandy and Brittany. The passage through the latter province is not one of the most enchanting reminiscences of travel – the Diligences going five miles an hour *exclusive* of stoppages, and the country as uninteresting as if it had been made by one of 'nature's journeymen'.[4] With delusive hopes of enjoying the scenery I had taken my place *en banquette*, and travelling like one of the *very* people, breakfasting in cellars with the conductor on three sous' worth of *café au lait*, or rather *lait au café*; gossiping with an English pilot who had somehow got out of his element thus far into the bowels of the land, but who spoke the language better than many more refined countrymen; falling asleep at night on the rough seats of the imperial, and putting my feet into the hats of ruffianly *commis-voyageurs*, who on awaking poured upon me a profusion of oaths, which I received with a composure that immediately procured me the reputation of being an Englishman, fortunately for me perhaps, as their respect for *le boxe* restrained them from proceeding beyond verbal hostilities. But with all this I was obliged to fall back on a pocket Homer before reaching Dinan. For the first time I began to read the Odyssey through from the beginning. It had for me all the interest of an old Romance, and forcibly recalled the boyish ardor with which I originally perused Robinson Crusoe. It may be supposed that I did not get it up very accurately, having neither Buttmann's *Lexilogus*, nor Scott and Liddell's Lexicon at hand.[5] All the doubtful words and passages I met with now, and during the succeeding month in Jersey I marked for future reference and looked them out in a heap on my return to Cambridge – a wholesale process productive of anything but accurate knowledge, as I found to my

---

4   [Shakespeare, *Hamlet* III.2.31.]

5   [H.G. Liddell and R. Scott, *A Greek-English Lexicon* (1843); P. Buttmann, *Lexilogus*, a study of words in Homer and Hesiod, first published in 1818–25 and in English translation in 1836.]

cost in the Tripos. But of this I thought little at the time. The book had a perfect charm for me, and when we arrived at Dinan I woke up from it and thought of the coming Mathematics with a shudder.

But at Dinan there was no more trace of our party than if the earth had swallowed them up. As the hotels of the town were not numerous, and the whole place easily run over, I could soon satisfy myself of this without applying to that ordinary substitute for Providence in a Continental town, the Police. However, I waited for two or three days, the environs being rather pretty, and then, in a great puzzle, proceeded to St. Malo (which dirty little town, by the way, contains, or at least did contain then, one of the best hotels in Europe), and there took boat for Southampton. There was an hour's landing at Jersey. I went on shore with an officer; we played two games at billiards, had returned on board, and the boat was just going to start, when my coach suddenly laid hands on me, and hurriedly stated – there was no time for a long explanation – how they had found it so dirty at St. Malo that they never went on to Dinan at all, and Jersey being a very nice place, they had determined to stay there. Jersey was just the place where I did not want to stay, having heard much of its abundant opportunities for idleness. But the whole thing passed in a moment, and before I could well open my mouth, I found myself and luggage on shore. In going ten steps we met a very pretty woman, soon another, then I saw a third in a shop; and one reason for staying at Jersey which had not been assigned flashed upon me.

I doubt if any spot on earth can claim a superiority to it in this respect. Nor is it deficient in other comforts and embellishments of life. Being very important to England in case of war with France, it is sedulously petted. Its inhabitants then enjoyed the benefits of free trade and protection together, actually selling the corn which they raised at protection prices in England, and importing corn for their own consumption, duty free, from the Continent. French wines, and gloves, and silks, they have without duty at French prices. The temperature of the island is very pleasant and equable all the year round; its scenery is necessarily on a small scale, the longest diameter of Jersey being but twelve miles, but it is exceedingly pretty. There are good saddle-horses to be hired, a phenomenon existing in few parts of the world. In short, it is a particularly nice little spot for a man of leisure to enjoy himself in, and one of the very worst for a man professing to study to pursue his studies in. The principal occupation of the inhabitants appears to be playing billiards, a practice which they are not backward to inculcate on strangers. The prettiness of the scenery and cheapness of the excellent hacks tempts one to be in the saddle half the day; the balmy and enervating air invites to early repose. It was a lucky thing for me that, before the end of a month, I quarrelled with my coach, which gave me a good excuse for leaving the party and the island; otherwise I should have come out a featherless biped indeed from the Degree Examination.[6]

---

[6] [I.e. 'plucked' (failed); alluding also to Plato's definition of Man as a featherless biped.]

18

Sawdust Pudding
with Ballad Sauce [1844]

On returning to Cambridge, near the end of July, I was fortunate enough to find a place in the team of a capital tutor, a Small-College man who had but six pupils, all going out this time, and five of them 'low men'. My sojourn at Jersey had only brought me through Algebra once more, and now, beginning with Plane Trigonometry, I resolutely encountered that nightmare of most classical men, the preparation for the Mathematical Tripos.

When the Classical Tripos was instituted (which was as lately as 1824), it was thought fit to impose as a condition on the candidates for it, that they should previously 'take Mathematical Honors', a phrase somewhat facetiously applied in their case, as it meant for most of them obtaining a place among the *Junior Optimes*, or lowest class.[1] The idea of this restriction was probably suggested by the previously existing one in reference to the Chancellor's Medals, the candidates for which were required to be *Senior Optimes*. Thus the Mathematical Tripos became, in fact, at the same time a test of merit for the Mathematicians and a pass examination for the Classical men, since none of the latter cared anything about being one place or twenty places higher or lower among the Junior Optimes; indeed, being a Senior Optime or not generally made very little difference to a Classic, unless he were a

---

[1] [The three classes of honours in mathematics were Wranglers (1st), Senior Optimes (2nd) and Junior Optimes (3rd).]

candidate for one of the Medals, it being so small a matter to him compared to his place in the other Tripos. Bearing in view the real difficulty which a majority of the Classical men had in getting up their Mathematics, as well as the uncongenial nature of the study, it is evident that the Mathematical Tripos could only be made useful as a pass examination by keeping the standard of a Junior Optime very low in comparison with what might be expected from men pretending to *Mathematical Honors*, and claiming to show a proficiency in Mathematics. The 'low' questions[2] were chiefly confined to the first day's papers, but there was enough of them for a man knowing his low subjects only, but those perfectly, to become a Senior Op., and not one of the last ones either. And this did sometimes happen by good fortune to an aspirant for Classical Honors, who had read only, as he supposed, Mathematics enough to get through. But as from the longest of these subjects not more than six or seven questions were set, an unfortunate who had spent some time on one of them might nevertheless very possibly fail to answer a single question proposed in it. If a man is 'plucked', that is, does not get marks enough to pass, his chance of a Fellowship is done for, even at Trinity, for Trinity Scholars when plucked lose their Scholarships. Some ten or fifteen men just on the line, not bad enough to be plucked or good enough to be placed, are put into the 'gulf', as it is popularly called (the Examiners' phrase is 'Degrees allowed'), and have their degrees given them, but are not printed in the Calendar, nor were they at this time allowed to try for the Classical Tripos. Being *gulfed* was therefore about as bad for a Small-Colleger as being *plucked*, since it equally destroyed his chance of a fellowship, but a gulfed Scholar of Trinity did not lose his Scholarship.

The requirement of Mathematical Honors from Classical Men was the great question of University Politics, so to speak, at this time. The sufferers' complaint may be briefly stated as follows: — 'This restriction is unjust to us and partial to the Mathematicians, who are under no corresponding obligation. It is true that they have to pass their Little-Go, but the acknowledged main difficulty in that is the *Paley*, which is as much a difficulty for us as for them. The Classical part of that examination is fixed and defined in all its details long beforehand; it is not more than a man with ordinary school-boy knowledge can get up in six weeks; a failure

---

[2]   The 'low subjects', as got up to pass men among the Junior Optimes, comprise — *Euclid*, first four books, sixth, and eleventh; *Algebra*, including Logarithms; *Plane Trigonometry, Conic Sections*, first three Sections of *Newton, Statics, Dynamics, Hydrostatics*, and *Optics*, so far as these can be carried without the Differential; frequently *Spherical Trigonometry*, and more rarely the rudiments of *Astronomy*.

in it is not irremediable, for should a man be plucked (which very seldom happens) at the first Previous Examination, he can pass in the October one without endangering his ultimate prospects; lastly, it comes in the middle of his University career, and leaves him his last and most important twenty months clear to devote to his favorite studies. Whereas the pressure of the Mathematical Examination comes upon us just at the time which we most want for our Classics. It is very general in its range of subjects, and very limited in the number of questions from each subject, so that to make sure of passing, we are obliged to get up twice or three times the amount that would be necessary if the range of questions were more accurately defined beforehand, or the low papers were longer. If of two men equal in classical talent and knowledge one has a better mathematical capacity than the other, so that he can get up the requisite quantity in four months, while it takes his competitor eight, he gains four months advantage over him in time to polish up his Classics, so that an irrelevant and unfair element is introduced into the test of classical merit. If any study has a prescriptive right to a privilege or bounty, it is ours, for we *continue* to study after entering the University, while many of the Mathematicians only *begin* there. A man may be a Wrangler the commencement of whose Mathematical knowledge was contemporaneous with his admission. But no one was ever placed in *any* class of the Tripos who came up to the University knowing only the elements of Greek grammar. The Classical man, if plucked, loses, so far as the tangible pecuniary recompense is concerned, the work of ten years or more; the Mathematician is not obliged to put in peril the result of four years' labor. Nor is it a small grievance, though sinking into insignificance alongside some others, that we are obliged to *stand up to be knocked down* – are published as 'Wooden Spoon', perhaps, or a few places above it, in an examination which for us is merely a pass, while on its face it professes to be only a test of merit, and is so for the majority of those in it.

However, we should not complain of these evils did the result of the compulsory study afford any compensation for them. But so far from our being able to perceive any mental benefit arising from the Mathematical course, whatever effect we are conscious of is absolutely injurious. We are puzzled and worried over intricate propositions, the truth of which we readily admit, but in which we can see no beauty and take no interest. The mind refuses to swallow the loathsome dose forced upon the memory. We forget Classics without learning any Mathematics. What we do get up for the examination we cannot be properly said to *know* – it is only held in solution, and when we have passed the ordeal for which it was destined, is precipitated immediately. Our very first object is to turn it out of our minds as soon as possible, that they may recover their classical tone.'

To this the Mathematical Dons would reply – so far as they condescended to express themselves verbally or in writing, for many of them, being in possession, were content therewith, and deigned not to give reasons – 'The object of a University is not to reward distinguished talent in any one particular branch, but to give a thorough and complete education to the mental faculties. The Mathematics are necessary to improve and develope the reason, as the Classics are to improve and develope the imagination. If the Mathematical experience of many begins after their entering the University, so much the more reason is it why we should make up for the neglect of the Public Schools, which have been and still are notoriously deficient in this respect. And it is the circumstance of having to begin here with the rudiments of Mathematical science, that makes the subject so distasteful to Classical men, compared with the languages of which they have long ago passed the rudimentary difficulties. If they would go back in recollection to their early school days, they would find themselves suffering as much then from grammars and nonsense verses, as now from roots and cosines. The small quantity of Mathematics required to pass a man among the Junior Optimes, need not at the most liberal allowance require for its preparation more than nine months of the thirty-nine which complete his course for the B.A. degree. If any instances of failure after honest application occur, these are exceptional cases, owing to nervousness, bad luck, or other causes, exactly such as sometimes throw a candidate for one of the Medals down into the Second Class of the Tripos, and which cannot be guarded against in any system. Moreover, there is a double moral advantage arising from the compulsory study of Mathematics. In the first place, it checks an arrogant tendency on the part of Classical men to consider their knowledge as *the* knowledge of all others and the one test of ability and cleverness, by exhibiting their deficiency in an equally extensive and important intellectual department. In the second place, having to overcome a difficulty and discharge a disagreeable task by ready application, gives a lesson of patience and confidence very serviceable in after life.'

Such, I fancy, would be admitted by those members of the Senate upholding the restriction to be a pretty fair summary of their arguments in favor of it. The dispute is a nice one to decide for it is not easy to find a judge at once competent and impartial. A man with a natural talent for Mathematics cannot easily so far put himself into the place of one naturally averse to and incompetent in them, as to appreciate the effects of their compulsory study upon the latter's mind. On the other hand, a Classical man has no right to decide against the use of Mathematics to himself until he has given them a full and fair trial. This I can certainly claim to have done. Having been initiated into Euclid and Algebra at school; having somehow gone through the Mathematical Course at Yale College without being able to perceive that I derived the slightest possible good from it; having faithfully attacked Algebra again from the very beginning, during the term previous to my first May at Trinity, and made an almost total failure; having renewed the attack three times subsequently, the last for six months together, and with so much success that I accomplished my object of getting through in Honors – I may say with justice that I have tried the experiment, and must say with truth that, so far as any intellectual discipline or improvement is concerned, a very large portion of the time so spent – certainly almost all of that spent in Analysis – was clear waste. But as the case of an individual, however well investigated in itself, may be anomalous and not available for general rules, let us examine carefully the positions of those who advocate the compulsory study of Mathematics to the end of the Undergraduates' career, and also the effect of the two courses of study – the Classical and the Mathematical – in developing the different faculties.

The fundamental assertion that Mathematics develope the reasoning powers, as Classics do the imaginative (or, as it is sometimes expressed, that Classics make men elegant and Mathematics make them accurate) is one of those stereotyped sayings which a great many people take on trust, but which will not stand the scrutiny of a vigorous inspection. In fact, it does not characterize *either* branch correctly. It may well be doubted whether any direct study can properly be said to improve the imaginative faculties – to increase the original stock of them possessed by any individual, or implant them where they do not already exist. If there is any such study, it certainly is not that of the Classics, which leads to the criticism and imitation of others' models rather than the creation of new ones. Taking imagination in the sense of *invention* or *originality*, it enters much more into Mathematical than into Classical pursuits; and if this invention, as exhibited in the working of problems, &c., could be imparted by study and practice to those naturally destitute of it, then we might say that Mathematics, and not Classics, improved the imagination. That Classical studies *correct* the imagination, is another proposition, and I believe a very true one; they give taste and style; their office is eminently aesthetic. If asked what are their effects and benefits, I should name this as the first; and for the second I should assign what is generally attributed to Mathematics – accuracy and discrimination in reasoning. That Mathematical propositions are in most cases perfect specimens of ideal demonstration and pure reasoning, is rather against than for them in this respect. There are, as a general rule, no shades of reasoning in Mathematics: a demonstration is either right or it is wrong. Sometimes, indeed, it may be arrived at in several different ways; but these are distinct processes, not modifications of the same one. The two most general forms of reasoning which we need and encounter in the practice of life, discrimination between quasi-synonyms and judgment from probabilities, are unprovided for by Mathematical training. The niceties and difficulties of Classical, particularly Greek syntax, are much better calculated to teach practical accuracy.

What, then, *are* the qualities of the mind most necessary for and most brought into play by Mathematical study? I should answer (setting aside the inventive power already mentioned, which, I think it will generally be conceded, is rather a pre-requisite for than a development of Mathematical proficiency) *method* and *concentration*; and I believe it will usually be found that those persons who are deficient in ability to acquire Mathematics, are also deficient in method and concentration. For myself, I always find the want of an orderly and regular sequence of ideas one of my greatest troubles in treating of a subject – what thought to put first, and how to connect the different heads. So much so is this the case, that, when younger, I used generally to write an essay in fragments and piece them together as best I could;[3] and even now, whatever I write about, I am continually obliged to leave out something pertaining to the subject, for want of being able to find an appropriate place for its introduction. And the next great difficulty is a want of concentration, an inability to keep my attention fixed upon one subject at a time until I have done with it. Now, one of the essential characteristics of Mathematical demonstration is the regular sequence of steps following one another in order; disturb this order, and the demonstration is not only vitiated but destroyed. Sometimes, indeed, where the solution is given beforehand, you may begin at both ends and work the equivalents till they meet, but even then the progress both ways is in regular and methodical order. Equally true is it – indeed it almost follows as a matter of course – that a Mathematical demonstration requires the concentrated and undivided attention of the person who is engaged on it; it is not like reading a passage in Classics, where, if you do not understand one line or sentence, you may pass it over for the time, go on to the next, and return again to the original difficulty after having made some progress elsewhere.

---

[3] [This was Bristed's procedure in writing *The Upper Ten Thousand*; and also his original plan for *Five Years*.]

But now, it may well be asked, since method and concentration are two most desirable qualities to gain, if these are particularly brought into play in Mathematical operations, is not the study an exceedingly useful one? The difficulties attendant on an answer to this question I am not disposed to underrate; that my answer will satisfy the reader I can hardly expect, as it does not in all particulars satisfy myself. Firmly convinced as I am that all the Mathematics which I read after a certain point were a sheer waste of time, still I cannot explain so fully as I could wish why this was the case, and is the case with all men of similarly constituted minds.

One thing is open and on the surface – the insuperable disgust to Mathematical study which a man of this class feels (and in this class I include not only those who like myself just scraped through, but a number of those who by dint of sheer cram or good luck succeed in becoming Senior Optimes). He cannot work himself up to an interest for the pursuit. When he succeeds in writing out a long formula with perfect correctness, he does not feel the same satisfaction as when he has turned off a good copy of verses, or a neat translation, or an essay that pleases him. The only gratification present to his mind is the consolation of having *shot so much rubbish*. Nor can this nausea be altogether accounted for by mortified vanity and the discouragement caused by a want of progress, for in many cases it absolutely increases with the progress made. I never felt so thoroughly sick of everything like a Mathematical book as just before the 'Great Go',[4] when my knowledge of Mathematics was greater than it ever was before or has ever been since – if we can apply the term *knowledge* to the quantity of Mathematics requisite to get a place among the Junior Optimes. But in truth such a man never has and never can have any Mathematical knowledge in the true sense. The amount of alien matter violently obtruded upon his mind never assimilates itself to his mental composition, is never unconsciously remembered, never becomes a part of his habitual associations. It is only held on to temporarily by an incessant mental effort; as soon as that effort is relaxed it departs, and there is no wish or impulse of the mind to retard its departure. He looks upon the Mathematical examination as a sort of fight with the examiners, in which he is to get through or get a Senior Optime as the case may be, with the least amount of knowledge and trouble; should he come out high among the Senior Ops, and beat a number of single men, he rather enjoys it as a joke upon the examination, a sort of irony of fate, and views it much as a billiard player would a *racroc* – a piece of

---

[4] [The degree examination, as opposed to the Little-Go (Previous Examination).]

luck but not at all a matter of pride. Cases are on record of Classical men who by a happy combination of labor and luck have become high Senior Optimes, consequently beating several candidates for Wranglerships, and nine months after have taken in no Mathematics to the Trinity Fellowship examination. And not only is the progress in this uncongenial study, slow, disagreeable, and elusive, but, so far from its strengthening the mind of the scholar for more appropriate employments, it actually weakens and unfits it. Fagging at Mathematics not only fatigues, but hopelessly muddles an unmathematical man, so that he is in no state for any mental exertion. It was the general complaint of men who had been working up Mathematics for the Trinity Scholarship, or going through a longer probation for the Senate House, that it took several days to recover the spring and tone of their minds when they set to work on Classics again. Indeed the infliction of a Mathematical course upon non-Mathematicians has always seemed to me like an attempt to implant in the mind new qualities, not to develope those which it already possesses. No doubt a man who can acquire a real knowledge of Mathematics is better off pro tanto for it, and if he has the requisites for this as well as those for being a good scholar, his mind is clearly more valuable than if it were only fit for Scholarship. But when a man has not these requisites, and after several fruitless attempts and eight or nine months final fagging, can only just achieve a Junior Optime, *quaere* if his time would not have been better employed in other studies allowed to be useful, more to his taste, and in which he makes infinitely more headway. By the time a youth has arrived at the age of eighteen or nineteen, supposing him to have received any sort of decent preparatory education, he will generally have found out what he can do, and what he cannot, and in which direction his forte lies, and it is then certainly the best individual economy to make the most of what is in him.

To the moral argument in favor of Mathematics, quizzical as it may appear to some, I am seriously inclined to attach considerable weight. That Classical men, loving and adoring their favorite studies, proud of their excellence in them, and thinking it a surpassing excellence, may often be tempted to look upon Scholarship as the one great test of merit, and that it may prove a beneficial corrective to step out into another mental region and find themselves mere children there, may be readily admitted.[5] Equally must we admit the benefit derived from overcoming a difficulty

---

[5] At the utmost, it only amounts to doing well, <u>the very same things</u> which others have done as well or better, say to be a 2nd Porson, and what is the good of that? (B)

of long standing and getting through with an unpleasant duty. It teaches patience during the struggle, and gives a healthy self-confidence after it. But it must not be forgotten that there are moral evils involved as well. One of them is the very serious trial of temper occasioned by Mathematical annoyances. The petulance and irritability thus engendered were matter of notoriety; indeed you could always tell when a Classical man was under the influence of a Mathematical examination in prospect, merely by observing his ordinary demeanor. There was also a great sense of unfairness – a feeling as if we were sacrificed to the Mathematicians, and the compulsory passing in Mathematics was a sort of bounty or protection upon them at our expense – which in some cases rose so high as to make it almost a personal matter. I have heard a man say he felt like going out and kicking the first Mathematician he met.

One undeniable and undenied effect of the restriction on Classical Honors at Cambridge was that it prevented a number of men from going out in Honors at all. These are generally not the very best Classics, for in their case the prize at stake is worth a great effort; but the B. No. 1 men, who bid fair to be low first-class men or good seconds. One of these men has been reading on for two years and a half, more or less regularly, till just as the men of the year before him are about to try their fortune, he begins to determine seriously on his own views and prospects. He takes his coach into council, who says, 'You ought to be a First Class, if you work for it; you must read so many hours a-day for this next year'. Off goes the student to his Mathematical tutor to see how much time must be taken off for the 'Mathematical Horrors'. He, after due examination of his pupil's ignorance, informs him that so many hours a-day for two or three terms will be necessary. With this report our Third Year man travels back to his Classical tutor, who replies, 'If this be the case – if you have to give up so much time to Mathematics, your First Class will be in danger, and on the whole I would advise you to go out in the Poll. Unless you are pretty sure of a First, it don't pay to go through the trouble of getting up Mathematics for the chance of a Second' (the coach himself has probably a lively reminiscence of his own labors to obtain a place some eight or ten above the Spoon). The pupil takes his advice, gives up reading for Honors, and goes out in the Poll, which is as much as saying that he does nothing for the last year of his College life.

I have said this is *undenied*. As an offset, however, it is asserted that the Mathematical Tripos is increased by numbers who, but for the compulsory restriction, would not go in it. But we have good reason to doubt whether these forced volunteers confer any very great honor or benefit on the

Mathematical Tripos. It is certain that they lower the standard of it, that is, of the lower places in it, and it is probably on this account that the inferior places are so little thought of in comparison with those of the Classical Tripos, a Senior Optime, for example, compared with a Second Class in Classics. Were the Mathematical Tripos confined to Mathematicians, there would be less disparity between the standard for the Wrangler and for the other Classes, and the lower places would be more honorable than they are at present, and more on a par with the corresponding ones of the Classical Tripos.

What, then, is our inference from the above? That to a large class of students, Mathematics are not only useless, but injurious, and should therefore be turned out of their education altogether? That in the University of Cambridge it would be desirable to open the Classical Tripos entirely, and allow Classical men to take their degrees without having read a word of Mathematics? By no means. So peculiar and extensive a department of reasoning as the Mathematical no liberally-educated student should be without some experience of, even though his experience may never fructify into knowledge. We must also remember that a boy is not exactly qualified to judge of what he can do or what he is fit for; it is at a more advanced age that the student is able to reason on the progress and capabilities of his own mind, that he can elect his forte and reject what is unprofitable. I am inclined to think that, supposing a boy begins to study the dead languages at eleven or twelve (which is early enough), he may well begin Euclid a year after, and Algebra at fourteen or fifteen; and from that age to go on for two or three years devoting about as much time to Mathematics as is now usually done in our Colleges, that is to say, from one fourth to one third of the whole period assigned to study. But if at the end of that period he be found to make little progress and take no interest in the study, he should be allowed an opportunity of passing a final examination in the lower branches, and then be permitted to take leave of pure science at the age of eighteen. And here again we should make a distinction as to the *kind* of Mathematics. That geometry is generally more popular and more easily understood than analysis is a tolerably familiar truth to all who have had much to do with liberal education; the simplest expression of this truth is the preference of Euclid to Algebra shown by Freshmen and schoolboys, and their quicker progress in the former study. The great power which Analysis gives renders it superior for high Mathematical purposes in any case where both methods are applicable; but as a fixed element of general education, geometry must be preferred.[6]

---

[6] For a thorough comparison of the two processes see *Whewell on Cambridge Studies*,

As to the course most desirable at Cambridge, it is well known that many young men come up with no knowledge of Mathematics except a very little Algebra and Euclid. It is a wise arrangement of the separate colleges to examine at the end of the first eight months on these subordinate branches, with the addition of Plane Trigonometry, thus giving the tyros plenty of time to study the rudiments without neglecting their Classics. By this time the student, with his tutor's assistance, has usually succeeded in giving the Mathematics a fair trial, and discovering whether he can go on with them to his own comfort and improvement, or not. It would appear then just and beneficial to all parties to *put the Mathematics into the Little Go*, as a Cantab would say; in other words, to demand such a modicum of low Mathematics as may be deemed a sufficient test, from all the students at the previous examination, and then leave the Classical men free to pursue their own peculiar study, and develop themselves in their own way, for the last year and a half without interruption.[7]

The two great hardships complained of by the Classical men were, first, that the Mathematical degree examination was too diffuse in its character to enable them to calculate accurately on passing it, and secondly, that it occurred just at the very time when it was most inconvenient. The first evil has been to a great extent remedied within a few years, and it is not improbable that the second grievance will be abolished at no very remote period.[8]

After the result of the Scholarship examination many of my friends had advised me to give up competition for Honors, and retire gracefully with flying colors. But I had several inducements to attempt going out in Honors. A little feeling of chivalry had something to do with it; I wanted to give one or two men whom I had beaten at the Scholarship a chance of doing better in the Tripos. A better reason was a natural curiosity to test my knowledge and fix my relative place more definitely. Partly from originally defective preparation, partly from the irregular and interrupted manner in which my studies had been prosecuted, my Classics were in the most unequal order, in some things standing very fair, in others hardly

---

Part I, pp. 38–63. [W. Whewell, *Of a Liberal Education in General: and with Particular Reference to the Leading Studies of the University of Cambridge, Part 1* (London, 1845).]

[7] This was done well before my time. (T)

[8] [Reform of the Mathematical Tripos was agreed on in 1846, just after Bristed left Cambridge, and came into effect in 1848. The examination was divided into two parts, elementary and advanced, honours in the first being a precondition of entry to the latter. See Ch. 27, and Warwick, *Masters of Theory*, pp. 101–2.]

well enough to be placed at all. I could not assure myself or others of my probable standing, the classical tutor's decision of last winter appearing in some measure contradicted by subsequent performances. Moreover, I really was very desirous of a First Class, and though not willing to risk my health reading for one, thought the chance worth some trouble as well as the risk of failure. But more than all, I was influenced by a sense of pique. There was a general impression that I could not get through, 'that is', said the Mathematical tutor in whose team I had ineffectually tried to work the summer before, 'not that you are *unable* to pass, but you will get disgusted and sick of the work, and throw it up before the time comes'. For this very reason I was resolved to get through. From my Jersey trip I had brought back only the discovery that I was strong enough to ride, and this greatly consoled me for all Mathematical afflictions. After cramming, and fussing, and 'writing out' three, four, five hours in the morning, it was a delicious luxury to mount a blood mare and gallop over that carpet-like turf which one finds nowhere but in England. A friend, who did not intend to go out in Honors, but was staying up this Long to study Hebrew, he gave out – the uncharitable said for another purpose – used to accompany me.

Even with this favorite amusement, restored after a deprivation of three years, it was hard to keep one's spirits up under the Mathematical burden. The feeling was exactly like that of eating sawdust. My mind could extract neither pleasure nor nutriment from the food presented to it; and yet this work did not occupy more than four hours a day of my time, some days not even so much. But those few hours daily exhausted me more than twice the time spent on congenial studies would have done. Apparently I had time to spare for Classics, and my Pembroke friend, who was now working a nice little team of three or four, begged me to come into it, or, at least, attend his examinations on Saturdays. But this I was forced to decline. To keep up the amount of energy requisite to carry me through the Senate House, it was necessary to abstain from any hard and systematic work during the rest of the day. It was desirable to unbend as much as possible. I read heaps of old ballads and romantic poetry – Motherwell, Shelley, Miss Barrett, sometimes Homer, soared up as high as I could from the disagreeable daily necessities of x and y into the cloudland of fancy and rhyme. Still it was not in human nature for a Classical man living among Classical men, and knowing that there were a dozen and more close to him reading away 'like bricks', to be long entirely separated from his Greek and Latin books. My library stood in the small room which was my winter snuggery. The summer apartment contained only a big standing-desk, the eternal 'scribbling paper' and the half-dozen Mathematical works required. A wise precaution, but it did not long avail. At first I admitted Homer to share my after-dinner hours with the old English ballads. Then, as I was anxious to do a good bit of Greek prose in the Tripos, wishing to make that one of my strong points, and liking the composition itself, and it had been told me by Travis, that the best way to acquire facility and elegance in it was to read plenty of good Greek prose – the Republic, for instance – I took the advice, *au pied de la lettre*, and began to read the Republic an hour after breakfast every day before attacking my Mathematics. In this way I cleared five books of it; after reading two or three I was tempted to try my composition, and used on the off-days, when I had no Mathematical paper to do with my coach, to work at Greek prose, chiefly with a view to *pace*, until I could beat the ordinary examination time. It turned out rather a bad speculation in the end, for practising first for rapidity and then for spicy words, I came to disregard accuracy of Syntax, and to make wrong or slovenly constructions. All my compositions (they were not confined to Greek prose) I put down in a book to have them corrected afterwards,[9] but the three weeks intervening between the two Triposes was a very insufficient time, to wash so much dirty linen either with comfort to my coach or profit to myself. Had I given less time to composition, and gone on more slowly and carefully under the supervision of a tutor, it might have turned out much better for me. But the fear that I should not be able to limit my time in Classics if I once began them with a coach always frightened me off; and my Mathematical friends assured me I was perfectly right. 'If you try to go on reading Classics with a tutor', said they, 'you may give up the idea of getting through in Mathematics'.[10]

And now what does this troublesome Mathematical course amount to? Of how much does it consist? Some general hints of its extent and scheme have already been given; let us now go over them in greater detail.

The subjects which a man who is merely a candidate *to pass* in Honors, whose only object is a place somewhere – Wooden Spoon if he can do no better (and not unfrequently he would as lief have that place as any other, particularly if it can be obtained at a comparatively small outlay of time and trouble) – are broadly defined as *everything inside the Differential*,

---

[9] [This book survives in Bristed's papers in the Beinecke Library, Yale University.]

[10] What a picture of a misdirected course of study in a most promising mind! It was sheer barbarism. However, he read a great deal harder than I did in the six months preceding the Tripos. (T)

which, however, is characterizing the schedule too liberally, as there are several matters from the Theory of Equations in Algebra to various introductory propositions in Astronomy which are quite independent of the Calculus, and nevertheless do not usually come into the future Junior Optime's scheme. What I prepared is a fair specimen of the usual amount, as follows: Euclid; first four books, sixth and eleventh. Algebra; as far as the theory of equations. Plane Trigonometry. Spherical Trigonometry. Newton's Principia; first three sections. Conic Sections. Statics; Dynamics; so far as they can be carried without the differential. Hydrostatics; Optics. (Descriptions of instruments enter largely into these four subjects, and are great godsends to the Classical men.) Ten subjects in all.

It must be borne in mind that most of these subjects are read very differently from what they would be with us. Thus, in Trigonometry, the Sines, Cosines, &c. are not *lines*, but *ratios*. Conic Sections are read entirely by analysis; though there may be a 'picture' to each proposition, the relations of the lines are expressed entirely by Algebraic formulae. But for the occasional recurrence of the terms 'parabola' and 'ellipse', a tyro who had read *Bridge*[11] would not be able to discover that *Hamilton*[12] was writing on the same subject. As Classical men, with very few exceptions, take more kindly to Geometry than to Analysis, this makes it all the harder for them.

On the other hand, it is admitted that the getting-up of a subject does not involve the knowledge of every page and every proposition in the ordinary text-books treating of it. As there is a certain run of questions from which examiners do not vary, these are marked for study and the others for omission (R and O are the usual marginal designations in pencil); and here it will be seen that much depends on the judgment and experience of the coach. Still it must not be suspected that there is any lack of generality in the Examinations. Suppose, for instance, there are seventy-five propositions in Conic Sections from among which questions in the Mathematical Tripos are usually set, and that the average number of questions is seven; this evidently leaves a pretty wide range. To make sure of the two questions in Spherical Trigonometry, on the first morning's paper, the candidate must have mastered forty pages of close print. Then, again, besides the text-books, there are manuscripts[13] containing variations and different methods

---

[11]　[B. Bridge, *A Compendious and Practical Treatise on the Construction, Properties and Analogies of the Three Conic Sections* (London, 1811).]

[12]　[H.P. Hamilton, *Principles of Analytical Geometry* (Cambridge, 1826).]

[13]　[See Warwick, *Masters of Theory*, p. 144.]

not to be found in the books, with which every man has something to do at some period of his course. Any such changes would not be allowed in Euclid or Newton, but in other places men are sometimes enabled to make a show of originality with them. On the whole, then, it may be safely said that the getting up of a subject is equivalent to getting up any one of the ordinary books upon it.

The library required for such a course is not very extensive. On each of the subjects comprised in it there are two or three books written by Mathematical Dons, and used indifferently according to the taste of different tutor and the previous purchases of different pupils. My stock consisted of – I really forget whose Euclid,[14] Wood's and Hind's Algebras, Snowball's Trigonometry, Hamilton's Conic Sections, Evans' Newton, Earnshaw's Statics, Earnshaw's Dynamics, Miller's Hydrostatics,[15] Griffen's[16] Optics, two or three other elementary works on Mechanics (one of them by Dr. Whewell), and two volumes of MSS. In addition to these, I borrowed a huge volume, called Pratt's Mechanical Philosophy. Most of these works were purchased at second-hand, some of them at fourth or fifth hand, an indignity which rarely befals Classical books.

The manner of going to work is somewhat this. As the public examination is to be all pen and ink, the private instruction to prepare you for it necessarily involves much similar practice. So you arrange with your coach, according to his ideas of what you ought to get up and your ideas of what you can or will get up, that you will be prepared next day or the day after in the Ellipse, or the First Section of the Principia, or all Algebra, as the case may be, and on that day he sets you in his own room a paper, perhaps of his own composition, perhaps an old College Examination one, on the agreed subject, containing ten or fifteen questions. You do as much of this as you can and as fast as you can, and leave your papers to be looked over in your absence by the tutor, who on your return next day explains the errors in them. Any difficulties in the text-books it is of course also his business to explain, but these are not of frequent occurrence; the trouble usually is not to *understand* but to *remember*.

How far is the candidate acquainted with these ten subjects, which we have intimated that he cannot properly be said to *know*? If his temporary mastery of them were complete, that is, if he could be sure of doing all

---

[14] Potts. (B) [The standard edition of Euclid (1845), by the Cambridge coach Robert Potts.]

[15] Nearly all wretched books. (B)

[16] Griffin. (B)

the bookwork that might be set from them, he would get just questions enough to make him a low Senior Op; even supposing he did no problems. But it may be supposed that, as a general rule, this never happens: so safe and thorough an acquaintance with the low subjects implies some ability to make use of their principles in problems, a Mathematical power, in short, which has already led the student to seek high Mathematical Honors. (I say as a general rule, for there are some cases of men with a low Mathematical or half-Mathematical sort of talent, so to speak, who can be absolutely perfect in low subjects, and break down when they come to higher ones.) A non-Mathematical man must read for twice as much as he expects to do; he can seldom make anything except Euclid and Newton quite safe, or calculate with certainty on doing much more than half of a subject which he has got up. Nor can he make sure of solving even *one* problem, though he may find as many as three within his capacity. His ambition is generally limited to doing 'riders', which are a sort of scholia, or easy deductions from the bookwork propositions, like a link between them and problems; indeed the rider being, as its name imports, attached to a question, the question is not fully answered until the rider is answered also. My experience was that I could floor a Euclid or Newton paper, and in any other subject, taking bookwork and riders together, do enough for half marks. The highest degree I ever heard of as being taken without the Differential was 10th Senior Optime, or in the first quarter of the Second Class. It was a case of extraordinary good luck as well as cleverness.[17] In general, a man who has any pretensions to a Senior Op's place, even one of the lowest, just to let him in for the Medal, will have made some little progress in the Differential Calculus (the term *Fluxions*[18] is never used), so that he can do a few questions in the subject itself and make some slight application of it in other branches.

As my Mathematics began to feel a little less shaky, and the desire of working up my Classics increased, and the pace of the men about me carried

[17]　I suppose he means Vaughan (in 1838), of Trinity bracketed Senior Classic. Possibly he may mean Penrose of Magdalene (1842). (B) [Charles James Vaughan, Trinity 1834, Senior Classic and 10th Senior Optime 1838; fellow of Trinity 1839–42, headmaster of Harrow 1844–59. Vaughan refused bishoprics, to the puzzlement of his friends, who were unaware that the father of a Harrow pupil with whom Vaughan had had an affair had threatened to expose him if he accepted preferment. Francis Penrose, Magdalene 1838, 10th Senior Optime 1842; distinguished architect and first director of the British School at Athens, whose building he designed.]

[18]　[The term used by Newton for the differential calculus.]

me along, and my health was decidedly improving, I now attempted a 'spirt', or what was one for me. Beginning with five hours and a half, I put on an extra half hour to my working time every three or four days until I had reached seven hours, at which point I remained for a week, and then suddenly gave way, broke down all at once, and was obliged to lie idle and recruit for some days. After that, I did not attempt more than five hours a-day till the Mathematical Examination, till then also I bid good bye to my Classics. This was about the end of the Long, and the beginning of our last Undergraduate term.

It was not an unpleasant life after all, that last Long; a good grievance which always gives one something to talk about, delightful weather, pleasant rides, occasional cobblers, and the mild excitement, like an innocent sort of gambling, which a man feels when working to save himself in one Examination and get credit in another.

19

On the Razor's Edge [1844-5]

A Saunter on King's Parade on Sunday Evening.

A busy time indeed is the term before going out to the 'Questionists Candidates for Honors'. Ants, bees, boat-crews spirting at the Willows, jockeys nearing the post and getting the last half inch out of their nags (though this last simile is perhaps more appropriate to the private tutors than to their pupils), are but faint types of their activity. They even break in upon their cherished hours of exercise. Lucky is the man who lives a mile off from his private tutor, or has rooms ten minutes' walk from chapel; he is sure of that much constitutional daily. They have little appetites for their not very tempting dinners, and grudge themselves their usual hours of sleep. The Classical men are rather the busiest; they have a double burden to undergo, and a most critical achievement before them – to get up Mathematics enough to pass, without sacrificing the time necessary to keep up their Classics to the proper point – the minimum of knowledge in the one case, the maximum of acquisition in the other. Of those *rarae aves* who are aiming, and with a fair prospect, at success in both Triposes, one hardly knows what to think. The reported saying of a distinguished Judge, who had himself taken the highest Honors of his year, in reference to a young relative of his then reading double, 'that the standard of a Double First was getting to be something beyond human ability', seems hardly an exaggeration.[1] We must suppose such men to be so strong-minded and hard-headed that they make their Classical reading an amusement and relaxation after their Mathematical work. But the mere and single Mathematician has anything but a holiday; indeed, as all his interests are concentrated in the approaching examination, he is the most anxious about the immediate result. To one danger Mathematicians are more exposed than either Classical or Double men – disgust and satiety arising from exclusive devotion to their unattractive studies. A high Wrangler[2] once told me, just before the examination, that he felt like wishing he had never opened a Mathematical book, and that he never wanted to see the inside of one again, so sick did he feel of the whole business. This was only a temporary state of mind, for he resumed his books in a few months, and ultimately became Lecturer in his College. This, of itself, shows how fatiguing the final spirt must be, when it could thus disgust a man with what was his favorite pursuit and final profession.

Some previous remarks may have tended to give the impression that the standard of the Mathematical Tripos is *throughout* a low one. I hasten to disabuse the reader of any such misconception. The standard of the lower places is low, because the last class has become in a great measure a *pass* Class for the Classical men, and the lower half of the second Class has not quite escaped the same fate; but to be among the first twenty or twenty-five Wranglers a man must have read Mathematics *professionally*, besides possessing a good natural capacity for them; and to stand among the best eight or ten he must be *remarkably* clever at Mathematics, with considerable industry and a good memory into the bargain. As expressed by numbers, the disparity between the top and bottom of the scale is not so enormous, the Senior Wrangler having perhaps 3,000 or 3,500 marks to the Spoon's 200; but the actual disproportion in knowledge is much greater, because, from the shortness of the time allowed, the highest men, rapid as their pace is, seldom have time to do all they know. And now comes an important question. When we speak of a standard as *high* or low, we have necessarily before our minds some test of comparison, and

---

[1] Alderman (Alderson?). (B) [Edward Alderson, Trinity 1804, Senior Wrangler, 1st Smith's medal and 1st Chancellor's medal 1809.]
[2] Walker? (B)

the one most naturally presenting itself in the present case is the standard of Mathematical attainment in other institutions renowned for their Mathematical teaching. How, for instance, would the Cantabs compare with the pupils of the Polytechnic? It is rather a delicate query for any one to answer, but especially for a Non-Mathematical man, who can only form an opinion of his own through inquiries from others, and comparison of their answers. A Cambridge man, who was Sixth Wrangler, once said publicly (in the columns of the *Times*), that perhaps the first eight or ten men on the Tripos might be considered respectable Mathematicians in France, and all the others would be laughed at; but what data he had for this opinion, or what qualification for judging beyond the fact of having been a high Wrangler himself, I was never able to ascertain. Another, who also stood high in Mathematics, and was a Fellow of Trinity, who had lived some time in France, was acquainted with several French *savans*, and had witnessed examinations at several French schools, went so far on the other tack as to maintain that one of the first eight or ten Senior Optimes would be a high man at the Polytechnic. These are the extreme opinions, somewhere between which the truth probably lies. A gentleman of the highest Mathematical attainments,[3] who has had an extensive foreign scientific correspondence, and wrote in Continental scientific journals when a mere youth, assured me as the result of his experience abroad, that the standard was nearly equal in the two places; that a high Senior Optime would be a respectable man at the Polytechnic, and a high Wrangler a very good man; that the best man of the Polytechnic might be Senior Wrangler, and *vice versa*. The unmathematical reader may perhaps be disposed to accept this opinion as that of a man having some authority; the scientific one may form an idea of the Cambridge standard for himself in a very simple way. A set of Mathematical Tripos papers (those for the year 1845) will be found in the Appendix.[4] Let him study these, bearing in mind the limited time allotted to each paper, so limited that he can scarcely appreciate its shortness without the actual experiment of writing one or two of them out;[5] and then consider that it is an ordinary thing for a man among the first ten Wranglers to floor the bookwork of the first four days; that it is not unusual for a man among the first six to do as many as twelve problems on one paper; that the Senior Wrangler of

---

[3]   Thomson? (B)

[4]   [Here omitted; in Bristed's first edition, vol. 2 pp. 399–428.]

[5]   Many of the high men write out their bookwork from memory faster than an ordinary person could copy the formulae from a book placed before him.

that very year did *all* the bookwork except three questions, and more than forty problems out of sixty, clearing *nineteen* on one paper in three hours – and he will then have some little notion of the extent of preparation and competition.

It usually happens that the Senior Wrangler is a long way ahead of the year, the opposite of what is observable in the Classical Tripos, where there are generally two men closely balanced and nearly equal. Among the first dozen seldom more than two very decided gaps occur, and frequently after the Second Wrangler nine or ten lie together so closely that, in sporting phraseology, a blanket might cover them. As there is no provision in the printed lists for expressing the number of marks by which each man beats the one next below him, and there may be more difference between the twelfth and thirteenth than between the third and twelfth, it has been proposed to extend the use of the *brackets* (which are now only employed in cases of literal equality between two or three men), and put together six, eight, or ten, whose marks are *nearly* equal. But the *penchant* of the general system is for keeping every man's individuality of place as much as possible, and the proposed change has not met with encouragement.[6]

The usual number of Wranglers – whatever *Wrangler* may have meant once, it now implies merely a First Class man in Mathematics[7] – is thirty-seven or thirty-eight. Sometimes it falls to thirty-five, and occasionally rises above forty. Perhaps from twenty-five to thirty of these are men known to have fair Mathematical standing, and generally set down as probable Wranglers, or having a right to expect to be. The others are outsiders, whose reputation before the examination did not equal, or whose luck in the examination more than equals their desert. A few of the Small Colleges will give a fellowship for *any* place among the Wranglers, but most of them require the Questionist to be among the first fifteen or twenty. Different Colleges assign different limits, which sometimes vary according to the number of vacancies and the supply of good men, though if there be a dearth of high Degrees among the B.A.'s of any college for some years in succession, the Dons of it usually make up the deficiency by electing members of other Colleges to their Fellowships. About six Wranglers on

---

[6] It is very dangerous to begin it, unless it is proposed to change the system. (E)

[7] The Questionists used formerly to *keep acts*, deliver Latin disputations, &c., which entered as an element into the result of the examination. All this is now agreeably compromised by the payment of two shillings.

an average go out subsequently in Classics, and half of these are in the Third Class.[8]

The Second Class, or that of Senior Optimes, is larger in number, usually exceeding forty and sometimes reaching above sixty. This class contains a number of disappointments, many who expect to be Wranglers and some who are generally expected to be. It has a fair sprinkling of Classical men, either candidates for the Medals, or who have made sure of getting through and had something to spare. The Third Class or that of Junior Optimes, is usually about as numerous as the first, but its limits are more extensive, varying from twenty-five to sixty. A majority of the Classical men are in it; the rest of its contents are those who have broken down before the examination from ill-health or laziness, and choose the Junior Optime as an easier pass degree under their circumstances than the Poll, and those who break down in the examination; among these last may be sometimes found an expectant Wrangler. As the gulfed and plucked men do not appear on the lists, and there is no particular reason for their being talked about unless they happen to be Classical, it is not very easy to arrive at their number. I fancy from ten to fifteen men are gulfed every year and about the same number plucked. This will make the average number of candidates for Honors rather above than below one hundred and fifty.

The mention of gulfed and plucked men brings me back to myself. About six weeks before the examination, having gone over all my subjects and beginning to review them, I wrote out all I could in several old degree papers, with a view of ascertaining how many questions I could answer. The result of my inquiries led me to the conclusion that twenty-four full questions or their equivalent, would get me safe through, while twenty would just land me in the gulf; and the result of my practice was that I could do just about the latter number. So there I was on the verge, touch and go. I had already thrown aside my Classics entirely, and now applied myself to the much execrated Mathematics with new diligence, polishing up my longer subjects with great zeal. At this time a lucky inspiration led me to get up Spherical Trigonometry; it was only a few days' work, and I have reason to believe saved me.

About ten days before the examination, just as I was beginning to make a visible impression on my work, and absolutely expecting not merely to pass, but to pass *high* among the Junior Optimes – not that it made much difference if I did, except for some small bets on my place – there came upon

---

8   Not at Trinity (or St John's?). (B)

me a feeling of utter disgust and weariness, muddle-headedness, and want of mental elasticity. I fell to playing billiards and whist in very desperation, and gave myself up to what might happen. At the same time or a little earlier, one of our Scholars who stood a much better chance than myself, gave up from mere 'funk', and resolved to go out in the Poll.[9]

It was a sort of melancholy satisfaction to me that there was a mortality, so to speak, among the examiners this year. Two out of the four[10] were taken ill, one some weeks before the examination, the other only a few days. In place of the former was appointed my friend E—— not to his extreme satisfaction so far as I was concerned, for the idea of helping to pluck me was not at all agreeable to him; instead of the latter, whose illness took the authorities quite by surprise and obliged them to choose at the last moment whomever they could get, was put on my own private tutor. He had five men going out besides myself, and certainly would not have been chosen, only it happened that the examination papers were already in type, so that he had nothing to do with setting them and was only called on to examine. I had therefore the opportunity of saying in joke that to pass so desperate a case as myself the Dons were obliged to put on my most particular friend and my actual private tutor.

The first Tuesday in January chanced to be an unusually fine morning. Every Questionist who could find a four-legged animal mounted that day for a ride, as a luxury warranted and an exercise demanded by the occasion. There was not a beast to be found in the livery stables. I borrowed a friend's horse – the emergency of the case justifying the atrocity – and rode him till I could hardly keep myself on his back, or he himself on his legs. Next morning before the clock struck nine, I was among the nervous throng at the Senate House doors, and it had hardly ceased striking when I was writing out at full speed the first proposition that caught my eye on the paper. The particular time of the year when the examination is held gives rise to an occasional source of failure of a rather odd sort. The Senate House being a large, airy, stone-floored building, can be but imperfectly warmed if the weather be damp or severely cold. Thus a man with any tendency to imperfect circulation becomes chilled, especially in his hands, and with chilled hands, he is disabled to a considerable extent from writing. The first year I was at Cambridge, one of our best Trinity men,[11] afterwards a

---

9   Fussell. (B)

10   Two of them are called *Examiners* and two *Moderators*, but their duties are substantially the same.

11   Preston or Richardson. (T) Preston (1841). I have often heard Preston say this.

Fellow, lost fifteen or eighteen places among the Wranglers, as he believed, and as his previous and subsequent successes entitled him to believe, solely from being frozen up. Fortunately the present January was remarkably mild and pleasant throughout to the great comfort of us Questionists. The low questions being nearly all comprised in the first day's papers, that day usually decides the fate of the doubtful men. They have, however, a few remaining chances in the following days of this week; among others, two propositions from the Eleventh Book of Euclid, invariably set on Friday morning. Having achieved about twenty questions on Wednesday correctly, as I hoped, among them two in Spherical Trigonometry which are supposed to pay well, I began to feel tolerably confident. Next day I did nothing, but Friday morning I made sure of the two propositions in Euclid, and that afternoon actually hit off a Euclid deduction, which, as it stood at the head of a problem paper, might be dignified with the name of problem. Greatly elated with this exploit, I copied it out in the most elegant penmanship I could achieve, and wrote under the Q.E.F. about the only decent Greek Iambic I ever composed:

> *Pollen opheilo tou problematos charin.*[12]

The same day I met E—— walking, who gave me to understand that I was probably safe; the only possible danger was that they might draw the line high up, and sacrifice a large number. This is one way, and probably the only way in which an examiner may befriend an examinee. Any attempt to mark unfairly or change relative places would be detected and exposed at once,[13] but the dividing lines between the Classes are not rigidly fixed by a certain number of marks, some slight variation is allowed according

---

(B) [Theodore Preston, Trinity 1838, 25th Wrangler 1841, fellow of Trinity 1842, Lord Almoner's Professor of Arabic 1854–71; Thomas Richardson, Trinity 1837, 30th Wrangler 1841, fellow of Trinity 1843.]

[12] ['Much thanks do I owe to the problem.']

[13] Something of this kind occurred while I was in the University. A Classical examiner having marked two Candidates belonging to his own College much higher than the other three examiners did, was suspected of partiality to them, and *non-placeted* (rejected) next year when he came up for approval. [Bowring identifies the examiner as 'Hildyard': James Hildyard, Christ's 1829, 2nd Classic 1833, fellow of Christ's 1833–47. In 1842 Hildyard, an obstreperous member of Senate, had tried to have another examiner removed: M.E. Bury and J.D. Pickles, *Romilly's Cambridge Diary 1842–1847* (Cambridge, 1994), p. 30; see ibid., p. 114 for Hildyard's own barring in 1844.]

to the general standard of the year,[14] and here he may take his stand for including the greatest possible number. It happened once that two of the Mathematical examiners were particularly interested in two Classical men; one had a Trinity friend[15] who was pretty sure of a Chancellor's Medal if he could get a Senior Optime, the other a Caius friend[16] who was safe for a First if he could pass among the Junior Ops. The two desiderata played exactly into each other's hands, for the further the lower line of the Senior Optimes could be brought down, the more men must be let through to make the last class of the ordinary size, and the more men were let through altogether, the larger number of Senior Optimes might be decently made. Between them they passed about twenty men who would otherwise have been gulfed, if not plucked outright, increased the Senior Optimes to the same extent, and indirectly added thirty per cent. to the Classical Tripos of the year.[17]

E—— had been studying character in the Senate House, and watching the faces, expressions, and modes of work of different men. An examiner has ample opportunity for this, having little else to do. His chief business is to see that no one brings in books surreptitiously. Any attempt at copying the self-interest of the candidates is sufficient to prevent among the higher men. Sometimes, however, when a Classic struggling to get through, sits next to an acquaintance who is to be a Wrangler, I fancy the latter may write his papers in a larger hand than usual and lay them 'convenient', as the Irish say, to his friend in difficulty. The general result of the alphabetical arrangement, however, is to place you between two strange men of two strange Colleges. Even in the lucky junction above mentioned, a good deal of discretion is requisite in the copier. It would not do for him to 'realize' any high bookwork or difficult problems. Not unfrequently – perhaps once in two or three years – a clumsy attempt of the sort is made; the ready apprehension of the examiner detects it at once, and the unlucky culprit is

---

[14] This is the chief obstacle to calculating a man's place beforehand with accuracy. He or his tutor may know almost to a fraction the number of marks he is likely to get, but they cannot tell how all the other men of the year will do.

[15] Gooden. (B)

[16] Drury. (B) [Benjamin Drury, Caius 1836, fellow 1842–97.]

[17] 1840, I can hardly doubt. Gooden was last but two of the senior ops, of whom there were over seventy. Drury of Caius was last but three of the junior ops. This is a strong confirmation of Bristed's accuracy? (E) [Whitting confirms the identifications, and adds that the examiners were respectively A. Smith of Trinity and A. Thurtell of Caius. Each examiner, that is, belonged to the same college as his protégé.]

filled with confusion by being called on to explain his own papers – which, of course, being unable to do, he is plucked without mercy.[18]

Sometimes an examiner is asked to explain the meaning of a question; but such a demand, which conveys an indirect criticism on the perspicuity of expression of him who set the paper, is not common, nor has an examinee usually any time to waste in asking for explanations. So E——, having nothing better – indeed nothing at all to do during the two and a half or three hours a-day when he was in attendance, studied the men at work and their different ways of looking and writing. We had three men out of Trinity, each aiming to be first of the College, but one had over-read himself and looked pale and ill,[19] another was seated next a Small-Colleger[20] who wrote about as much and as fast as himself – he was likely to be made nervous to a detrimental extent by this proximity. These speculations were justified by the result; the third man,[21] who had not been first in any of the College Examinations, but was now in perfect order, healthy, and cool, beat his opponents by two and four places, respectively.[22] But E——'s great fascination was the head Johnian. The best man from John's is a candidate for Senior Wrangler[23] pretty much as a matter of course, that College having a patent as it were for turning out Senior Wranglers, just as Trinity has for Senior Classics. This present year, however, one of the Small College men[24] was a real Mathematical genius, one of those men who, like E—— himself, are said to be 'born for Senior Wranglers',[25] while the Johnians were believed

---

[18] There was one in our year (1844) by a man Hislop who sat next to the SW Hemming. (B) [Hislop, as one might expect, cannot be traced.]

[19] Grant? Sargant? (W); Grant, Sargeant (B). [Alexander Grant, Trinity 1839, 7th Wrangler 1845, fellow of Trinity 1847; Henry Sargant, Trinity 1841, 9th Wrangler 1845.]

[20] Scratchley, Queens'. (W, B) [Arthur Scratchley, Peterhouse 1841, migrated to Queens' 1842, 10th Wrangler 1845, fellow of Queens' 1845–9.]

[21] Blackburn. (W, B) [Hugh Blackburn, Trinity 1841, 5th Wrangler 1845, fellow of Trinity 1846.]

[22] One full question in *high* bookwork will often give a man two or three places among the Wranglers.

[23] Parkinson. (W) [Stephen Parkinson, St John's 1841, Senior Wrangler 1845; fellow of St John's 1845–71.]

[24] Thomson (E, B); Lord Kelvin! (T) [William Thomson, Peterhouse 1841, 2nd Wrangler 1845; Professor of Natural Philosophy at Glasgow, 1846–99, President of the Royal Society 1890–5. Famous for his work on the Atlantic submarine cables and for degrees Kelvin.]

[25] Parkinson. (B)

to be short of good men and owned it themselves. But now their best man suddenly came up with a rush like a dark horse, and having been spoken of before the Examination only as likely to be among the first six, now appeared as a candidate for the highest honors. E—— was one of the first that had a suspicion of this, from noticing on the second day that he wrote with the regularity and velocity of a machine, and seemed to clear everything before him. And on examining the work he could scarcely believe that the man could have covered so much paper with ink in the time (to say nothing of the accuracy of the performance), even though he had seen it written out under his own eyes. By-and-by it was reported that the Johnian had done an inordinate amount of problems, and then his fellow-collegians began to bet odds on him for Senior Wrangler. But the general wish as well as belief was for the Peterhouse man,[26] who, besides the respect due to his celebrated scientific attainments (he was known to the French Mathematicians by his writings while an Undergraduate), had many friends among both reading and boating men, and was very popular in the University. His backers were not disposed to give him up. 'One problem of his will be worth half a dozen of the other man's', said they; and there were grounds for this assertion, some of the problems being more difficult, and therefore marked higher than others, so that four on a paper may pay more than ten.

Saturday afternoon finishes the work for the majority of the candidates. The papers set on the Monday and Tuesday of the week following contain only about one low question a-piece, to amuse the mass of the Questionists during the half-hour before the expiration of which they are not allowed to leave the Senate House. At the end of this half-hour a general rush is made, and five sixths of the men take their departure. The last two days, in fact, serve chiefly to determine and arrange the places of the first twelve or fifteen men. To a low Wrangler, not to say a Senior Optime, they make no material difference. On Wednesday morning the coaches used to be crowded (it is the rail now) with Questionists going down, home, or elsewhere to amuse themselves and divert their anxiety, as they best can during the nine days that intervene. A few of the Classics fall to work immediately, even during the last two days of the examination.

I went down to London – the Cockney talks of his Metropolis as the place to which all the world comes up; the University man, with equal arrogance, makes his headquarters the highest part of the earth, and goes *down* everywhither from it – taking a Theocritus in my pocket; dined about

---

[26]   Thomson. (B)

with friends and went to see *Antigone*, which was just then one of the lions, and received with a furore that showed how extensively Classical tastes are diffused among the educated classes in England.[27] One interesting effect of the acting on a modern stage of this ancient play was, that it brought out the points, and showed how far Sophocles wrote for the galleries *ut ita dicam*. One line which drew down the house,

> That is no State where only one man rules,

afforded a ludicrously melancholy example of popular inconsistency. The very people who cheered this sentiment had, the but a few weeks before, been 'hooraying for His Majesty Emperor of all the Rooshas.'[28]

Before the Mathematical list came out, I was back at Trinity, and trying to put my Classics in order; the only thing I had then to attend to

---

[27] [Mendelssohn's version, performed at Covent Garden in January and February 1845.]

[28] I may be pardoned for introducing here a little anecdote connected with this potentate's visit to London, which, though not particularly relevant to anything in the present book or chapter, strikingly illustrates the dumminess of a certain class of the English population. A fashionable snip, who had authority for calling himself 'breeches-maker to H.R.H. Prince Albert', had an order to prepare some finery for the Emperor. A Polish officer, the ruin of whose country had not so far involved his own as to deprive him of the ability to sport a good coat sometimes, was having his measure taken at this aristocratic establishment, when the glitter of a sumptuous, gold-embroidered pair of unmentionables caught his eye, and he inquired for whom the gorgeous garment was intended. The shopman, in a tone of awe befitting the subject, informed his customer of their exalted destination. 'For the Emperor, eh!' said the Pole, bottling up his patriotic indignation as he best could, 'well, I hope they will suit him'. Having said which in an accent of extra sarcasm, he stalked haughtily away. Unfortunately, the gallant exile's imperfect pronunciation, or the excited imagination of the shopman, had erroneously provided the prominent verb of the sentence with an initial aspirate, and the terrified underling hastened to his master, declaring that the officer had just left the shop with fell intent to shoot the Emperor! As soon as the astounded master-tailor recovered the use of his faculties and legs, he ran off to the police, and the police ran off after the conspirator, whom they speedily brought before the nearest magistrate, and with him 'a couple of daggers'; which, as proofs of his wickedness and part of his apparatus for shooting the Emperor, they had taken into custody also. After the worthy magistrate had been sufficiently horrified at these implements of artillery, they turned out to be *ornamental paper-knives*, such as are common enough in ladies' writing-desks. The Pole had no difficulty in making a satisfactory explanation, and the tailors and policemen were heartily laughed at – and served them right; don't you think so, reader mine?

was Composition, in which, except Latin prose, I had never been good, and was now terribly rusty. My Pembroke friend (now promoted to the Tutorship of another College)[29] was absent on business, to the great disgust of his five pupils, of none more than myself, for I had relied very much on his assistance. We fled in different directions; I took refuge with one of my former coaches, the majestic 'Jupiter'. About the result of the Degree Examination I felt no disquietude, having pretty well made up my mind that I was to get through, and *where* I was made little difference – the Wooden Spoon would answer as well as anywhere else. Indeed, I gave out that it was the place I had read for, and some hints let drop gave me reason to suspect that the examiners would assign me that distinguished situation if they could find a reasonable excuse for so doing. E—— had, indeed, a theory of his own 'that no clever man could be plucked, if he gave himself any trouble not to be', which he applied to myself in a flattering enthymem, 'You need not be afraid, for' &c; while, on the other hand, I was conscious of not having done too much, nor all that little too correctly. On the whole, there seemed a probability of my being selected to represent the minimum amount of knowledge, even leaving out of consideration that the examiners prefer, *ceteris paribus*, to put a Classical man into the forlorn hope, as he may make a joke of it, while a 'single man' coming out at the end is only made a joke of himself.

At nine on Friday morning, just sixteen days from the hour when the examination began – an interval which will not appear too long when it is remembered that nearly one hundred and fifty men have to be placed in individual order of merit – the list, signed by the examiners, is posted up outside the Senate House. The friends of the candidates, gownsmen and gyps commingled, throng about it, the result spreads in all directions, and in a very short time the booksellers have it fairly printed in two or three forms, among others on sheets of letter paper ready prepared for mailing. I was quietly seated at breakfast, when my gyp entered to announce that I stood 112th, and also that the Johnian was Senior Wrangler.[30] Soon after, the same friend who had reported the result of the Scholarship to me came in and stated, with some *naiveté*, that he had begun to look from the end of the list up, knowing he would come to my name sooner in that way, and that he had arrived at me *very soon*. After which, he proceeded roundly to anathematize the Johnians, who had completely stolen a march on the rest of the University, and were not satisfied with their unexpected gain

---

[29] Trinity Hall. (W)
[30] Parkinson. (T)

of the first honor. 'Some Johnian, invented on purpose',[31] was third, to
the extreme discomfiture of another high Small-Colleger and of our best
three Mathematicians, the highest of whom stood only fifth,[32] with a third
Johnian just below him. When I obtained possession of a list, about mid-
day, I found there was only one man between me and the Spoon. It is not
every Questionist that hits so near his place. There were fourteen plucked
and fifteen in the gulf, so that of 143 candidates 31 did less than myself,
that is, less than the equivalent of twenty-four questions. There were but
five Classical men victimized, two of them probable First Classes.[33]

A new Tripos list affords a man well up in *Calendar* and College
gossip a good half-hour's amusement in studying the lucky bits and the
disappointments, the outsiders who have come up, and the men who
have been sold. Many of the last suffer either from wilful idleness, or
egregious over-estimation of their own attainment – fostered perhaps by
want of judgment and perception in their tutors. Only two places above
me was a Small-Colleger who had been confident of a high rank among
the Senior Optimes; he was so upset by the disappointment that he dared
not communicate the result to his father or show his face at home. Several
supposed Wranglers had tumbled down to Senior Optimes, and some whose
hopes and expectations did not rise above high Senior Optimes found
themselves elevated into Wranglers. More than one Questionist saw, to his
disgust, another man who had sat next him in the examination and covered
much less paper come out twenty places over his head. The very worst man
in a Cambridge examiner's eyes is he who does a great deal, but much of
it wrong, and much of it inaccurately. Probably fifty questions and eight
average problems,[34] so done as to get full marks, will bring a Questionist

---

[31]   Peirson. (T) [Robert Peirson, St John's 1841, 3rd Wrangler 1845, fellow of St
John's 1849–55.]
[32]   Blackburne (not Colin, who was 8th in 1835). This is about the 1845 tripos.
(T) [Hugh Blackburn.]
[33]   Poor devils! (T)
[34]   The proportion of problems to bookwork done by the candidates is very various.
The latter shows more reading, the former evince more natural Mathematical ability.
It is by them that an outsider, who has not read high, frequently gets a good place;
his bookwork, for instance, might only be good enough to make him thirtieth
Wrangler, but he does twenty good problems, and so climbs up among the first ten.
On the other hand, it sometimes happens that the third or fourth Wrangler does
no more than five problems on all the three problem papers – in fact, is beaten in
problems by some Senior Optimes – but such a man will floor the bookwork of the
first four days, and do a fair proportion of that set on the last two.

comfortably among the Wranglers, but a great many who think they have done more than this find themselves low Senior Ops, or even worse.

The unexpected award of the Senior Wranglership was the great surprise of the year, and subject of conversation, for some time. It was said that the successful candidate had practised writing out against time for six months together, merely to gain pace, and had exercised himself in problems till they became a species of bookwork to him, and thus he attained the prodigious rapidity in solving them which enabled him to do nineteen on one paper of three hours, thirteen on another, and nearly as many on the third – more than two thirds of the whole number set. The Peterhouse man, who, relying on his combined learning and talent, had never practised particularly with a view to speed, and perhaps had too much respect for his work to be in any very great hurry about it, solved eight or nine problems leisurely on each paper, some of them probably better ones than the other man's, but not enough so to make up the difference in quantity. Both men floored all the early bookwork, the Johnian presumably getting full marks, and T——[35] perhaps some extra marks for style.[36] In the high work of the last two days the Peterhouse man beat his opponent, but he could not have been very far ahead, as the Johnian did all but three questions out of the four papers, and came out on the result of the whole examination three hundred marks in advance.

The disappointed candidate, however, was not without a chance of partially retrieving himself the very next week in the examination for the Smith's Prizes, which is considered by the knowing ones a better test of excellence than the Tripos, as it embraces a higher class of subjects, and the element of speed does not enter into it to such an extent. T——'s friends, as well as himself, awaited the result with a mixture of hope and fear. In the end he had it all his own way, and beat the Senior Wrangler in the proportion of three to two. But this was a subsequent consolation; for the present the triumph rested with the Johnians.

---

[35] T—— is Thompson, Peterhouse, <u>much</u> the greater man. (T) [William Thomson.]

[36] It is possible to *beat a paper* or get *more than full marks* for it. This apparent Hibernicism is thus explained: – The ordinary textbooks (Earnshaw, Griffen, Wood, &c.) are taken as the standard of excellence, and a very good man will sometimes express the operations more neatly and cleverly than they are worded in these books, in which case he is entitled to extra marks for style. This was the case with E—— in his Senate House examination. One of the examiners gave him extra marks for all his bookwork.

20

How I Came To
Take a Degree [1845]

Reading the List of Names of those who have passed.

When I put on my Bachelor's gown next day in the Senate House, it was with a feeling of some satisfaction at having mastered a formidable difficulty, and the little margin I had to spare rather enhanced this satisfaction. Looking upon the Mathematical examination as Classical men often do, in the light of a fight with the examiners, I had gained the day. Moreover, I felt entitled to say that, low as the standard of a Junior Optime is compared with the *professional* acquirements of the upper men, I had gained a knowledge, though indeed but a temporary one, of a considerable amount of low Mathematics, more than the majority of our students ever grasp at one time, more than when at Yale I should have considered myself or been considered capable of; for to cram up certain pages of a subject and recite them from day to day, is a very different thing from being able to write out any question at random in the subject. And I repeat it, that for an unmathematical man it is not an easy thing to become even a Junior Optime, and as it demands a fair acquaintance with the low subjects, so it requires a considerable expenditure of time and trouble. I was then rather proud of my Bachelor's degree; and yet there were circumstances connected with it that ought to have made me rather ashamed of myself.

That certain political and religious oaths are among the conditions of some of the English academical degrees is generally known to the American reader; the particulars are not so well understood. We are all aware that at Oxford the Thirty-nine Articles must be signed in advance. Hook's irreverent joke has taught us that.[1] At Cambridge it is different. When the Freshman puts down his name on the College books he is not required to sign anything. During his first term he matriculates, and then affirms (*profitetur*) that he will keep the statutes and maintain the privileges of the University to the best of his ability,[2] which does not mean much, a great portion of the statutes, both College and University, being notoriously in point of fact and practice obsolete, and never thought of except when some theological squabble or ultra martinetism on the part of a new Don brings them into notice. A Trinity Scholar on being elected swears that he will take the Bible for his rule of faith, and that he believes the royal authority to be supreme, *and by no means subject to the jurisdiction of foreign bishops* (externorum Episcoporum jurisdictioni minime subjectam), a hit at the Pope, which I imagine any good Protestant, republican or not, would rather go out of the way to swear than otherwise. But on taking his B.A., the Questionist must sign a declaration that he is a *bona fide* member of the Church of England, and also take the oaths of allegiance and supremacy.

Before taking the degree, it will be observed, not before going in to the examination for Honors. The effect of this is, that though a Dissenter or a foreigner cannot take a degree, he may be Senior Wrangler or Senior Classic, for the admission to the Classical Tripos depends not upon having taken the B.A. degree, but upon having passed the examination for that degree; indeed he may take all the University Honors except the Smith's Prize and Chancellor's Medal, the institution of which prizes is so worded as to make only Bachelors eligible for them, and a theological prize or two of no great repute. But as the Fellowships are given to none but Bachelors, he is ineligible to them. This is not merely a possible case, but has actually

---

[1] [Theodore Hook matriculated from St Mary's Hall, Oxford. Asked by the Vice-Chancellor if he was prepared to sign the Thirty-Nine Articles, Hook replied, 'Yes, forty if you like'.]

[2] Here is the Professio faithfully copied, no punctuation and all from the printed form. 'Cancellario procancellarioque academiae Cantabrigiensis quatenus jus fasque est et pro ordine in quo fuerim quamdiu in hac republica degam comiter obtemperabo leges statuta mores approbatos et privilegia Cantabrigiensis academiae quantum in me est observabo pietatis et bonarum literarum progressum et huius academiae statum honorem et dignitatem tuebor quoad vivam meoque suffragio atque consilio rogatus et non rogatus defendam. Haec omnia in me recipio et polliceor me fideliter esse praestiturum.'

occurred; a Jew was Second Wrangler in 1837, and a Quaker Fourth the year before.[3]

The origin and reason of this restriction are evident. It was at first intended as a safeguard against the Romanists, and afterwards kept up to prevent them and Dissenters generally from obtaining *a share in the government of the University*. For as the University is governed by those Graduates who choose to retain their names on the boards, giving degrees to Dissenters would be putting a portion of the University's destiny into the hands of men who might be hostile, and at best are not necessarily friendly to the religion which the University professes and is bound to uphold. It appears to me that this restriction has been subjected to much unmerited abuse, and that it is not antediluvian or bigoted, but simply self-defensive. If the connexion between Church and State were dissolved, and the Established Church abolished, this restriction would of course be swept away, and many other things with it; but so long as the Established Church exists I do not see how the Church Universities can admit Papists or Dissenters into their Senates.

In regard to foreigners belonging to the same church the restriction is less necessary and defensible, but it must be remembered that such cases are of very limited occurrence, and that the institutions of England are not in general encouraging to foreigners; everything, from a University to a hotel, is solely calculated for the wants and benefit of the natives. Selfish and barbarous as such ideas must seem to the disciples of universal philanthropy and fraternity, a reflecting *native-born* American, in view of the effects which an indiscriminate reception of foreigners, so as to place them almost immediately on a level with the original inhabitants, wrought in his own country, may perhaps suspect that the prudence of the English practice goes a great way towards making up for its unloveliness.

It may indeed be urged that the University and College regulations might be so altered that a degree should not necessarily confer a vote, and that, as in the case of Fellowships, the presumed original idea and intention that the Fellows should be in Holy Orders, has been so far departed from that in some Colleges the Fellows need not take Orders at all, in others not for

---

3   [James Joseph Sylvester, St John's 1831, 2nd Wrangler 1837; Professor of Natural Philosophy, University College London, 1837–41; Professor of Mathematics at Johns Hopkins University 1877–83; Savilian Professor of Geometry at Oxford 1883–97. He took his Cambridge degree in 1872, after the repeal of the Test Acts. William Aldam entered Trinity in 1832 but did not matriculate; 4th Wrangler 1836; MP for Leeds 1841–7, High Sheriff of Yorkshire 1878.]

seven years, while there are actually *Bye Fellowships* which give their holders the dignity of the title without a voice in the College government, some rules might easily be generalized to apply to the parties under consideration. To this it may be answered that whatever real and desirable distinction the University confers consists not in the degree itself, but in the place occupied on the examination list, since the M.A. degree can be obtained by any one who has taken a B.A. on paying a certain sum and performing some trifling ceremonies, and the ordinary B.A. implies only an amount of knowledge of which, if it be harsh to call it contemptible, it may at least be said that it is nothing for any person to be proud of; and that such half measures as giving degrees which should not confer the full customary privileges, or Bye-Fellowships with their nominal salaries and inferior position, would not be accepted as completely satisfactory, and would only encourage renewed demands for a more thorough change.

Originally intending to leave the University as soon as the Classical Tripos list was out, my only anxiety about the question of a degree had been whether the want of one would prevent me from going out in Classics, and having once ascertained that it would not, I had taken no further thought about the matter. But this autumn my views underwent an important change. I wanted to keep my scholarship, and thought what a nice little head-quarters my Trinity rooms would be while making excursions upon the Continent. Sometimes I had hopes that my place in Classics would justify my reading for a Fellowship. The Enemy always knows where to have a man, and is fertile in sophistic and Jesuitical snares to delude moral men. At first I had serious intentions of taking the oaths without scruple or pause. I was in an awful state of disgust with matters at home on account of the recent Presidential election. The consternation and despair into which a large portion of the Whig-party were thrown by the defeat of Henry Clay[4] will not readily be forgotten by any one who was old enough at the time to take an interest in public matters, which in our country does not imply a very advanced age. But the terrible prostration of heart with which it affected a certain class in the Northern states, and particularly in New York, has not been generally appreciated out of that class, nor am I aware that it ever found distinct public expression; perhaps the nearest approach to such expression was contained in the concluding numbers of the most elegant, gentlemanly, and every way respectable journal that our

---

[4] [Clay had failed in two previous attempts at the presidency, in 1824 and 1832; this was his final attempt.]

city ever boasted, which expired in pure disgust and despair, as it were, a few months after Polk's election.[5]

I was one of those who, in popular phrase, swore by Henry Clay, and the blow fell on me with peculiar force for two reasons. First, being a non-resident, I had not an opportunity of observing those sudden premonitions of calamity which did something towards preparing those at home for the shock; secondly, I had been in the habit of making Henry Clay's election the universal answer to all objections against America. 'We were unfortunate. Harrison died, and the other man betrayed us. Consequently, there has been a great temporary demoralization. Only wait till Clay is President, and you'll see how gloriously we shall get on.' When, therefore, the much desired steamer brought defeat instead of victory, when the test which I had myself selected turned out against me, the exultation of my anti-Republican acquaintances was undisguised, and my dejection utter and unmitigated. I had not a word to throw to a Puseyite.

Already in an unfavorable mood of mind, I was not likely to have my spirits raised by such epistolary intelligence as I received from home. Cicero's letters at the worst time of the Caesarean and Pompeian troubles could hardly present a more melancholy and disheartening picture. The feeling of our New York Whigs was very different from what it would have been in the event of Martin Van Buren's re-election.[6] That would have been Paradise in comparison. By the elevation of Polk they saw themselves given up to the mercy of Irish aliens and rampant slaveholders. War with England and the indefinite extension of slavery, were all but inevitable. They put no longer trust in anything, not even in their leaders. Nor did Whigs only feel inclined to despond. There were many Democrats who thought the casting-off of Mr. Van Buren by his party a foul wrong, as they afterwards testified at the ballot-box, and who at the same time saw in the anti-rent agitation – an agitation encouraged by professed members of the Whig party – a local evil more dangerous than any federal one. In short, a large proportion of the wealthiest, best educated, and most estimable men in our State seemed verily to have despaired of the Republic. And what gave an apparent confirmation to their doleful views was the absence, except in a very few cases, of any immediate personal calamity or wrong to induce a

---

[5]   [James Polk, 11th president of the USA, 1845–9. Bristed is probably referring to the *New-York American*, founded in 1819, whose final issue appeared in February 1845, three months after Polk's election.]

[6]   [Van Buren was 8th president of the USA, 1836–40, but failed of re-election in 1840; he was unsuccessful again in 1848.]

prejudice of grief. I was seized with the infection, and dreaded little less than proscriptions and *novae tabulae.*

Could the croakers of that time have looked forward six years, and seen the political sky cleared of almost every cloud that then overhung it – our credit restored abroad, our influence and name respected, a Northern Whig President[7] in power, Daniel Webster at the head of the Cabinet, in their own state a gentleman like Hamilton Fish[8] fulfilling successively the gubernatorial chair and a seat in the Federal Senate – could they have foreseen these things, their fears might well have appeared childish and unfounded. Yet were these fears not altogether groundless and chimerical. The dangers they dreaded really existed; their error was not putting sufficient faith in the counteracting Providence of God. We were truly threatened with the indefinite extension of slavery and preponderance of the slave power. The romantic discovery which placed California on the side of freedom, making that state at once a barrier and an antagonist force, could not have been anticipated by any calculation; and we may hope that some equally effective interposition of the Divine arm, to crush the intrigues of Romanism, will ere long manifest itself. The desponding ought to have trusted that God would not forsake a land containing so many Christian men, and so much true religion and philanthropy; that our country, raised up for great political and religious ends, would not be lightly forsaken by the Supreme Being.

But that winter was a time of darkness at home and abroad. We had a lamentable foreign reputation, especially among those who had been our warmest friends. The two great parties in England had undergone a singular change of feelings toward us. The Liberals talked and acted as a man might to an ungrateful friend or *protégé* who had turned out badly. The more an Englishman had leaned towards Radicalism, the prouder he had been of any instances of good government and prosperity in the United States, as they tended to promote his principles at home, and the more bitter was his disappointment when the conduct of some parts of our Union furnished the Conservatives with an argument against our institutions. *The most bitter things that were said against America at this time proceeded, with scarce an exception, from English Liberals.* The Tories and Conservatives, on the contrary, as if grateful

---

[7]   General Taylor. (T) [General Zachary Taylor, elected 12th president of the USA in 1849, died in office the following year after eating cherries and milk on the Fourth of July.]

[8]   [Fish was governor of New York 1848–50 and later a US senator, serving as Secretary of State under Ulysses S. Grant.]

to our Republic for having unwittingly furnished them with weapons against Democracy, were far more inclined than formerly to be just and generous to the individual citizens of it, especially when such individuals belonged to the minority party, for then they regarded them as a sort of victims, and too good for their country.

At the same time it is true now, and it was true even then, that Englishmen, whatever their political opinions among themselves, or their expressed opinions with us, are always flattered when an American sides with them. They are really jealous, though they would not own it even to themselves, of our preference for the French; and with all their suspicion of foreigners, the greatest compliment an American can pay them is to take up his residence in their country, or say anything that induces a suspicion of his having such an intention.[9] And it now happened that many of those about me, seeing how disgusted I was with the real or supposed state of things at home and our unlucky reputation a-broad, did their best to persuade me to take a degree, which they looked upon as a sort of earnest that I would continue among them. They were not indeed my best and most intimate friends, or the men of most ability among my acquaintances; from some of these I received different and better counsel. 'Why should you be so downcast about an election?' asked one; 'I am sure I wouldn't annoy myself if O'Connell were premier to-morrow.' And the same or another man, after a long discussion of the matter with me, expressed his conviction that, upon my own showing, there could never be any serious encroachment on the rights of property in a country which had so many small proprietors. And although these conclusions were a little too philosophical, and not altogether borne out in practice, the Papal Aggression excitement being a sufficient refutation of the first, and the Anti-rent iniquities of the second, still they were far nearer the truth and more worthy of serious consideration than the arguments by which I was assailed on the other side. But the strongest of these arguments were supplied by my own pique and disgust. 'What's the use of standing on such a punctilio?' said I to myself. 'Your countrymen, in disavowing the Native American party, have repudiated their own nationality, and put the foreign settlers over their own heads. The boast of

---

[9]   When Mr. Everett was replaced ['I.e. displaced': B.] at the Court of St. James, a report was circulated that he intended to remain in England as a private gentleman. This report I heard from several quarters, and was frequently questioned about it. It is hardly necessary to say that nothing had been said or done by our Minister or his friends to give foundation or countenance to such a rumor; it arose entirely from the desire of the English to retain him there.

the Irish in New York, that they controlled the Presidential election, has been verified. Protestantism is at a discount. After all, a man's religion is dearer to him than his country. Better be Queen Victoria's subject than John Hughes's slave.[10] Our people declared that their franchise was not worth having when they thus sent it a-beggaring. Nor ought I to entertain any sentimental scruples about professing a temporary allegiance to a country which I may be ultimately compelled to make my abode.' Still I could not bring myself to take the oaths. Then the tempter hinted a most Jesuitical medium, a way to avoid all practical difficulty, though, like most similar compromises, it would probably have united all difficulties, if any practical ones had existed, or had there been any other than a moral objection in the way. It was this. The oaths at Cambridge had come to be such mere formulae that people cared very little about them, and hardly knew what they swore. In the Senate House, after the Senior Wrangler has presented himself alone, the rest of the men are sworn in batches of a dozen each, the oath, or part of it, being read to them, and a Testament handed round to be kissed. I might go up with the rest and pass the book by, which there was every opportunity of doing without detection, so that I could thus get the degree without taking the oath of allegiance at all. This I finally did, and in one sense the experiment was perfectly successful; no one of those in authority ever noticed my evasion, either at the time or afterwards. But it did not escape observation in all quarters, and a great deal of the moral influence which I had heretofore possessed was lost at once.

Many persons will think me foolish for relating a circumstance so much to my own disadvantage; but reflection has convinced me that where the recital of a young man's errors contains nothing in itself mischievous, it is part of his duty and expiation to relate them as a warning to others. Besides the obvious moral of never giving up the ship, there is another to be drawn from my misadventure.

Let every young man beware how he violates his integrity or deviates from a straightforward, honest course in the smallest matter. The temporal consequences may not be injurious, nay, may even for the time being bring the convenience or advantage expected. But the consciousness of aberration from the path of honesty will continually oppress him; he will have lost irretrievably the pride of rectitude – a pride which is honorable and righteous, and has nothing reprehensible in it. My conduct on that occasion has been a continually recurring source of mortification to me, which the

---

[10]   [John Hughes, first Catholic Archbishop of New York 1850–64.]

lapse of years cannot obliterate, and the recollection of it has frequently interposed to check me in plans of improvement for myself and others.[11]

---

[11]   [In his third edition, Bristed adds, 'Two or three years ago, the whole machinery for conferring BA degrees was brought to a stand by a Jew's coming out first in the maths tripos. As the Senior Wrangler has to take his degree *alone* and *before all the others*, he is an essential and indispensable part of the programme. It was necessary to pass a special 'grace' or note of the senate, in order that Mr H—— might take his degree *without* the oaths'. As Whitting notes, this is Numa Hartog (Trinity 1865), Senior Wrangler 1869. The Test Acts prevented him from obtaining a college fellowship, and the publicity about his case contributed to their repeal in 1871.]

21

The Polloi and the Civil Law Classes

Nos numeri sumus.

Horace.

During the week of interval between the examination for Mathematical Honors and the publication of the Honor list, takes place the examination of candidates for an ordinary degree, popularly called the *polloi*, and by abbreviation, the Poll men. Their number is greater than that of the candidates for Honors in the proportion of four to three, but as the range of subjects is more limited, the papers shorter, and the examiners more numerous, the classification of the men goes on nearly *pari passu* with their examination, and the list is issued on the same day as that of the candidates for Honors. There are on an average about two hundred Poll men, and it is a most striking instance of the minute subdivision in vogue at Cambridge examinations, and the introduction of competition wherever possible, that *every one* of these two hundred men is arranged in order of merit according to his marks, except some fifteen or twenty who have just succeeded in passing, and who are bracketed together at the end, and familiarly known as the 'Elegant Extracts'.[1] The head man is called Captain of the Poll, which

---

[1] I write of this arrangement as one actually existing, though in strict correctness I should use the past tense when speaking of it. For the alterations which have been

is deemed among the non-reading men almost as great an honor as Senior Wrangler or Senior Classic among the reading ones.

As an impression appears to prevail in some literary quarters of our country that the great bulk of English University students study and know very little, and the hard-reading men are very few in number, it may be worth while to look once more at the facts and figures of the case. The proportion of Honors men to Poll men is, as has been already remarked, in round numbers, one hundred and fifty to two hundred, or three to four, that is, three sevenths of the whole. Now, though most of the Junior and some of the Senior Optimes have not worked hard at *Mathematics* throughout their whole Undergraduate course, we have to take out of these the Classical men, who have been busily employed in their pet pursuit. Still, after allowing for these, there may remain some thirty idle men on the Honor list, and against these we must put about the same number of reading men among the *polloi*. For insufficient preparation of some Poll men, particularly those who are *opsimatheis*, and have taken up the Church late in life, gives them enough to do in preparing for their Little Go and Degree examinations, after the time occupied by the College examinations is deducted. There are also many men every year contending for the Captaincy of the Poll, some for the honor, such as it is, others because it will help them to get Poll pupils afterwards. The first thirty men, or so, in the Poll, have their subjects polished up with great care, and may be called all but perfect in them. (I had personal assurance of this from a friend who was one of the Poll examiners.) We have, therefore, *three sevenths* of the Undergraduates faithful students, while about one man in nine (that is to say, all the First Class of the Tripos, and nearly all the Wranglers) is a *very hard* student. I imagine there are not many Universities or Colleges in the world of which more could be said with truth.

The fixed subjects for the Poll examination are the Acts with all the History, Geography, Antiquities, and 'cram' generally pertaining thereto; Paley's Moral Philosophy, three Books of Euclid, Arithmetic and low Algebra, and certain portions of Mechanics and Hydrostatics. The movable subjects are a Greek and a Latin author as in the Little-Go. These are declared two years in advance, so that there is plenty of time to polish them up.

Besides the degree in Honors and the ordinary degree, there is but one

---

made in the Poll, see the chapter [27] on 'Recent Changes at Cambridge'. ['Elegant extracts' is taken from Vicesimus Knox's book of that title (1784, often reprinted), a collection of English pieces for reading and reciting.]

other way of obtaining a B.A. It is in *Civil Law*. Not more than a dozen or fifteen men – sometimes not so many – avail themselves of this outlet, which is generally considered something even below the Poll – unjustly I suspect, for the candidates must at least have attended the Professor's Lectures for three consecutive terms, to say nothing of what is required in the examination. The lectures generally follow the order of subjects in Halifax's *Analysis of the Roman Civil Law*. The principal text books in my time were these:–

Corpus juris Civilis. Harris's *Justiniani Institutiones*. Taylor's *Elements of the Civil Law*. Heineccei *Antiq. Rom. Syntagma*. – *Elementa Juris Civilis*. Vinnii *Comment. in quatuor Libros Institutionum*. Burn's *Ecclesiastical Law*. Blackstone's *Commentaries*.

22

The Classical Tripos [1845]

A Clasical Tripos.

Cave ne titubes.

HORACE.

Mind your eye!

H. Walker, Esq.

The time now drew nigh when the few picked men, who had resisted the temptations of idleness and escaped the perils of Mathematics, were to fight out their last great battle. Trinity Scholars, University Prize men, outsiders from Small Colleges, double men (these the fewest of all) mustered from all quarters. We made a very small show numerically, only twenty-six candidates out of the whole year, which might be set down in round numbers at three hundred and fifty men. At least five who had intended to augment our number were killed off in the Mathematical Tripos. *Nineteen* of us were reading for the First Class, so that there was a pretty extensive prospect of sells.[1] Out of the twenty-six sixteen were Junior Optimes, so that allowing a few to be trying their luck in Classics only for the chance of piecing out an inferior Mathematical degree, it was pretty clear that full half of the candidates had read Mathematics for no other purpose than to enable them to display their knowledge in the Classical Tripos. Of the

---

[1] [Disappointments.]

remainder, five were Wranglers, four of these Double men, and the fifth a favorite for the Wedge.[2] Two men who had been rivals all the way through school and through College were racing for Senior Classic.[3] After these two more were known and spoken of as nearly equal, and then 'it was any one's place'. The First Class was likely to be small, the year not being a good one on the whole; what little strength it had was in Trinity; our College supplied fifteen of the twenty-six candidates, thirteen of them reading for the First Class, and only four sure of it.

So said ordinary gossip; for all these probabilities, the merits of the year at large and of the different men in it, are eagerly discussed and canvassed beforehand, not only by the parties interested and their immediate friends, but by reading men generally. Still, however the candidate's chances may be made to fluctuate by such relative circumstances, his own positive fund of knowledge and readiness in expressing it must be his main reliance, and accordingly he now works with a will if he ever did in his life.

Any one whom business or pleasure has led to drive habitually a fast trotter on the road can testify to the continual care and practice necessary to keep the animal in proper condition; how he must be a good horse in the first place, and then regularly worked, must be fast and enduring, and not nervous or easily frightened in a crowd, and ready to go his best at any moment. I really cannot conceive any better comparison for the training to which the Cantab with an examination in view subjects himself – especially when that examination is the Classical Tripos, which covers more ground than any other.[4] I might carry out the analogy, and say that in both cases much depends on the skill of the driver. Many a man has owed several places, perhaps the difference of a class, to the skill of his coach.

Three things are requisite in the Tripos: first, an accurate knowledge of Greek and Latin Syntax, and a corresponding dexterity in unravelling difficult constructions. Without this groundwork no man can be sure of a good place. Next, the aspirant must be skilled in Composition, must be able

---

[2] [The name given to the lowest-scoring successful candidate in the Classical Tripos: after the first incumbent of the position, Hensleigh Wedgwood, in 1824. Cf. the 'Wooden Spoon' in the Mathematical Tripos, a position achieved in 1860 by Wedgwood's son Ernest – a unique family double.]

[3] Rendall & Holden. (B) [Frederick Rendall, Trinity 1841, Senior Classic 1845, fellow of Trinity 1846–8; Hubert Holden, Trinity 1841, Senior Classic 1845, fellow of Trinity 1847–54. The two men were bracketed as Senior Classic.]

[4] Except the University Scholarship, and Medals, where the prizes are limited to one or two of the candidates, and the competition not general.

to write Latin and Greek Prose, Greek Iambics, and two or three kinds of Latin verse. Thirdly, he must have a very large vocabulary, so that he will seldom meet with a word which is not familiar to him. A fourth requisite which might occur to the reader – the knowledge of archaeology, law, history, &c., all that is comprehensively and not altogether fairly designated as *cram* – does not enter very largely into the qualifications for the Tripos.[5] The questions set by way of riders to the passages given for translation are not numerous, nor do they bring many marks. In this respect, there is a great difference between the Cambridge Tripos and the Oxford Schools.

In comparing these different elements of success, it has often been observed, and I think with justice, that writing Greek and Latin, particularly Greek and Latin verse, occupies too high a place. The Composition papers counting at least two fifths of the whole, a boyish knack in the manufacture of verses often gets the better of a more mature knowledge of language. I have known a man whose translations were only ordinary Third Class standard get himself a good Second by a brilliant copy of Elegiacs, the remains of his schoolboy proficiency; and one of my acquaintances, who stood third in his year on several of the translation papers, but being a Double man had no time to practise Composition, fell to a low place in the Second Class.

At Oxford a candidate for the First Class selects his twelve authors. At Cambridge he reads as much as he can. Though able to work but a few hours a-day, I was a fast reader when at work, and had covered a fair amount of ground. Since entering the University I had either read for the first time or reviewed the following authors:

Homer: all the Odyssey, Books XIII and XXIV of the Iliad. The Homeridian Hymns.

Hesiod: Shield of Achilles, Works and Days.

Aeschylus: all (seven plays).

Sophocles: all (ditto).

Aristophanes: all (eleven plays).

Euripides: Medea, Hippolytus, Ion, Bacchae, Hecuba, Phenissae, Cyclops.

Pindar: all. Theocritus: all.

Herodotus: Books I and VII, with numerous extracts from the others.

---

[5]   We had a History paper, most unfairly undermarked. (T) [This was introduced in 1849.]

Thucydides: Books I, II, IV, VI, VII, and all the difficult passages in the other three.

Xenophon's Banquet.

Demosthenes: the five *Aphobus* and *Onetor* Orations, the De Corona, the *Parapresbeia*, the Ad Leptinem.

Plato: Phaedrus, Phaedo, Protagoras, Gorgias, Symposium, Theaetetus, Sophista, Politicus, Five Books of the Republic.

Aristotle: the Rhetoric, Five Books of the Nicomachean Ethics.

Theophrastus's Characters.

Lucretius: Book I. and extracts from the others.

Catullus: all.

Virgil: the Georgics, Six Books of the Aeneid.

Horace; all. Juvenal: all. Persius: all.

Propertius: Books I. and IV.

Plautus: all (twenty plays).

Martial: all the Epigrams more than four lines in length.

Cicero: the Tusculan Questions, De Natura Deorum, De Divinatione, De Officiis; the Archias, Balbus, Muraena and Cluentius.

Livy: Books I and XXXI.

Besides these, there were some subjects not strictly available in the Tripos, such as extracts from Callimachus and Apollonius Rhodius, fragments of Alcaeus and Sappho, and several books of Athenaeus.[6]

It will be observed that the above list includes no portion of my previous preparation for the University. Some of my school reading, e.g. Sallust and the earlier books of the Iliad, I had a real knowledge and memory of. But the books comprising the course at Yale College I could not be said to have *read* in the Cambridge sense, with the single exception of Tacitus, an author whom I had much fancied, and worked up his History, not with a

---

[6] [Trevelyan ticks the books he had read: all those listed except Aristophanes and some of Homer. He adds, 'I did this and sometimes more but no Propertius. Theophr. Char. not read, but I read it afterwards in Jebb's edition [1870]. Oddly enough at that time I had read hardly any Cicero, and no Livy since leaving private school'.]

view to the limited requirements of the recitation room, but according to my own idea of how he ought to be studied and translated.

With these additions made to the above list, it will tolerably well represent the reading of a candidate for a good place in the Tripos. Of some authors, such as Aristophanes and Plautus, there was more than the usual amount; of others, as Herodotus, Demosthenes, Cicero, and probably Thucydides, rather less; and, generally speaking, I was better read on the higher authors, or those which come later in a student's reading, than on the more ordinary ones. On my knowledge of Aristophanes, Theocritus, Pindar, Plautus, &c., I relied perhaps too much. Some of the books in the list I of course knew better than others, but perfection in them all would have given me but a moderate chance had I depended only on finding pieces set which I had read. In the long authors, every man must trust to his general knowledge; of Herodotus I had read but two Books, yet it was not easy to find a passage or even a word in him that puzzled me, I was so well up in his peculiar dialect. My great deficiency was in Composition; the only kind which I could do well and accurately was Latin prose; at Greek Iambics, Greek prose, and Latin verse I worked all day, but with very moderate success. Our year, in spite of its bad reputation, showed an unusual independence of coaches. Most of the best men read by themselves during this month, dispensing with all assistance. This increased the uncertainty of speculation on their positions.

The examination was to begin on Monday. The Saturday immediately previous I devoted to a long ride in company with two fellow-sufferers, according to the Cambridge tradition that a man should he nearly idle for the day or two just before an examination – a theory, however, which very few have the courage and coolness to put in practice. For next week I had made all preparations in the most artistic way; moved my bed into a room with a fire-place, invited a different friend to dine with me every day, and projected a series of nice little dinners to make up for my long abstinence.[7] (Before the examination a man is on diet; during and after it he requires to be well fed.) On Sunday, I had intended to go to St. Mary's[8] as usual in the morning, and be systematically idle for the rest of the day; but the fit came too strong upon me, and I fell to writing Elegiacs, and afterwards looking over marked passages.[9] If there are no Sundays in

[7] We had the <u>same</u> little party of four – covered by a 12s 6d order from the Kitchens. (T)

[8] [Great St Mary's, the university church, opposite the Senate House.]

[9] As a Cantab reads, he marks any particularly strange word or difficult passage

revolutionary times, there are very apt to be none the fortnight before a Cambridge examination.

But Sunday work is seldom of any profit, even temporally speaking, and mine was no exception to the rule. It would be as great a bore to the reader as to myself were I to recall in detail all the chances, perils, and disasters of that week; how, when I had carefully practised writing Elegiacs, and acquired a tolerable command over them, Hexameters, of which I had not written three copies in two years, and probably not five in my life, were set the first morning; how, after lying awake from nervous excitement the whole night before the Greek Iambics, I dozed off towards morning and very nearly overslept the paper; how I was *frozen up* [10] on Thursday morning, the weather having changed from mild to very cold, as if for my special discomfiture, so that half my Greek Prose went up nearly illegible and without accents; and the report spread that I had broken down completely, or, as a Johnian elegantly expressed it, was *squashed*. Suffice it to say, that the five days were over at last, and I was left nearly delirious. A friend, who had been ill himself during an examination, and could therefore appreciate my condition, carried me out for a long walk on Saturday morning; that night I made up for the lost sleep of the six preceding, and on Sunday was in my usual state, with the exception of a propensity to eat and drink all that came in my way, which lasted a full month till the waste of the system had been repaired. [11]

The same evening I called on my right-hand neighbor in the examination, whose style of work, busy as I was, had occasionally fallen under my notice. He was one of the candidates for Senior Classic, had read almost everything, and written verses ever since he was twelve years old. [12] His learning was great, his Composition wonderfully rapid and elegant, his taste generally unexceptionable; but he was not very clear-headed or

---

for future reference; this is a great assistance to hint in running over an author rapidly. *Interleaved* copies of works are very common, and besides these, many men keep note-books to set down at length any difficulties they meet. To have 'got up' a book thoroughly, almost means that you have prepared a new edition of it.

[10] [The Senate House was unheated, and the candidates often found it difficult to write. It was claimed that on occasion, the ink froze in the inkwells.]

[11] I have dreamed of the Tripos examination ever since (1861–1910) though I was at the top of my health during it. (T)

[12] ['Holden', comments Ellis, adding that the 'respectable mathematician' is Rendall; Bowring and Whitting agree. Trevelyan adds that Rendall was his first-form master at Harrow.]

accurate, and therefore always liable to make slips of the pen. His rival
was a respectable Mathematician, and had just taken a Wrangler's degree,
was much behind him in speed, elegance, and quantity of knowledge, but
fearfully accurate, and never forgetting anything he had once learned. My
neighbor, who knew exactly his own strong and weak points as well as
those of his old schoolmate[13] and antagonist, endeavored to overpower him
by weight of learning and brilliancy of execution. He had read almost every
single passage that was set, and to show that he had done so, wrote at the
head of every translation paper he sent up the author's name and that of
the particular book or play. The bit of Theophrastus which was set us on
the last day he had by good fortune read over the very night before. As I
was pretty well up in it myself, though my acquaintance had not been so
recently renewed, I felt no hesitation in glancing at his work since I did not
wish to borrow from him. He was writing his notes *in Latin*, and getting
up his paper exactly as if he were editing the extract. It deserves to be
enumerated among his claims that he wrote a beautiful hand, delicate as a
woman's, and withal very legible. After all he was only bracketed Senior
Classic, some errors of syntax in his Greek Iambics,[14] and other inaccuracies,
having brought him down to the level of his less learned and showy, but
more safe competitor.[15]

He was very fond of English poetry. *Some* allusion to the examination it
was not possible to forego, but we soon disposed of the shop with our tea,
and then read, criticized, and very generally talked over the poets of the
new school – Shelley, Keats, Tennyson, Miss Barrett – for some hours, till,
as I rose to go, somewhere about the witching hour, he stopped me with,
'Now stay a little longer; I have some capital brandy that was sent me by
a friend – *an old parson in the country*'. The 'old parson in the country' was
sufficient guarantee for the orthodoxy of the liquor, which indeed proved
worthy of its clerical paternity. So we sat well into Monday morning,
drinking grog and talking of all the poets in all the five or six languages
that we knew more or less about. Such are a reading-man's relaxations after
the intense examination work.

The Classical examiners are not bound to declare the result of the Tripos
on any specified day. They consequently take their time about it, getting
up amicable little fights among themselves as to the comparative merits of

---

13   [Holden and Rendall had both come from King Edward VI School, Birmingham,
then ruled by Arnold's pupil James Prince Lee.]

14   I only got 52 out of 150 for those. (T)

15   [An example of Rendall's compositions is omitted.]

different men. They are usually a month in deliberation, although the four Composition papers are the only ones which they *all* examine; each one is sole arbiter of marks on the paper and a half of translation which he sets. Meanwhile some of the expectants have the additional amusement of going in for the Chancellor's Medals. On the present occasion but three candidates presented themselves, and two of these were morally certain of the two medals beforehand. The rest of us had nothing to do but to worry ourselves looking over the papers, finding out mistakes, and speculating on our chances, or else, more wisely, to leave the place, and forget the whole subject as far as possible. I went to London, saw various sights and acquaintances, and afterwards visited a friend who was then a private tutor at Eton, the opportunity being a good excuse and occasion for what I had some time wished – a little personal insight and examination into an English Public School.

23

A Visit to Eton.
English Public Schools

A Parliamentary return of all that is taught at Eton during ten
years of pupilage in the nineteenth century, ought (if anything
can) to surprise the public into some uneasiness on the subject.
Edinburgh Review, Jan. 1845.[1]

It is a singular spectacle for an American to see numbers of youths eighteen
or nineteen years old, who in his own country would call themselves and
be called young men, leaders of fashionable society perhaps – going about
in boyish costume, and evidently in the status of boys. What increases the
singularity of the appearance is that the Englishman's physical development
is more rapid than that of the American – of the Northern States, at least;
thus the Etonian of nineteen is as old in appearance as the New Yorker or
Bostonian of twenty-one. They all wear white cravats and black beavers;
caps are forbidden, otherwise there is no uniformity of costume, and the
juvenile round jacket is as common as the manly coat upon strapping young
fellows nearly six feet high. Still, however you may *dress* persons of that
age, it is not possible to confine them entirely to the discipline of boys; the
upper forms will walk out into the town of Windsor, and should one of

---

[1]   [A quotation from William Empson's review of A.P. Stanley's *Life and
Correspondence of Dr. Arnold, Edinburgh Review* 81, pp. 190–234, at p. 228.]

them meet a tutor he takes refuge in a shop, the tutor, by a long established fiction, making believe not to see him.[2]

There are always several hundred boys at Eton; at that period (1845) it numbered more than seven hundred. About one tenth of these are *Collegers*. These *Collegers* are the nucleus of the whole system, and the only original part of it, the paying pupils (*oppidans*, *town-boys*) being, according to general belief, an after growth. They (the Collegers) are educated gratuitously, and such of them as have nearly but not quite reached the age of nineteen, when a vacancy in King's College, Cambridge, occurs, are elected Scholars there forthwith and provided for during life – or until marriage.

The number of masters is but small in proportion to that of boys, nor is the average fairly distributed; one master may have forty pupils under him. This is one of the most obvious defects of the system. Formerly, there were many private tutors, who might in some degree make up this deficiency; but as these gentlemen were found in some instances to have too comfortable a time of it, regulations were made obliging them to keep the same hours at night with the boys, and in other respects circumscribing their liberties, in consequence of which their numbers rapidly diminished, and at this time there were but three, each attached to his particular boy. That Classics form the staple of education at Eton, is known to every one who has heard of the place; it was, therefore, matter of no small surprise to me to be informed – and indeed to see with my own eyes – that the Classical course was of a very obsolete and defective description, the text-books old-fashioned, chiefly selections, and those not always of the best authors or the best parts of them. Latin versification still flourishes; it might be unjust to say that everything else is sacrificed to it, but it is certain that other and less doubtful elements of Scholarship are somewhat neglected for it. Of Mathematics there is not a great deal to be said – for there is very little done.

Passing to the more general branches of education, it is singular to find *no instruction whatever given in English Grammar*. But this singularity is not confined to Eton; it extends to all the English schools, public or private, that I am acquainted with. English Grammar is not one of the branches of the English school *curriculum*. When I mentioned this omission to my English friends, they generally turned it off with some mild joke about its being necessary for us in America to learn English Grammar at school, because English was a strange language to us; but the peculiarity of their practice seemed never to occur to them. I fancy it does not correspond with that of

---

[2]   [This practice was known at Eton as 'shirking'.]

other nations. French Grammar is certainly studied, and with much care, in the schools of France.

In Ancient History the boys were well read, and would have been in Modern, only that something was given them for it which *Punch* could hardly have caricatured. Just at that time the Puseyites and Young England had become most rampant and wanton in their perversion of historic facts and extravagance of historic fancies, and Eton was not untouched by the prevailing epidemic. I saw a sort of historical manual written by one of the under-masters (no friend of mine, thank Heaven!) which contained such utter absurdities, both in the preface and the body of the work, that I should hardly be believed were I to relate them. It is proper to say, however, that the book attracted so much unfavorable notice that the compiler was obliged to remove his most glaring mis-statements in a subsequent edition.[3]

The study of the Modern languages had received an impulse from some Prizes instituted by Prince Albert, and was beginning to attract a tolerable share of attention.

My informant considered that the subject best taught was – what I should hardly have expected – Geography. It was not merely learned from books; much attention was paid to drawing and copying maps.

As to the morality of the school, my friend's impression was not the most favorable. One instance in particular, which had recently occurred, made a strong impression upon him, and upon me when he related it. A boy, whom he knew very well, found a pencil-case and advertised it through the proper channel and authority. *More than a hundred* boys applied for the article, and some of them from their descriptions were evidently making the wildest shots at it. With all due allowance for the juvenile propensity to lose pencils, one cannot avoid the conclusion that at least three fourths of these youths were trying to get possession of what did not and could not belong to them.

This brief notice of the great foundation of Eton, the school where the sons of the nobility are educated, does not present a very pleasant state of things. I can only say that my impressions have been set down according to my best recollection of them. Some things I noted with my own eyes; others may perhaps have been unintentionally colored by my informant. He was

---

[3] [C.J. Abraham's *The Unity of History; or Outlines of Lectures on Ancient and Modern History, Considered on the Principles of the Church of England*, published at Eton by the school bookseller E.P. Williams in 1845; 2nd edn. 1846. In the preface the author debunks Voltaire, Gibbon and Hume; the book is violently anti-Catholic. Abraham later became Bishop of New Zealand.]

a King's College, London, man, an Evangelical, and one of the Cambridge Apostles; on every account, therefore, disposed to be very critical in his standard both of intellectual and moral training, and not at all favorably biased towards Eton.[4] At the same time, I did not rely on his opinion only. Happening to know some of the Under-masters, truly excellent and religious men as well as good scholars, I drew from them indirectly that the moral condition of the boys was far from satisfactory. It is but just to say, however, that they did not allude to the frequency of gross vices, but rather to habitual carelessness about truth, deception of teachers, tyranny of older boys over younger (though the *fagging system* is allowed on all hands to be very much humanized), and other sins which are apt to be prominently exhibited in large congregations of boys, and which Arnold in more than one place has so feelingly deplored.

When, in writing this chapter a few months ago, I came to arrange my knowledge and recollections of English Public Schools, and put together the different impressions I had received from one quarter and another, it became evident that I still wanted considerable light on the subject. Instantly I wrote off to two friends, one an Eton man, and actually connected with Eton at the present time, the other a Shrewsbury man, Fellow of Trinity College, and making a name in the literary world.[5] The nature of the inquiries which I put will be tolerably plain from the replies themselves, which I received by return of post, and have no hesitation in printing, as they contain nothing personal or which can possibly give offence to any one, and tell the story much better than I could. The Etonian shall have the precedence from the greater length and earnestness of his communication.

My Dear B.

Our whole number of boys is about six hundred. It has not fallen below this for eight years. Six years ago it was as high as seven hundred and seventy-seven. At present it is about six hundred and thirty.

The Scholars or Collegers are seventy. The founder evidently contemplated the accretion of pensioners, 'juvenes commensales', just like a College at Oxford or Cambridge. It is believed that there were 'oppidans,' or pensioners, almost at the beginning.

We have a Head Master, with twelve assistants, for the Upper School, which contains six hundred boys. These are not equally divided. The Head Master has no more than thirty boys. The next two or three divisions seldom

---

[4]   [The only Apostle who fits this description is Frederick Gibbs.]
[5]   Johnson, Clark. (B) [William Johnson, W.G. Clark.]

reach 40. But the tenth contains seventy-eight, and has ranged above 60 ever since Christmas. The lower school, a separate establishment, contains at present about thirty boys; it used to contain from one hundred to one hundred and fifty in old times. They retain the whole staff, whether the ranks are full or not, i.e. the Lower Master (Magister Ostiarius, or '*usher*', you see the derivation with the French 'huissier') and four assistants. So that we have eighteen regular Classical Masters, wearing Academical dress. Besides this, there are five Mathematical Masters, all graduates, with extra masters for languages, &c., quite enough.

No boy can enter the lower school after his thirteenth, nor the upper school after his fourteenth year. The great mass of boys come at twelve and thirteen. No one, I think, ever comes to school *under six*; this only happens with residents; seldom does a boy enter under nine. I am not aware of a minimum of juvenility. The lower school professes to be preparatory from the rudiments. I suppose a boy must be in trowsers and know how to read.

As to what a public school is, consult Sidney Smith in the Edinburgh for 1810.[6] I do not accept his definition as quite satisfactory. A public school, as a peculiar institution of English society, is a place in which a boy is at once in a class under a master who acts for the head-master, and subject to a tutor who acts more specially for the parent or guardian. There are but three schools that come under this definition – Harrow, Eton, Rugby. These three seem to me to be very similar to Oxford or Cambridge in the Middle Ages, in the period between the first institution of colleges and the decay of the University 'Schools'. As an undergraduate (say in 1500) got his chief teaching, and made his chief display of knowledge in public with a Professor, whilst he prepared his work, cultivated his speciality, and underwent discipline in a college so an Eton, Harrow, or Rugby boy, attends the one school chapel, shows up exercises, is examined in his lessons according to fixed routine, contends for honors, takes degrees (what we call 'removes', *e.g.* changing from lower boy to fifth form, from one who is fagged to one who fags), with (apud) the Head Master or his assistant, whilst at the same time he receives catechetical instruction in religion, prepares most of his lessons, and gets his exercises looked over, &c., with his tutor, whether he boards in his house or not. The tutor also corresponds

---

[6] [Sydney Smith, 'Public schools of England', *Edinburgh Review* 16 (1810), pp. 326–34. Smith was with Richard Payne Knight and Francis Jeffery the leading contributor to the *Review* in its early years, and notorious for his attacks both on English academical institutions – especially Oxford – and also on the power and income of bishops.]

with the parent, watches over money matters, and attends to the *pros ho hekastos pephuke* [individual talents], superintending and guiding all those more optional studies for which the school (= the University) gives leisure and encouragement. Sidney Smith wrote, perhaps, before tutors began to attempt much in this way, though even then there was some attention paid to individuals.

Eton is less symmetrical than the other two, in so far as she retains *Dames'* houses cheaper than tutors' houses. About one hundred and thirty boys board with Dames, having tutors to whom they pay £10 or £20-a-year for tuition, paying the Head Master £6 a-year, and leaving him to pay his assistants. An assistant gets from the Head £44 a-year, working perhaps twenty-four hours a-week in class with seventy-five or seventy-eight boys. Then we live by our pupils. As we do each other's work, each boy gets what he wants, not caring how the money is distributed.

At Eton a boy changes his division and comes under a new Master every half year, retaining his tutor. The tutor is not merely an agent for the parent, but the boy's natural defender and friend ... At Eton you get much more help from your Tutor in preparing lessons and exercises than at Rugby. Rugby men who have lived years with us, and thoroughly studied our practices, prefer our *tutorial* system, though they think our school system inferior as regards the cultivation of the intellect.

It is this duality, this polarization between the public authorities and the more private or more Collegiate discipline, which seems to me (not now for the first time) to constitute the differentia of a public school. It shows itself in this way – a boy does not look upon his tutor as a schoolmaster; he is to him a gentleman whom he knows just as he knows his father's friends, whom he can ask to his father's house, from whom he claims hospitality as soon as he has left school, if he ever revisits Eton. Again, he is proud of the house he belongs to, as a man is of his College; though in cricket and football clubs, in regular 'long boats', and aquatic sweepstakes, in running and leaping races, he competes with the whole school, yet he belongs to a football club in the autumn, which includes the twenty or thirty boys boarding in his own house, and thus matches are made between houses as between colleges, and his society is found chiefly in his own house, though not exclusively (much less in summer than in winter). Again, the school examinations are conducted in a more professional or business way than the private tuition – no great regard for peculiarities of character, for moral superiority, &c.; a boy is plucked just as at Oxford if he falls short of the minimum from whatever reason; on the other hand, if he gets into a scrape, his tutor is applied to for his character, and can generally, if he thinks it right, extricate him, and set him right in the eyes of a Master who may have thought ill of him ...

What Sidney Smith says of its roughness, its similarity to a forest or to a savage life, is at present almost entirely inapplicable to Eton, and, I believe, to Harrow. Rugby is rougher – the boys in a tutor's house are more left to self-government.

Shrewsbury is one of the many endowed grammar-schools founded in or soon after the reign of Edward VI. Its only claim to publicity is, that for one generation it drew pupils from all parts of England; whereas most grammar-schools, such as *Bury St. Edmonds, Tiverton* (in Devonshire), *Oakham* and *Uppingham* in Rutland, draw boys from their own localities. A school like Shrewsbury flourishes only when very well officered, unless it has a very rich endowment, plenty of Scholarships to give away at the Universities, as Merchant Taylors' sends men to St. John's College, Oxford ...

Repton, I believe, differs from Shrewsbury only in being less famous. It may become famous and so far public by achieving conspicuous success at Oxford and Cambridge, but not so famous as Shrewsbury was twenty years ago, because it has now so many competitors. Shrewsbury grew fast, whilst Eton and Harrow were vegetating slowly – before Rugby arose – before any other old grammar-school bestirred itself.

It is customary to reckon *Winchester* and *Westminster* as public schools. Every year at Lord's cricket-ground, which is the ground of the Marylebone Club and the Newmarket of cricket, a week is given up to the 'Public School Matches'. ...

At Cambridge we Etonians are charged with levity, and with that kind of impudence which shows itself in ten Eton men talking Etonica at a party without caring for what is due to the other four men present.

The two great evils of the place, which are now attracting every one's attention, are these: (1) Mathematics are not compulsory and general; (2) There is too much money spent by the boys, too much self-indulgence ... And we ought to remodel our chapel service, so as to have a short service every day, and not school-days without prayer and holidays with too much of it. Finally, we ought to have fewer holidays ...

The real reason for sending a boy to Eton is that he will there find, not the best teaching nor the best discipline, but the best society. I suppose, however, that Harrow is just as good in this respect, or very nearly so. The only difference is that they have not so large an admixture of poor gentlemen's sons. They have nothing in lieu of our seventy Collegers (who, being elected by merit, are really picked boys, the competition being very keen, fifty candidates for ten vacancies every year), and the candidates for College, and other frugal boys, living at Dames' houses.

There has been an alarm about Eton being a Puseyitical school. Harrow has gained thereby, having a contrary reputation. The truth is that neither school has any distinctive religious character, any more than the London Clubs or the English aristocracy generally. Both schools, I believe, fairly represent English society in its good and its evil ...

Perhaps I ought to tell you that a boy in a tutor's house, at Eton, costs his father altogether, including all his personal expenses, such as clothes, journeys, pocket-money, medicine, on an average not less than £200 a-year. Many boys, however, spend £30 a-year in pocket money, some £50 ... Yours, sincerely, W.J.

Some passages in the above letter I have been obliged to omit, as their tone of eulogy, however sincere on the writer's part, might seem extravagant to a reader not under the influence of similar feeling. My Shrewsbury friend has treated the subject in a somewhat lighter vein and his views do not precisely correspond with those of the Etonian.

My dear B,

The term 'Public School', in its proper sense, is applied to all schools which have an endowment for the Master, and where the education is for boys. The term is a translation of 'libera schola', about the meaning of which there has been a good deal of discussion lately in the Court of Chancery. The Head-Mastership is in the gift of Trustees, whose choice is limited by charter to an MA, B.D., or D.D. of Oxford or Cambridge. These trustees are country gentlemen, or burgesses, who don't see the use of Latin and Greek, and want to turn the foundation into a commercial school, on which point they join issue with the Head-master. They get a dictionary, look out 'libera', and find that it means *free*. The Head-master[7] maintains that it means *liberal*, and assumes that a liberal education excludes the *three R's*, and all that could fit a man for standing behind a counter. *Adhuc sub judice lis est*, and as the judex is the Lord Chancellor, it is like to remain under him till it is addled.

In common parlance 'Public School' is only applied to the *larger* endowed schools. Thus, there is a small Grammar-school with an endowment of fifty marks per annum at Boughton cum Bangaway; no one calls it a Public

---

[7]   [Benjamin Kennedy, headmaster of Shrewsbury 1836–66: see his *Libera Schola* (London, 1862).]

School: suppose a lease falls in, and the revenue becomes £3,000 instead of £33. 6s. 8d., a good scholar gets the Headship, boys come by hundreds, and call themselves 'Public School men' *nem. con.*

I have heard Winchester and Eton men maintain that the term 'Public School' ought only to be applied to those two foundations which have a College, or *close* and *free* school distinct from the *open* and costly school *pasi koinen enapotisai chremata* [open to anyone who can afford it] (you remember the Collegers and Oppidans at Eton), and also a College at the University appropriate to them, New College and King's. But no one else recognises this limitation. Shrewsbury is a public school in precisely the same sense as Harrow or Rugby, though the numbers are not so great nor the endowment so large. It acquired what celebrity it has, first under Dr. Butler[8] (afterwards Bishop of Lichfield) and secondly, under Benjamin Kennedy, though the numbers are much diminished.

It was founded, like many others, by Edward VI out of the spoils of the Monasteries. I don't see how Repton can be called a private school, being endowed; unless one calls it so as a mark of contempt for its scanty numbers. In all old towns (with very rare exceptions) are to be found endowed schools, generally connected with the municipality when there is one, not at all with the parochial system. Most of these schools are in a state of effeteness for want of the sinews of learning – money. Very often the founders left an estate to the borough magistrates, charged with a fixed payment to the Master of the school, fifty merks a-year say, which was a handsome sum three hundred years ago, but is hardly enough to find one in cigars now-a-days.

Suits have been set on foot in some cases to compel the holders of the estate to comply with the spirit of the Founder's will, and pay as large a proportion of the rent as fifty merks a year was then. This has occurred at Ludlow. Sometimes the Dean and Chapter have been made patrons of the school, and have played the same dodge, e.g. at Rochester, where W——,[9] one of our Fellows, Headmaster of the school, is carrying on a *guerre à mort* with the Cathedral dignitaries. There was a debate about it in the House lately.

Eton and Westminster are both Colleges, though at Eton there is a School besides. The reason of their being coupled together is, I suppose, the old custom of rowing matches on the Thames, from which, both at

---

[8] [Samuel Butler, headmaster 1798–1836.]

[9] Whiston. (W) [See R. Arnold, *The Whiston Matter. The Rev. Robert Whiston versus the Dean and Chapter of Rochester* (London, 1961).]

Oxford and Cambridge, the two rivals join and form boating-clubs – you remember the Third Trinity.

James I. wanted to make Trinity College the same appendage to Westminster that King's is to Eton, or New College to Winchester; but some College Hampden[10] resisted and defeated him.

Ever yours, truly, W.G.C.[11]

I make no attempt to reconcile any contradictions in the three different accounts now laid before the reader, but merely present them and leave him to judge for himself. It is certain, however, that Eton, which has not been out of fashion for a hundred and fifty years, stands pretty nearly 'at the top of the tree'. The other schools differ very much in reputation and in the characteristics of their pupils, as observable at the University.

Westminster was once the Court School, and for a long time rivalled Eton, but is now in a terrible state of decay. The position of the school in the heart of a great city had doubtless something to do with corrupting the boys' morals, but would not entirely account for their low and ungentlemanly habits; nor could their general ignorance of everything but vice, be attributed to any other cause than gross neglect on the part of those who had the control over them. Even the Westminster Collegers who were annually elected to the three close Scholarships at Trinity, and who might reasonably be expected to present the best specimens of the school, rarely did anything to distinguish themselves in the legitimate pursuits of the University. Within a few years Westminster has acquired a new Head-Master.[12] If a conscientious man, he has such a work before him in the reformation of that school as no one would envy, and none but a very conscientious or a very bold man, or both, attempt.

Winchester has now less than two hundred pupils. Few of these come to Cambridge. They have a College of their own at Oxford (New College) which stands in the same relation to them that King's College, Cambridge, does to Eton, and which naturally takes their best men. A friend of mine who professed to know something about Winchester summed up his opinion

---

[10]   It was Whitgift (Archbp of Canterbury), then Master. (B)
[11]   W.G. Clark. (W)
[12]   [H.G. Liddell, co-editor of the dictionary Bristed refers to as 'Scott and Liddell' (1843); appointed in 1846, he served until 1855 when he became Dean of Christ Church, Oxford.]

of it in this sweeping sentence, that it was 'stationary, illiberal, rough, coarse, and limited'.

Harrow had the reputation of being a great place for the quasi-aristocracy – the sons of rich commoners – as Eton is for the sons of Noblemen. The Harrow men at Cambridge in my time were usually unfortunate, starting with a good reputation and breaking down in the long run. When Frederick Peel missed his Scholarship he was supposed to be going the same way, but he broke the charm by his First Class in the Tripos. This school also has gained a new Head-Master within a few years – I use the term *gained* designedly, for the present incumbent is C.J. Vaughan,[13] whose name will be familiar to all attentive readers of Dr. Arnold's correspondence. Under his auspices the most favorable results may be hoped for, if he does not disappoint the expectations which his own character and Arnold's friendship for him have raised.

This brings me to *Rugby*, so interesting from its association with the name of Arnold. (He died in 1842, and many of his last 'Sixth Form' were my contemporaries or nearly so at Cambridge.) The Rugby men were in general less brilliant and quick than the Etonians, good sound scholars, but not remarkably showy or striking; the Rugby exhibitioner at Trinity was usually in the First Class of the Tripos, but not very high on it. But they were men of great weight and character; they seemed to have been really taught to think on ethical as well as purely intellectual subjects better than any set of young men I ever knew; they had better grounds for their belief, and always appeared to have looked into the reason of what they said or did, and to go back to first principles. Their veneration for Arnold's memory was unbounded; they spoke of his loss as a personal calamity, as one might speak of a near relative's death; and you could always recognise a Rugby man's room by the portrait conspicuously suspended in it. It was sometimes objected that the influence exerted by Arnold over the minds of his pupils had been too great – that it destroyed their originality and self-dependence. This was a common saying of the Apostles; I do not think it evinced their usual discrimination. Surely the liberal, independent, no-party nature of Arnold's mental and moral constitution, which prevented him from ever thoroughly acting with any side in politics, and made the Whigs afraid to give him a Bishopric, *could* not impress on the minds of his scholars any blind partisan bias in politics or religion, such as a violent Puseyite, or Young Englander, or Calvinist, or Republican might have done. What he *did* impress upon his pupils was a love of truth, a reverence for

---

[13] [See p. 111 n. 1; p. 204 n.17.]

reverend things, a philosophic habit of investigating principles, which tended to give them the reality of that 'earnestness' which some of their despisers only pretended to possess or fancied they were possessing.

Shrewsbury, of which we have had occasion to make frequent mention, is one of the very first schools that a Freshman hears of in connexion with this Prize or that Scholarship.[14] Even Eton does not send up such a proportion of the Cambridge Classics – in fact I doubt if any three schools together do, Eton included. The Shrewsbury men at Cambridge had a reputation for two things particularly, writing Greek Iambics and playing whist; but their general line was minute accuracy of Scholarship.[15] It may be inferred from this that they excelled in Greek rather than Latin and their precision in Greek syntax was carried out to a refinement and minuteness hardly paralleled even in Law or Mathematics. In most things they displayed a hard and subtle acuteness, such as one is accustomed to deem a national characteristic of Scots rather than Englishmen: this showed itself in their very relaxations. Whist, I have said, was their favorite amusement, and they played it purely for amusement; the few shillings at stake could have had little to do with the interest displayed. I often watched a table or two of Shrewsbury men before and after supper, and it was singular to see such youths playing nearly as scientifically and quite as silently as the oldest and most experienced hands, never making a gesture of impatience or exultation, or opening their mouths except during the deals.

It was said, and with reason, that they crammed too much for the one object of the Classical Tripos, and devoted too much time to making themselves machines for the construction of Greek Iambics. For instance, they read too little Homer at school through fear of becoming too familiar with Heroic Greek to the injury of their Attic. It was owing to this Homeric deficiency and their not being quite up to some of the other schools in Latin verse,[16] that a Shrewsbury candidate for the Bell Scholarship was usually unsuccessful, while he as usually beat one or both of the Bell Scholars in

---

[14] It is remarkable that Shrewsbury of late years when two thirds less in numbers (100 to 300) gets <u>absolutely</u> more university honours than it did in my time (1830 to 1834), under Butler's presidency, and yet those are generally called its palmy days. (H)

[15] It was said of a Shrewsbury man who was Senior Classic in my time, that he had never been known to make a mistake in a Classical paper during his whole University career. ['I deny <u>that</u>. Vide Camb. Univ. Calendar', comments Bowring, who adds 'Cope': Edward Meredith Cope, Senior Classic 1841.]

[16] [H.J. Hodgson loyally protests, 'I deny this: vide Sabrinae Corolla'. *Sabrinae*

the Classical Tripos. Their accurate habits were of great service to them in Mathematics; they seldom read for high degrees, but were always pretty safe to get through or be Senior Optimes as their Classical prospects required. Apart from this necessary digression they in most cases confined themselves vigorously to their Classical studies, but after the Degree and the Tripos they expanded and developed with great rapidity, taking in a variety of miscellaneous knowledge, and displaying a number of qualities and capabilities for which one would not have been disposed to give them credit previously. They afforded the most striking example of what is a common feature in English education, a mental development held in abeyance and working unseen under the pressure of study, which starts out into full life on the removal of the pressure.

I have been thus particular in speaking of Shrewsbury, because the peculiar style of Scholarship which originated there has invaded and pervaded that of Cambridge, where Latin Composition and 'cram' have yielded the first place to Greek Composition and metaphysical syntax – in brief, Greek has got the better of Latin, and language of matter.

The King Edward VI School, Birmingham, had a great reputation which began within late years, in fact after I entered the University. In five years it sent up five scholars of the highest order, of whom all were Fellows of Trinity, four Senior Classics (alone or bracketed) and two Double Firsts, besides some high Wranglers, for Mathematics as well as Classics were well attended to there. They were mostly what would be called *slashing* men who could do a great deal and do it well, though there was considerable variety among them, little uniformity of method and much originality. Thus the two candidates[17] for the head of the Tripos in one year whom I have already mentioned as very different in their style and forte, were from the Birmingham school.

Repton, where Peile[18] the editor of Aeschylus is Head-Master, though a small school, was sending some very good men to Cambridge a few years ago.

While speaking of English schools it would be unjust to pass over one immortalized by the quaint genius of Lamb and in which the circumstance

---

Corolla, a collection of Latin and Greek verse by Shrewsbury men, was published in 1850; three further editions followed.]

[17]   Holden and Rendall. (B)

[18]   [T.W. Peile, headmaster 1841–54. His edition of the Agamemnon appeared in 1839, his Choephori in 1840.]

that one of my most intimate and valued friends[19] was educated at it, often made me feel something like a personal interest – *Christ's Hospital*, otherwise known as the *Blue Coat School*. It is purely a charitable establishment; the pupils have retained their distinctive dress (a blue gown, yellow leggings, and no hat) ever since its foundation, and are obliged to wear it continuously even in vacation time, and when absent from London. This school has several very good Exhibitioners[20] at different Cambridge Colleges, some of them worth as much as £100 a-year; these are frequently filled by crack men, both in Classics and Mathematics – more frequently the former. This may be deemed no wonder when the worldly prospects of these youths depended so entirely for a favorable start on their academic success. It was more surprising to find in them a great deal of general knowledge, a love of poetry,[21] refined taste, and often a touch of romance in their characters, altogether coming up to one's ideal of the poor scholar, such as is oftener met with in novels than in real life. There was a distinctive peculiarity in their external appearance by which they were easily recognised. Closely cropped hair constituted a part of the school regulation costume; on their emancipation into the University they let their locks grow to the longest extent permitted by the usages of English civilization.

The reader may have observed that, with one or two exceptions, the schools enumerated are distinguished for Classics alone, and he may ask where the Mathematicians are trained. They certainly do not, as a general rule, come from the Public Schools. Many of them are fitted in private; some of those who enter at the Small Colleges are very deficient in Classics, nor do they read any at the University except their First-Year College subjects and Little-Go authors. Many come from King's College, London. This is the Established Church part of the London University, in opposition to University College.[22] The students attend like scholars at a day-school, or the students of Columbia College; it is somewhat as if Columbia should prepare pupils for Yale or Harvard. Many of the King's College London

---

[19] Maine. (B)

[20] An *Exhibition* is something like a College Scholarship in the gift of a particular school, but the Exhibitioner has no privileges beyond the pecuniary emolument, and it does not interfere with his sitting for an ordinary Scholarship.

[21] This was very remarkably the case with Maine. (B)

[22] [The University of London opened in 1828, its Anglican rival King's College in 1831. When a new body, the University of London, was given a charter in 1836, they became constituent colleges, the original University of London becoming University College, London (the comma was later dropped).]

men are capital scholars, though not being equal to the Public School men in Composition, they seldom take the very highest places on the Tripos; still they had one Senior and one Second Medallist during the interval between 1839 and 1849. In Mathematics they were very successful, and turned out a number of high Wranglers; they had the Senior Wrangler twice while I was at the University.[23] Professor De Morgan is the great Mathematical coach there,[24] and it is probably the only place where Mathematicians enjoy a preparatory drill in searching written examinations, corresponding to that of the Classical men at the Public Schools and as similar as theirs to what both have to experience in their University course.

The '*Colleges*' now founding all over England, e.g. at Brighton, Marlborough, Liverpool, Birkenhead, Fleetwood, are great schools, but not at all like Eton or Harrow, or any of the old public schools, great or small, any more than the London University is like Oxford or Cambridge. In some respects they have the advantage, being cheaper, more systematic, and attending better to Mathematical studies.

Durham University, which was established to supply a cheaper place of education for North-Country clergymen than the two old Universities, is still in its infancy, and one seldom hears much about it. I believe it answers its purpose pretty well.

While speaking of English preparatory places of education it may be well to say a word of the Scotch Universities respecting which some curiosity is occasionally manifested by our countrymen. I knew several Cantabs (North-Country men and Scotchmen) who had been at Glasgow, which they regarded as a preparatory school. From their report I should imagine that the Scotch Universities occupied an intermediate position between ours and the English, in point of classical and rhetorical attainments, age of pupils, and soundness and variety of studies. There are some very good schools in Scotland, one in particular (though I cannot now recall the name and locality of it), which sends a number of good men to Cambridge and Oxford; but though taking good places, they did not come up to the English standard of the highest excellence in scholarship. From what I know of Trinity College, Dublin, I should be inclined to say the same of it as of the Scotch Universities. Some of its graduates, indeed, will tell you that the standard of the Fellowships and other chief Honors there is higher than that of *any* academical institution in the world (I have seen

---

[23] Cayley 1842, Henslow 1846. (B)

[24] [Augustus De Morgan was in fact Professor of Mathematics at University College, not at King's.]

this assertion publicly made in print); but undervaluing himself is not an Irishman's fault. I owe my 'rudiments' to a Trin. Coll. Dub. man, and am not disposed to speak lightly of the classical acquirements of its members, but truth compels me to say that their Greek does not appear to be of the first water. The Cantabs used to say of them that they were always writing Greek verses in some magazine, and never printed a copy which did not show a fundamental ignorance of the laws of syntax and prosody.[25] It is a peculiarity of this institution that the *Fellows are allowed to marry*, probably by way of asserting a Protestant principle.

---

[25] See some pertinent examples in specimens of Sergt Murphy and Mr Kenealy's composition given in a review of *Arundines Cami* published about 1841 or 1842 in Dublin University Magazine. (B) [The review, probably by Edward Kenealy himself, appeared in the magazine in February 1843 (vol.14, pp. 121–41). Kenealy later achieved notoriety as defence lawyer for the Tichborne claimant.]

24

Being Extinguished [1845]

Succefs

Failure

During the week I spent at Eton, it was expected that the result of the Tripos would be declared; but the absence of an examiner put it off for a week longer. More fidget and more speculating. After my mishaps in Greek Prose and Latin Verse, I ought to have made up my mind to die decently, but then I was conscious of having sent up a rather neat bit of prose, and Iambics that were a little above my average – so said a friend to whom I showed the rough copy. Re-examination of the translation papers disclosed some glaring mistakes, but every one makes mistakes, except now and then a Shrewsbury man. The betting was against me, but there was some money on me even. The examiners were more taciturn than usual and let nothing be suspected beforehand. The only generally received rumor was that Frederick Peel (who had been working like three horses all the Long) was coming up wonderfully and going to be *the* successful outsider of the year; and this rested more on the firm conviction and positive assertions of his coach than on anything that had leaked out.

At last it was unofficially announced that the Tripos would be out on the morrow. All that night I sat up playing whist with two or three interested parties, and two or three not interested, who had benevolently sacrificed themselves for the occasion. Our host was a good-natured Mathematician, still taking it easy after his successful exertions to obtain a place among the first twenty Wranglers.[1] We played straight on from 10 p.m. till 6 a.m., only stopping to put coal on the fire from a diminutive scuttle, or champagne into ourselves from a large pewter mug.[2] Then we went to dress, for the daily clean shirt is part of an Englishman's religion, and after that to chapel. Most of the competitors were there, and a very pale, uneasy, used-up set we looked. I was particularly struck with the appearance of one young man of Irish extraction, a hard student, but not naturally clever, who finally came out third Classic and Second Medallist.[3] He was ghastly pale and seemed hardly able to stand. Poor fellow! he had another source of anxiety that we knew not of. For some time he had been on the high road to Rome – very secretly – and was then practising various ascetic acts of devotion and penance. About a year after he went openly over to the enemy, leaving an Orange father to bewail his untimely fate.

After chapel, to breakfast with what appetite I might, and then to billiards – anything to pass away the morning. It was nearly the dinner hour when I strolled down, for the third or fourth time, in the direction of the *quasi-*University Bookseller's, where the Tripos list was always posted.[4] A great crowd surrounded the shop as was customary on such occasions; a Trinity man whom I knew was emerging from it, 'Where am I?' 'Second in the Second Class.'

On hearing this double mediocrity of position assigned me I had need of all my philosophy. Though from the first the limited time I was able to read had made the chances greatly against me, and other things had combined to let me down gradually, I certainly was considerably sold by the final result – indeed I don't know if I ever was as much so before or since. However, I disguised my mortification, and pushed my way in. The first acquaintance I saw was a Small Colleger, who had last year taken two of the Browne's Medals, the Greek and Latin Odes, beating our best

---

[1]   Latham? (W), Latham (B). [Henry Latham, Trinity 1841, 18th Wrangler 1845; fellow of Trinity Hall 1848–88, Master 1888–1902.]

[2]   The big, glass-bottomed pewter mug is an article of furniture to be found on almost every Cantab's premises. Its primary and ordinary use is for imbibing beer; on unceremonious occasions it serves for the reception of any potable fluid.

[3]   Knox. (T, W, B) [Thomas Knox, Trinity 1841, 3rd Classic 1845; converted to Catholicism in November 1845, later Superior of the London Oratory.]

[4]   [Deighton's, in Trinity Street, publishers of the *Cambridge University Calendar.*]

Trinity men, and whose name was now just above mine, leading off the Second Class.[5] He was standing up like Miss Barrett's 'statue thunder-struck', overwhelmed by the shock, but expressing no emotion. When he caught sight of me, his feelings first found vent at the presence of one so nearly in the same predicament, and he broke out with 'I *do* think they might have drawn the line a little lower!'

All the men of the year who had taken University Prizes (except one unfortunate 'gulfed' in Mathematics) were in the Second Class, namely the Small Colleger aforesaid, myself, and my quondam Methodist friend, who had contributed so much to the introduction of sherry-cobblers.[6] One of the examiners afterwards told me that all this Second Class (twelve out of twenty-four – two men were not placed) lay very close together, so that there was but little difference between the first and last man in it. Peel had leaped the gap, and was the last of the six who composed the First Class. Should this gentleman carry out in Parliament the habit he had at the University, of failing when he was expected to succeed and succeeding when he was expected to fail, he will be a very bothering man to both friends and opponents.

If inclined to take refuge in the proverbial consolation of misery, I had certainly company enough. Not only had *every man* in the Second Class cherished some hope of a First, but one of the aspirants to that honor had dropped into the Third.[7] Such accidents are not uncommon with Double men, who, in working up their Mathematics the last year, are apt to let their Classics go down.

In one respect the standard of the Classical Tripos is higher than that of the Mathematical; more knowledge, both positively and comparatively speaking, is required for the lower places. The first man of the Third Class approaches much nearer to a Classic[8] than the first Junior Optime does to a Mathematician, and his marks bear a much larger proportion to the Senior Classic's than the other's do to the Senior Wrangler's. The same difference extends throughout; the last man of the First Class is much better in his line than the last Wrangler in his; and the Small Colleges, which give their Fellowships according to the Degrees, show this by requiring a candidate to

---

[5]   Newport, Pembroke. (B) [Henry Newport, Pembroke 1841, headmaster of Newbury Grammar School 1849–52, of Exeter Grammar School 1852–76.]

[6]   Fussell. (B) [James Fussell, who appears in Ch. 14.]

[7]   Russell (St Johns). (B) [Henry Russell, St John's 1841, 26th Wrangler 1845; fellow of St John's 1849–86.]

[8]   [A member of the first class in the Classical Tripos.]

be in the First Class of the Tripos, or – not merely a Wrangler, but – among the first fifteen or twenty Wranglers, thus putting the First Class in Classics and the first half of the First Class in Mathematics on an equality.

I have said that for an unmathematical man it requires a good deal of honest hard work to get a place anywhere on the Mathematical Tripos. I conclude this chapter by saying that to take even a good Second in Classics, one must, as a general rule, have read a large quantity, and be able to display a considerable knowledge of the Ancient Languages. No one knows how hard a First Class is to obtain, unless he has either *just got it* or *just missed it*.

25

Reading for a
Trinity Fellowship [1845]

A Long Farewell.

It was such as literary society ought to be, composed of men
of real learning; of friends confiding in the mutual esteem
entertained by all undisturbed by ambitious quacks or impudent
pretenders.

Griffin's *Remains.*

Sell or no sell, the affair was definitively settled. 'All the king's money and
all the king's men' could not give me the chance over again. The first effect
of my disappointment was that it made me resolve to leave Cambridge
at once. I packed up my books – a couple of trunks contained with ease
the rest of my effects – sent them in charge to a bookseller, and waited
on our College tutor to resign my Scholarship. He refused to present my
resignation, and begged me to wait awhile, intimating his expectation that
I would stay and read for a Fellowship, and his belief that there were not
more than four men in the year who stood a better chance (there were

ultimately but four Fellows out of our year).[1] After my Classical degree, this seemed a mere compliment and *façon de parler*; still, as there was no pressing necessity for my resignation, I consented to withdraw it, and went off on a fortnight's run through Belgium and France. Before that fortnight was over, my feelings underwent a change. The first impulse passed away, and I found myself attracted back to the old place. Of a Fellowship I had the faintest possible chance, not worth taking into account, but the reading for one would be profitable and not unamusing; the pursuit and acquisition of learning had become a pleasure to me; I had formed some very agreeable friendships with men whose professional occupations would retain them at the University; I was not in sufficiently strong health to travel to the best advantage, and could recruit better during the coming season at home (which Cambridge had now been to me for three years and more) than elsewhere. So, on the whole, I resolved to return thither, for a while, at least, as a Bachelor.

The principal business of a Trinity Bachelor Scholar in residence (no Bachelors, except Scholars and Fellow-Commoners, are allowed to retain their rooms in College beyond the term subsequent to that in which they take their degree) is reading for a Fellowship. The M.A. *incepts* in about three years and two months from the time of taking his first degree, though he does not become a *full* M.A. till the July following – three years and a half in all. The Fellowship Examination is held in October, so that a candidate has three chances during his Bachelorship. Success on the first trial is rare, except in the case of a Senior Wrangler, or high Double First. A Senior Classic, unless a high Wrangler also, is seldom chosen the first time. This happens not from the preponderance of Mathematics in the examination (for the reverse is the case), but because a *Trinity* Senior Wrangler is usually a very superior man generally, not behind-hand in Classics, and often first, or among the first, on the Metaphysics paper.

The Examination consists of Classics, Mathematics, and a number of subjects conveniently comprehended under the title of Metaphysics. The Classical Examination nearly resembles that of the Classical Tripos. The Composition is about the same in amount, but the Translation papers are only three in number, two Greek and one Latin; and there is a long paper of general questions in Ancient History, Antiquities, Philology, Civil Law, &c – a 'cram' paper in short. One extract from the Greek verse paper is to be translated into English verse. Under these circumstances, a man who has taken a high Classical degree rather seeks to review and polish up than

---

[1] Blackburn (?5th Wr) Grant (7th Wr), Holden and Rendall Sen. Classics. (B)

enlarge his reading; but a Mathematician, especially if he has come to the University tolerably well prepared in Classics, and temporarily neglected them to read Mathematics for his Degree, will often extend his knowledge of Greek and Latin considerably. A Mathematician *very* deficient in Classics stands little chance, unless he be first-rate indeed in his branch, and also very good on the Metaphysical paper. I imagine Classics weigh at least as much as the other two together.

There are only two Mathematical papers, and these consist almost entirely of high questions; what a Junior Op. or low Senior Op. can do in them amounts to nothing, and the Classical men usually cut them entirely.

The third branch of the Examination comprises several subjects more or less connected among themselves.

1st. The History of Metaphysics. I say the *History* of Metaphysics, because an explanation of the theories of different schools rather than a support of any particular one is expected.

2d. Moral Philosophy, considered not only in an historical but also in a practical and, so to speak, polemical point of view.

3d. Political Economy, considered, like Metaphysics, rather in an historical than a partisan light.

4th. International Law.

5th. General Philology.

It is possible that questions are sometimes set on this paper not strictly reducible to any of the above heads. It intentionally covers a great deal of ground, one of its objects being to bring out clever men and men of general and, at the same time, deep reading beyond the immediate sphere of Classical and Mathematical studies. Except in Moral Philosophy, there is no preferred class of opinions. In Ethics, the dominant school was anti-Paley – that of the *independent* moralists, as they were called at Cambridge, among whom Butler occupies a high rank, and Whewell, as one of his interpreters, no contemptible one. No particular opinions being prescribed in the other subjects there are of course no particular text-books – no substantially similar courses of reading for all candidates. The only works which can come under this category are, Dr. Whewell's *History and Philosophy of the Inductive Sciences*, and *Moral Philosophy including Polity*. His double position – as Professor of Casuistry in the University, and Master of the College, has procured him this distinction, and you may always be sure of finding several questions set from his books.

In general the *Greek* and *English* authors are those most attended to. Plato and Aristotle, in their ethical, metaphysical, and political speculations, come in for a large share of attention; and with them, consequently, their historians and commentators, particularly Ritter. Cudworth is a favorite author. Mill's Logic became a standard work immediately on its publication. The older Scotch Metaphysicians are not in high repute. Cousin is read to some extent; Comte, I fancy, not much. The German Transcendentalists are not very deeply dipped into; most men were afraid of them. The Trinity receipt for getting-up Kant was, read the first forty pages of the 'Kritik' *and the Index.* There are generally two or three men who acquit themselves very stylishly on this paper, and cover a great extent of ground in the three or four hours allotted to it. An acquaintance of mine,[2] who stood first in Metaphysics, and gained his Fellowship by it, confined himself chiefly to one question, an ethical one – in discussing which, he took up and answered, piece by piece, a recent article in the Edinburgh which had attracted his attention. Probably the paper which he sent in would have made a respectable pendant both for quantity and quality to that which had suggested it. Another man, who was second in the same examination, wrote up not only all the paper, but all the *ink* within his reach.[3]

The average age of taking the B.A. may be set down at twenty-two years and three months, so that a Trinity man usually borders upon twenty-five when he attains the dignity of Fellow. The Fellowships are tenable for seven years from the time of taking the M.A. to such of the Fellows as do not go into Orders; those who do, may hold them till death or matrimony. For a Barrister this seven years' Fellowship is just the thing, as it gives him a support (£200 a year) long enough to start him in his profession, and carry him past thirty, by which time he has usually begun to do something if he ever means to, nor are the two or three years spent in procuring it by any means wasted,[4] the training being in many respects calculated to fit him for his vocation.

The number of vacancies varies from three to eight, averaging five, so that about one of three Scholars becomes a Fellow.[5] All the Scholars, however,

---

[2] Gibbs? (B) [Frederick Gibbs.]
[3] Walker? (B)
[4] I doubt this. (B)
[5] In our year 1844 only five. (B)

are not candidates to the end. Some never feel warranted in going in at all; others go in the first year and then give up.

The majority of candidates take pupils. This is considered, when a man has *good* pupils (and with a good Degree he can exercise some choice in the matter) rather a help than a hindrance. Sometimes a Bachelor who has set his heart on being a Fellow, continues to read with his private tutor, but this is considered *infra dig.*, and seldom practised.[6] Tutors have been known to refuse such applications. A modified form of coaching somewhat more common is where two friends assist each other reciprocally. But in general the Bachelor is expected to rely on himself.

I remained in Cambridge nearly the whole summer of 1845, a capital specimen of an English summer, for it rained every day without exception, and my daily ride combined the additional advantage of a shower-bath. My amateur Mathematical coach, who was now making his last spirt for a Fellowship, used to accompany me on these excursions, and we always expected the ducking as a matter of course and prepared ourselves accordingly. A Jew would not have given ten shillings sterling for both our wardrobes. My studies during this time were a great amusement as well as occupation. Into the Metaphysics proper I did not go far, in fact all my performance in that line was to read three or four hundred pages of Mill's Logic. This was chiefly owing to my curiosity to finish some of the works of Plato and Aristotle which I had begun the previous summer – the *Republic*, the Nicomachean Ethics, the Politics – and these books being read not merely for the language, but with more attention to the subject-matter than if they had been got up merely for Tripos purposes, looked indirectly towards the Metaphysical course. In the afternoon and evening I reviewed some of Cicero's more difficult Orations in company with my friend, thus at the same time paying off my old debts to him and keeping up my fluency in Latin Prose. With the same double purpose I used to revise his Latin Prose Composition, but a shot which I made for the Members' Prize proved unsuccessful. Also I made my first regular attack on Italian along with another friend[7] who had taken the highest Classical Honors, and was now resting after his toils in the *otium cum dig.* of a Small College Don. But neither of us went very zealously at our new pursuit, and our acquaintance with the tongue of Dante never became, to borrow a very old Joe Miller,

---

[6]   Charles Sargeant read Classics with Tom Taylor for his Fellowship. (B) [Charles Sargent, Trinity 1839, 5th Wrangler 1843; fellow of Trinity 1843.]

[7]   Maine, then of Trinity Hall. (B) Atkinson (now master) of Clare? (T) [Edward Atkinson, Clare 1838, 3rd Classic 1842; fellow of Clare 1842, Master 1856–1915.]

a speaking acquaintance. There was a tempting Fellows' garden belonging to his College, that overhung the Cam, with a carpet-like green to play bowls on, a mossy wall on one side and all sorts of vines with variety of flowers creeping over it, and a little table under a big tree, just the place to sip claret and eat huge strawberries. There we used to drop our Italian grammars, forget how *tre viaggiatori trovarono un tesoro*, and talk criticism and aesthetics till we had fairly talked each other out; and some months after his part of the conversation would meet me, like an old friend in a strange place, when I opened a new Edinburgh or Fraser.[8]

The Bachelor in most cases gives himself a kind of half holiday his first summer, as, not expecting a Fellowship at the first trial, he does not particularly lay himself out for one. Thus the men about me were more assimilated to my habits of half-work, and I had more opportunities of observing what had often struck me before – the development which takes place in an Englishman's mind after the age of twenty-two when he recovers in two or three years all the ground which he *appeared* to have lost as compared with an American, Scotch, or Continental student and gains a great deal more. The new traits of character, mental and moral, the new capabilities and veins of thought which were then displayed, the way in which they sucked up, as it were for mere amusement, different kinds of knowledge from all quarters – all these things were most interesting to observe.

It has been mentioned that some Bachelors sit in the first examination who do not present themselves at the succeeding ones.[9] Sometimes the reverse happens, and a man who wishes to reserve himself for the second trial does not show his hand at the first. This was my case; six weeks before the time I was in Switzerland, where, and in Italy, I passed the autumn and most of the winter. Even among these new scenes the reminiscences of the study clung to me; I carried along a volume of Plato and another of Thucydides, which were oftener in my hand than in my trunk. Before

---

[8] [Atkinson is not listed as a contributor to either journal, or indeed any other, by the *Wellesley Index*. Maine published in several periodicals, but his listed contributions do not fit Bristed's account, and a reference to him would surely have been more specific than 'another friend'. (For bibliographies of his work, see G.S. Feaver, *From Status to Contract: a biography of Sir Henry Maine, 1822–1888* (London, 1969), pp. 331–9; A. Diamond (ed.), *The Victorian Achievement of Sir Henry Maine* (Cambridge, 1991), pp. 402–14.) Bristed may mean simply that Maine's thinking was up with or ahead of the current arguments of the day.]

[9] This was the case with Hotham. (B) [Henry Hotham, who appears in Ch. 9 as 'Rothermann'.]

leaving Cambridge I had sent in an essay for the *King William*, a prize left
for the competition of Trinity Bachelors by some good Protestant; and at
Rome I heard of my success. March found me in my old quarters again,
reading Plato's Laws and making an analysis of them as I went on, while my
evenings were employed in a critical perusal of the Epistle to the Romans,
in conjunction with a friend who was reading a little Theology not professionally. But the time had arrived when it was necessary for me to decide
a question on which I had been pondering for several months, whether I
should 'gang or bide'. Loving the place as I did, I could not disguise from
myself the fact of my being in a false position there. I would rather have
been a Fellow of Trinity than anything which I could rationally hope to
be in my own country, and there was a chance, though a very remote one,
of my getting a Fellowship; but long before that was determined, I must
have become an Englishman out and out, by process of gradual assimilation.
Five years' residence where a man is an alien in religion may not altogether
qualify him to be a citizen, but when he is of the same religious persuasion
with those about him, and both he and they indifferent in politics, it begins
to have a marked effect. I say *indifferent in politics*, for the adiaphorism of
the better class in England at that time,[10] was hardly credible to one who
had first seen them in 1840 and 1841. They went pretty much where Sir
Robert Peel[11] chose to lead them, and the liberal, or so called, interests were
sufficiently in the ascendency to please any but a very strong Radical. News
from America began to sound to me like news from abroad. I no longer
took a personal interest in it. When unable to bear the voyage homeward
I had longed passionately after my native country; now that I was able to
go, I had lost all inclination. My Cambridge friends were fast filling up
the place that had been occupied by my relatives at home. External events
hastened my decision. The Oregon difficulties were looking very black.[12]
Nothing that our papers or publications *said*, seemed half so like war as
the silence of the English. A settled idea appeared to pervade the country,

---

[10]   1845–6. (B)

[11]   [Prime Minister 1841–6.]

[12]   [Oregon County (or Columbia District as it was known in Britain) was a region
in the NW part of the US, to which both Britain and the US had claims; in 1818
they had agreed on a system of joint occupancy. In 1844 the Democratic presidential
candidate James Polk asserted the American claim to total control; he then won the
election of 1845. The boundary dispute was settled in 1846, when the 49th parallel
became the boundary between the US and Canada. Bristed was not a supporter of
Polk: see p. 224 n. 5.]

that we – or a majority of us – were determined to have a war, that it was not their fault and they couldn't help it and must only be ready for it when it came.

It was like tearing myself up by the roots to leave Cambridge. I gave in my resignation this time without recall, and took my name off the boards. My tutor argued with me for some time, and at last finding my determination not to be shaken, admitted that I was quite right to go. Then, by way of re-asserting my nationality, I put up a motion at the Union (the questions for debate are always proposed in the form of motions), that the American claims in Oregon were just and reasonable, or something to that effect. The subject was discussed in a rational tone, and the majority against us very small. Finally I took leave of my friends in a series of dinners, leaving them as last memorials a French dish (*bisque d'écrevisse*),[13] and an American one (cocoa-nut pudding), that there might be a pleasant memory of the transatlantic in their mouths. On a fine May morning I took my last walk in the grounds of Trinity; they had never looked more beautiful. Sorry as I then was to quit the spot, I have never once regretted that I did so.[14]

---

[13] Known at the kitchen before Bristed's day. (T)
[14] Read the whole book again to this point at Christmas 1910, with the Cambridge Calendar. A most remarkable account of a more than remarkable society. It had better have stopped here. I wonder whether the notes are [by] Mr Thomas Flower Ellis, to whom the book belonged. (T)

26

The Study of
Theology at Cambridge

Were a German scholar to give his opinion on our universities,
he would say that they constitute only a philosophical faculty
with a small intermixture of theology.

Journal of Education, Vol. X. p. 69.

The American, and to a great extent the Continental, idea of a University,
is an institution for purposes of liberal education, which, besides a *general*
academic department, comprises three special faculties, Law, Physic, and
Divinity, to which the other faculty is deemed preparatory. The existence
of these separate faculties is generally considered with us the distinctive
mark of a *University* as opposed to a *College*. Judged by this rule the English
Universities would be represented in them by the slightest vestiges. Thus at
Cambridge there is a Professor of Civil Law who lectures and examines a
class of about twenty-four men a-year, and a Downing Professor of the Laws
of England, who does not lecture or examine at all – at least, he did not
in my day. The Professors of Botany, Chemistry, and Anatomy, have classes
varying from three to thirty. Medical school, in the ordinary sense of the
term, there is none. Ask an English University man why these things are
so, and he will answer that it is because the purely professional part of Law
and Physic cannot be taught anywhere so well as at the metropolis, where

the great hospitals and great courts are. With Divinity the case is different. A large number of the University graduates, probably more than half, being destined for the Church, and the chapels, clerical dress, and general routine of the place, adapting it well for getting up the mere formal part of the profession, that study is necessarily pursued to a considerable extent. Even here, however, the University does not pretend to *complete* the professional education, each bishop holding private examination, by his chaplain, of the candidates whom he admits to Holy Orders.[1]

1. A certificate of attendance on the Divinity Lectures is requisite to obtain the College testimonials for Orders; lectures are therefore very numerously attended, and by not a few Undergraduates.

2. The exercises required for Degrees in Divinity are Latin theses, and the only remains of the old system of 'keeping acts', which is now represented in the Degrees in Arts merely by payment of a small fine.

3. Hebrew is not *essential* to admission into Holy Orders. Probably half the candidates have not studied it. But it is coming to be more and more required by the bishops in their theological examinations. I think it may be assumed that the study of Hebrew is more advanced in this country than in England. Several English scholars have admitted as much to me. On the other hand the Alexandrine Greek, particularly the Greek Testament, is more carefully and accurately read there than here. Some portions of the Testament, the Acts for instance, are worked up with very great care, every subject relating to them, critical, historical, geographical, antiquarian, controversial, being elaborated with the utmost pains.

4. In 1846, was established an annual voluntary Theological examination, open to all graduates at any time after taking their B.A. This examination consists of the Greek Testament, certain assigned portions of the early Fathers, Ecclesiastical History, the Church of England Articles and Liturgy. The names of those who pass respectably are published in alphabetical order. There is a subsequent examination in Hebrew for such as choose to present themselves, and to which Bachelors in Civil Law are also admitted. Many of the Bishops now require that candidates for Orders in their dioceses shall have passed this voluntary Theological examination before presenting themselves to be privately examined by the chaplain.

---

[1] [Omitted here is a bald summary of chairs, their duties and the syllabus of professorial lectures, taken from a syndicate report of 1842.]

5. There is no specified time necessary to be spent in preparing for Orders. Any B.A. twenty-three years old, and having the necessary Professorial and College certificates, may present himself, subject to the particular conditions of his Bishop.

27

Recent Changes at Cambridge

Probably most persons will allow that a great degree of caution
is requisite in legislating on the subject of education.

Whewell.

A large class of hasty reasoners are accustomed to talk and doubtless to
think, of the English Universities as old hulks water-logged, or run aground
in the stream of modern improvement, regions systematically opposed to
emendation, and uninvaded by the much boasted-of 'march of intellect',
where the same things are taught in the same way year after year and age
after age. How far this reproach may be applicable to Oxford I shall not
pretend to say, but there certainly never was an academical institution less
liable to the charge than Cambridge. I will venture to say that there is
not an American College which has experienced during the last ten years
so many and so important changes, additions, and improvements, as that
great University. Nor is this to be wondered at when we consider that the
governing body comprises men of different pursuits and preferences, Classics,
Mathematicians, and Divines in large numbers, Metaphysicians and Casuists
more numerous than an outsider or one superficially acquainted with the
place might suppose, followers of natural science, less influential than the
other classes, yet not without their weight, all eagerly on the look-out for
any improvement in their favorite branch, and equally so for an occasion
of urging their claims to greater attention and privileges. The clever men
who remain attached to the University are very soon put in possession of a

share of the governing power. Some of the most important examinations are conducted by men under thirty,[1] so that different ages, as well as different tastes and abilities, are brought into contact and collision.

The changes which the principal examination for the Degree of B.A. underwent since 1800 and previous to 1840, are thus detailed in a Report, for the year 1849, of the *Board of Mathematical Studies*, which Board is itself a recent institution:

In 1808, the examination of the candidates for Honors commenced on the first Monday in the Lent Term; three days were devoted to Mathematics; and the candidates having been arranged in *Brackets* according to the result of the examinations on those days, the order of their merit was finally determined by examinations of the Brackets on the following Friday. Each candidate was examined 18 hours in the course of the three days, of which 11 hours were employed in answering questions from books, and the remaining 7 in the solution of Problems. The number of candidates that obtained Honors in that year was 38. In 1828, when the number had increased to 90, the examination commenced on the Friday preceding the first Monday in the Lent Term, and extended over four days, exclusive of the day of examining the Brackets; the total number of hours of examination was 23, and the time assigned to Problems remained the same as in 1808. By regulations which took effect in January, 1833, the commencement of the examination was placed a day earlier, the duration was five days, and the hours of examination on each day were 5½. Thus 4½ hours were added to the whole time of examination, 4 of which were appropriated to the answering of questions from books, and the remaining half-hour to the solution of Problems. The successful candidates in that year amounted to 105. In 1835 the number was 117, and the examination, for the convenience of the examiners, began on the Wednesday of the same week, without alteration in other respects. In January, 1839, there were six days of examination, beginning on the Monday preceding the first Monday in the Lent Term, and the total number of hours of examination was 33, of which 8½ were given to Problems. The first day of examination was altered in 1841 to the Wednesday week preceding the first Monday in the Lent Term. The number on the list of Honors in 1840 was 146.

Of the alterations relating to the classification of the candidates and the mode of proposing the questions, the following are those of chief importance. Previous to January, 1828, the candidates were divided into six classes, determined by the Exercises in the Schools; different printed

---

[1] The College annual examinations are so commonly. (B)

Problems and *viva voce* questions were proposed to different classes, generally taken two together, and the only questions proposed to all in common were the *Evening* Problems. In the year above named, important regulations, confirmed by Grace of the Senate, Nov. 13, 1827, came into operation. The classes were reduced to four, determined as before by the Exercises in the Schools. On the first two days all the candidates had the same questions proposed to them, inclusive of the Evening Problems; and the examination from books on those days excluded the higher and more difficult parts of mathematics, with the view of securing an object which, in the opinion of the Syndicate on whose recommendation these regulations were adopted, was highly desirable, viz. 'That the Candidates for Honors may be induced to pursue the more abstruse and profound mathematics to the neglect of more elementary knowledge'. Accordingly, on the first day (Friday) the questions from books extended to such parts of pure Mathematics and Natural Philosophy as do not require the Differential Calculus, and on the Saturday were added parts of Natural Philosophy somewhat more advanced, and the simpler applications of the Calculus. On Monday, the first and second classes were examined together, and the third and fourth together, in questions from books and in Problems; and on Tuesday, the second and third were examined together, and the first and fourth separately, in questions from books. The questions which had previously been given out *viva voce*, were *printed*, in order to make generally known the questions proposed in each year, and, by thus directing the reading of the students, to produce more fixity and definiteness in the mathematical studies of the University. The printed papers also afforded the opportunity of ascertaining by inspection that the examination embraced in due proportion all the ordinary subjects of mathematical study. No change was made in the substance of the examination; the questions inserted in the papers being, like those which had been proposed *viva voce*, propositions contained in the mathematical works commonly in use in the University, or simple examples and explanations of such propositions.[2] For the purpose of preventing those who had attended to a part only of the subjects from having any undue advantage by this mode of conducting the Examination, it was especially recommended that 'there be not contained in any paper more questions than students well prepared have been generally found able to answer within the time allowed for such paper.' At the same time a discretionary power was given to the Examiners of proposing additional questions *viva voce*, if any

---

[2] [On the wider context of these changes, see Stray, 'From oral to written examination'.]

candidate should before the end of the time have answered all the questions in the paper. This power, however, was not continued in the regulations of 1833, nor in any subsequent regulations. With this exception, the preceding regulations may be said to have determined the principles on which in the main the examinations have been since conducted; and for this reason it has been thought right to insert them at some length in this Report.

By regulations which came into force in January, 1833, the same questions were proposed to all the classes during the first four days. The order of difficulty of the questions on the first three days was the same as it had previously been on the first two days; but on the fourth day the examination extended to subjects of greater difficulty, care, however, being taken to insert into the papers some questions suitable to the lower classes. On the fifth day the examination was conducted according to classes.

In January, 1839, the division into classes was discontinued, and the same questions were proposed throughout the examination to all whom the Moderators judged, from the public Exercises in the Schools, to be qualified for examination as candidates for Mathematical Honors. The order of difficulty of the questions was regulated nearly as before, questions selected exclusively from the higher parts of the subjects being proposed only on the sixth day of the examination.[3]

The examinations as they existed from 1840 to 1846 have been described at length. During the last four years, from 1846 to 1850, several alterations, some of them very important, have been made.

In 1846 the great Mathematical examination for Honors was re-modelled; it was split into two parts and its time lengthened from six to eight days.[4] This was *a pass examination for Honors*. After an interval of eight days the examiners published an alphabetical list of those who had so acquitted themselves as to deserve Mathematical Honors, and such Classical men in it as only wished to pass were then sure of being Junior Optimes. The candidates for higher Honors then had an examination for five days in the higher subjects, after which all the men on the first list were classed according to the examination of the whole eight days. At the same time the arrangement of the *polloi* was made into four classes, the men in each class placed alphabetically, and the gulfed men were required to pass the non-mathematical part of the Poll examination before their Degrees were allowed them.

---

[3] [The excerpt from the Report ends here.]
[4] [Omitted: a long list of syllabus topics.]

The advantages of this change in the Honors examination were very great. The Classical men found themselves in a far better position, having their requisite field of Mathematics accurately marked out, at the same time that the number of questions in it was enlarged; while they stood a chance of knowing what they did get up much more thoroughly and with more satisfaction to all parties. In respect to those who were candidates only for Mathematical distinction, an occasional abuse of the old system was effectually guarded against. It had sometimes happened that men with more ambition for University Honors than Mathematical ability or steady application, had, though deficient in their low subjects, managed to secure respectable places by lucky speculation in cramming parts of high ones. By making all the candidates pass a preliminary examination in the low subjects this occurrence was at once prevented.

But the Classical men were not satisfied with the point they had gained. They continued to agitate the question and finally in 1849 opened the Classical Tripos to the First Class of the Poll and the men gulfed in Honors. This change was effected in the face of strong opposition, and some have prophesied very deleterious consequences from it. For my own part, I doubt whether it will have any effect for good or evil. The grievances of Classical men in my time were these; first, the *uncertainty* of the amount of Mathematical reading required of them; secondly, the annoyance of the Mathematical examination coming so soon before the Classical. The former was remedied by the change of 1846, the latter was not remedied by the change of 1849.[5]

In 1848 it was provided, by way of giving the professors something more to do, that all candidates for an ordinary Degree should, during their Undergraduateship, be obliged to attend for at least one term the lectures of one or more of the following Professors [a list of thirteen chairs, here omitted.] Also, that all students going out in Civil Law and not taking a First Class in that faculty, should, before receiving their Degree, attend for one term the lectures of one or more of the first eleven Professors above named.

The Classical Tripos received in 1849 the addition of a paper of questions in Ancient History – an addition not made before it was wanted, as minute scholarship was threatening to banish, under the invidious name of 'cram', all antiquarian learning from the University.

The Little-Go did not escape notice among all these alterations. Old

---

[5] [In 1854 it was agreed to remove entirely the mathematical bar on entry to the Classical Tripos; this change came into effect in 1857.]

Testament History, Arithmetic, and two Books of Euclid were added to it. Ecclesiastical History was also added to the fixed subjects for the Poll. Such a general stir woke up the King's men, who voluntarily put themselves on a level with the other Colleges by renouncing their privilege of taking Degrees without passing the examination.

But the most important change was made in 1848 by the establishment of two new Triposes, those of the *Moral Sciences* and the *Natural Sciences*.[6] The former includes Moral Philosophy, Political Economy, Modern History, General Jurisprudence, and the Laws of England; the latter, Anatomy, Comparative Anatomy, Physiology, Chemistry, Botany, and Geology. They are open to all Bachelors.

On the benefits to result from the establishment of this latter examination it may be premature to offer an opinion; that of the former is clearly destined to be of much importance and value. It is, in fact, nearly equivalent to carrying out for the whole University the course of reading pursued for the 'Metaphysical' papers in the Trinity Fellowship. There are but two objections to its becoming immediately popular. One is the want of pecuniary stimulus, direct or indirect, to the successful candidates. This will be obviated in time. There is no want of liberality on the part of Englishmen to encourage every form of learning. Dr. Whewell himself has here led the way by founding two annual prizes of fifteen guineas each for the two candidates who pass the best examination in Moral Philosophy. The other is one which I do not know if those actually on the ground have paid much attention to, but it struck me, looking at it from a distance and remembering my own experience, with great force. The examination is held just between the Mathematical and Classical Triposes, and consequently those who are very anxious or at all doubtful about their Classical Degree will hardly be able to attend to it.

Such are the changes recently made by the University within itself. But an external force has lately been brought to bear on it, not altogether unnoticed on this side the water. I allude to the Commission appointed within a year, and now, I believe, in session.[7] Some people both in and out of England think that this Commission will have very much the effect of running a railroad through a long secluded tract of country, and that something very stunning is to result from it. Others believe it merely a tub for the whale, such as English Whig Ministers delight in, and the end of which will be – just nothing. Should any positive state interference, such as a section of

---

6　Law Tripos? (W) [This came later, and was first examined in 1858.]

7　[The Royal Commission report on Cambridge was published in 1853.]

the Radicals desire, really be attempted, I leave Professor Maurice (whose very able Lectures on Education are less known than they deserve to be) to state the probable consequences.[8]

---

[8] [Omitted here is a lengthy extract in which Maurice argues for parliamentary support for the universities; the text largely consists of a quotation from a parliamentary committee report on education of 1835. In Bristed's 2nd edition it is on pp. 308–11. Maurice published several lectures on education in the late 1840s.]

28

The Cambridge System
of Education in its
Intellectual Results

There are some subjects in treating of which we can plunge *in medias res*. The subject of this chapter is not such a one. We must, in discussing it, bear in mind the Frenchman's advice, to 'begin at the beginning' before investigating the merits of any particular scheme of education, we must understand clearly what we mean by education and what we consider to be the object of it. This going back to first principles is, doubtless, a great bore in many cases, as where the Congressman, recorded by Sands, began his speech on a question of paying Pennsylvania Avenue with a historical dissertation on the Constitution of the United States; and such an announcement made formally at this stage of a book is very like admonishing the adventurous reader who has travelled so far that now is the time for him to repose after his labors. Nevertheless, it is very necessary on some occasions, if he would avoid that satisfactory state of things which is called in Latin *controversia*, and in English *cross-purposes*. For the term *education* is a tolerably comprehensive one, covers a great deal of ground, and may be taken in a great many different acceptations. Ask one man to define *education* for you, and he will tell you (truly enough, too, in one sense) that everything which a man passes through in his life is a part of his education for this world or the next. Ask another what he understands by education, and he will answer your question most Socratically by another, or a string of others, – 'education of whom, and for what? – a lawyer's education, a doctor's, a merchant's?'

And if you tell him 'a man's', he will be still less able to give you a direct reply. Ask a third what the end of education is, and he tells you, *ore rotundo*, that it is 'to qualify men to do good', which is a magnificent sentiment to hear, only if you come to cross question this gentleman as to the particular kinds of 'good' that men are to be qualified to do, you will find them to include robbery of private individuals, resistance to public authority, and a general propensity to upset everything established.

There are certainly some very odd ideas on this same subject of education afloat among us. Here, for instance, is a passage which I find in a book called *Hints towards Reforms* (p. 211), a series of lectures and discourses delivered by Mr. Horace Greeley, editor of the *New York Tribune*.[1]

The youth who fancies himself educated because he has fully mastered ever so many branches of mere school learning, is laboring under a deplorable and perilous delusion. He may have learned all that the schools, the seminaries, and even our miscalled universities, necessarily teach, and still be a pitiably ignorant man, unable to earn a week's subsistence, to resist the promptings of a perverted appetite, or to shield himself from such common results of physical depravity as Dyspepsia, Hypochondria, and Nervous Derangement. A master of *Greek and Hebrew* who does not know how to *grow Potatoes*, and can be tempted to drown his reason in the intoxicating bowl, is far more imperfectly educated than many an unlettered backwoodsman.

Now, as regards the 'intoxicating bowl', it is certainly a terrible defect in a man's *morale* that he should habitually get drunk. So it is, for that matter, that he should habitually advocate Anti-Rentism, or any other species of robbery; but I do not perceive that his education has *necessarily* anything to do with the one or the other. He may have a hereditary propensity to drink or plunder which no education can eradicate, and which can only be repressed or punished by other influences, or he may have started in the world a sober and honest man, and have afterwards become perverted by warping influences. But I wish to call particular attention to the words which I have italicized, and the proposition which they convey, to wit, that to grow, or, in more correct English, to *raise* potatoes (to the dignity

---

[1] [H. Greeley, *Hints Towards Reforms* ... (New York, 1850; 2nd edn 1857). Greeley was the leading editor of his day, and also an influential politician. One of the founders of the Liberal Republican party, he failed in his bid for the presidency as its candidate in 1872.]

of which vegetable Mr. G. has further testified by the big P he employs in spelling it) is a more essential branch of education than Greek and Hebrew.

Now, methinks, a reader of ordinary capacity and reflection, if he had his attention attracted by such a passage, and were led to compare for himself the relative value of the two things referred to as elements of education, would, in the first place, be likely to inquire the amount of labor and time respectively necessary to become a master of the two things. And I fancy the result of his examination would be that a thorough knowledge of Greek and Hebrew requires assiduous application to them for a number of years, probably seven or eight, at least, while the Science of Raising Potatoes may be conquered in a few seasons, perhaps months, taken at intervals. And this consideration would not improbably lead him to the conclusion that, so far at any rate, the scholar had acquired the more valuable part of education, because, supposing them compelled to change places, he could learn to raise potatoes much sooner than the potatoe-grower could learn Greek and Hebrew, provided their abilities were equal. This, then, would suggest another question, as to the relative amount of mind and capacity requisite to make a Greek scholar and a raiser of potatoes. To this, I imagine, he would not be very long in finding an answer, that to make a Greek and Hebrew scholar a man required to be, not a transcendent genius certainly, but a person of fair capacity, rather above than under the average intellect; that to be a scholar is not *tou tuchontos*, in plain English, possible for every man that you may pick up in the street; that if the scholar is not necessarily a Mercury, neither is he such a stick as can be made out of any wood; and much more to the same purpose, which Mr. Greeley himself would hardly make bold to call in question; while, on the other hand, it would appear to him, that any man not naturally an idiot is capable of being instructed in the cultivation of potatoes, as the example of the Irish peasantry fully shows, who excel in that cultivation, though very poorly off for intellectual endowments. Hence the conclusion would not unnaturally follow, that the knowledge of Greek and Hebrew was in itself a stronger evidence of a man's being something out of the common than the knowledge of raising potatoes, and therefore more valuable to a man in giving him a start in life.

Further, as *education* must be admitted, from the nature of the case, to have some effect on the material subjected to its influence, our reader will be induced to ask, how far the study of Greek and Hebrew, on the one hand, and the learning to raise potatoes on the other, respectively improve a man or a nation, morally or mentally. And here, I think, the result of his investigations will be, that the study of Greek and Hebrew has been generally allowed to improve the intellectual faculties – what faculties it improves, or to what extent, may be a mooted point, but that it does improve some of them, and in some appreciable degree, is almost universally conceded, and that nations famous for their knowledge of Greek, such as the Germans and English, hold a high intellectual rank in other respects; whereas in the culture of potatoes there is nothing that necessarily improves a man intellectually or morally, and in the case of a nation devoted to it, the Irish aforesaid for instance, it has been allowed on all hands to retard the moral, mental, and even physical improvement of the nation; so that here again he will be apt to conclude that the Greek and Hebrew have the best of it.

But there is another light in which the student may view the question. He may look at it as a mere matter of dollars, and those dollars gained by no indirect process, but the immediate fruit of the two pursuits. To be sure this is a dreadfully low way of regarding the subject, but we had better come down to it for the satisfaction of those who profess to be nothing if not practical. Even weighed in this balance, I think the Greek will preponderate over the potatoes. Putting out of the question any other mode of 'realizing' his literary acquisitions, a good scholar can always get his living as a teacher; I do not say a thoroughly comfortable living or as good a living as he ought to have in all cases, but a better living than a man can get by raising potatoes; and in any civilized country can command the services of more than one potatoe-raiser. Many a scholar may have difficulty in helping himself in some of the most ordinary occurrences of every-day life, and still be driving a very lucrative trade by his scholarship. I knew a Senior Wrangler so green in all apparatus relative to horses, that once when we were riding out together and his curb-chain unfastened, he very soberly set to work to refasten it *over the animal's nose*; but this very man was making more money at the time than the sharpest hostler at the most frequented livery stable ever did.

And this brings on one question more; in what condition of society will the knowledge of raising potatoes be of more pecuniary advantage to its possessor and more value to the community generally than the knowledge of Greek and Hebrew? And the answer is most obvious: in *the very first and primitive* stage – in an unsettled country – in the backwoods of a newly discovered territory – among that shipwrecked crew on a desert island whom Locke took as an example of his fancied 'state of nature'. There all men are hewers of wood and drawers of water, tillers of the soil, shooters of wild beasts or savages. There all elegancies of mind or body are out of place and premature, because every one's attention is absorbed in satisfying the immediate wants of life. There the confectioner and the scholar, the French milliner and the German metaphysician are alike useless drones; the carpenter is a prince (as he was in Homer's time), and the historical painter cumbereth the earth. There and there only is Mr. Greeley's assertion a correct one.

By the time the student has carried his speculations thus far he will be able to appreciate pretty correctly the comparative value of the Greek preferred by his humble servant the author, and the potatoe-raising commended by Mr. Greeley; and he will also have had a neat illustration of a position maintained by many wise and good men – that Socialism tends to put the lowest kind of work above the highest, and therefore, so far from advancing, as it pretends to do, the course of civilization, goes directly to pervert and retard it, and to throw the world back to the ages of barbarism.

Returning from this partial digression and turning to a much higher being in the scale of animated nature than Mr. Greeley, we find this idea in the lectures of Professor Maurice, of the London University;[2] that from all the various systems and definitions of education ever proposed may be evolved three distinct doctrines; the first, that the end of education is *development of the faculties*; the second, that it is the *restraint* of certain faculties; the third, that it is the giving of information. (This is not the order in which he enumerates them, but as it is their historical order, I prefer stating them so.) For illustrations of these three principles carried out purely – so far as it is possible to keep them unmixed – he refers to Athens, Sparta, and the modern Utilitarian school.

The first and second of these principles appear to be in direct contradiction, but it is the first and third which really clash for the second looks chiefly to a particular set of faculties, different from those which are the main object of the first. In other words the idea of *development* has more reference to our *intellectual*: that of *restraint* more to our *moral* education. As a general rule there are more mental faculties that require *developing* and more moral propensities that require *restraining*. The illustrations chosen by the Professor show this; the Athenian education wonderfully sharpened the intellect at the expense of the morals, the Spartan education left the intellect untouched; it is no exaggeration to say of the Lacedemonians that they were *illiterate on principle*; whatever in their education was not physical, was moral. Such being the case, I put out of question for the present the second principle, not because a man's moral nature is not, in my estimation, of infinitely more importance than his intellectual, but for the same reason

---

[2] [See p. 277.]

that in examining the other two principles I shall set aside the questions of *physical* development and of information on subjects pertaining expressly to the *physique* of the student, although I hold that the body is the very first thing to be attended to for if a man's body is not in good working condition, he will seldom be able to apply himself so as to improve his mind to the best advantage; and if his *physique* is much out of order, his *morale* is very apt to he injuriously affected But I regard the improvement and education of the mind as the special business of a College or University; just as I would say that the special business of one particular Faculty – a Law school, for instance, is to teach law; and I should expect the graduates of a given College or University to be men of more intellectual power and refinement than the mass of the community; if they were not, I should immediately conclude there was something wrong in the University course; but if they were not stronger or healthier, or more moral men than the rest of the community I do not say that I should be perfectly satisfied, but I should be inclined to withhold my censure as long as they did not fall *below* the average in these respects, nor should I immediately set down their want of physical and moral superiority as the fault of the Institution. In all this I may be wrong; however, my plan has at any rate the advantage of enabling us to consider one thing, at a time; to examine by themselves the intellectual advantages or disadvantages of the Cambridge system and then to compare them with those of any other, first similarly examined apart.

Now the University of Cambridge adopts the *first* rather than the third of the theories above enunciated as the true theory of a liberal education. It does not propose to itself as its primary object the giving of *information*, but rather the developing and training of the mind, so that it may receive, arrange, retain, and use to the best advantage, such information as may be afterwards desirable or necessary – such information as it may be the business of professional teachers to supply it, or its pleasure to collect for itself. For this training the University has decided, not in blind obedience to precedent, for the subject is undergoing discussion within its precincts every day – that classical and mathematical studies are the best means, and it undertakes to teach them thoroughly. Here, at the outset, a difficulty arises which is satisfactorily provided for. Neither the preparation nor the abilities of those who enter on any college or university course at the same time being equal, it is a question with all academical authorities, how to make a class work together so that the dull ones shall not retard, nor the bright ones hurry the rest, and that all shall be kept busy without any being overworked. Now the Cambridge system, by its examinations of different kinds suited to different degrees of preparation and capacity, and by its private tuition (which is an integral part of the system, though existing unofficially), has provided for educating every separate student in accordance with his antecedents and capabilities, and ingeniously combines the advantages of a public and a private education. The student then may learn more or less, but whatever the amount, he is expected to learn it *thoroughly*. Hence, as the first effect, he acquires habits of extreme mental accuracy.

At our colleges it is so arranged that all the students go through the same course, at least during the most important years of their undergraduateship, and necessarily some go through it well and some ill; it is too much for some, and not half enough for others. Now at Cambridge precisely the reverse of this takes place. A student may go through a very limited or a very extensive course of reading, but whatever he passes an examination in he is required to do and know well. Even the examinations which are disparagingly known as 'pass' ones, the Previous, the Poll, and (since the new regulations) the Junior Optime, require more than half marks on their papers, and the way in which a slovenly and inaccurate man loses marks would astonish a great many of our students if subjected to them. And as we ascend to the honor examinations, the demand for precision increases with the field for its exercise, till we arrive at cases of High Wranglers who have made not one single decided mistake in their six days' work, and of Senior Classics who 'floor' the Tripos papers without an error.

It is unnecessary to enlarge on the value to its possessor of such a habit of reading, thinking, and writing accurately. I will merely allude to one of its advantages. A Cantab is most careful in verifying references. He will not take a thing at second-hand if he can go to the original source of it. Hence he is little liable to be imposed upon by the ignorance, real or assumed, of others, or to be the innocent medium of currency for other men's blunders. I believe that a historical, antiquarian, literary, or statistical error, put forth in print or public speech, is sooner and more certainly detected in England than in any other country, and that this is owing to the influence of Cambridge men and Cambridge education.

But the English student does not only read his subjects accurately; he reads them comprehensively, and so that he can apply them. It is, indeed, impossible to avoid the imparting, in some instances, of partial and exoteric information; but as a general rule it could never be said of the Cantabs what has more than once been said of American college students, that theirs is a knowledge of particular books rather than of subjects. And in no place of education is there less parrotry, less exercise of memory, as distinguished from the acquisition of knowledge, than at Cambridge. The nearest approach to it is the case of the classical men who get up only Mathematics enough to pass as Junior Optimes. Even here the knowledge, though temporary, is real for the time; it is not retained in the mind, because it is immediately afterwards crowded out by more interesting matter; but these men really understand their subjects for the examination, and can work, if not problems (which are the last test of a man's mathematical knowledge), at least examples, deductions, and riders in them. Let me give an instance or two of what I mean by applying knowledge. A student for classical honors in his second or third year may be utterly unacquainted with some long author like Plautus. He reads two or three of the comedies, and gets them up so carefully that he has acquired a good insight into the author's vocabulary and peculiarities of phrase and construction, so that he will make a very fair translation of a passage from any of the other plays which he has not read. Take a Cambridge Second-year man and an American graduate, both disposed to study Plato; let the former read four dialogues, and the latter eight, which will take them about the same time, each reading in the way he has been accustomed to; the Cantab from studying half the quantity, will know more about his author than the American, and will translate and explain a passage at random from any of the other dialogues. If our Cantab be a mathematical man, his skill in the application of his knowledge will be still further increased by the symmetrical arrangement of it.

Again, the Cambridge student acquires manly habits of thinking and reading. He becomes fond of hard mental work, and has a healthy taste in his mental relaxations. The trash of the circulating library he despises as he would sugar candy. No works of fiction but the very best, and those rarely, are to be found in his room.[3] His idea of light reading is Shelley's or Henry Taylor's poetry, Macaulay's Essays, a leader in the Examiner, a treatise on Ethics or Political Economy; he would laugh at you for calling this 'reading' in the University sense, or study. Such a taste is indeed late in forming; when nearly a man in size and looks he is still disposed to be idle and schoolboy-like in the intervals of his hard work, and at eighteen is behind an American or Scotch youth in general information; but the habit of mind once started, he goes on drawing in knowledge from all quarters at a vast rate, and whatever he does take into his well prepared mind assimilates itself with matter already there, and fertilizes the whole, and fructifies; nothing of what he reads is thrown away.

Now the general and final effect of this energetic, accurate, and comprehensive style of working, is that the Cambridge student exhibits great

---

[3] It was a rule of the Union Library to admit no novels, and so strictly was the rule observed that it was with great difficulty Walter Scott's could be introduced.

power and rapidity in mastering any new subject to which his attention is necessarily turned. If he has to acquire a foreign language or a new science, to become familiar with the elements of a difficult profession, like that of the law, or even to learn the details of a large business establishment, in any case he takes cleverly hold of the first principles, and then proceeds accurately, but speedily, from step to step, till he has attained the desired knowledge.

From many striking instances within my own observation, only one remove from it, of the way in which a Cantab carries a thing through, let me relate an event that occurred just before I entered the University. A high Wrangler, then a Trinity Bachelor, went to see a relative who was largely engaged in the manufacture of plate glass.[4] While lionizing the premises, he learned that the chief difficulty and expense lay in the *polishing*. Forthwith our Trinity man sets himself to get up the subject, and after he has acquired all the information he can from those on the spot and such other sources as are available within a short time, he goes to work to calculate the formula of a law according to which two plates of glass rubbing together will polish each other. The result was an improvement which realized a handsome fortune for the manufacturer, who did not forget how he had obtained it, and evinced his gratitude in a substantial manner.

And now let us see how such a man will write on any subject – the consideration of which I may seem to have unduly delayed, for the first and almost the only test of a young man's ability that occurs to many of us (except making a speech) is his writing. What training has he had for this? Directly very little; he may not have written a dozen set essays – nay not half a dozen – all the time he was at the University. But he has been accustomed to reproduce the thoughts of others, rapidly, tersely, and accurately, upon paper. He has never had room for verbiage any more than for ornament. He will have a tendency to say whatever he says correctly, concisely, and pointedly. He will not write fluently at first, for want of practice – nor elegantly, for he has not cultivated the graces of style, but he will write understandingly and from a real, conscientious study and knowledge of his subject. He will be ready to detect misstatements, inaccuracies, and false logic in others, and for himself will not be likely to commit an *ignoratio elenchi*; to miss the drift of a question – to find fault for instance with

---

[4]   No. James Chance – now a member of the firm at Birmingham. The 'relative' was his own father. (H) [James Chance, Trinity 1833, 7th Wrangler 1838, later head of the family firm, Chance Bros.; with Faraday experimented with dioptric lenses for lighthouses.]

literature *for not being science*, as a very showy writer on this side the water did not very long ago.

As to his style it will soon improve – thanks to another result of his education without which those mentioned would be very imperfect – an elegant and refined taste which arrives late at maturity only to approach nearer perfection. His mind is imbued with the influence of the choicest classic models, *through which he reads and by which he interprets those of modern literature*. Applied to his case the argument so often urged against the study of the Classics in our Colleges, 'that they are forgotten in a few years', would be false and meaningless. His Latin and Greek are not forgotten. They stick to him through life. They explain his reading and adorn his writing. They bring him into fellowship with the scholars, the men of elegant literature, *the gentlemen of the intellect* throughout the world. He does not have to hunt after Classical quotations and allusions to be brought in as bits of 'business' for the purposes of making an impression on others still more ignorant than himself; they drop from him as naturally as a figure or an antithesis, and he feels they will please men of his own stamp, because he feels pleased to meet them elsewhere: they are his *phonanta sunetoisin*, vocal to the intelligent, though for the multitude they may need interpreters.

This is a brightly coloured picture that I have drawn; are there no dark shades in it? Have I represented a man educated *kat'euchen* [according to our prayers] just as I should wish my son or yours to be in every respect? There *are* one or two little deficiencies to consider, which we will look at in all candor.

The first may have been anticipated from my silence. The two great results of College education which most of our people, including most of the students themselves, look to, are public speaking and writing. Whatever else a young man knows how to do, he must be able to write fluently and showily and to address a meeting. Now the Cambridge system of education is certainly not calculated to make public speakers. By this I do not mean that it will spoil a man who has the material of a real orator in him as much as the system of a New England College will spoil a man who has a tendency to be a good scholar; but that it is not favorable to the production of those pretty good debaters and ready haranguers whom our places of instruction turn out in such numbers. I have mentioned in a former chapter that some of the cleverest men in the place despised and undervalued public oratory on principle; and the authorities do nothing to encourage it, except giving here and there a College prize.

But it is not merely in this negative way, and from want of opportunity and encouragement to practise frequently, that the young speaker suffers.

The education he goes through is positively unfavorable to fluency on his legs. The habit of weighing every word accurately, may be all the better in the end for a man who has real oratorical genius, but is certainly all the worse for an ordinary debater. The general run of public speaking requires redundancy and repetition, nor does it admit a fastidious choice of words except in some elaborate concluding period. Just before leaving Cambridge I found myself falling off in ability to address an audience, and that in a greater degree than the mere want of practice would account for.

This admission will settle the business in the eyes of some; they will deem it enough to counterbalance all the benefits claimed for the Cambridge system. My own opinion is, and I shall endeavor to prove it farther on, that we value this faculty too highly and pay too large a price for it. Still there is a medium here as in everything else; viewing the art of public speaking merely as an *accomplishment*, it deserves more attention. A gentleman at a public dinner, for instance, ought to be able to extemporize some appropriate observations when called upon without stumbling over his own words and making himself and every one else uncomfortable, as an Englishman is apt to do on such occasions. And here, I think, lies the English error on this point; they regard a certain proficiency in public speaking as a purely professional matter, for the barrister or Member of Parliament to learn subsequently to his academical course. But *besides* its professional value it is an accomplishment which a highly educated man may be expected to possess, and should therefore form part of a liberal education.

The second deficiency is one rather more complicated and not so easy to explain or understand. I may state it thus – *a tendency to make men too exclusively consumers and not sufficiently producers of knowledge*. The Cambridge man is great in acquiring a mastery of a subject and using it for his own benefit, in his profession for instance, but his inclination to promulgate his acquisitions and the fruits of them to the world, does not keep pace with his ability to do so. We see this exemplified in the resident Fellows, who, reading as many books as the German professors, write a great deal less. It is not idleness that causes this; between teaching and study their time is pretty well filled up; the indolent and rusty Don who does nothing but drink port and play whist has become nearly a tradition. It is not any selfish or priestly feeling in regard to knowledge – no, men are more ready to communicate information when you ask it of them. The tendency in question rather springs from false modesty and an excessive fastidiousness produced by hypercriticism. Accustomed to scrutinize with the greatest severity the performances of others, the English graduate is not indulgent to his own. He is just as hard upon them, and more dissatisfied with them.

A friend who was with difficulty induced to write a few pages now and then for a Mathematical journal which he did with great clearness and force, once said to me on the occasion of my having a prize essay printed, 'I should not like to publish anything myself; when you put a thing in print *it seems as if you were perfectly satisfied with it*, and I never am with what I write.' This is the spirit that keeps many a competent man from making a name among the scholars and literary men of the civilized world. It is true such a man has a plausible excuse. He may say that since 'of making books there is no end' and the majority of those published are perishable and of small value, he will play a wiser part by not adding to the number; that he had better be a reservoir to supply the streams of his neighbors, informing and improving his immediate associates by his conversation and unwritten learning. But surely when there is room for a new book on a new subject or an old one that has long lain fallow; when new lights can be thrown upon old questions; when in short a man has acquired a certain combination of knowledge and ideas not to be found in any book, and the acquisition of which he feels would be beneficial to others as it has been to him, ought he not to write a book, his time, and means, and other circumstances permitting? I am very much inclined to think so.

To sum up, it may be said that, as the utilitarian system inclines a student to communicate more knowledge than he possesses, the English University system will sometimes hinder him from communicating what he has.

29

Physical and Social Habits of Cambridge Men, Their Amusements, &c.

Cricket on Parker's Piece.

Mens sana in corpore sano.

Horace.

Some remarks already dropped here and there may have given the reader a hint of the comparison between the intellectual teaching of Cambridge and that of some other places to which I am proceeding, and which is one of the principal objects of this work. Before arriving at this, however, it is necessary to look at our English friends all round, physically, socially, morally, religiously.

To a vegetarian, a teetotaller, a 'eupeptic' of any sort (lovely names these are, and show a sublime taste in the people who invented and use them) and, I fancy, to a New Englander generally, the Cantab's life would not appear the most regular, nor the kind of one best adapted to promote health, strength, and longevity. He is never up before half-past six in the morning, and seldom in bed before twelve at night. He eats a hearty dinner of animal food at 4 p.m., drinks strong malt liquors with it, and not unfrequently strong wine after it. He is not shy of suppers and punch. He often starts himself for his morning's work with the stimulus of a cigar. He reads nine hours a day on a 'spirt' the fortnight before examination, writes seven hours a day or more against time during the examination week, and the week after that does nothing but jollify.

Yet this very man takes better care of himself and has a more philosophical system of living than many a conscientious and painstaking ascetic, who has spent half his life in declaiming against the wickedness of alcohol and tobacco. For eight or nine months of the year he is in a regular state of training; if he had to walk a match the only change necessary would be for him to drink a little less. His seven hours of sleep (a rather scanty quantity, but enough for most men in good health)[1] are always the same seven hours of the night. The sponge bath and horse-hair glove are among the regular and daily accessories of his toilet. His breakfast is light and simple – a buttered roll and a cup of tea – and when he is at it he does not worry himself about anything else. He is discreet in his position when at work, and knowing that he has to stoop forward in writing at the examinations, does most of his reading leaning back in his arm chair or standing at a high desk where he strengthens his legs and eases his chest at the same time. After he has dined you could not bribe him to engage in any exertion of body or mind for at least two hours. The most he will do is to lounge to the Union and read the papers, or he may look over some easy and familiar book in his own rooms. But above all, his exercise is as much a daily necessity to him as his food, and by exercise he does not understand driving in a carriage, strolling about, or even playing billiards. 'Constitutionals' of eight miles in less than two hours, varied with jumping hedges, ditches, and gates; 'pulling' on the river, cricket, football, riding twelve miles without drawing bridle; all combinations of muscular exertion and fresh air which shake a man well up and bring big drops from all his pores, are what he understands by his two hours exercise. See one of these men stripped and observe the healthy state of his skin – that is enough to demonstrate that he is in good condition, even should you overlook his muscular developments.[2]

---

[1] There can be no Procrustean standard for such things. Some men will be satisfied with six hours, others require eight and a half. I have reason to believe that the average amount of time which a Cambridge reading man passes in bed is rather under than above seven hours.

[2] [For a good discussion of the Cambridge combination of intellectual and physical exercise, see Warwick, *Masters of Theory*, pp. 176–226.]

The staple exercise is walking; between two and four all the roads in the neighborhood of Cambridge – that is to say, within four miles of it – are covered with men taking their constitutionals. Longer walks, of twelve or fifteen miles, are frequently taken on Sundays or days succeeding an examination. The standard of a good walker, is to have gone, not once but repeatedly, fifteen miles in three hours, without training or being the worse for it next day. A number of my acquaintances professed to be able to do this. After walking comes boating or 'pulling', which is *the* sport par excellence of an English University, as sword exercise is of a German (this was the illustration given me by a man who had been at both). The men put themselves into extra training for the Spring races, eschew pastry (which an Englishman never takes much of at any time, generally eating cheese where an American does pie) and confine themselves to a small quantity of liquid, usually malt liquor, during the day. Besides these races, the Cam is always full during the warm season, of men pulling up and down, sometimes one, sometimes two in a boat. Some of the reading men work very hard in the boats. Two Smith's Prizemen and one Senior Classic[3] were prominent boating men during the three years from '42 to '45. Cricket, football, fives, all games of ball in short, are popular in their season. There is not so much riding as might be supposed, considering that there is not one Englishman in five hundred of the University-going classes, who cannot ride and does not like to.[4] The expense is the reason generally alleged, and under the circumstances it shows more self-denial than University men usually have the reputation of. There is sufficient business, however, for five or six livery stables,[5] those who keep their own horses being mostly the Noblemen and Fellow-Commoners, and a few of the Fellows. Englishmen have a patent for making any sort of horse leap, and when your Cantab gets on a hired horse, with his own spurs, to take perhaps the first ride he has had for three months, the amount he will get out of him is incredible, and the amount he gets out of himself somewhat remarkable. I recollect once being, with some other men, nine hours on horseback during which time we took no refreshment and did not once dismount. The whole distance ridden was not more than forty miles, but having to wait some hours for the steeple chase we went to see (and some of the leaps in which we took) our animals had the pleasure during that interval of walking about with us on their

---

[3] Denman. (B) [One of the Smith's prizemen was George Hemming, Senior Wrangler and 1st Smith's prizeman 1844.]

[4] Nonsense. (T)

[5] More now, besides the private stables of each college. (T)

backs. When there is ice enough, which does not happen every winter, the Cantabs are great skaters, and stories are told of their performances in this line which I will not repeat, for they sound very large and I could not positively authenticate them. There is a certain amount of fencing and sparring practised, more of the latter than the former, not a great deal of either. It is almost a *sine qua non* for a Cantab's exercise, that it should be in the open air. He never minds the weather, or thinks of putting off his constitutional because it rains.

It may be asked whether, allowing that from this regularity of exercise a high standard of strength and endurance results, the general health of the men is also good. For health and strength do not *necessarily* go together: in our country we meet many persons of great activity and a considerable share of downright strength, who are nevertheless always out of order and ailing. I have no hesitation in saying that the health of the Cambridge men is on a par with their strength, and such as might be expected from it by an ordinary observer. Dyspepsia is almost unknown, bilious attacks are not common, consumption scarcely ever heard of.[6] Sometimes a man gets a temporary affection of the heart from pulling too much, or from some irregularity in his way of life. Sometimes he has a nervous attack from over work just before, or over excitement at an examination. These are the most general forms of illness, and usually but temporary in their effect. When a death occurs it is almost always either from accident or wilful dissipation.

I was anxious to obtain the statistics of Undergraduate mortality, for the purpose of bearing out my statements on this point by the actual figures; but I could not get them, simply because none have ever been kept. Some of my medical friends made shots at the question from their own experience, and agreed in an average of three deaths a-year; but this, among a population of eighteen hundred, must be below the mark. Of the 'year' that entered with me at Trinity (that of 1844)[7] three men died before the time of graduating, but two of these were lost by accidents;[8] of the year before (that of 1843), and of the year after, in which I finally went out (that of 1845), there was not a single man who died. I doubt if this ever happens at Yale College (where the number of students is nearly the same as at Trinity) for two out of three successive years. During five

---

[6]   [Alexander Gooden often suffered from constipation: see Smith and Stray, *Cambridge in the 1830s*.]

[7]   1840–1844. (B)

[8]   One, Jermy, was killed by Rush. (B) [Isaac Jermy, Trinity 1840, BA 1844; murdered in 1848, with his father, by their tenant-farmer John Rush.]

years that I passed at New Haven, there was not a graduating class that had not lost at least three members.

Indeed a man must be healthy as well as strong – 'in condition' altogether to stand the work. For in the eight hours a-day which form the ordinary amount of a reading man's study, he gets through as much work as a German does in twelve; and nothing that our students go through can compare with the fatigue of a Cambridge examination. If a man's health is seriously affected, he gives up honors at once, unless he be a genius like my friend E——,[9] who 'can't help being first'. To go on with half reading, and take a place below his own standard, as I did, is what an Englishman is too proud to do.

Why are the Cantabs in such good physical plight, when they have neither dietetic lectures nor voluntary societies? All that you will hear in the way of precept is a tradition or two, such as that eight hours a-day, 'coach' and all, is a proper amount of work for a reading man, or that it is not safe to read after Hall (i.e., after dinner). Regular exercise is the great secret. But why do they exercise so regularly? First of all, it amuses them: where so many different kinds of exercise are attainable, every man must find some kind that he likes, and that he pursues without thinking all the time that it is for his health – which is one reason why it does him good. These young practical philosophers have wisdom enough to see that it is not enough to exercise the body unless the mind is interested and diverted at the same time; and they carry out this principle even in the 'constitutionals': a man will not walk out alone, for then he might still be thinking of the problems or the verses he was lately working at; no, he takes a friend with him, and they two talk on some subject of the day, politics or literature, or at worst 'shop', such as who are likely to be the next Scholars – anything but their actual studies. Now this seems so obvious a dictate of common sense, that the acting in accordance with it may appear to involve no remarkable stretch of wisdom, nay, I may be thought platitudinous for enlarging upon it at all; but I do insist that the principle deserves our attention, inasmuch as some professed luminaries of reform among ourselves have strangely ignored it, and with a short-sighted utilitarianism started a precisely contrary doctrine. The proposition has been distinctly laid down by persons of different schools, from an Episcopal bishop to a Socialist of no particular religion, that there should be no such thing as pure relaxation, but that when students are not at study they should be at *work* – actually employed in manual labor. This is really using a youth at one of the most critical and important periods of

---

[9]   Ellis. (T)

his life worse than any person of common intelligence or humanity would use a horse.

The doctrine is brought forward partly to carry out a fancy that some people have of *asserting the dignity of labor* – of making out that manual occupation is something very fine and glorious, not for its results, but for and in itself; and therefore they would make students work *for the mere sake of working*. Such a fancy is equally repugnant to reason and Scripture. The necessity of labor was part of the primeval curse, and all beauty, or glory, or dignity pertaining to labor depends on the *ends* to which it is the means. I may respect most sincerely the man who drives a dung-cart, if I know that he supports a sick relative or educates a child from the fruits of his toil, but driving a dung-cart is a very undignified pursuit for all that. Most manual labor is in itself disagreeable; men submit to it because it is necessary and profitable, not for any merit or attraction that it has in itself. So they are delighted to obtain physic when ill by reason of the results they expect from it; but no one would say that taking castor-oil is its own reward.

To help along this crotchet comes the just-see-before-your-nose-and-no-farther sort of idea that all time not spent in doing something tangible is lost. There is sometimes a useful lesson to be got out of a joke. Let me repeat a very old one for the benefit of these utilitarians.

A country manager saw that the trumpets of his orchestra were not taking part in an overture which the other musicians were executing. He rushed upon them and inveighed at their idleness. 'But', said one of the assailed, 'we have fifteen bars *rest* here'. 'Rest!' retorted the other, 'I don't pay you ten shillings a-night for *resting*; blow away!' How the *rest* of the trumpets should be essential to the harmony of the piece was beyond his comprehension.

It is well known that scarcely one third of an entering class at West Point graduates, and any cadet, or any person with the place, will tell you on being asked the reason, that it is the union of hard study and military drill (which amounts to a species of work) that causes so many to break down. A West-Pointer has told me that, after drilling, the men are so fatigued, in mind as well as body, that it takes them some time to settle down to study. I do not presume to find fault with the system at West Point, which is a peculiar one for a peculiar purpose. Its first object is not to educate young men, but to provide the U.S. Army with first-rate officers. The Government, having its pick out of a large number of applicants, has a right to sacrifice many of them for the sake of getting the best possible men for its own wants; but a system which sifts out, in a course of four years, more than two thirds of those subjected to it, would never answer for a system of general education.

In schools where a rigid system of gymnastics is made the substitute for ordinary boyish recreations, the result is apt to be that, the play having been turned to a study, *the study degenerates into play.*[10] Pestalozzi's establishment at Yverdun was a striking example of this.[11] In short, it is a safe rule to lay down, that, to keep a student in good working order for a length of time, the harder he applies himself to his studies while studying, the more diversion he requires when taking exercise.

The sensible example of their Seniors does a great deal to encourage these young men in taking healthful exercise. The Master of Downing[12] is noted as the best skater in Cambridge, and may be seen cutting figures on the Cam during any hard frost. The Master of Trinity[13] is a crack horseman, and few men of his weight in England can take a leap better.[14] An English tutor or lecturer has no sham dignity which makes him fear to demean himself by joining in the sports of undergraduates, and consequently none of the undergraduates themselves think these sports undignified. Still less are they withheld by any religious scruples. That it is wrong for a clergyman to ride, or that walking for exercise on Sundays is a species of practical infidelity, are propositions that they would be slow to admit. I remember once accompanying a college lecturer and tutor, a very young man, but whose merits and good character had gained him rapid academic promotion, on a long Sunday morning constitutional between our early breakfast and St. Mary's at 2 p.m. We had been discussing all manner of ethical and theological questions, and thought we had passed the time rather profitably than otherwise, when suddenly something put me in mind of New Haven, and I said to him, 'Do you know, M——, where I was when a boy they would think we had been spending this morning very wickedly?'

He looked several notes of interrogation at me.

'Because,' I continued, 'we have been walking.'

---

[10]   The same is pretty much the case at Bruce Castle [in] Tottenham. (B) [Rowland Hill's progressive school.]

[11]   See *Fraser's Magazine*, vol. xliii p. 631. [vol. 43, June 1851, pp. 631–42: the article, 'A bit of our boyhood', is anonymous and the author has not been identified.]

[12]   [Thomas Worsley.]

[13]   [William Whewell.]

[14]   Quite the contrary. (T) [Trevelyan may have been thinking of Whewell's death in 1866, after falling from his horse. In his own copy, Whewell wrote 'Oh!!!' next to this sentence.]

'What! do they think it a sin to take a walk? Do you mean this operation we have been performing?' as if there must be some other recondite meaning beside the ordinary one, so incredible did what he had just heard appear to him. I assured him such was the case. 'Well,' said he, after a pause, 'I wonder if they eat their dinner on Sunday?' Here were developed two traits of the Cantab – his appreciation of the necessity of exercise, and his contemptuous rejection of sham.

From the exercises of the Cantabs one naturally comes to their amusements, under which head I include all relaxation which is not hard bodily exercise, and all in-door occupation which is not study. I have mentioned that there is a good deal of whist played by a certain set of reading men, especially on Saturday nights. But there are many laudably ignorant of the game, though they have no holy horror it or of those who play it, and I never once heard a set homily against cards from any one all the time I was at Cambridge. Non-reading men play vingt-et-un to a considerable extent, but for the lowest possible (sixpenny) points. Gambling is certainly not a prevalent vice in the University.[15] The same class are also fond of billiards, but not so much so as young Frenchmen or Americans. A reading-man seldom patronizes the billiard-rooms, for the simple reason that, if he does, he soon ceases to be a reading-man.[16] The chess club at Cambridge is a small one, but tolerably supported.

The English are not a musical people, as those of them who know anything about the matter admit themselves. Cambridge does not differ from the rest of the island in this respect. It is rare indeed to hear a Cantab sing.[17] Were he to do so in the streets at night, like a Continental or American student, he would be set down for mad or drunk. Now and then a *very* boating man will favor you after his liquor with a song of the sort that had better be left unsung. Or if the University man attempts an instrument it is usually one of the most painful description, such as the cornopœon, which when played by a master of it is only one degree on the right side of torture to hear, and when, as is usually the case, imperfectly understood by the attempter of it, is worse than a dozen donkeys.[18] Once a Trinity man

---

[15]   This varied excessively. (T)

[16]   In my day it was usual for reading men to play a couple of games at billiards between hall and chapel. I have played scores of games with Jebb. (T) [Richard Claverhouse Jebb, Senior Classic 1862, fellow of Trinity 1863, Regius Professor of Greek 1889–1905.]

[17]   This varied much in the different sets. (T)

[18]   [Usually spelled 'cornopean': the British equivalent of the *cornet à pistons*.]

set up a private organ,[19] and used to perform the Morning Hymn before chapel, in consequence of which be received *sixty-five* anonymous notes in one day, and at last, if I recollect rightly, the authorities were obliged to interfere and put a stop to the nuisance.

Painting is better appreciated, though very few have time to cultivate the national ability for sketching or the means to possess many original pictures. But some first-rate engravings are almost a necessary part of the University man's furniture. These generally run in three classes – religious subjects, such as the most noted works of Raphael and Titian; Landseer's animals; and historical incidents or portraits of great men.

But as may naturally be expected in a University, most of the amusements are of a literary character. There is a great deal of the old standard literature read, and new books of value are keenly criticized in conversation. Book-clubs are formed, and as the works of the day pass from hand to hand they supply the members with subjects of conversation when two or three of them are taking a quiet cup of tea (each man furnishing his own commons – bringing his little milk-jug and his share of bread and butter as well as of knowledge). There was a club in Trinity, that met once a week to read Shakspeare. Conversational criticism on books, informal discussion of literary, ethical, metaphysical, religious subjects – discussion in which men seek for truth rather than victory, and speak from a full mind rather than with a ready tongue – is a necessity of the highly educated Englishman, his evening's amusement, his opera.

Such talks, whether two, three, or more be present at them, usually result from some previous arrangement made in Hall for instance, or during a walk. It is not considered exactly the thing to tumble in upon a man in the evening without warning, unless you have some particular reason for it, or he is your particular friend. He may be reading or preparing to read. Generally, however your Cantab takes care to guard against such a surprise by 'sporting' himself in.

If you call on a man and his door is sported, signifying that he is out or busy, it is customary to pop your card through the little slit made for that purpose. About these cards there is one little peculiarity. An English visiting card has the prefix of 'Mr.' not the name alone as with us. But a University man always omits this prefix; if he happen to be using his 'town' cards, he will draw a pencil through the engraved 'Mr.' The more usual way however is to have blank cards, and write on them your name

---

[19]   Guillebaud or [? Meltion]? (B) [Henry Guillebaud, Trinity 1835, 15th Wrangler 1839, fellow of Trinity 1841.]

(and College if visiting a man of another College) in pencil. There are some of these little peculiarities in addresses, signatures, &c, worth noting as part of the Shibboleth by which our countrymen and the English may be distinguished. An Englishman having a middle name, sometimes writes his two initials before the family name, but more usually leaves the second initial out. Thus Mr. John James Brown will sign himself 'J. Brown'; and put 'Mr. J. Brown' on his card. The practice, of writing or printing the first name in full with the middle initial, 'John J. Brown,' as with us, is not common. The custom of leaving out the middle initial sometimes puzzles those who do not understand it, and is a frequent source of ambiguity. I was myself led into error by it in regard to my friend Hallam; his name was Henry Fitzmaurice: from his leaving out the middle initial I fancied he had dropped his middle name through some dislike for it. I knew two Englishmen travelling in this country who had the same family name and the same first initial, which was enough to make some confusion probable, but their habit of omitting the middle initial which distinguished them made it ten times worse, and they were continually being mistaken for each other.

Never address a letter to an Englishman as 'Mr. John Brown' or 'Mr. Brown', unless you want to insult him, but always 'John Brown Esq.' or '—— Brown Esq.' if you do not know his Christian name. It makes an important practical difference to an Englishman, by the way, whether he is legally rated as 'Esquire' or 'Gentleman', the former class being exempt from some burthensome jury duties to which the latter is subject.

Talking of addresses reminds me of a queer style some of the Dons had of beginning a note or letter to a pupil, 'My dear Mr. So and So', giving the recipient an impression for the moment that he was honored by some lady's correspondence. Probably they intended something patronizing by it; a friend of mine who received a note beginning thus, commenced his answer with the same form, and the Don was much disconcerted.

If an Englishman puts 'Mr.' on his card, he does not put 'Sir' into every sentence of his conversation, as some of our people do. I have sometimes wondered whether this continual introduction of the vocative was a polite Gallicism (since the French use 'Monsieur', about as frequently in conversation), or whether it springs from our debating society and public meeting habits, regarding every one addressed as a president or chairman to be made a speech at. It certainly has a very stiff effect at all times, and sometimes a very ludicrous one. I have known southern and Western gentlemen whose conversation seemed to consist of successive enunciations of 'Sir!' with few words between to connect them.

Of other tastes, habits, and peculiarities of Cambridge men, I do not know that there is much to be said, beyond what may have already been inferred by the reader in the course of this work. They are perhaps rather less conventional than the general run of Englishmen, and pass Sunday in a more Continental manner. They spend little in personal equipment, and I do not remember ever hearing a remark made of or to a man on the subject of his dress. They are generally very gentlemanly in their behavior – unless they happen to be drunk, and some of them even when they happen to be. They have an accurate sense of public propriety in most cases. You will not see a tipsy student out of doors in Cambridge oftener than in New Haven. You will never hear a man swear in broad daylight. It is not considered manly or gentlemanly to walk in front of the College buildings uttering monstrous oaths, as many of our southern students consider it. Nor will you ever hear a man openly avow himself a disbeliever in the truths of Christianity.[20] Some may say that this does not necessarily involve a panegyric on the Cambridge students, and only arises from their want of thought on the subject, a proposition to which I do not assent, believing that as a general rule there are no men who take their opinions on less evidence and investigation than infidels, and that men who, like poor John Sterling,[21] refine away all their belief by over-speculation are rare exceptions.

---

[20]   Rather too common at present. (T)

[21]   [Sterling had entered Trinity in 1824 and became president of the Union Society in 1827, when he also became an Apostle. His magnetic personality and brilliant exposition of often changing opinions inspired many of his contemporaries. In 1838 he founded a dining club (the Sterling Club) which functioned as a kind of informal extension of the Apostles. Sterling died in 1844; on the Sterling Club, see Allen, *Cambridge Apostles*, pp. 182–97.]

30

On the State of Morals
and Religion in Cambridge

Chapel Time

"A num'rous crowd arrayed in white
"Across the green in numbers fly."
(Byron)

A theologian in liquor is not a respectable object.

Thackeray.

I approach this part of my subject with very great hesitation and reluctance. In the first place, it is not pleasant, after having said many things in praise of an institution to which one is warmly attached, to be obliged to say anything in strong and positive dispraise of it. But there is a much stronger reason for this feeling on my part. The very fact of a man's writing upon matters of religion and morality looks like his setting up a claim to be a particularly moral and religious man. Any approach to such a claim may well provoke severe scrutiny, and there are some direct confessions as well as indirect admissions in the course of this book which will not bear any very rigid test. In admitting this I do not allude to any places where the *Latex Lyaeus* is spoken of as an ordinary beverage and a promoter of festivity;

in other words, where drinking wine is mentioned, and not mentioned as a sin, although well aware that many good people would consider me, as a necessary consequence of this, little better than an infidel, and totally disqualified from giving evidence on ethical or theological points. Allowing such persons all credit for sincerity, and wishing them a little more charity; honoring them for their temperance, and trusting that they may learn to extend a little of it into other matters – their judgment of others, for instance – I cannot accept their primary article of faith, or put myself under their jurisdiction. There are other things which touch me more nearly, such as having walked round an oath and taken a degree under false pretences – a piece of Jesuitism for which I shall never forgive myself, and of which no other person can judge more hardly than I myself do. Besides this obvious instance, there are doubtless others of commission and omission, in the facts told and in the way of telling them, which may make me appear a very Catiline complaining of sedition if I do anything which resembles sitting in judgment upon others.

Yet it is manifestly impossible to pass over this branch of our subject *sicco pede*. Admitting, as indeed we have already laid down, that the special intent and primary idea of a University is to educate liberally the intellect, still the moral and religious condition of so many young men – the pick of their generation too, in more ways than one – must needs be a very important consideration; and when we take still further into account that this University is one of the great sources whence the National Church derives its teachers, the absolute necessity of saying something on this point must be apparent. No sense of personal deficiency shall prevent me from speaking out. Some suspicions might be brought on both myself and my *Alma Mater* by silence – on myself as utterly indifferent to the state of morals in a place so long as the intellect was cultivated and the animal well provided for; on her, as allowing a state of things too bad to be mentioned and in regard to which silence was the safest defence.

A young man passing as I did from an American College immediately to an English University, will certainly be astonished at some and shocked at many of the differences he notices in the habits of those about him from what he has been used to consider as the proper practice of students. That decanters and glasses should be among the articles directly recommended by the tutor's servant who assists him in furnishing his room – without any objection, too, from the Evangelical friend who assists him in his purchases; that he should be able to order supper for himself and friends out of the College kitchen, and his College tutor, so far from appearing as a bird of ill omen to mar the banquet, will perhaps play a good knife and fork at it himself – all this seems odd to him at first, but he readily comprehends that the system is one suited to the more advanced age of the students, and one which by refusing to make decent merriment a *malum prohibitum* within the College walls, deprives them of excuse for frequenting external haunts of dissipation. By-and-by, however, as his experience increases, he finds that this liberty is often abused into the most shameful license. The reading men are obliged to be tolerably temperate, but among the 'rowing' men there is a great deal of absolute drunkenness at dinner and supper parties. And, after making all allowance for the peculiar climate which admits of stronger and more copious potations than ours, and the fact that an Englishman never drinks *before* dinner, still it must be allowed that there is a prevailing tendency to drink rather more than is altogether beneficial even among those who are never actually intoxicated. In a mere physical point of view this is greatly to be regretted. If the temperate libations of our students could be superinduced upon the wholesome food, leisurely digestion, and regular exercise of the English, we might expect as the result astonishing specimens of health and strength.

And, even with the chances which they thus throw away, they are splendid instances of physical development; but unfortunately their animal passions seem to be developed almost in a corresponding degree. The American graduate who has been accustomed to find even among irreligious men a tolerable standard of morality and an ingenuous shame in relation to certain subjects, is utterly confounded at the amount of open profligacy going on all around him at an English University; a profligacy not confined to the 'rowing' set, but including many of the reading men and not altogether sparing those in authority. There is a careless and undisguised way of talking about gross vice, which shows that public sentiment does not strongly condemn it; it is habitually talked of and considered as a thing from which a man may abstain through extraordinary frigidity of temperament or high religious scruple, or merely as a bit of training with reference to the physical consequences alone;[1] but which is on the whole, natural,

---

[1] It is a striking proof how physical considerations with an Englishman are apt to overcome all others, that a student will frequently remain chaste or not, entirely in accordance with the result of some medical friend's opinion as to the effect it will have upon his working condition. There was one well known case in my time of a man who preserved his bodily purity solely and avowedly because he wanted to put himself at the head of the Tripos and keep his boat at the head of the river. He succeeded in the former and more important object, but failed in the latter because there he had to depend on the cooperation of others. [Ellis disagrees: 'His motive

excusable, and perhaps to most men necessary. One of my first acquaintances at Cambridge, the Fellow Commoner next to whom I sat in Chapel, had not known me two days or spoken to me half a-dozen times before he asked me to accompany him to Barnwell one evening after Hall, just as quietly as a compatriot might have asked me to take a drink; and though it would certainly be unfair to take this youth as a type of all Cambridge, yet, just as a foreigner on being invited by a Southern or Western gentleman to 'liquor' soon after or perhaps before breakfast, might conclude that to drink in the morning was not an uncommon thing for an American, and that a tolerably large class of persons were in the habit of doing so – the proposition made to me in so off-hand and matter-of-course a way might justify the conclusion that the practice was sufficiently common – as indeed subsequent experience fully proved.

Now, if I did not feel more the friend of Truth than of Cambridge; if I could consider myself the advocate of the University, seeking only to make out the best case for my client; if I thought it profitable employment to weigh different sins against one another, with a view of estimating their comparative enormity or veniality (which I do not, believing that from such kind of casuistry sprang directly the worst abuses of the Jesuit school) – under any of these circumstances I should not be at a loss to make out a defence of Cambridge morals, on the principle so frequently adopted among us when assailed by foreigners – the *tu quoque* style of argument, or parrying one accusation with another. I might say that these young men, so inferior to ours in purity, were superior to them in some other moral

---

was a much higher one. Novi hominem'. Bowring comments, 'This was Denman, but some of his friends said it was a mere put off to conciliate his rowing pals.']

[Warwick (*Masters of Theory*, pp. 214, 219) argues that the reference is to George Hemming, and adduces in evidence W. Thompson's *Life of William Thomson* (London, 1910), p. 36, where Thomson is quoted as saying that Hemming 'won't pull in the College boat on account of the kind of men of which the clubs consist usually'. If the man referred to is one of the leading rowers mentioned by Bristed on p. 292 – two Smith's prizeman and a Senior Classic – then both Denman and Hemming qualify. George W. Hemming, St John's 1840, was Senior Wrangler in 1844; George Denman, Trinity 1838, was Senior Classic in 1842. Denman rowed in the Oxford and Cambridge boat races of 1841 and 1842, and won the Colquhoun sculls in 1842; Hemming was no.1 in the Lady Margaret, i.e. St. John's, boat in 1842, and no. 7 in 1843. Warwick states that Hemming is 'easily identified' (ibid. p. 214), but the evidence of the two Trinity annotators points rather to Denman, as perhaps does his greater prominence as a rower. Moreover Bristed, Bowring and Ellis were more likely to have known about a Trinity man than about a Johnian.]

qualities; that they minded their own business, and told no lies or scandal of others; that the whole University of Cambridge does not contain as much hatred, envy malice, and uncharitableness, and general ill-feeling as an American College; that I was personally acquainted with many men who thought no more of committing fornication than a Southerner would of murdering an Abolitionist, and yet were models of honesty, generosity, truth, and integrity: that men are frequent among us, not only in youth but at a more advanced stage of life, spotlessly pure, rigidly abstemious, making great personal and pecuniary sacrifices in the cause of philanthropy, who are nevertheless greedy of scandal, careless of truth, with very loose conceptions of the obligation of contracts or the duty of citizens to the government. I might set off the integrity of one country against the purity of the other, and say, that if the Englishman is apt to forget that his body is God's temple, the American is equally apt to overlook the assertion, on equally high authority, that what cometh *out* of the mouth defileth a man.

But such arguments, which though very briefly sketched above are certainly not understated, rather go to point out to us our own errors than to excuse those of the English students, and are very like ignoring the question at issue. They prove, indeed, that all the moral virtues are not comprised in purity and temperance, but not that temperance and purity are not requisite in a place making any pretensions to morality. Here are some hundred young men getting drunk systematically, making one another drunk, with the eternal joke of blacking with burnt cork the first man's face who loses consciousness, making any stray 'snob' whom they catch drunk (a poor wretch of a tramp was killed my first year by some Trinity men, to whose rooms he came begging, and who gave him three quarters of a bottle of port), unmanning and un-gentlemanizing themselves to any extent. This is a bad state of things, and there is no getting over it. If they are very nice, honorable, and upright men when sober, more shame for them to degrade themselves systematically. I say systematically, for any man who *habitually* gets drunk must set about it with a certain system and previous design, since it requires but a moderate amount of common sense and experience to tell him how much he can carry. Here is a gross vice, the forbidding of which was one of the peculiar features of Christianity and has always been one of its leading distinctions in practical morality from all other religions, made a matter of habitual practice and a subject of familiar conversation. Can this go on in a place devoted to the education of Christian youth, without great blame being attributable *somewhere*? But the worst is not told. Many of the men whose undergraduate course has been the most marked by drunkenness and debauchery, appear, after the 'Poll' examination, at Divinity lectures – step out of Barnwell into the Church, without any pretence of other change than in the attire of their outward man – the being 'japanned', as assuming the black dress and white cravat is called in University slang.[2] Even a little hypocrisy would seem decent in such cases. The idea of going into Christ's ministry as a mere business, of being 'put into one of the priests' offices for a piece of bread', without feeling specially inclined to and qualified for such a work, is sufficiently abhorrent to people brought up in our way of thinking, even when the hireling shepherd is a map of correct moral character; but when his life for years has been giving the lie to every word he will preach, *can* language be strong enough to express our emotions of grief and indignation? Is it possible to exaggerate, is it more than just possible to caricature a state of things which can give rise to such occurrences as the following, which (except that the real names are changed and the coarse language of the narrator slightly modified) is literally set down as I heard it told? –

'You want to know what this row was between Lord Gaston[3] and Brackett – well, it happened this way. Brackett had brought his *chère amie* down from London. Gaston made her acquaintance. Brackett goes there one night and finds the door locked; so he kicked the door open, and gave Gaston a black eye. Then Gaston wanted to challenge him, and said he didn't care whether he was turned out of the University or not (this is the penalty for being concerned in a duel); but his friends agreed that, *as Brackett was going into the Church*, they had better make it up,' &c.

Or this – to take a much milder instance – at which, also, I was present. A Bachelor, whose life had been rather a notorious one, was about to be presented to a curacy. A friend inquires into the value of it, and comes to the conclusion that he has something better at his own disposal. 'You are to get ninety pounds a-year at Oakstone, and no parsonage. Now our place is worth a hundred, *besides* the house, which is a very nice one – big enough

---

[2] [In 1833 R.M. Beverley had described Barnwell as 'a town set apart and devoted to sin', and reported that it was customary for undergraduates to go there to visit the prostitutes after Sunday evening chapel. He also cited the case of an ordained college fellow who 'walked abroad in Cambridge with his mistress on his arm'. *A Letter to His Highness the Duke of Gloucester, Chancellor, on the Present Corrupt State of the University of Cambridge* (London, 1833).]

[3] Hannington. He and Jas Buller were a nice pair! (B) [Henry Hannington, fellow of King's 1820–70; James Buller, fellow of King's 1833–56. The remoteness of the pseudonyms, from the real names in this case presumably reflects the scandalous nature of the anecdote.]

to take pupils and all that sort of thing.' The to-be-ordained pricks up his ears at the prospect. 'And the parish is really a nice one', continues the friend, 'but there is one drawback I must tell you in candor. There is an old woman lives near by, who makes it a principle always to quarrel with the parson.' The parson in prospect inquires the name of this formidable elderly lady. It is the mother of a celebrated novelist. 'Well to be sure,' says the aspirant to the cure of souls, 'she is a – – – (I leave the reader to fill in the three monosyllables); but – a hundred a-year – and you said the house was in good order?'

Now it will not do to cite against such cases instances where itinerant preachers under the voluntary system, in this country or other countries, have turned out to be rogues and impostors; to speak of the notorious Maffit,[4] or an almost equally notorious Temperance Lecturer. Such men are rare exceptions; they are vaguely connected with some religious denomination, or, perhaps, actually repudiated by that to which they profess to belong; they spring from the low and ignorant, and find their victims in the class from which they sprang. There is no comparison to be instituted between them and the number of high-bred youth who every year are trained as gentlemen, receive a liberal education so far as they will avail themselves of it, and then enter deliberately on a mockery of the sacred profession, with a great body of clerical teachers looking on, and abetting, as it were, in the desecration.

It would be more to the purpose to show that this immorality was partly, or in a great measure, owing to causes over which the University or its individual colleges can have no control. And certainly there are some antecedent and independent causes. A great deal of the mischief is done, that is to say, the seeds of dissipation are implanted beforehand, at home or at school. The moral education of English boys is very much neglected, especially that part of education which consists in example and

---

[4] [John Newland Maffit(t) (1795–1850) was a well-known Methodist clergyman, editor of two Methodist magazines and in 1841 chaplain to the US Congress. In 1848 he became involved in scandal after marrying his second wife, the 17-year old stepdaughter of a Brooklyn judge. The title of a work published in the same year tells (almost) all: *Rev. John N. Maffit, and his Late Unfortunate Marriage, a Narrative of All the Facts Relative to his Marriage with Miss Frances Smith of Brooklyn, N.Y. – their Private Correspondence and the Cause of her Death, as Published in the Police Gazette.* Maffit was alleged to have persuaded Frances Smith into marriage with bribes (a watch, a grand piano and $7,000, delivered by another Methodist minister), and then to have murdered her.]

in removing temptation out of their way rather than debarring them from it. The principle, *maxima debetur puero reverentia*, which even a Heathen[5] was able to see the wisdom of, is very little borne in mind. If boys can be made *manly*, that is to say, courageous, honest, and tolerably truthful, the formation of habits of purity and self-denial is altogether a secondary matter. Grown people, old, grey-headed men, encourage boys to drink, and talk before them as the fastest specimen of Young America would not talk before his younger brother. A stranger, with no further knowledge of the subject than he would gain by reading any good sermons addressed to boys, Arnold's at Rugby for example, could not but remark the progress made in vice at an early age by the inmates of a public school, and the trouble which a conscientious teacher has with them in combating the fearful delusion, evidently derived not merely from the practice, but from the admitted theory of their elders, that indulgence in sensual vices is not incompatible with a Christian life.

But there is another cause more deeply rooted and growing directly out of the aristocratic constitution of English society. It is the low estimate which men in the upper ranks of life form of women in the lower. The remark has often been made, and with perfect truth, that that spirit of chivalry which makes every man the protector of every woman,[6] is a peculiar feature of American civilization. In some European countries it does not exist at all; in others, as England, it is limited to a certain class of society.[7] That shop-girls, work-women, domestic servants, and all females in similar positions, were expressly designed for the amusement of gentlemen, and generally serve that purpose, is a proposition assented to by a large proportion of

---

[5] [Juvenal, *Satires*, 14.47.]

[6] With the melancholy exception of one class, the disgrace of which exception we northern men are fully conscious of. Yet I would not advise an Englishman to lay too much stress on it, as it might provoke other comparisons not too favorable to his own country.

[7] It may be observed that a poor woman in England is just as likely to be maltreated by men in her own walk in life as by those in a higher, only the ill-treatment takes another form, that of brutal usage. The cases of aggravated assault and battery upon women that come before the London Police magistrates are positively startling in number and degree. In truth, the animal vigor of the Englishman is apt to degenerate with the lower classes into sheer brutality; and of this open brutality, especially as exhibited towards women, there is probably more in England than in any other country in Europe, except perhaps Russia. [For a recent discussion of attitudes to male violence toward women in 19th-century England, see M.J. Wiener, *Men of Blood: Violence, Manliness and Criminal Justice in Victorian England* (Cambridge, 2004).]

Englishmen, even when they do not act upon the idea themselves. You meet the position, either directly expressed or implied (more frequently the latter), both in their conversation and their writings. A very clever and interesting traveller in Norway, when discussing the morality of different classes of the population there, observes, 'the servant-girls are what servant-girls are everywhere', as if there *must* be but one standard for women occupied in domestic service, and that necessarily a standard of degradation! And in a popular novel published some years ago, I recollect that an old gentleman lecturing his nephew says to him, 'You seduced a servant. I know young men are young men, *and servant-maids are not Lucretias.*' Then he goes on to say, that what he *does* blame him for is abandoning his illegitimate child without support.

Once as I was walking in the outskirts of Cambridge with a friend, a man strictly moral in his life, we came upon a group of children at play, mostly girls ten or twelve years old. 'Poor things!' said he, 'there go prostitutes for the next generation.' It was the first thought that occurred to him on seeing these daughters of the people.

The English upper classes are tolerably moral in their own sphere. Their women are well brought up. Their young men respect ladies; perhaps it would be more correct to say *they are afraid of them.* But whatever the exact sentiment may be which actuates him, the young Englishmen has not as a general rule the Frenchman's *veni, vidi, vici* persuasion that every lady he meets is bound to fall in love with him. But the virtue of a housemaid or a milliner-girl is a thing inconceivable to him; he has no more conception of it than, I suppose, a native of New Orleans would have of the virtue of a Quadroon. Yet he does not entertain any corresponding scepticism as to the possibility of moral excellence in the other sex of the laboring class. He does not think that a poor man must necessarily be dishonest or mendacious, or may not be altogether a very good Christian. Still less does he fancy that he has a right to insult or ill-use him. If he did, the first clown who gave him a threshing, or the first magistrate before whom he was brought up for a breach of the peace, would soon convince him of his error. But that a woman from among 'the common people' should be anything but a *common woman* he will be slow to believe. Female virtue he deems a luxury of the wealthy.

A third cause has been assigned, which to me seemed *not* an independent one, and, going directly to aggravate rather than lighten the responsibility of the University. It has been said by some of the Evangelicals that nothing can be done to improve the state of morality in the Universities so long as the present Church system continues – so long as men will go, and are allowed to go into the Church merely as a means of support, and just as they would take up any other profession, or rather, with less thought and preparation than they would devote to any other profession. Now, granting that the connexion between the Church and the Universities is not one of the most vital and intimate character, still it would hardly be possible to say that they are so far disconnected and independent of each other that a vitiated state of things in the University may be thrown off and charged upon a general error in the practice of the Church. Let us, however admit that this is another cause of immorality, making three in all, beyond the University's control. How does this affect its responsibility?

It appears to me that the ruling class in the University generally, and more particularly in the particular Colleges, is not exonerated by the existence of these external and prior causes. For surely it is the business of the University to improve and make the best of bad material that comes into its hands. In matters intellectual it not only admits this duty, but acts up to it. One of the essential objects of the University of Cambridge, as claimed for it by Dr. Whewell and others, is to correct the imperfect and one-sided teaching of the public schools, to supply their Mathematical deficiencies for instance. And though (to repeat it for the second time) the moral education of its members is not the University's primary and special object; yet it is an object too important to be ignored by throwing off all short comings in it upon the antecedents of the students. What steps does the University take to keep Undergraduates out of mischief? It appoints two Proctors, with their deputies, who on alternate nights, accompanied by their servants or lictors (popularly denominated *bull-dogs*), make the tour of Barnwell suburb and other suspicious places, and apprehend any women who may be seen openly enticing gownsmen, or any gownsmen detected in improper localities. Now I do not doubt but these gentlemen perform their disagreeable duties with much diligence, that they prevent some vice and detect more; but were I asked honestly my opinion of their practical efficacy, I should say that they were not equal to the amount of police work they took in hand,[8] and that they were more successful in catching

---

[8]   Every Master of Arts is armed by the University with Proctorial power. How much this amounts to in practice a single instance will show. I was coming home one evening with a friend when we were set upon in the regular Haymarket or Regent street style by two women of the town who accompanied us for at least half a mile. As they really were a serious annoyance to us, I very innocently asked an M.A. whom we happened to meet (also a personal friend) to exercise his Proctorial power and make them go away under pain of the *Spinning House* (the Bridewell or House of

small offenders against University rules – pouncing upon a poor fellow like myself for instance, who had crossed the street after candle-light without his cap and gown, and fining him six-and-eightpence – than in checking or punishing men of profligate habits. The previous character, moreover, of some of the persons who hold the office, is such that their appointment can only be justified on the principle of setting one delinquent to catch another. Were the University really inclined to go energetically about the work, it might be no very violent exercise of its almost despotic power in the town – I say almost despotic, for the town officers are sworn in by and subject to the University authorities, and the Proctors have a right to enter any house or premises (except the precincts of King's College) in or within a mile of Cambridge – put down all disorderly houses and expel from the place all the notorious prostitutes, of whom there are nearly a hundred at the lowest estimate as well known as if they were under a Parisian registration. From the University at large let us turn to the particular Colleges, for they in their individual capacity are concerned with the worst blot on the system – the admission of improper characters into the Church. The candidate for Orders must have *testimonials from his College*. What are the requisites for these? What they may be theoretically I do not know, but practically they come to this – that he must have kept a certain number of chapels and communions. I have known men who at a pretty advanced stage of their Undergraduate course committed open acts of profligacy and disorder – by open acts I mean such as attracted the notice and incurred the censure of the College – but whose testimonials were not thereby forfeited or suspended. There is, I believe, but one case on record where a Trinity Fellow was refused testimonials;[9] of graduates not Fellows, only one case has occurred since 1840, and that not on moral grounds, but for Romanistic tendencies. It was a consolation to see that a candidate could be stopped for anything. And if any offence against morals is committed in their own order, how do the Dons treat the delinquent? A tolerably strong case occurred in my time. A young woman of previous good character went to a Fellow of Kings to procure an order of admission to the chapel on Sunday evening. He made

---

Correction for such characters). He took it as a very good joke, and began bantering the women and encouraging them. And indeed the idea of an M.A. exercising such power, is a mere joke; the Proctor himself is nothing without his *bull-dogs*, and the gowns-on sometimes escape from or resist even those.

[9] [Thomas Burcham, Trinity 1826, 3rd Classic 1830; fellow of Trinity 1832; Recorder of Bedford 1848–56, Southwark police magistrate 1856–69. He was refused testimonials in 1839: Smith and Stray, *Cambridge in the 1830s*, p. 166.]

her drunk and seduced her. The reader will probably agree with me, that if the corporation of Kings had expelled him from their body it would not have been a punishment beyond his deserts. What did they do? They suspended him from his Fellowship for two years, which was equivalent to a fine of £400 or thereabouts.

After what I have said of Cambridge morals, to say anything of Cambridge religion may appear to some superfluous. They may be disposed to pronounce summarily that, admitting a certain outward decorum, the absence of noon-day profanity or openly avowed infidelity, there must be an utter want of spiritual vitality in such a place. Let us not, however, be too hasty in our conclusions.

We have been speaking of men who were more or less depraved and immoral when they became members of the University. Let us take the case of a sincere practical Christian who enters, and examine what influences will be at work upon his spiritual life. In the first place there is certainly a danger that his standard of holiness will be lowered by the many examples of vice around him; that he will fancy himself fulfilling the requirements of religion when he is only preserving those of morality. This is a great and obvious peril on which it is needless to enlarge.

Then (especially if he be a clever man) comes the temptation to intellect worship. It is a temptation inseparable from academic institutions, where the advancement of the intellect occupies the first place in the public attention and the *egregia ingenii facinora* claim the first rewards. Hence he is in danger of falling into the error, so fruitful of evil, of supposing that by improving his intellectual, he will, *ipso facto*, improve his moral nature. This supposition is not peculiar to students at old universities; it is one of the *falsisms* of the utilitarian school that we most frequently hear announced in all solemnity of language: it is also most plausibly supported by the generally acknowledged result of experience that a certain amount of wisdom and intelligence seems necessary for the consistent practice of virtue, as we sometimes meet men who are familiarly said *not to know enough to be good when they want to be*.[10] But how unsound a supposition it is any scholar's acquaintance with Athenian literature and history may convince him.[11]

---

[10] I have often been struck with a remark of Dr. Arnold's to the effect that men ought to pray for judgment and understanding more than they do. The idea may seem strange; it would not be difficult to represent it in a ridiculous light; yet I am convinced it is one worthy of deep consideration. Solomon prayed for understanding, and his prayer was approved.

[11] One immediate consequence of intellect worship is that it makes men under-

But the picture is not without its bright lights. The prospect of the religious Undergraduate is not altogether gloomy. He is not deprived of that great support and consolation, the presence of co-workers in a good cause. There are some places of education at which it is next to impossible (humanly speaking) that a young man should live without being corrupted by the *universal* example of those around him. He can only preserve himself by turning recluse and living in a state of negative if not positive hostility to his natural companions. Now Cambridge is not such a place. A young man who enters there and is disposed to find a *truly* 'good set', can find one, or indeed have his choice among several sets of really virtuous and religious men. It was my comfort to know many right worthy the name of Christians according to the highest standard that was ever lived up to; men of no particular clique or theological school, but holding various opinions and coming from various places and teachers; pupils of Arnold from Rugby; Evangelicals from King's College, London; other King's College London men of the Eclectic stamp, followers of Professor Maurice, who looked at from a Presbyterian point of view might be called High Churchmen; Eton men who were yet more eclectic and had trained themselves *nullius jurare in verba magistri*. Men who differed in many things but agreed in being sincere Christians whether you regarded their faith or their practice; and whose conduct strikingly exemplified that *common sense of religion* which is so conspicuous in the writings of Whately, Arnold, and other liberal Churchmen, and of which a really good Englishman, when you find one, presents the very best specimen in his life. They seemed every day to solve that most difficult problem of 'being in the world, not of it'. Their progress in human learning did not make them forget that the fear of the Lord is wisdom and to depart from evil is understanding; nor did they deem that their pure lives and immovable principles gave them a license to be uncharitable and censorious. They made no parade of their religion on useless occasions, but when it was wanted it was never wanting. The recollection of some such men must have been present to Thackeray,

---

estimate women. The depreciating spirit to which I refer may be observed in men of very pure and strict lives; it does not, like the libertine's, sneer at woman's virtue; but while admitting her moral superiority, underrates its importance among the elements of society; nor does it avoid her with monkish asceticism, but rather treats her with slightly contemptuous patronage as one might a child. This topic seems irrelevant in a religious discussion, but there is one point of view where it has a direct bearing – the prejudice which men of strong intellect frequently conceive against evangelical doctrines, because these doctrines are especially popular among women.

when after scorching and withering with his sarcasm all classes of society in England, he suddenly stopped at the clergy and began to praise them. The remembrance of what some few among that clergy were, disarmed the universal satirist.

Why such men have not more influence in reforming the evils about them is a question easier to ask than answer. The existence of evil is the one great theological difficulty, as Whately well says, and the apparent non-success of good men in overcoming evil is but one branch of this difficulty. After all, they may do much that does not appear on the surface. It is so in their after life. Many of their good deeds survive them, it is true, but are not heard of in their time so as to redound to their credit. A clerical hypocrite is detected in some wickedness; he is brought into court; the newspapers are full of it; the enemies of the church, or of religion, or of both, exult. A pious clergyman devotes every spare minute of his time not occupied in parochial duty to the drudgery of taking pupils, that he may support schools for the advancement of knowledge and true religion, and may combat the Papist influences that have pre-occupied his ground: no one knows anything about it, except a few of his parishioners and intimate friends.

In looking over this chapter (probably the worst written in the book, though it has cost me more trouble than any other) it occurs to me that among the many faults which may be found with it, there are two particularly likely to be dwelt upon: the occasional use of coarse language, and the treatment of the whole subject in a meagre and inadequate manner. To the first charge I reply: English vice is a coarse thing; it is as well perhaps that it should be so; that men who *will* be vicious should be so in a coarse way, that they should get drunk on bad liquor, and keep company with the commonest harlots: for so they at least act the part of Helots, and enable a young man's taste to be a powerful auxiliary to his virtue. But this vice, being so coarse a thing in its nature, cannot be described without some coarseness; yet, though my language may be rough and inelegant, I deny that it is anywhere indelicate or voluptuous. In answer to the second charge, I can only repeat my original plea of incapacity; the consciousness of which incapacity yielded only to the impossibility of omitting the subject entirely from a work like this.

But with regard to the *theological* disputes at Cambridge, which have a historical, rational, and common-sense point of view quite independent of their religious nature, I feel able to speak more in detail; and these deserve to be the subject of a new chapter.

31

The Puseyite Disputes in Cambridge, and the Cambridge Camden Society

It is not hazarding too much to predict that a school which peremptorily rejects all evidences of religion except such as, when relied on exclusively, the logical canon irreversibly condemns, which denies to mankind the right to judge of religious doctrine ... must, in the present state of the human mind inevitably fail in its attempts to put itself at the head of the religious feelings and convictions of Great Britain; by whatever learning, argumentative skill, and even, in many respects, comprehensive views of human affairs, its peculiar doctrines may be recommended to the acceptance of thinkers.

Mill's *Logic* (1843).

The era of my residence in Cambridge was in one respect fortunate: it enabled me to witness a great struggle between reactionary and progressive principles. Anglo-Catholicism and Young England were in all their glory when I arrived there; they were both pretty well on the wane when I left.

The aim of the Anglo-Catholic (more generally known as the Oxford School, or by the popular nickname of *Puseyites*) may be briefly characterized thus: it was to bring the Church of England continually nearer to the Church of Rome without actually going into it. But as constructions of this sort, though possible and familiar enough in Mathematics, are not always exactly feasible in real life, it turned out that many of those concerned in the movement found themselves over the line before they were well aware of it. This, I say, was the general aim; there were some few exceptions whose Anglo-Catholicism had a certain 'finality' in it, and who maintained to the end a commendable distrust of the Pope while they would have had no objection to become a sort of Popes themselves. The writings of these exceptional characters have done the defenders of Puseyism good service in this country, and elsewhere among Protestant populations. Let it be said that the Oxford school favors the Romanists, and straightway their partisans will quote you a few sentences from Mr. Sewall,[1] and then *solventur risu tabulae*. But, as a general rule, so marked was the tendency Rome-ward that not a few believed the leaders of the movement to be *Jesuits in disguise* – a theory containing perhaps no inherent improbability, but not to be accepted in the absence of some positive proof. A more practical and plausible way of explaining the phenomenon, and which many adopted, was that the Oxford movement was a reaction from the Evangelical, as that was from the formalism of the old 'High and Dry' party, and as the present Protestant excitement is from Puseyism itself. But since the human mind, in this age of progress, revolts at the thoughts of absolutely retrograding, it was supposed by many that the Anglo-Catholics had invented or discovered some new ideas – a delusion which they themselves countenanced by talking much about 'developments'.

Yet after all there was nothing unphilosophical in the prevailing opinion that Puseyism was only a revival of the exploded doctrines of former days. The reproduction of error in the moral, political, and religious worlds, is a phenomenon that has already occurred too often for us to be startled at its occurring once again. A man's belief in physics is purely a matter of reason, in morals it is very often one of sentiment. When you have established a principle in mathematics or natural philosophy there is an end of it; you have gained so much clear ground for all future time. Not so in politics or religion. There a principle is established, or an error put down by a vast preponderance of evidence, but not by an irrefragable certainty of proof. The demonstration and refutation often take a practical form in their most important stages, as the English after much discussion *practically* disproved the divine right of kings by getting rid of James and prospering under William, the logical part of the proof being arranged afterwards. So, after the new principle has been triumphant for some time,

---

[1] [William Sewell, professor of moral philosophy at Oxford 1836–41. Sewell was sympathetic to the Tractarians, but was strongly anti-Catholic, and took an independent line in his writings on religion.]

the error is forgotten, but *the refutation is forgotten with it*, though men may be practically living on its results. By-and-by, since individuals are found in all ages with the same mental constitution and tendencies, the forgotten fallacy starts up into notice again, not unfrequently announcing itself as an original discovery. Then the process of refutation has to be gone through over again. The theological student soon observes how ancient heresies, Sabellianism for instance, are continually coming up again under pretence of being new discoveries in theology. The political student (I mean the man who investigates the history and science of governments with a higher view than that of making merchandize out of local and temporary party disputes) must be struck with the admixture of ancient fallacies in the social system of many a new light of the age. The Young England movement in politics, which though not coextensive with, ran parallel to the Oxford movement in theology, has been shown not to have originated a single new suggestion; even Mr. D'Israeli's brilliant discoveries how the Whigs wanted to make a Venetian government of England, &c., were derived straight from the time of the Stuarts and even from sayings of the first Charles himself. It must be remembered too in respect to Puseyism, that the abuses which it sought to restore in England had never been in abeyance throughout Europe. The original source of evil, the Romish church, had always existed, not at all times with full energy to work mischief, but always with the potentiality of and inclination for mischief.

It has been mentioned that the Anglo-Catholic movement was viewed by many as a reaction from Evangelicism. The Anglo-Catholics from the first attacked the Evangelicals in one of their main strongholds, their influence with the female sex. On the ladies they brought a double battery to bear, not only appealing to their *feelings* as the others had done, but also addressing their taste. With similar aesthetic arguments they attacked men of an elegant and somewhat effeminate turn of mind, and won over many pretty scholars and neat antiquarians. By 'developing' the same idea a little, inveigling against the coarseness of Puritanism and Evangelicism and giving out that theirs was the religion for a gentleman, they found favor with many persons in the upper classes generally, and made sham converts of many toadies of the aristocracy. To men of stronger minds in or destined for the church, they exhibited stronger and more congenial persuasives. They stimulated their ambition by suggesting, rather than distinctly explaining, the great power which the Oxford system would place in the hands of the clergy. A thoroughly excellent and conscientious man, one of my most valued friends, who was infected with Puseyism in the early part of his College course and afterwards happily recovered, confessed to me that this consideration had had the utmost weight with him, and would continually interfere to bias his judgment, in spite as it were of himself. And in politics, while encouraging all in the upper classes who were disposed to favor retrograde movements, they recommended themselves to the lower orders as their best friends, and to those who sympathized with the lower orders as the true social reformers.

By an able use of these means the Anglo-Catholics had, in the years '42, '43, and '44, acquired a strong foothold all over England, and at Cambridge they had established an influence more dangerous to the church and nation at large than the power which they wielded at their original headquarters of Oxford, for the best and ablest young men of our University seemed to favor their views when they did not actually embrace them. The principal instrument by which the Oxford party planted themselves in Cambridge, and which by a righteous irony was afterwards made the occasion of their signal discomfiture, was the *Cambridge* Camden Society.

This *Ecclesiastical* Camden Society at *Cambridge* had no connexion with the *Literary* Camden Society at *London* for the publication of Historical Documents, Diaries, Letters, Poems, Political Songs, &c., &c., heretofore only existing in old manuscripts. It is proper to mention this at the outset, because the identity of name has caused much confusion even in England.

The *Cambridge* Camden society was instituted in May, 1839, ostensibly with a view to 'promote the study of Ecclesiastical Architecture and Antiquities, and the restoration of mutilated Architectural Remains'. It professed to be nothing more than this, and its printed laws contained nothing dubious or objectionable. And though many religious persons might expect that such an association would indirectly attempt something for the spiritual benefit of the church, yet so long as it confined itself to its avowed line of architectural study and material decoration, no one could strictly find fault with it for omitting all mention of the vital truths of religion, any more than we could with justice reprehend a professedly *critical* editor of the Greek Testament for having embodied no theological matter in his notes. But the craft and artifice of these men was, that they first inculcated a taste for mediaeval art and architecture, for ancient church ornaments and furniture, *as a purely aesthetic and antiquarian matter* totally independent of theology, and then, after a taste for, and interest in and attachment to these things had been formed and established, endeavored to deduce from them an adherence to those religious and political errors which were contemporary with that art and architecture. In this they used a certain degree of caution, though here and there a phrase, such as 'the errors of the Reformation', 'the usurpation of William', peeped out from the very first. There was a marked and tolerably regular progress discernible in the publications of the society for which its committee was responsible, and in the publications of leading members of it to which it lent its sanction indirectly in every way without openly assuming the responsibility of them. From abusing Dissenters they proceeded to abuse Low-Churchmen, from abusing Low-Churchmen to abusing the old High-Churchmen; from non-reproval to cautious praise, from praise to recommendation, from recommendation to adoption of numerous Popish practices.

The state in which the Camdenians found many of the candidates for Orders gave them a great leverage in their operations. It has been mentioned with what utter deficiency of moral, not to say religious qualification, numbers of rash young Englishmen enter into the sacred profession every year. There seemed to be, and doubtless was among a large number, a practical conviction of the apostolic succession and its legitimately deducible consequences; a belief that some mystic influence was conveyed in ordination – some special grace which would sooner or later sanctify the recipient. And doubtless it sometimes happens in God's Providence that a bad man is converted to the truth by talking and preaching about it; but the experiment is a fearful one for the congregation, and thrice fearful to the minister. Now the whole Puseyite scheme, by substituting an essential and inherent virtue in the order for the necessity of virtue in the individual, provided an unchristian minister with a sop for his conscience. But the Camdenian development of it did more; it gave him something to do, and aroused the cravings of his better nature. For every man not utterly hypocritical or careless will, on finding himself in a position the duties of which he is unqualified to fulfil, endeavor to find or contrive some substitute for them; if he cannot be a true pastor, he will like to play at being one. If now you can persuade him to adopt Gothic architecture for his creed, and mediaeval restorations for his reforms; if you can convince him that rood-screens and floriated crosses are great articles of faith, and that preaching in a surplice or using altar-cloths of a particular color on particular saints' days occupy an elevated position in the list of good works, that it is a sacred duty to – not 'orient himself' like Horace Mann's young man, but 'orientate' his church, and that the destruction of a pew or gallery is of more importance than the reformation of a sinner; – then you have satisfied him at a cheap rate; he has his Body of Divinity speculative and practical, which gives him sufficient occupation yet does not interfere with his old desires and inclinations. And this was the *proton pseudos* of the Camdenians, the fundamental charge that would have remained against them even had

there been no connexion between them and Rome – had there been no
popery in the substitution of 'altars' for communion-tables, no priestcraft
and monkery in the separation of the clergy from the laity by partitions and
the men from the women by localities at church, had the Romish Church
been out of the way altogether – that they converted theology into a matter
of garniture and ceremony, and what with crosses and triangles, poppy-
heads and gargoyles, fishes and salamanders, made it as much a collection
of absurd conventionalities as Heraldry is, or, to adopt the comparison of
Rogers in the Edinburgh Review, as much a science of symbols as Algebra
all but the demonstration.[2]

For some years the Camden went on very triumphantly, and the Puseyites
seemed likely to make Cambridge their *point d'appui.* At their original
head-quarters they had sustained some decided defeats, such as the election
of Garbett as Professor of Poetry instead of their candidate Williams, and
the suspension of Dr. Pusey. At Cambridge they had lost nothing, having
refrained from such trials, which might bring out the full force of the older
members of the University against them, and chiefly confined themselves
to winning the younger. Their operations were not unobserved throughout
the country; Evangelicals, Eclectics, and High Churchmen of the old school,
all thundered away at them. Now and then the monthly preacher at Great
St. Mary's[3] attacked them on their own ground; but they were not moved
thereby in practice, though very much smashed in argument, and obstinately
refused to die when their brains were out – no wonder, since the reason
of a thing was with them a reason against it, and one of their fundamental
arguments was to deny the validity of argument.

While these men were in the full tide of success I always expected their
shipwreck was nigh at hand. That the English nation was going over bodily
into the arms of the Romish Church never entered into my apprehensions
– that my intelligent friends whose reason had been clouded by the mists
of Tractarian sophistry would see clearly again before long was my constant
expectation. I wish my faith in everything I ought to have believed in

---

[2] [Henry Rogers, 'Recent developments of Puseyism', *Edinburgh Review* 80 (Oct.
1844), pp. 309–75. Rogers wrote (p. 369) that 'Amidst crosses, crucifixes, triangles,
anchors, doves, fishes, and garlands, theology promises, like algebra, to be entirely a
science of symbols; but, unlike algebra, to have nothing to do with demonstration'.]
[3] The colleges successively appoint one of their non-resident graduates to preach in
the University Church for four or five Sundays. One of the Esquire Bedells (honorary
attendants on the Vice-Chancellor) said that he heard a new preacher every month
for thirty years, and thanked God he had some religion left.

(things political, I mean) had been as strong as my faith in the defeat of the Puseyites and the upsetting of the Camden.

In the Spring of 1844 Camdeno-Puseyism was at its zenith. It was then the University debating society passed that remarkable and irrational vote that monasteries ought to be re-established! But in the Autumn of the very same year a reaction began to show itself. Though too busy with my own affairs to notice much of what was going on around me, I could not help observing with great satisfaction that some of my best friends whose Puseyite tendencies I had deplored, were fast returning under the sway of charity and common sense. Soon the crash came on from without. It was more or less precipitated by an event of no very great importance in itself, but which, like many other trifling occurrences, led to a discussion of great principles.

The Church of the Holy Sepulchre in Cambridge was in the year 1841 very much out of repair; in fact a part of it had actually fallen in, and there was danger that the whole would come down. Some of the Camden Society came forward and offered not merely to repair the fallen part, but restore and beautify the whole church. The parishioners, who were the reverse of wealthy, gladly assented through their vestry, and the Restoration Committee appointed began to raise subscriptions and carry out their design. More than *four thousand pounds* were raised and expended in this restoration, which occupied more than two years and converted the church into what one person might call a 'perfect gem', and another a 'perfect toy', according to their views of such restorations. Some of my readers are doubtless acquainted with the *Temple Church*, which is one of the lesser lions of London; those who are will have some idea of the appearance which the 'Round Church,' as St. Sepulchre was commonly called,[4] assumed under the hands of its restorers. The often mooted point of the propriety of such exquisite decoration, and its good or bad spiritual tendency, it is not necessary to discuss here at length. This much, perhaps, a man without previous bias might admit, that there is at least no more impropriety in a number of individuals spending money upon a church than in any one of them spending it on his own house, and that to build a beautiful church is

---

[4]   It is sometimes mentioned in old deeds as 'ecclesia rotunda'. The more ancient part of the building is an exact circle. There are three similar round churches in England, those of Northampton, Little Maplestead, and the Temple (in London); none of them are as old as St. Sepulchre's, which was most probably built in the first half of the twelfth century, though the precise time is not known. Vide Le Keux's *Memorials of Cambridge*.

prima facie, and until some improper motive can be clearly assigned for it, an act in honor of God. The usual objection against making a show-place of a church proves rather too much, for experience shows that all churches possessing beauty, whether of external architecture or interior decoration,[5] will and must be to a certain extent show-places; and this we can only escape by carrying out the theory of the Methodists (which even some of them have begun to deviate from in practice) that an edifice for the worship of God, must be as ugly and barn-like as possible. For my own part I should as soon think of separating the sexes at church or obliging the women to wear veils because men sometimes come there merely to look at them. As to the qualifications and provisos in the case, ordinary judgment will supply those, such as that the expenditure of art and wealth *should* be for the glory of God and not for the glorification of any set of men, priests or others, and that such decorations should not be considered a part of or a substitute for vital religion, that encaustic tiles should not be placed alongside of faith and charity, or stained glass accepted in lieu of gospel preaching.

The incumbent of St. Sepulchre's was a non-resident. It must not be supposed from this, however, that he was an idle ecclesiastical dignitary, wallowing in luxury and so forth – one of those over-paid do-nothing priests that radicals like to dilate upon. His whole church emoluments did not exceed £150 per annum. £150 is not a very exorbitant salary for a clergyman in any country. But he was certainly a non-resident, and being in addition a man of small stature,[6] it is just possible that the Camdenians overlooked him altogether and never took him into account in their restoration measures. His curate was a Small-college man who used to write bad Latin in his Proctorial notices when he filled that office, two adequate reasons for considering him a cypher also. Towards the close of the year 1843, the incumbent made the discovery that the vestry had broken up the old communion table and erected a stone altar. He demanded that this should be removed, and as, after much correspondence and 'fuss generally', his request was not complied with, went to law – nominally with the church-wardens who had been put forward as a convenient stalking-horse, but

---

[5] A person disposed to hypercriticism might perhaps draw a distinction between the two, and say that the exterior architecture cannot withdraw the attention of the worshippers within from their worship, as the interior decoration does. But a church magnificent without and bare within, rather tempts strangers to remain on the outside of it, so great is the feeling of disappointment excited by the want of correspondence.

[6] Who wore bright blue breeches to the horror of the Camdenians. (B)

virtually with the Camden Society. These legal proceedings had the effect of stopping the consecration of the church (and consequently the celebration of divine worship in it) for more than a year, during which time the dispute was not confined to the courts but flowed over into the newspapers, and embodied itself in various periodical articles and even pamphlets. So far as the mere fact of stone altars existing in churches was concerned, the society had decidedly the best of it. They collected some two hundred cases, and among them the church of Mr. Close, the famous evangelical preacher of Cheltenham, which contained a very elaborate modern built altar. The altar put up in the Round Church moreover might have been called almost anything. It was a horizontal slab supported upon three perpendicular ones, open in front and not solidly attached to the wall behind. It looks as if the Society must have brought the trouble on themselves by blazoning and boasting of the gift of money for an 'altar' and its substitution for a table. They had a way of making even desirable changes as disagreeable as possible to Protestants by their way of urging them; thus they recommended the abolition of pews not merely because they disfigure the inside of a church and promote an unchristian exclusiveness in worship, but *because they had originated with the Puritans.* It will be borne in mind that the name by which the thing was to be authoritatively called was the point at issue here, rather than the nature of the thing itself. An altar may exist through some fancy of an architect, as in Mr. Close's church, without any special meaning being attached to it; but if a table be formally rejected and the substitution of an altar insisted upon, it must be from some definite idea attached to the thing.[7] What is that idea? An altar is strictly and originally that on which *sacrifice* is offered, and the consecration of the elements on an *altar* implies that our Saviour was not sacrificed once for all, but is crucified afresh every time the sacrament is celebrated; which is sheer Popery. Although the Court of Arches ultimately decided against the churchwardens and the objectionable article was removed, yet the many precedents adduced by the society, the liberal manner in which they had beautified the church, and some other circumstances, caused public opinion to deem it nearly a drawn battle. Nevertheless this contest was in an indirect way fatal to the society – not through their pecuniary losses, though these were considerable – but because it involved a more thorough examination of their Romanizing tendencies and practices among persons rather inclined to be Adiaphorists in church

---

[7] On one occasion of a similar dispute, the incumbent was satisfied with having a wooden top affixed to the disputed piece of furniture to show that it was not meant for an altar.

matters. The result was that the archbishops, several bishops, the chancellor and vice-chancellor of the University formally withdrew their names from the list of patrons. The Protestant members of the society (about one seventh of it) did the same, and nearly all the withdrawals were accompanied by publicly assigned reasons. The Camden tumbled from its pride of place, and as is usual in this world's affairs, now that it was going down hill every one was ready to lend it a kick. One of the smallest possible straws may be taken as an indication of the direction in which the *aura popularis* now set. Our Epigram Club had a bare majority so far favorable to Puseyism and Young England that it would accept nothing reflecting very severely upon them, and several Epigrams had been refused admission into its record-book on this account. But now (this was in the spring of 1845) one of us sent in a ballad on the defeat and embarrassments of the Camden – an atrocious piece of doggrel in itself, compared with which even the verses of the Camdenians, such as Mr. Neale's,[8] might pass for something like poetry; – nevertheless it was accepted almost without opposition, so evidently in accordance was it with the popular sentiment.

The president of the society recommended that it should dissolve itself. As there were some legal difficulties in the way of doing this without the consent of all the members, it still continued (and for all I know, continues to this day) a sort of existence under the name of the 'Ecclesiological, late Camden'; but its meetings were no longer held in Cambridge, and it soon ceased to hold any public meetings at all.

---

[8] 'That worthy Pindar of Puseyism' as the Edinburgh called him. ['... in the "ballads" of such men as Mr Neale, that worthy Pindar of Puseyism, we find a bigotry of which contempt itself could say nothing more bitter, than that it is perfectly worthy of the doggerel which embodies it'. Rogers, 'Recent developments of Puseyism', p. 370. 'Puseyism' was coined in the late 1830s to denote the Romanising tendencies of Newman, Pusey and the other Tractarians at Oxford. John Mason Neale (Trinity 1836) was a talented classicist whose incompetence at mathematics prevented him from entering the Classical Tripos in 1840. Having moved from evangelicalism to Anglo-Catholicism, he was one of the founders of the Camden Society. He later became a prolific author of hymns, novels and works on the Eastern church.] I annex the chorus of the ballad in question, quite enough to show that it was not approved on its literary merits.

> Sing pygostole, chalice, and pyx
> Sing roodloft and credence with glee, sir,
> Did ever you see such a fix
> As that of this so-ci-e-ty? sir.

The Master and Fellows of Trinity fired a last shot after the retreating enemy, by refusing to give testimonials for orders to a leading member of the Camden Committee, who had advocated in his writings a scarcely disguised Romanism.[9] This kicking-out a traitor who was preparing to desert, and only waiting to do a little more mischief, was a surprise and discomfiture to both Puseyites and Romanists; it had probably the effect of hastening the entire perversion of some of the former, whom the English church decidedly gained by losing.

The decline of Puseyism throughout England was simultaneous with the blow it received in Cambridge. True, it still exists, but with greatly diminished influence and power of mischief. The numerous perversions to Romanism which took place during the years '46 and '47, though they gave the impression that the Tractarian heresy was spreading, were in truth signs of its losing ground. Some ultras of that school, finding that they could do nothing more in the Church of England and were rapidly becoming more and more insignificant there, went openly over to that communion to which they had virtually belonged for some time previous.

With the exception of Mr. Newman, they were no loss in the way of talents, and generally they were no loss at all, except for the wealth which, in some instances, they transferred to the enemy. The old lady of Babylon always keeps a good look-out after the sinews of war, and in this respect the apostasy of some titled members of the English Church is certainly to be regretted.

People who were watching in 1844 for the next reaction in that Church feared it might be German neology. It was thought some of the younger Oxford men had an ominous inclination that way. The reaction that came over the whole people of England of indignant resistance to Papal aggression was not foreseen, partly because the amount of impudence that called it forth was indeed hard to anticipate.

With a few words on this subject of papal aggression I will close the present chapter. The matter is not irrelevant, for it was doubtless the Puseyite movement that encouraged the Pope to his insulting attempt;[10] and it is so generally misunderstood in this country that I cannot refrain from using

---

[9] [Benjamin Webb, Trinity 1838, BA 1842; co-founder of the Camden Society with John Neale. In 1843 the two men collaborated on *The Symbolism of Churches and Church Ornaments*. Romilly reported that 'He used at [Trinity] College to be called 'Blessed Benjamin': his dress was very peculiar and intended to designate ultra-highchurchism'. Bury and Pickles, *Romilly's Cambridge Diary*, pp. 208–9.]

[10] [The re-establishment in 1850 of a Catholic hierarchy in England.]

my humble endeavors to set forth the difficulty in a truer light than that in which it is usually represented by editors and their correspondents.

Much would-be ridicule has been expended on the folly of being alarmed at a *name*. 'The Pope does not try to dispossess the English clergy of their revenues', says one (admirable moderation on the Pope's part!); 'he only calls his vicars Bishops of Manchester, Westminster, &c. The other day he created an Archbishop of New York, and we never made any fuss about it. How admirably does our republican security of religious liberty contrast', &c., and then comes a comparison much to John Bull's disadvantage. Now the two cases stand on an entirely different footing. With us no religious sect has any direct connexion with the government (and only one sect – the universally aggressive one – has tried to have any indirect connexion), consequently there may be any number of bishops of different sects in a place, calling themselves bishops of that place without interfering with one another in the eye of the law, or intruding upon the ground of the magistrate. Thus John Hughes signs himself 'Archbishop of New York'; everybody knows this means merely that he is Archbishop of the Romish church here; that he has no jurisdiction over Protestants, nor can interfere with them or their clergymen. There may be a Protestant Episcopal, a Methodist, and a Romish Bishop of Massachusetts or Boston, and the Governor of Massachusetts feel no apprehension. But in England the National Church is part of the state; the bishop has temporal as well as spiritual jurisdiction. Any man who sets himself up as a bishop alongside of him is encroaching on his political authority; it is like Mr. Dorr declaring himself Governor of Rhode Island, which title, I presume, he would not have been allowed to retain even had he refrained from attempting at once to seize on the ensigns and munitions of government.[11] And were the Romish pseudobishops allowed to keep quiet possession of their new titles, they might before long proceed to usurp territorial jurisdiction and ecclesiastical revenue as a consequence of them (for these priests are clever hands at 'trying it on'), and it would not be altogether contrary to the spirit of the British Constitution that they should do so.[12] Now if a man turns

---

[11] Thomas Dorr (1805–54) was a reformist politician who pressed for the introduction of universal white male suffrage in Rhode Island in the 1830s. This was rejected, and in 1841–42 he led an armed insurrection (the Dorr Rebellion) to achieve his aims. Dorr was jailed for life in 1843 but released in 1845.

[12] It is true that their designations are not the same as any *now existing* in the Established Church. But some of them are taken from places where it is very likely that there *will be* English bishops; Manchester for instance. [The see of Manchester

round and says, 'But this is all wrong; there ought not to be any connexion of Church and State, and the English should abolish theirs', this is begging the question. The English State Church may be a bad one, but at any rate it is the church of the majority and the church of the government, and while it is so, government and individuals must accept it as a fixed fact, just as we do slavery in our southern states, or universal suffrage, or naturalization of foreigners. If we are jealous of the interference of strangers on the subject of slavery, which every man at the north allows to be a terrible evil, why should we be surprised at the indignation of the English when strangers meddle with the prerogatives of their church, a matter much more immediately connected with the government (for it is universal throughout the country, while slavery here is only partial and local), and which they regard as one of their greatest blessings?

had in fact been established in 1847; the first bishop was James Prince Lee, formerly headmaster of King Edward VI School, Birmingham.]

32

Inferiority of our Colleges
and Universities in Scholarship

In comparing University education – that is to say, the highest and most
liberal style of education – in England and in our own country, it is but
natural, since Classical studies professedly lie at the foundation of it in both,
that we should begin by contrasting the pupils' proficiency in such studies.
What English scholarship is, the reader may have had some opportunity of
judging from the preceding pages. What American is we shall now proceed
to examine.

As I am about to say a great deal that is unusual, unpopular, and pretty
sure to give offence, it may be as well, by way of preliminary, to anticipate a
summary way of disposing of all my remarks, likely to be adopted in certain
quarters. It is a stock argument against any man, possessing, or supposed
to possess an independent property, and having ever travelled or resided
abroad, when he makes any assertion not flattering to the popular vanity
– an argument which may be briefly expressed thus: This man cannot give
any valuable information to American citizens, because from his position
and associations he does not know what the duties of an American citizen
are. It is imputing voluntary or involuntary *incivism* to every well-educated
and travelled gentleman, and thence deducing the conclusion that nothing
which he may say on any question of practical importance is entitled to
consideration.

People who reason thus, overlook one very important element of the
question. The probability of a man's giving important information or
valuable advice on any point, depends not merely on his opportunities to

know and understand the truth concerning it, but *also* on his being free to tell so much truth as he does know. If he is under any strong bias of personal interest; if his pecuniary resources or his prospects of political advancement are likely to suffer by his telling unreservedly what he believes to be the truth, then his witness will be worth less than that of a man with less knowledge but more independence. An editor is certainly not in the position most favorable to the promulgation of unpopular truth, neither is a politician. The circulation of his paper or his availability as a candidate are considerations that will continually interfere with the convictions of his reason. No one who is directly dependent on the public for support dares to tell it the truth at all times. He who is indirectly dependent, like the man of business or the professional man without private means, is more at liberty, but not completely so. And when a man of either class has, by the exercise of his talents and industry, gained fortune and reputation, so that he may say what he thinks without danger and with a chance of effecting something, the probabilities are that, if a public man, he has so long habituated himself to the promulgation of the popular rather than the true, that his mind will continue to work in the same track; and that if a private one, he will be principally inclined to indemnify himself by the material comforts which wealth affords for the trouble he took to attain it, and will prefer a quiet life to the trouble of communicating his convictions to others.

In short, a man who has nothing to expect or fear from the public, who never intends to depend on their suffrages for anything, who does not practise politics or literature for a livelihood, who is not in danger of injuring his business by uttering unpopular opinions, who is not struggling for a place in fashionable society, and therefore not obliged to toady any individual or any set – such a man is almost the only one who can afford to speak the truth boldly, and is more likely than any other man to tell the truth, supposing that he knows it.

But why should he not know it? Is it on account of his wealth? Does that disqualify him from understanding republican institutions and what is good for republicans? I fancy there are too many men making or expecting to make fortunes for such a doctrine to be universally or very generally admitted. Moreover, if it be true, the Republic is not only certainly in danger, but must have contained the seeds of dissolution from its commencement, since the number of rich men among us has constantly increased and is increasing, in spite of laws, customs, and sentiments[1] most

---

[1] [Trevelyan rightly inserts 'not' before 'most'. The error was noted at the end of the 2nd edn, but was not corrected in the 3rd edn.]

favorable to the distribution of wealth. Is it because he has travelled and lived abroad ? Let us take the extremest case. Suppose an American boy to have been left at a foreign school, to reside there during seven of the most important years in his life, to have partially forgotten his native language, so that he speaks a foreign tongue habitually and from preference, and has acquired the habits of his foreign schoolfellows and teachers. It may be urged with some plausibility that his education has not helped him to become the best kind of American citizen. But look a little further. A foreigner comes hither – one from the same country where this boy was educated; all these disqualifications exist in him to a much greater degree, yet after a few years' residence he is admitted to all the privileges of a citizen, and may hold any office except that of president. How thrice ridiculous to maintain that a portion of the American's previous life spent abroad incapacitates him more than the *whole* of *his* does the foreigner. It is worth noticing, too, that the persons most zealous in suggesting the *incivism* of wealthy and well-educated men among their own countrymen, are usually those most patronizing of emigrant foreigners, are Democrats first and Americans afterwards, and value their country chiefly as a refuge for the radicalism of the world. Suppose an American, from living or travelling abroad, has even acquired some foreign habits, that he drinks coffee when most of his countrymen take tea, or *vice versa*, or wears a hat of a slightly different shape from the ordinary one, is he therefore unable to sympathize with his fellow citizens, or to understand what is for their advantage? Have our adopted fellow-citizens no foreign habits? Do not some of them get drunk and riot, and abuse Englishmen and Protestants, and lie and cheat at elections here, exactly as they did at home? If we reject all reference to our naturalization laws, on the ground that they are a *fait accompli* and do not prove any principle, then we have the broad question – Does personal knowledge of another country disqualify a man for giving an opinion on the affairs of his own? Now I should be far from maintaining the opposite extreme to the opinion I have been combating, by admitting that foreign travel is necessarily a benefit to an American. There is a common-place of a certain class of men – two or three certain classes indeed – I heard it so often from countrymen whom I met abroad, and during the period immediately succeeding my return home, that I could calculate with almost mathematical certainty when it was coming. It usually runs in these words: It is a good thing for a young man to spend some time abroad, and see something of foreign countries, *because* he usually returns with a better appreciation of his own. Now this I take to be quite as erroneous as the opposite conclusion. If the young man have some taste with not much principle, if he be only on the look-out for the pleasures of sense and worldly amusements, he will by no means return to his country better satisfied with it; on the contrary, he will have eaten of the lotus in Paris or some other continental city, and be always looking back to it with regret. But an earnest man (to borrow a phrase from my friends the Apostles)[2] will be much more likely both to understand the deficiencies of his countrymen from living among people who have what they have not, and to appreciate their strong points from living among people who do not possess what they have.

Lastly, is a man less able to understand the duties of an American citizen, or to give his fellow-citizens any advice, because he has received an elaborate liberal education? Is he, for instance, less acquainted with political philosophy because he has studied the ancient writers of it as well as the modern, instead of the latter only, and those at second or third hand through the columns of a newspaper or a Congressional speech? Is he less able to judge of the tendencies of Popery in this country, because he has mastered its history and traced its workings in other countries, or the follies of Socialism because he has read the Fifth Book of Plato's Republic and Aristotle's answer to it? If so, the old Tory slander becomes a truth. Republicanism is not favorable to education except in a low and limited form.

I protest therefore against being read out of court by any of those persons who have given themselves a patent for looking specially after the public interest; and if any one of them, editor, lecturer, hack politician, or other sort of demagogue, who has just intelligence enough to be deceived by an American edition of the Cock-Lane ghost,[3] and just learning enough to tell his hearers that Plato proposed in his Republic the abolition of all family ties (which is just as correct as it would be to say that the Romish Church imposes celibacy on all its votaries) if any such man is prepared to attack me in the outset with the assertion that I do not know how American citizens are educated or how they ought to be, I tell him beforehand, in the plain language which it would do people of his stamp good if they heard oftener, that it is because I know too well both the ills existing and the probable results of a better system, because my advice tends to spoil his trade, that he would like to keep me from being heard. And now to the subject of this chapter.

Were I to be questioned by an educated foreigner, an Englishman or Frenchman, German, Hollander, or Dane, upon the standard of scholarship

---

[2] [See Ch. 12 for Bristed's encounters with the Cambridge Apostles.]

[3] [The reference is to a notorious scandal of the 1760s. Cock Lane is near St Paul's Cathedral in London].

in our Colleges and Universities, I should be obliged to answer, not having the fear of King Public before my eyes, that it was exceedingly low, and that not merely according to his idea, but according to the idea of a boy fitted at a good school in New York.[4] When I went up to Yale College in 1835, the very first thing that struck me was the classical deficiency of the greater part of the students and some of the instructors. A great many of the Freshmen had literally never heard of such a thing as prosody; they did not know that there were any rules for quantity: it may be imagined what work they made with reading poetry. Nor could their teachers, in many instances, do much to help them; one of our classical tutors did not know the quantity of the middle syllable in *profugus*, almost the first word in the Aeneid.[5] The etymological part of Greek grammar (to say nothing of the syntax) was very imperfectly understood by the majority, and of those who made pretensions to scholarship there were not ten in a class who could write three consecutive sentences of decent Latin prose. The system of choosing the tutors to whose care the two lower classes were entirely committed, was enough to destroy any chance of rectifying the errors of bad and insufficient preparation. They were elected from the graduates who had taken a certain stand on the average of all their College course – say the first fifteen. Now a student might get among these fifteen – the 'oration men'[6] – by excelling in classics alone with very little ability in or taste for mathematics, or *vice versa*; but he was obliged to take such tutorial vacancy as came to him in his order of seniority; so the mathematical man might be set to hear classics or the classics[7] to teach mathematics. The consequence of which was that not only the bad men did not improve, but the good ones were generally pretty well spoilt by the time they came to the Greek professor's hands in the third year. Not only was the course for all the students limited to the

---

[4] [Rev. Huddert's school: see Bristed's account of his schooling at the beginning of Ch. 2.]

[5] [It occurs in the second line. All three syllables are short. Bristed might have added that the famous William Paley, when giving a Latin speech in Cambridge in 1795, had similarly pronounced the word with a long middle syllable; a mistake which was immediately publicized by witty verses – in Latin, of course.]

[6] [Superior performance was rewarded by invitations to give public orations. Bristed had encountered a similar system at Trinity, where he himself had given declamations.]

[7] ['Classic' = student of classics; a common nineteenth-century usage. The latest citation in *OED* is from 1933, but I heard it used by the master of my Cambridge college in 1966.]

same books, and very small in quantity, so as to keep it at the level of the worst prepared (among whom were generally a large number of 'benefi-ciaries' or charity students), but this small quantity was badly learned and taught;[8] a student with classical tastes had no encouragement for getting up his classics properly, for he had no chance of showing his scholarship or doing himself justice – his tutor could not appreciate him; consequently if ambitious, he was easily tempted to seek distinction in other things, the various associations for the cultivation of 'speaking' and 'writing' in which the College abounded. The only extras in which the scholar could exercise himself and attain honor were the three Berkleian premiums. Two of these were for Latin composition in the first and second years, and some queer things occasionally happened in the adjudication of these. Just after I left in '40 or '41, some enterprising youth sent in an exercise in Elegiac metre, a variation which so astonished the examiners (the compositions being usually in prose) that they gave it the first prize. It was published in the College Magazine, and lo! every pentameter except two or three had a radical defect in the metre – a spondee in the fourth place instead of a dactyl, e.g.,

> Invalidos artus *labentemque* pedem.

He might well say 'labentem pedem', sure enough.[9]

Nevertheless, after all this there was still a possibility of our learning something in the last two years from some of the professors; but to put the finishing stroke to us, by the beginning of the fourth year we were supposed to have become finished scholars, and further instruction of us in Greek and Latin was given up. When the third Berkleian praemium was open for competition towards the close of this year – involving an examination in three Greek and three Latin subjects, with seven months of idleness (except

---

[8] The only part of the first two years' course generally well learned was the *Satires of Horace*, thanks to Professor Anthon's labors, for which New England students are generally anything but grateful. [Charles Anthon, a prolific author – or assembler – of classical editions, was Professor of Greek Language and Literature at Columbia, 1830–67. His complete edition of Horace, first published in New York in 1830, went into more than a dozen editions, was pirated in England and spawned smaller editions. Anthon had taught Bristed at Columbia; the latter's mention is part of his consistent praise of Columbia at the expense of Yale. For Anthon, see M. Reinhold, 'Charles Anthon', in W.W. Briggs (ed.), *Biographical Dictionary of North American Classicists* (New York, 1994), pp. 19–20.]

[9] [The Latin = 'weak limbs and a tottering foot'; Bristed's point is that the second half of the line applies only too well to the author's grasp of 'feet' (metre).]

three hours' lectures a day) to prepare for it, it sometimes happened that not a candidate presented himself! Yet the prize, as it was the only Classical one in the year and gave some opportunity of showing scholarship, much more than the daily recitations which fixed the 'appointments'[10] or regular College Honors, ought to have excited some competition, to say nothing of its pecuniary value to those remaining in residence, which must have been an object to many of the theological students residing after their graduation. I never heard of more than one candidate except in 1839 when I went in myself along with a friend,[11] and the professors, after examining us both for the usual time allotted to one (four hours for six subjects, one of which was the whole Iliad!), divided the prize without any further attempt at discrimination of our merits.

How much temptation there was in such a state of things to read anything not included in the regular course may easily be conceived. How much was known of authors out of the course, one little incident will suffice to show. A student writing in the College Magazine, quoted the lines from Lucretius,

> Tu pater es rerum inventor, tu patria nobis,
> Suppedita praecepta tuis, rex inclyte chartis

as a *modern* distich.[12] From the context in which he had found it there was nothing very remarkable in his making the mistake, but it was a little singular that no one in the place ever detected it for three years, and I presume no one has up to the present time. Fancy such an error passing unnoticed in a foreign University. Or fancy a Bachelor who wished to carry out his Classical studies, reading by himself for six months in a University town *because he could find no one to teach him*, as actually happened to myself.

Such was the condition of Scholarship at Yale ten years ago, and if I wanted to spoil a boy who promised to make a good scholar, I could not think of a more certain way than sending him to an institution so conducted.

---

[10] ['In many American colleges, students to whom are assigned a part in the exercises of an exhibition or commencement, are said to receive an *appointment*'. B.H. Hall, *A Collection of College Words and Customs* (Cambridge MA, 1856), p. 11.]

[11] A.R. Macdonough, now of the New York bar, a gentleman of fine Classical tastes, and who under any system which gave those tastes encouragement might have become a superior scholar. He had a way of reading off Cicero *ad aperturam* into elegant English, that would have made an Oxonian's mouth water.

[12] [Lucretius *de rerum natura*, 3.9–10.]

I speak within limits in asserting that he will not make as much progress in the whole four years as he ought to do in one, and *may have* made in one before or after quitting the College. A little strong language will I trust be pardoned from one who has himself been a victim of the system.

Yale is the largest College in our country, and one of the two most distinguished. The result of my inquiries has not led me to believe that Harvard is any better off. That the other Colleges throughout the country, many of which derive their instructors from these two great New England Colleges, are if anything in a worse state, may be easily inferred.

There is one exception which for the honor of our city I am proud to insist upon. Columbia College, New York, has always exhibited in its Classical instruction a marked superiority to the other similar institutions of our country. It is a fact which deserves to be more generally known than it is, that the standard for admission into the Freshman class at Columbia is higher both in Classics and Mathematics than at any other College in the United States.[13] Unfortunately its position in the midst of a large city prevents it from entering into competition with other institutions, limits its pupils to the sons of residents in the city, and in fact makes it only a very superior day-school for New Yorkers.

But has there been no improvement in the last ten years, a space of time in which our countrymen can do so much? I rejoice to say that there has. Under the auspices of the new President of Yale[14] there is more encouragement for, and consequently improvement in certain branches of classical learning than at any former period. Having occasion two years ago to examine some of the best in the Junior class who were candidates for a Scholarship, I was agreeably surprised at their proficiency in Greek prose, while in some of their earlier studies, Virgil for instance, they were as deficient as the students of my time.[15] The Scholarships, five in number, nearly all founded by the President himself, must have a good effect in

---

[13]   When I fitted for Columbia – a preparation which was all but sufficient for the Sophomore class at Yale – three books of Xenophon, three of Homer, three of Euclid and Algebra as far as Quadratic Equations, were among the subjects required. Now, I believe, *either* the Euclid *or* the Algebra, *either* the Xenophon *or* the Homer, will be accepted. Even this lower standard of admission is beyond that of the New England Colleges.

[14]   [Theodore Dwight Woolsey (1801–89) was Professor of Greek at Yale 1831–46 and President 1846–71. Bristed often corresponded with him; *Five Years* is dedicated to Woolsey.]

[15]   [Bristed is here uncharacteristically modest, in not mentioning that this was the

the end, by giving the best men a motive for reading beyond the regular course. But allowing these favorable prospects, and supposing that other institutions have improved equally (which may be doubted, since whatever has been done at Yale is owing chiefly to the exertions of one man, its new head), our colleges are very far behind what they should be, judging not merely by a foreign standard, but by that of the best schools in New York or Boston.

It may seem very unpatriotic to say all this, but when people are not generally awake to their own deficiencies their eyes ought to be opened, and their real friend is he who tries to do this, not he who, by claiming for the country what it does not possess, makes it and himself ridiculous in the eyes of foreigners, and tends to make them sceptical in regard to its real merits. Talk to a stranger of our chivalry towards women, our sympathy between classes, our benevolence for public objects, the diffusion of rudimentary education among the masses, &c., and he may be well disposed to believe you; but if you tell him at the same time that 'So-and-So is a great scholar', when his works prove him to be a very inferior one, or that 'Classics are on the whole as well taught at Yale and Harvard as at Oxford and Cambridge' (I have heard this roundly asserted, by a public man too), and your foreigner says to himself, 'Here is my informant grossly astray on a subject of which I can judge at once; may he not be equally mistaken in some of the other excellences which he attributes to his countrymen?' The English have injured their character by a similar mistake of claiming too much. Insisting on a superiority in the arts of life – in dress, cookery, and furniture, which they do not possess, and their claim to which is so readily disproved, they have caused foreigners to distrust their pretensions to higher excellences which are less obvious on the surface, and require longer and deeper experience and examination to appreciate.[16]

Bristed Scholarship he founded in that year, for sophomore performance in Greek. For some years he himself set the papers and examined the candidates.]

[16]   I.e. Mr Bristed went to England to astound the natives with his knowledge of 'dress, cookery, and furniture', and returned to America to astonish his countrymen with 'those high excellences etc.' (E)

33

Supposed Counterbalancing Advantages of American Colleges

The great comedian of Athens saw that the feeling of their own insight and profundity rendered his countrymen a prey to the vulgarest delusions. The great philosopher of Athens whom that comedian ridiculed, saw still deeper into the meaning of the same fact – saw that the most clever and enlightened of the youth of Athens could talk about all manner of things, but knew nothing whatever of themselves!

Maurice's *Lectures on Education.*

Admitting that our colleges do not teach Latin and Greek so well as the European ones, the natural and ordinary defence is, that they teach other things, and those on the whole of more value, better. Let us examine the particulars of this defence. What are the other things taught? – are they better taught? – and are they more beneficial as means of liberal education?

And first, in relation to Mathematics. There used to be, and probably is still, a vague general impression at Yale, to the effect that the Mathematical course there is a very difficult and thorough one – that, in fact, Mathematics constitute one of the crack points of the institution. This fancy certainly derived some support from comparison with the Classical course, *as compared with which* the Mathematical was undoubtedly a good one. But that did not prevent it from being very bad, as tried either by an ideal standard, or by those existing in other countries. How *far* it reached is sufficiently shown by the fact that the Differential Calculus, the vestibule as it were to all high Mathematics, was among the *optional* studies at the end of the third year. The Valedictorian at the completion of the course, or the man who gained the first mathematical prize in the second year, need never have studied it. Nevertheless, a course of Mathematics stopping short of the Differential may be a very good one so far as it goes. But this was not the case with the course at Yale College. In many of its stages it was liable to the same reproach as the classical, of being a study of *books* rather than *subjects*. The learning and recitation of portions from day to day (for the annual examinations were little more than a form, and had no effect on the college honors) encouraged a habit of cramming from one day to another. A great deal of the work in the second or third year consisted of long calculations of examples worked with logarithms, which consumed a great deal of time without giving any insight into principles, and were equally distasteful to the good and the bad mathematicians. In fact, while the course was, from its daily recurrence throughout three years, and the amount of figuring it involved, more disagreeable to classics than a more difficult and rigorous investigation of principles requiring less dead mechanical work would have been, the best mathematicians of the class always grumbled at it quite as much as the best linguists did at the classical course. They complained, that with the exception of two prizes for problems during the Freshman and Sophomore years, and an occasional 'original demonstration' in the recitation-room, they had no chance of showing their superior ability and acquirements, that much of their time was lost in long arithmetical and logarithmical computations, that classical men were continually tempted to 'skin' (copy)[1] the solutions of these examples, and thus put themselves unjustly on a level with them; and much more of the same sort. I am strongly inclined to think that a course of mathematics, covering as much real ground as the present one of three years, might be put into two without infringing more than at present on the special pursuits of the more classically disposed students, and with positive benefit to the whole body. As it is, any student who enters upon his Senior year at Yale has *nominally* gone over a greater amount of mathematics than

---

[1] [As a song at the Yale Biennial Jubilee of 1855 put it, 'There was plenty of *skin* with a good deal of Bohn' – referring to Bohn's series of classical translations, much in use as cribs. Hall, *College Words and Customs*, p. 431.]

one of the *polloi* at Cambridge – twice as much at least; but it does not follow that he really knows more or has enjoyed more of the peculiar benefits of mathematical training. I suspect that a man in the first class of the 'Poll' has usually read mathematics to more profit than many of the 'appointees', even of the 'oration men' at Yale.

Secondly, as regards the sciences in general. The fact that during the last year various courses of lectures are delivered on the natural and moral sciences, attendance on these courses not being optional as at an English University, but compulsory on all the students, will doubtless be considered by many persons a great point in favor of our Colleges. For my own part I look upon it as one of their greatest mistakes. The idea of being able to impart any adequate or permanent information to a large body of students in twenty-five lectures a-piece on a dozen different sciences, almost any *one* of which is work for a quarter of a man's lifetime, seems to me altogether visionary and chimerical. There are perhaps eight or ten of the hundred students present at each course who take an interest in the particular science, and derive some appreciable benefits from the lectures. It requires very little practical acquaintance with the working of the system to ascertain that most of the auditors consider the lecture merely as part of a routine which they are obliged to go through. In Professor Silliman's laboratory, I recollect, the lively manner of the lecturer, his deserved personal popularity, and the additional attraction of an extra audience of school-girls, caused his lectures to be attended *to*, as well as attended, but I doubt if his hearers carried away any very lasting impressions.[2] At Professor Olmsted's lectures, the students were inclined to go to sleep.[3] At those on Botany, such as had not an amusing book to read or an opportunity for reading it without being very openly seen, used to withdraw themselves from the rooms by very undignified and irregular methods. Ever and anon the professor's voice was heard in sharp digression from his stamens and pistils, 'Mr. Monitor, look sharp! there's another gentleman jumping out of the window.'[4]

---

[2] [Benjamin Silliman (1779–1864) had been appointed in 1802 the first professor of 'chymistry and natural history' at Yale. A pioneer of American science, he was the first person to fractionate petroleum by distillation.]

[3] [Denison Olmsted (1791–1859), professor of mathematics and chemistry at Yale from 1825, of astronomy and natural philosophy from 1836. Olmsted was famous for his work on meteors.]

[4] [This was probably Charles Upham Shepard (1804–86), who had taught botany in the 1830–1 session, and natural history from 1833 to 1847. His *Treatise on Mineralogy* (New Haven, 1832–5) went into several editions.]

Let it be admitted, however, that to have attended a certain number of lectures on scientific subjects is one of the desirable accomplishments of a liberal education – nay, more, that it may sometimes evoke talent in the direction of some one science, which but for this accidental opportunity might never have been developed. Let us have the lectures then, by all means; but to make such lectures – for which no preparation is required and at which no notes are taken, which involve no reading before or after and merely break in upon the student's day for two or three isolated hours – to make them a substitute for hard work and mental training, has surely a perilous tendency to effeminate the student's mind and give him desultory habits of thought. The youth who, under such a system of classical and mathematical training as has been described, is ludicrously enough supposed to have acquired a sufficient knowledge of classics and mathematics, arrives at the end of his third year. Then the faculty virtually tell him, 'You are a finished scholar and mathematician – all you have to do for the next year is to pack in all the sciences by means of lectures on each one three times a week during a term or two. All we ask of you is to attend a lecture of an hour's length three times a-day, and in the intervals you may read reviews and work them up into speeches and essays for your debating society.' What should be an afternoon or evening amusement is made the work of the day.

I think a careful inquirer will find that the great *savans* of Europe have not been trained on such principles. Most of them have begun by being good mathematicians and in many cases good scholars also; and at a maturer period of life they have brought well-disciplined minds to the particular study of their special pursuits.

Thirdly, there is a prevailing opinion among our students (how far it is accepted in other quarters of the community I will not pretend to say) that, in consequence of being left so much to themselves during the last year of their course, and of not overvaluing the College course at any time, they have much leisure for the perusal of literature and general improvement of their minds and acquisition of miscellaneous knowledge, in which respect they have the advantage over the English student.

Now as respects literature this is altogether a mistake. There certainly is *a kind* of literature in which our students are more at home than the English. They read more newspapers; they read more magazines; they read more political pamphlets; they read a great many more novels; they are well up in all that floating small literature of the day which an editor or periodical critic has to wade through as part of his business, and which any other man, especially any *young* man who wishes really to improve his mind, is much better without. But of the standard and classic literature of the language they do not read more – or know more. They are not better acquainted with Shakspeare and Milton, with Wordsworth and Tennyson, with Bacon and Locke, with Gibbon and Robertson. They are not *by any means* so well acquainted with the old English Dramatists, the old English Divines, the essayists and political writers prior to Queen Anne, or the best ethical and logical writers of the present day. They take much of their knowledge at second hand from the English reviews – reviews which the Cambridge man reads indeed with pleasure, but which from his previous acquaintance with the texts and sources of them, he regards as subjects of his own criticism rather than authorities or oracles. They read rapidly, indiscriminately and uncritically.

As to any superiority in miscellaneous information which the American student may have over the English one, much of this exterior knowledge is not owing to his collegiate training or want of training at all, but to his home and vacation life, the greater variety of people he encounters in his ordinary intercourse with the world. So much of it as is attainable from books, the English student picks up later in life, when he is better able to make use of it.

Fourthly, in all our Colleges English Composition and Public Speaking are encouraged in every possible way, both by the authorities and by associations of the students themselves, from the very beginning to the very end of the course. At an English University there is very little encouragement for either English Composition or Public Speaking. But to speak and write well, it is said, are the great aims and requisites of the minister, the lawyer, and the political man of any sort. They are the principal means of obtaining fame and power in a free country, and therefore are the highest intellectual ends of man; and that is the best education which best prepares the student for them.

Here we are arrived at the strong point of our Colleges and Universities. For it is the immediate object of an American College practically (whatever it may be with some of its Faculty theoretically) to make the students fluent speakers and ready writers, just as it is the immediate object of an English University to turn out good scholars and mathematicians. And the object is certainly accomplished: our Collegians learn to think on their legs and handle a pen with dexterity at a remarkably early age. The end proposed also, is a higher object to an ambitious young man. To aim at being a great author or orator, seems nobler and grander than to solve problems or read Aristotle in the original. As this is a very important matter, let us examine it in detail, beginning with a view of the effect which the admitted end of our collegiate education has upon our collegiate system as its workings are developed in one of the New England Universities.

Almost from the beginning of their course, certainly from the third term of their Freshman year, all students ambitious of distinction are, by common consent, divided into two classes, called in their own phraseology *scholars* and *writers*. The former class includes, by a singular extension of the term, Mathematicians as well as Classics – all, in short, who are prominent candidates for College honors; the latter, those who undertake to distinguish themselves in English Composition, either in the weekly readings of it before tutors and professors, the numerous debating societies among the students (into all of which orations and dissertations enter largely as part of the exercises), or the columns of the College Magazine.[5] Sometimes a youth attempts to distinguish himself in both departments, and the attempt when made is frequently successful; but, as a general rule, the two classes of aspirants for fame are distinct. Closely connected with the 'writers' are the speakers. Excellence as a debater, even when unaccompanied with a reputation for writing well, is much prized, and the happy possessor of both faculties is one of the College geniuses. The writers, including the speakers as subordinate to and in many cases coincident with them, are – and it is to this I wish to call particular attention – infinitely more honored and esteemed and envied and looked up to by the great bulk of the students than the 'scholars' or College appointees. The Freshman's object of reverence may perhaps be the 'Valedictorian'; but by the time he is well launched in his Sophomore year, his admiration is transferred to the 'First President' of the Brothers' or Linonian Society, the 'First Editor' of the *Yale Literary*, and the 'Class Orator'.[6] Supposing a student to have received the 'appointment' of an Oration from the Faculty, and also to have been elected Editor of the Magazine by the students, he and his fellows would consider the latter a far greater honor than the former – so far above it that the two could hardly be put in comparison. In short, the distinctions conferred by the

---

[5]   [For an analysis of 19th-century views on debating, see S. Farrow, 'Debating and its discontents', *Language and Communication* 26 (2006), pp. 117–28, who discusses Bristed's views.]

[6]   [The Society of the Brothers in Unity (1768) and the Linonian Society (1753) were the two leading student societies at Yale. When the university library was established in 1871, they donated their own books to it; they are now housed in the Linonian and Brothers Reading Room in the Sterling Memorial Library. The *Yale Literary Magazine*, to which Bristed several times contributed (see Bibliography A2, 1838–41), had been founded in 1836.]

students on one another are more prized than the distinctions conferred by the College authorities on the students. So much so is this the case, that the prizes given by the Faculty for English Composition are not accepted among the students as tests of the best writers.

This state of things is induced by several different causes. The Faculty promote it indirectly by the inferiority of their Classical and Mathematical instruction, and by leaving the students so much to themselves during their last year. They promote it directly in more than one way: by giving 'compositions' and 'disputes' and 'declamations' so large a place in the College exercises of the second and third years, by making the right to deliver a speech (at Junior Exhibition or Commencement) the highest reward for proficiency in College studies, by formally acknowledging the existence of the larger debating societies in such acts as giving 'half-lessons' for the morning after the Wednesday night debates. The existence of so many charity-students or 'beneficiaries', comparatively old men and more likely to shine in writing and speaking than in the late-learned elements of Latin and Greek, also does much to promote it.

But whatever the causes, an outsider – one who had not the previous bias of being brought up under the system – looking at it from an external point of view, would be apt to say, 'Here is a most anomalous and abnormal condition of things for an academical institution. The students have set up their judgment against that of their instructors. They declare that the means of education proposed for them by their teachers are the more ignoble, and those proposed for them by themselves the more worthy. They make themselves judges beforehand of that which it is the business of their tutors to qualify them for judging of. And their instructors receive these claims with assent – reluctant assent perhaps – but certainly not opposition, not even a negative one. What is this but self-condemnation on their part?'

It is not impossible, however, that the students, inadequately provided for by their teachers, may have provided for themselves a good means of education. Let us, therefore, examine the effect of practice in English Composition and Public Speaking, from an early age (say fifteen) as prominent elements of a liberal education.

First of all, it may reasonably be doubted whether the cultivation of two special talents which border closely on the domain of genius, and high excellence in which very few men can reasonably hope to attain, ought to be made the corner-stone of a general education. The very fact that it is a greater thing to be an orator than a scholar, is a positive reason for giving classics a preference over oratory in a *University* course. Not only does your end answer the proposed conditions better, but you have more likelihood of arriving at it. You cannot make every third man in a class a great orator or author, though you may give him a fluency and confidence in talking platitudes or a knack of stringing together common-places on paper; you can make every third man of a class a respectable scholar. Were it possible to send forth every College graduate throughout the country an orator, it would not he desirable. It would be an unfortunate example of mental alchemy.

'If all were gold then gold were no more wealth.' Could we turn out every graduate a moderately good classic, we should give a taste and tone to the intellect of the country that would have a most favorable influence on oratory and authorship.

Let us look a little further. The immediate effects of the system we admit to be dazzling. The American student in his Senior year (when he may have attained the age of nineteen or thereabouts) has a readiness of tongue and pen, a confidence on his legs and a general dexterity of argument, unparalleled by his contemporaries in any part of the world. He will make speeches and write essays that are astonishing for one of his years when compared with the productions of older men about him. He seems to have shot up into full mental stature before he has reached the limit of his bodily growth. In all mixed society he will throw an English youth of the same age utterly into the shade. But let us examine how far this precocious splendor has any solid aliment or permanent source.

The Englishman's tardiness of development is in a great measure intentional. He is kept back to take a good start. He leaves school at the period of life when the American leaves College. Up to that time his studies have not been such as he can make an immediate display before the world with, but have rather been directed to strengthening and polishing his mind for future use. At the University his aim is to excel in the studies prescribed by the authorities of the place, not in something different from and partly antagonistic to these. However well-prepared he finds numbers in advance of him, and can never complain that he does not know what to learn or can find no one to teach him. Whatever his school reputation, his vanity is sure to be speedily checked, and first of all by his private tutor, who 'slangs' him for a mistake here or an inelegancy there. Then he makes mistakes in examinations also, and 'loses marks'.[7] If a thriving

---

[7] ['Mark' in the arithmetical, rather than simply indicative sense was perhaps seen by Bristed as a non-standard usage. The examples in Hall's *College Words and Customs* (1856) are all from the 1840s; the range he reports, from 0 to 4 at Yale, from 0 to 8 at Harvard, suggests a crude scheme little developed from the earlier 'mark of

public-school classic and ready to carry all before him in that line, he is still obliged to read mathematics, to feel his inferiority at first and perhaps at last to occupy a subordinate place in them. If he has cleverness there is no lack of room to display it, but it is necessary that he should work hard also; there are great rewards of reputation as well as substantial emolument for the combination of intellect and industry, but none for disconnected and single exhibitions of brilliancy. The tendency of every influence about him is to make him cautious, self-critical, and self-distrustful, careful and elaborate in his acquisitions, and consequently when he learns anything he takes hold of it as with a vice; when he says he knows it, you may be sure he does. And when he becomes a high Wrangler or First Class man, he does not infer that he is therefore bound to be a great statesman or orator at once, but only that he has good talents, a fair power, and regular habits of work, by which *if he continues to work*, he is likely, in course of time, to succeed in his profession. Or if he fails to take the stand he hoped, he can never charge his examiners with unfairness.

Our student, on the contrary, is from the first surrounded with influences calculated to excite and flatter his vanity. If he comes to College from a good school in New York or Boston, the chances are that he is set under a tutor who knows less of the rudiments of scholarship than himself. Hence the first lesson he learns is to despise his teachers. He hears it said all about him that the College appointees are for the most part poor dull fellows who never do anything to distinguish themselves in after life, that an Appointment is only worth taking as a mere extra if it can be got without taking much trouble for it, and that *writing* and *speaking* are the proper objects of his ambition. And the opinion respecting the appointees is partly true; a successful mediocrity not much beyond what is required for the Captaincy of the Poll at Cambridge (if we except regularity of attendance at recitations) has no great charm for a boy who is clever, and well enough prepared for something better. Thus he is led to depreciate the honors given by the authorities, and seek for distinction in another quarter. He aspires after those rewards which are in the gift of his fellow-students, and which he himself has a share in bestowing on others. He becomes habituated to making speeches and reading compositions before audiences of from thirty to a hundred, whose capacity to be critical is not equal to their disposition, and whose disposition is modified by their mutual interest; now and then

---

approbation'. In England the modern (arithmetical) sense can be found in the early 1820s; the underlying changes in practice probably date from the 1790s. See further Stray, 'From oral to written examinations'.]

he makes an unusually showy effort, and is applauded for it. His friends and acquaintances have not the same ability to find faults in his performance that a tutor has to correct the exercise of a pupil, nor does their position enable them to speak so freely without the risk of giving offence or incurring the suspicion of jealousy. If he succeeds in winning these popular honors, they are almost the exact counterpart of similar ones in maturer life. He writes smart articles in the College magazine and is made editor of it; he gets a reputation for speaking in his debating society and is elected president, just as he might get sent to the state-legislature when a man, for speaking well at public meetings. If he fails, his failure may be owing not to want of merit, but to want of popularity, or to intrigue and jealousy, of which there is always a great deal at work. Thus he brings the great world into the academic shades, and aims at being a public man while he should as yet be but a hard-working student.

And here his unguided and indiscriminate reading involves him in a double error. Not only is the object of his aim prematurely high, but the ideal of that object becomes continually lowered for him. He does not appreciate what he seeks to be. Though professedly working to form a style, he does not properly study the best models or confine himself to them. He swallows a great deal of second and third-rate matter. He acquires a childish fondness for metaphors more or less mixed, and generally for all sorts of figures, as if they were the sole test and standard of excellence in composition. In short he aims at *fine* writing, and sits down not to express his ideas on a subject, but to *write a piece*. So, in oratory, he knows little, except at second-hand, of Demosthenes and Cicero; rather more but not too much about Burke. He does not confine himself to the best models of his own country. He possesses well-thumbed copies of Webster's speeches and Everett's Orations,[8] but he will turn from these at any time to the last imperfectly-reported stump speech – especially if he can utilize anything from it at the debating society. A secret conviction is generated in his mind that *he* could do nearly as well in their place as many of the men whose performances he reads – which may not be so very far from the truth – and here again his vanity is gratified. Moreover as his experience leads him to suspect that people are much in the habit of talking and writing about things of which they have but small knowledge, he comes to the conclusion that very small knowledge of a subject is necessary to qualify a man for talking

---

8 [Daniel Webster (1782–1852) was famous for his oratory, especially for his speeches to Congress. Edward Everett (1794–1865), who succeeded Webster as Secretary of State, provided a biographical memoir for vol.1 of his *Works* (1851).]

and writing about it – he will consider himself prepared to discuss any point in metaphysics, for instance, after going through a course of *Stewart's Outlines*.[9] The real acquisitions of a Senior Class in a New England College bear a lamentably small ratio to their conceit of knowledge.

One thing they certainly have mastered – the art of electioneering. They have learned a great deal of human nature, as regards the way in which men can be 'got round' and votes influenced. One of our large Colleges is an excellent school for a professed politician; whether this fact is particularly honorable to them, or whether that occupation is a particularly honorable and desirable one for all or many students, may admit of a doubt.

This brings us to another evil springing directly from the early and constant practice of writing and speaking. It encourages a *sophistic habit*, most dangerous for a very young man to acquire, since it puts him in an unfortunate frame of mind for the reception of knowledge and truth. I use the word *sophistic* not without direct reference to its origin, and to the intellectual training of the young Athenians by their itinerant professors – a training not far from having its counterpart among ourselves. What was this system as we deduce it from contemporary writers, especially Plato, who, indeed, often illustrates it himself unintentionally in his own course of argument? The Sophist was a professor of mental and moral philosophy; he taught his pupils to argue on all points of metaphysics and of ethics, including politics – to argue readily, dexterously, captiously, the discussion often declining into the merest hair-splitting and verbal quibbling. Victory, not truth – to effect a presumption rather than to secure the acquisition of knowledge, was the end of debate. The benefit proposed, sometimes without an attempt at disguise, to the pupil was, that he should be able to humbug the people and get on in the world (that is the plain Saxon of it), which he was to accomplish by being always ready to talk about anything, and never at a loss for a plausible argument.

Our young men leave college imbued with debating society formulae. Their very slang is redolent of the society – its phrases are the phrases of their every-day life. If three or four of them are in a room together, one cannot say to another, 'Smith, shut the door, please', without putting it into some such form as 'I move Mr. Smith shut the door', or 'I move Mr. Smith be a committee of one to shut that door'. They are always ready for

---

[9]   [Dugald Stewart's *Outlines of Moral Philosophy*, a major statement of the Scottish common-sense school, first appeared in 1793. It was a much-used textbook in the New England colleges, particularly in an edition introduced by James McCosh, president of Princeton.]

an argument, and will tackle a man of any age if there is a chance of a discussion. Recondite disquisitions are not to their purpose; but any popular question, such as a man can talk of from review and newspaper reading, they delight to raise a controversy about. They evince a great dexterity in taking exceptions, and are as quick to find instances against the generalizations of others as to draw imperfect generalizations themselves.

Many years ago the father of a young Englishman who had distinguished himself at the University, and given other indications of uncommon talent, having destined his son for public life, wrote to a friend, an eminent Scotch advocate and politician, for advice how the young man should be trained to make him a successful orator. The answer, which was long preserved in the family, contained these suggestions among others, – 'He must seek the conversation of older men, and talk at them without being afraid of them; he must talk a great deal merely for the sake of talking; he must talk too much in company.'[10]

The person who related this to me was most struck with the apparent paradox of the last clause – the ludicrous idea of the future orator *never talking enough* until he had *talked too much*. I was impressed by a different thought – the exactness with which our collegians anticipate this advice for themselves and carry it out. They talk at older men without being afraid of them; they talk a great deal for mere practice in talking; they talk too much in company.

Now the young man to whom this advice was given had the foundation of a thorough education whereon to build his rhetorical superstructure, varied knowledge to adorn, and a superior intellect to illuminate it. He started on a large capital in every point of view. If therefore he acquired a sometimes inconvenient habit of talking too much in company, there was still a probability that he would say much worth hearing; if his conversational sparrings with older men involved some violation of modesty, they were at any rate not likely to be disfigured by egregious errors. But when a youth acquires this talking facility and propensity without a proper training and knowledge to support it – when most of his authorities are at third or fourth-hand, hearsay, or in the last newspaper article, or the confused recollection of what was at first imperfectly read, it follows inevitably that he must make many mistakes which his verbal dexterity will be continually brought into requisition to protect. And from this combination of inaccuracy

---

[10] Should the reader be curious to know the result of this advice, it may be said that the subject of it has only attained moderate success as a public speaker, though in some other paths to distinction he stands among the foremost men of the age.

of detail with facility of expression results one of our great national faults, a tendency to defend rather than prevent mistakes; plausibility in explaining away or glossing over an error rather than caution in guarding against the probability of its occurrence.

This feeling which, like the Spartan's conception of honesty, or the Parisian's of conjugal fidelity, places the evil of error, not in the original commission, but in the subsequent conviction of it, stands directly in the way of individual and national improvement. Its favorite mode of argument is the *ignoratio elenchi*, the ignoring of the main point in dispute, and joining issue on some irrelevant accident; of it and its favorite form of this mode is the *tu quoque*, a digression upon some personal demerit of the opponent.[11] Thus both literature and politics are debased, and honest criticism or difference of opinion converted into matter of individual quarrel.

After all, the strongest objection to this literary precocity is that it defeats its own object. The ambitious student begins at the wrong end. He acquires manner before matter, and has a style in advance of his thoughts. His untimely blossoms do not fructify. His graces and ornaments of trope and metaphor, like the flowers which a child sticks into the ground to make a garden, grow faded and lose vitality for want of root and nutriment. He repeats his ideas, or those of others.[12] He wrote fluently at eighteen, at twenty-six he writes a trifle perhaps more fluently but in no respect better. Some years ago, I heard an Italian say that his country produced many young artists of great promise, but none of them ever came to maturity. I thought at the time it was pretty much the same with our College geniuses. The class below me at Yale, out of a hundred members, had thirty poets – that is to say, men who had written *and published* verses. This is an extreme instance; but the number of 'great writers' in my time (eleven years ago) at that College was very large. The number who have since attained any substantial literary distinction I could count on one hand and have some fingers to spare.

The best education has its limits, and very marked ones. No physical

---

[11]   As if, for instance, one should say, by way of invalidating any of the conclusions in this book, 'The author was at an English University himself, and does not afford us a favorable specimen of a Cambridge graduate, or appear to have profited much by his stay there.'

[12]   Barefaced copying from books and reviews in their Compositions is familiar to our students, as much so as 'skinning' their mathematical examples. It is in a manner forced upon them, by being expected to *write* before they have anything *to write about.*

training can develope an ordinary man into a giant or a Hercules. No intellectual training can *make* a genius. The error of our system is that it makes a great many ordinary men suppose themselves to be geniuses, while at the same time it does not develope their ordinary abilities in the best way.

I have often been surprised (until from the frequency of the phenomenon it ceased to surprise me) at the altered impressions made on me by these College geniuses in after life. I do not refer to their position or want of position in the world, so much as to the effect which their conversation had upon me. They seemed to have *come back to me*, if I may be allowed to use a sporting phrase.[13] Their remarks seemed trivial and common-place, their ideas limited, till I was tempted to look down upon those whom I used to look up to. And more than one such man has confessed to me his regret at not having made better use of his College opportunities, and devoted himself more attentively to the legitimate studies of the place; and has owned his reluctant conviction that the time which he anticipated was borrowed at usurious interest and the apparent gain had turned out a real loss.

The truth of what I have asserted, namely that our literary precocity overreaches itself, may be brought home very briefly to every unprejudiced and capable man. We accustom our youth to the practice of Composition much sooner than the English do theirs. Do we on the whole write as well as the English? Will any candid and well informed man say, from his heart, that the average of our books published every year is equal in quality to the average of theirs, or that the average quality of our newspaper and periodical literature is anywhere near theirs? I think every man who can afford to have a conscience will admit that there is a difference in their favor, and a greater difference than can be accounted for by the absence of an International Copyright Law.[14] Yet, in order to justify our practice, we should expect as a result a very decided superiority to the English – unless we suppose an original inferiority of material. But the natural quickness and cleverness of the American mind are universally admitted. Our most bigoted enemies have never charged us with incapacity or stupidity. Our keenness of intelligence is all but proverbial among the nations. The

---

13   [That is, fallen back.]
14   [The Berne Convention, which established an international copyright system for books, dates from 1886. Towards the end of his life Bristed was secretary of the committee of the International Copyright Association, on whose behalf he published 'International Copyright … Popular delusions on the subject', *The Galaxy* 10 (Dec. 1870), pp. 811–18.]

inference seems unavoidable that there is something better in the English mode of training.

But our public speaking! *There* we have them! *There* we are unapproachable! Certainly this is our peculiar national excellence. Our few real and great orators will sustain a comparison with the few real and great orators of Europe; this much we may safely claim for them, and this is as much as will be conceded by the rest of the world. But it is in the general diffusion of a certain rhetorical facility, in the ability of every educated American to think and talk *on his legs*, that our superiority to Europeans consists. And doubtless it is a very convenient accomplishment for a gentleman to possess, one which an American is often proud of abroad, or before foreigners at home. But (leaving out of consideration much of the price we pay for it as has been dilated on in the last few pages) it may be doubted whether the practical benefits accompanying its exercise are very great or altogether unmixed; whether our national speech-making talent does not, in some situations, cause an immense waste of time and ruinous delay of business, while in others it mocks both speakers and hearers with a delusive show of improvement. As to the combinations of writing and oratory, made to serve indifferently for either – the *logoi epideiktikoi*[15] so much in vogue among us under the different names of 'Addresses', 'Discourses', 'Orations' and 'Lectures' – they are usually undertaken because the author received a flattering invitation and felt bound to put together an hour's worth of something – or because it was an easy and pleasant way of making pocket money – or because it was a cheap and convenient way of advertising something that he meant to bring out in book shape afterwards, and so make money of twice – or for any reason rather than an earnest desire and intent to teach the audience anything or make them think; and attendance at such Addresses, &c, is as much mental dissipation as the Frenchman's theatre or the German's concert.

There is one evil result of our national over-encouragement to oratory which has not yet been touched on; but to this it will be more convenient to recur in the next chapter.

[Added in third edition:

The larger debating societies at Yale have recently died out, but this is not so much a change for the better as it looks. They have succumbed,

---

[15]   [Epideictic speeches; that is, ceremonial public oratory, as opposed to forensic oratory.]

not to the pressure of the regular college studies but to the multiplication of the smaller and more secret societies.

I have been informed that at Harvard the societies never occupied the same prominent position as at Yale. If true, this is a good *a priori* argument in favor of the Harvard claim to superiority in the more regular academic business.]

34

The Advantages of Classical Studies, Particularly in Reference to the Youth of our Country

Haec studia adolescentiam alunt, senectutem oblectant, secundas res ornant, adversis perfugium et solatium praebent, delectant domi non impediunt foris.

Cic. *Pro Archia.*

The cultivated world, up to the present day, has been bound together, and each generation bound to the preceding by living upon a common intellectual estate. They have shared in a common development of thought because they have understood each other. Their standard examples of poetry, eloquence, history, criticism, grammar, etymology, have been a universal bond of sympathy, however diverse might be the opinions which prevailed respecting any of these examples. All the civilized world has been one intellectual nation, and it is this which has made it so great and prosperous a nation.

Whewell, *On University Education.*

We have thus far proceeded on the supposition that classical studies form a necessary and important part of a liberal education. But there is a class of persons (not very numerous or influential perhaps, but still too much so to be passed over in silence) who would join issue with me on this first principle. They would deny the utility of classics as a general collegiate study, and affirm that the error of our Colleges is, not the classical deficiency of their course, but their admission of Latin and Greek at all as a necessary element of that course.

One is certainly tempted to take a high tone in replying to such objections, and to treat them very summarily. Our first impulse is to tell the objectors that the almost unanimous voice of the civilized world has established the study of the classics as a requisite element of the best education, and that for us to act differently would be to proclaim and make ourselves boors. But as there are those with whom prescription has no weight but is rather an objection, we will try the study in question on its own intrinsic merits, first examining and rebutting the charges brought against it, and then asserting its positive excellences. We have a right to call on the other side to make the attack, as we are *in possession*.

There are one or two *moral* objections which it may be as well to begin with disposing of. First, it is said that the ancient authors are corrupting and unfit for young men to study or read, on account of the occasional indecencies to be found in them and the debasing mythology which they uphold. Now as regards the mythology, that any one was ever injured in his faith or morals by reading that Jupiter married his sister and had a number of other wives in addition seems hardly a matter to be argued seriously. If such things suggest any thoughts to a youth they are most likely to impress him with the necessity there was for a revelation, when he sees that the wisest heathen nations could make no better religion for themselves than such stuff as this. As to the grossness of the ancients, if we are to lay down as a rule that a young man is to peruse nothing which a young lady in white muslin may not read aloud to a family circle, we shall make great havoc among the literature of all languages, our own not excepted. What does harm in most cases is not grossness but *voluptuousness*; and there is very little voluptuous writing in the ancients. It would hardly be overstating the case to say that of the properly *classical* authors, Ovid is the only one who represents vice in a luscious and attractive form. Three chapters of almost any French novel, or two hours' walk on the Boulevards of Paris, will put a young man in more danger than all the Aristophanes and Juvenal he can read in a year. Yet a father who prevented his son learning French on account of the risks his morals might run from an acquaintance with Gautier or Paul de Kock, would be deemed by most people over-scrupulous, and a tourist who should fear to visit Paris because there are unchaste pictures in the shop-windows there, would incur not altogether undeserved laughter. The student is not *compelled* to wade through any of the filth he sometimes meets with – nay, with expurgated editions, he may not even be aware of its existence. For my own part, however, I think it not only permissible but actually desirable that he should read *something* at least of the very worst that is to be found in ancient literature. It is a disgusting but wholesome preventive dose against intellect worship. Most conscientiously can I say that nothing has ever more strongly impressed me with the utter incompetency of the highest intellectual refinement, unaided by true religion, to preserve man from the lowest degradation of vice, than studying Athenian life in Plato and Aristophanes, and marking how these 'gentlemen and scholars', as they called themselves (*kaloi k'agathoi*), these men of cultivated minds and refined manners, gave themselves up to shameless depravity.

There is also an opinion existing in certain quarters, which however we more usually see insinuated than openly expressed, that Classical studies have an anti-republican tendency. Any well defined *argument* to this effect I never recollect to have read, but much vague suggestion and declamation; still it is easy to conceive some reasons, such as they are, in support of the opinion. The Toryism of an historian like Mitford, or a commentator like Mitchell;[1] of Blackwood's Magazine, also famous for its Classical articles; of the University of Oxford, and nearer home the marked old Federal leanings of the majority of students in our eastern and northern Colleges, might be pressed into the service and make a plausible show. But there is a much stronger array of cases on the other side. Against the name of Mitford may be put those of Thirlwall, Arnold, and Grote, the first two independent Whigs, the last a Radical.[2] If the great Athenian satirist found a Tory

---

[1] [William Mitford's *History of Greece* (10 vols, 1784–1818) was notoriously anti-democratic, in marked contrast to a later and more famous work, George Grote's *History of Greece* (12 vols, 1846–1856). On the contrasting political stances of the two Histories, see F.M. Turner, *The Greek Heritage in Victorian Britain* (New Haven, 1981), pp. 192–233. Thomas Mitchell (1783–1845) was best known for his editions of Aristophanes, whose conservative political views he applauded. Bristed refers to Mitchell's editions below.]

[2] [Connop Thirlwall (1797–1875), author of a *History of Greece* (8 vols, 1835–44) which was eclipsed by Grote's. Thomas Arnold (1795–1842), best known as headmaster of Rugby School 1828–42, was like Thirlwall a devotee of the German historian Reinhold Niebuhr; both men belonged to the 'Liberal Anglican' movement. George Grote (1794–1871), remembered now largely for his History, was a banker and radical politician.]

Commentator in Mitchell, he has found a liberal one in Walsh,[3] who is actually at this moment I believe a resident in if not a citizen of our republic. The Edinburgh is a fair set off to Blackwood.[4] If Oxford seems sunk in antediluvian Jacobitism, Trinity, the great Classical College of Cambridge, has always been a notoriously Whig corporation. That the majority of our own College Students incline not merely to conservatism but to obsolete Federal politics, on which account our Colleges are not over-popular with the Democratic party, is true; but the reason of it is substantially the same with that which causes the German students to be the constant terror of their despotic or semi-despotic governments, or which made the mass of English Under-graduates liberal when the popular sentiment of England was Tory, and now makes them conservative when the popular spirit is liberal. All educated young men have a tendency to be in opposition, and to criticize the existing order of things; they see (not perhaps without some exaggeration) its faults, to which they have not yet become habituated by custom and experience, and they acquire a strong though temporary bias towards the other extreme. Nor is this to be regretted, when we consider the tendency of all governmental institutions to intensify their own abuses.

That Classical reading helps to make students hostile to ultra-radicalism, ochlocracy, and socialism, may at once be admitted, inasmuch as it helps to make them gentlemen and sound-minded men; and this is a result to boast of rather than apologize for.

But the objections to the study of Greek and Latin are mostly founded on *intellectual* grounds. I shall not pretend to take them up in the order of their popularity or plausibility, but only to enumerate and answer them as they occur. Some of the more familiar have a certain amount of truth in them; but it is derived from and tells against, not Classical studies in themselves, but *the imperfect way in which they are pursued at our Colleges.* Thus we hear of the painful drudgery to which Collegians are subjected, their

---

[3] [Benjamin Dann Walsh (1808–69) was 5th Classic in 1831 and a fellow of Trinity 1833–8. In 1837 he published a critical pamphlet on the University and the first part of a translation of Aristophanes. In the following year he married, forfeiting his fellowship, and emigrated to the US. Walsh tried farm and lumber dealing, but eventually became an expert entomologist, ending up as the first State Entomologist of Illinois and founder editor of the *American Entomologist*. See C.A. Sheppard, 'Benjamin Dann Walsh: pioneer entomologist and proponent of Darwinian theory', *Annual Review of Entomology* 49 (2004), pp. 1–25.]

[4] I believe even the *Democratic Review* has learned the difference between these two periodicals.

repugnance to crabbed roots and musty Lexicons, and the cruelty of forcing on their fresh and ardent minds such uncongenial occupation, their want of all interest in their text-books, &c. Now this *may* be the case with us, but the very last complaint of a Cambridge Don would be that his pupils did not take interest enough in their Classical studies.[5] He would rather be afraid of their taking too much interest in them, to the exclusion of other branches of mental discipline in which he wished them to be exercised. Again it is said, and nowhere more frequently than among College under-graduates themselves, that those who take high College Honors do not usually make a figure in the world afterwards; whence it is inferred either that Classics stultify the men who study them, or that they so disagree with clever youth that these refuse to make progress in them. This again may be true here, but it is certainly the very reverse of the case in England, where the number of men who have distinguished themselves at the bar, in the Senate, or in certain walks of literature, after taking good degrees at the University, is wont to be dwelt on with pride by the defender of the old system; while the opponent of it takes a very different stand from the depreciator of Classical training here, and, admitting the future success of distinguished Collegians, tries to show that the sequence was not altogether a consequence. So too, we hear the question triumphantly put, 'What use *can* there be in our young men taking several years to *learn* what they forget in a much shorter time after leaving College?' It may be true – I fear it is true, that very many of our students forget in eighteen months what they have been supposed to learn in three, four, or five years; that there is very often not that difference observable between the graduate and the non-graduate of thirty which there ought to be – or in fact no observable difference at all in their Classical knowledge. But it is not so with the English, the French, or the German student in after life. He remembers and knows what he studied at College, better than he does anything else except his immediate daily occupation, whatever that may be, in which he is necessarily more freshly prepared than in any other subject. To say of the majority of foreign University graduates that their Classics are to them but 'a foggy reminiscence of dull days wasted and dry tasks slighted', would be simply not true. And if the majority of our graduates forget their Classics in so short a time, it is because they have never really learned them. The fault is in the imperfect and inadequate mode of teaching, not in the thing taught or supposed to be taught.

---

[5] Such of them, that is, as will study at all. Under *any* system there will unfortu-nately always be a class with whom *any* study is a weariness to the flesh.

We now proceed to the arguments against classical studies, which, if well founded, would hold good against them, however well taught. That which may be said to include, or at least to lie at the root of all the others, is that they do not form the basis of a practical education – that they do not contribute to such an education in any degree – that they do not make practical *men*.

To appreciate this objection it will be necessary to examine what is meant by a 'practical man', and how far the making of practical men ought to be the object of a liberal education.

The sort of 'practical man' who most ostentatiously appropriates the name to himself is also, perhaps, the variety most usually held up as a type of the species. He is the 'self-educated' man, which is very much to his credit so long as he does not therefore pretend to know better than men who have learned a great deal more by the help of others. He is also a 'self-made' man generally, and 'the architect of his own fortune', which is also highly creditable to him so long as he does not insist on being able to do everything because he has advanced his own position in the world. Sharp-witted, industrious, and indefatigable, he makes a capital electioneerer or agitator of any sort, a first-rate hand to 'keep the pot boiling', whatever the fuel may be; and if you can attach him as jackal to the right sort of lion, may do a fair amount of good. But the worst is that he is pretty sure to set up for a lion himself, and then his want of ballast, of foundation, of theoretic knowledge, of esoteric knowledge of any one thing, is continually leading his quickness into sad blunders, and causing a great part of his energy to be misdirected. He has overcome the empirical difficulties of his own case, but for all philosophical investigation he is utterly untrained. He has a vast conceit of his own acquisitions, and a very inadequate conception of the limits of human capacity. Hence this man, whose boast it is to be eminently practical, runs off instantly into the wildest speculations. He cuts up society as one would cut up a pie, and proposes to pull down the fabric of ages with less ceremony than a careful landholder would observe in removing an old fence. Such a person may possibly be the best that could have been made out of his antecedents; but it by no means follows that men with better antecedents should aim at being like him. He is the result of necessity making the best of a bad bargain; not a desirable product of instruction, or a model for teacher or student. He does not come up to the poet's definition of a man. He may be a being of very large discourse, but he cannot look before and after. Such men it is not the tendency of classical studies to turn out. So much the better for those studies.

In another not unfrequent sense of the term, a practical man means a good man of business, that is, a man sharp at a bargain and clever at making money. Doubtless there are means of education more favorable to the development of this faculty than the study of Latin and Greek. If we take two boys at sixteen, and send one to a college and the other to a counting-house, it is not improbable that in eight years the latter may be making his thousands of dollars for the other's hundreds. And if any father believes that making money is the great end and object of civilized man, and means to bring up his family accordingly, it certainly will be a waste of time to teach his son classics. They might, perhaps, divert some portion of his time from the ledger.

But if it be asserted or insinuated that a classical education makes young men dreamy, or visionary, or idle, that it disposes them to shirk their daily duties, prevents them from acquiring regular business habits, or interferes with the exercise and development of their common-sense in the ordinary affairs of life – all this, I positively deny. On the contrary, I am convinced by my own case, as well as that of others whom I have observed, that it has great efficacy in giving even a constitutionally idle man regular habits of work. The care and accuracy which it inculcates and the taste which it forms, are often of great practical benefit. If classics were better and more generally studied among us, one of the very first effects would be that the Congressional and State Legislature speeches would be cut down to less than half their present dimensions, to the corresponding gain of the nation's time and money.

But the objection comes up under another form. The study of the ancient languages does not, it is said, *positively* tend to unfit men for practical life, but it impairs their efficacy by occupying the time in which they might acquire other more useful branches of knowledge. Thus, to teach our young men Latin and Greek, it is said, is to teach them *words* – they should not learn words but *things*. Such a saying may be very effective when artfully introduced as an *obiter dictum*, but it will hardly bear examination and discussion. That our students ought not to *learn words* and use them as the substitutes for, instead of the expression of thoughts, is at once admitted; it was one of our arguments against the 'speaking and writing' system. But that they should learn the *meaning of words* is of the utmost importance towards their understanding the meaning of things, for the latter often depends on the former.[6] A large proportion of the disputes among men

---

[6] For example, the reader may remember having seen in a chapter [Ch. 31] how the name of a piece of church furniture involved one of the staple differences between Protestantism and Popery.

are uselessly prolonged, if not originally caused, by their not comprehending one another at the outset, so that there is a deep philosophy in the common euphemism of *misunderstanding* for *quarrel*. Some of the most ordinary terms in every-day discussion – *church, state, civilization, society, aristocracy, democracy* – let any man consider the variety of complex ideas involved in every one of them – the different definitions that different people of his own acquaintance would give of every one of them – and then say that the knowledge of the *meaning* of words is not of the greatest value. Did I wish to throw dust in the eyes of a body of readers or hearers, I should not wish for a better set of men to operate on than such as had only been sedulous to learn things – isolated, unsystematized facts, and had overlooked the meaning of words as a trivial knowledge. I think I could manoeuvre with definitions and shift premises so that they should be satisfactorily deceived without a suspicion of it. The apprehension of scattered facts is no more an education than loose bricks and mortar are a house; they are but rubbish covering the earth till you know how to put them together. Or does a *knowledge of things* mean that a man is to be able to do as many things as possible for himself, to be not only his own waiter and wood-sawyer, but his own doctor and lawyer and washerwoman, perhaps! This is one of the utilitarian schemes of education; if it could be carried out, the immediate effect would be to render men independent of one another, and thus dissolve society (which is by its very constitution a system of mutual dependence) into its rudest elements. (Another incidental proof that our disciples of 'progress' are progressing in the way exactly calculated to re-barbarize mankind.) But we shall be more likely to come at a clear understanding of the matter by inquiring what studies those who object to a classical course would substitute in our Colleges for it, as 'practical' ones. And here let us premise by observing that if we are to turn out the Classics on this account, we must, in consistency, send the mathematics after them, for every objection that can, on practical grounds, be urged against classics applies to mathematics in a tenfold degree. They are far more distasteful to the majority of students, more engrossing in their demands on the attention, harder to acquire, easier to lose – a boy who has read Homer *well* at school will know it tolerably all his life, but a good geometrician will soon cease to be perfect even in his Euclid if he does not keep constantly refreshing his knowledge – they are utterly useless in immediate application to our every-day pursuits. There is indeed a popular presumption of their utility, arising from the fact that *arithmetic*, which is the introduction to them, is also concerned in making money, but that is about the amount of the connexion between them and practical life. The classics may seem to have little enough to do with it, but they have obviously more than that. The author wants a motto for a chapter, the preacher has occasion to refer to the 'original Greek' of a passage, the lawyer finds a scrap of Latin in one of his 'under-done pie-crust' colored books, or the clerk in the newspaper which constitutes the bulk of his literary relaxation, the orator rounds off a handsome period with a quotation from Cicero, which the reporter makes two or three mistakes in taking down and the compositor two or three more, in setting up. But what parson, or lawyer, or merchant, or politician, or essayist, or poet, is ever called upon in the course of his ordinary life and business to write out an equation, or draw a hyperbole, or prove the parallelogram of forces? If the classics are to go overboard as not sufficiently practical, the mathematics must keep them company.

What then is left for our students to study? 'The literature of their own language for one thing', says one. Now it has been already intimated that no class of men are better read in the valuable parts of English literature than the hard-working classical students at Cambridge, and no men better prepared to profit by that reading, which is to them a relaxation from, not a substitute for, severer studies. But if we put *Belles Lettres* in the place of mental discipline, if we admit as part of the student's hardest work the reading of English authors with a view to their beauties, and the hearing lectures on them, then he will seek his *relaxation* in the trashiest and idlest reading. Just as surely as the greater includes the less, will the presence of a classical element in our College course do more than its absence to secure a proper acquaintance on the part of our students with such vernacular literature as is worthy to be read.

The *natural sciences* are insisted on by some as calculated above all other studies to improve the mind as well as impart useful knowledge. The immense value of these sciences to the world no rational man will deny. Their contribution to the progress of civilization it becomes no man to underrate. But their desirability as the predominant and original element of a liberal education by no means follows as a matter of course. The mere popular rudiments – the experiment and diagram part of most of them, are sufficiently interesting to enter among the relaxations of the industrious pupil, who will indeed be pretty sure to acquire a knowledge of them somewhere whether they are taught at College or not,[7] but do not deserve the name of

---

[7]   This is a point seldom taken into account, but telling very strongly against most of the substitutes proposed for the classics – Belles-Lettres, popular results of science, even the modern languages. It is very much more probable that young men who begin

serious study; for the willfully idle, they are no more temptations to study than classics or mathematics would be, but rather a confirmation of their idle habits. But to attain or approach a mastery over any one science is a very different matter, and falls to the lot of a few. The details demand an uncommon faculty for and interest in the minute observation of nature. The systematic comprehension and colligation of these details I will not say absolutely requires, but certainly is very much aided by a thorough training of the mind according to the more orthodox methods. We have already in another place adverted to the folly of supposing that a youth *learns* half-a-dozen sciences by attending a brief course of lectures on each. But let the time be as much extended as by the substitution under consideration it would be, so that something more like a knowledge of these sciences might be acquired; still I maintain that a young man whose education has been composed wholly or chiefly of instruction in the natural sciences, is not a *liberally* educated man. He will be apt to have acquired most *illiberal* opinions of all other branches of learning. He will be likely to underrate outrageously (even to ignoring its value entirely) all knowledge except such as is based on observation and experiment, or inductive reasoning and (real or supposed) tangible proof. He will be in danger of doubting all fixity in principles of knowledge, or principles of moral and religious truth – of supposing that 'ethics and theology are progressive sciences' as much as chemistry or geology. He may even be led to despise the standard literature of the civilized world, because much of it was written before the discovery of gravitation or the invention of the steam-engine; as if men went to a poet or dramatist to learn astronomy or mechanics from him – a misconception of uses so ludicrous that were there not instances of it on record, it might well be deemed incredible.

Mental Philosophy has been proposed as a substitute, sometimes for Classics, sometimes for Mathematics. The value of Metaphysical studies I would not for a moment underrate, but it seems to me evident that they should be considered a crowning pinnacle, not a corner-stone of liberal education. Their abstruse nature, the logical clearness of conception which they demand, the variety of illustration from other sciences and branches of learning, which they not only admit but require, the instability of systems and the want of universally admitted truths to found systems on

---

by studying the classics will pick up these other things, incidentally or subsequently, than that, if they begin with these things, they will be willing or able to learn Latin and Greek at a later period. The information will come after the discipline much faster and easier than the discipline after the information.

respecting them – all appear to point out that a thorough preparatory training *in both Classics and Mathematics* is requisite to their being pursued with advantage.

The Modern Languages are frequently proposed as a substitute for the Ancient, and of all substitutes have the strongest claim. Their study appears to differ from that of the Classics more in degree than in kind. It teaches universal grammar, verbal analysis, accurate comparison, discrimination of differences – though to a less extent; it enforces the perusal of good models of taste, though not so good ones; it puts the students into communication with the intellect of other nations, though not of other ages; while, at the same time, its immediate results to the traveller or the inhabitant of a metropolitan city answer the requisition of our practical friends.

I am fully prepared to admit that a young man *may* read German instead of Greek, and French and Italian instead of Latin, in such a way as to derive more benefit from that course than a very large number of our students do from their Greek and Latin one; but this would be an exceptional case – and I think that even such a student would be ultimately led to take up Latin and Greek at a greater expenditure of time than if he had begun with them. Looking at the question generally, the difficulty which presents itself is this: That part of the study of Modern Languages which answers to the study of the Ancient, and the practical part of them – that is, the being able to speak them with fluency, are in a great measure independent of each other. The practical part is learned only by practice – by talking yourself and hearing others talk around you. The pronunciation, which is half the battle, can only be acquired in this way. All of us must have met with men who could read French easily, nay, had read a fair amount of French literature; yet could with difficulty put two sentences together correctly in conversation. A New Yorker generally speaks better French than a Londoner, because he is more in the habit of meeting Frenchmen and persons who speak French. Spanish is more generally spoken in New York than in Boston, on account of our commercial intercourse with Cuba, Mexico, and South America, and the number of natives of those countries constantly to be found among us; while Spanish literature is more read and better understood in Boston than in New York. A Cambridge First Class man suddenly called on to talk Latin to a Hungarian or German scholar will bungle very much at first; he will not converse half as fluently as a New Yorker will in French with a Frenchman; yet the Cantab really knows more Latin than the New Yorker does French – that is to say, he can read Latin with less danger of meeting a word that he does not know the meaning of, translate it more accurately, and write it more elegantly and grammatically than the other can French. It is useless to multiply examples – the distinction is sufficiently evident.

Now, if the critical study of Modern Languages were chiefly attended to at our Colleges, it is probable that the advances made by the students in the practical use of them as a medium of direct communication with foreigners, would not be so rapid as altogether to satisfy the advocates of this study on practical grounds. They would run the risk of being much disappointed, when the College Junior, who had been reading and writing French for a couple of years, was unable to converse familiarly with the first Frenchman he encountered. Their object would not be attained, while that of the advocates of the mental discipline afforded by the study of languages would see their end working out somewhat as before, only with inferior tools.

This is one danger. The opposite one, though less imminent, is more formidable – that the Modern Languages might be studied only for practical use in conversation and the commonest forms of writing. Such an education would do well for a man of pleasure or a commercial traveller; I would not recommend it to any one else. If speaking foreign languages were any test of intellectual progress, the Russians ought to be ahead of all the rest of the world, for there are no such practical linguists as the better class of Russians. They talk French like Parisians, English like Englishmen, German like Germans, Italian like Italians. What does it profit them? Simply that their bodily comforts and personal consequence are somewhat promoted by it when they travel. What have they done for literature, for freedom, for true cultivation of any sort? What do they take home from their travels? A knowledge of French wines and silks, perhaps of Italian music: of the thoughts that shake empires and create intellectual and political revolutions, they appropriate none.

Finally, are we to substitute for Greek and Latin not one only, but all or several of the studies enumerated? This is the dream and wish of many reformers, the ambition perhaps of not a few students. Doubtless we are a very clever people, but not sufficiently so to make universal geniuses of all our Collegians. For a man to 'make omniscience his forte', as Sydney Smith phrased it,[8] he must have extraordinary talents of many different kinds, and in addition, an uncommonly good constitution to be able to stand the hard work which the acquisition of so much knowledge requires even of the most talented men. Of such favored mortals, there are perhaps a

---

8 [Here, as in Ch. 11, Bristed gets Sydney Smith's saying about William Whewell the wrong way round: see p. 88 above.]

dozen in an age. Nay more, we shall find that these very men began their multifarious learning with learning the Classics. Take some of the names that naturally occur to us: Macaulay – he was a crack Classic University Scholar, and Fellow of Trinity; Humboldt – he is a scholar as well as a *savant;* Brougham – his scholarship may not be of the utmost accuracy, but no one would say that he had not received a fair Classical education, and did not know a considerable quantity of Greek and Latin. I do not know if the attempt was ever made to turn out a man or a set of men who should know *omne scibile except* the Classical languages and literature; till the experiment has been tried, and tried successfully, we have good reason to believe that it would be trying to put up an immense building without any foundation.

Early in this chapter it was remarked that our opponents might justly be called upon to begin the attack, as Classical studies were in possession. But it would be doing those studies injustice to rest their claim on this negative and incidental ground. I therefore now proceed to the positive part of the argument, and assert roundly that the study of Latin and Greek, carried out further and more thoroughly than it now is in any of our Colleges, would be peculiarly calculated to benefit our College-going youth, and through them our whole country.

One of the greatest difficulties in the way of a man's daily and progressive development as a man is the constant pressure of his professional or business avocations. The merchant has to look after his cargoes and keep his bank-book straight, the broker to watch the stock market, the clergyman to write his sermons and mind his parochial affairs, the lawyer to bandy words in court, the editor to abuse the other side in politics – every man has a tendency to become absorbed in his particular pursuit, and the cleverer and more ambitious the man, the stronger this tendency usually is. He becomes hampered by the formulas of his profession. He 'talks shop' in and out of season. He associates with those similarly occupied, and they all help to render one another more one-sided. The *Idols of the Tribe* overshadow him, and pervert and illiberalize his understanding. And this is particularly the case with us, because an American, more quickwitted and energetic and ambitious than any other man, throws himself into whatever he undertakes more earnestly and completely. Some there are, however, who having either acquired or inherited as much wealth as is sufficient for their wants, are tied down to no exclusive pursuit. These ought to be more liberal and unprejudiced, more literary and generally accomplished, larger and loftier in their views, more *men* in short than any other class: frequently, alas! they are the very reverse. Absence of daily toil gives them no positive bond of sympathy. They have not been educated to enjoy or profit by their leisure; their only centre of union is a well-spread banquet; they can only find their level in frivolous pursuits and amusements of doubtful value, even as relaxations.

Now what we want to remedy this evil is something which shall cultivate those intellectual faculties and tendencies, and supply those intellectual wants that are common to all intelligent and reasoning men *as* men; that are common to men of all professions; something that shall give men of all professions a common ground to meet on in leisure moments; that shall rival and counteract the enticements of the pleasures of sense or the repose of idleness; something that shall give men of leisure a mode of spending their time profitably to themselves, and at least not injuriously to others.

In some countries this desideratum is supplied by the love of art. All the educated classes are amateurs of music, painting, and sculpture; all members of the educated classes, however different their professions, have this point of contact. The merits and influence of such a taste, it would be irrelevant to discuss here, since an enthusiasm for art is not and cannot be made a trait of any people sprung mainly from an Anglo-Saxon stock. Our common subject must be something more dependent on the purely intellectual and logical faculties. Society makes various efforts to supply itself with such a general topic. Politics, discussed with all our national fury of exaggeration, dividing the community into two parties ready to spring at each other's throats, contribute very little to the pleasures of social intercourse or the improvement of our higher mental faculties; pecuniary subjects do indeed excite an interest common to all men, but the very reverse of an ennobling or liberalizing one.

Now this common bond which we want, a good classical education supplies. The learned languages were the depositories of a past world's intellectual wealth during the long night of the Middle Ages. They obtained a universal foothold as instruments of a liberal and literary education, when the modern languages of Europe not only contained no literature of their own, but were not out of their embryo state, unformed and unsettled. By and by those modern languages became, like their respective countries, organized and defined in their limits, and polished by cultivation. They became fit vehicles for a native literature, and such literature sprang up in them. But, flowing directly from classical literature, it continued in every case to retain some tincture from the original source; with the distinct impress of nationality are always to be found blended some features referable to the common stock. From Greece through Rome was Europe civilized; from Europe America. There is a direct intellectual succession (far clearer to trace than the vaunted Apostolic one) from the Athenians to ourselves; the scholars of the world have been its trustees. The classics are the golden chains that bind together the past and the present, the east and the west of literature. Classical education gives men a common taste and sympathy for literature. It not only makes them like to read, but teaches them how to read; it enables them to understand books, and understand one another when they talk about books.[9] And it is because the acquisition of such an education does *not* require any pre-eminent talent, because any one – *ego vel Cluvienus*[10] – who is not positively *below* the average of intelligence can acquire it with the necessary time and trouble – it is precisely on this account that it is valuable to the majority of men in the better ranks of life, to *ordinary* doctors, *ordinary* lawyers, *ordinary* merchants. But especially valuable is it to men of no profession, as supplying them with some gentlemanly occupation and amusement, besides eating and drinking, dressing, and dancing. Even its moral benefits to such men in giving them something to do, and a taste for doing something, and thus guarding them from some of the temptations to which idleness is peculiarly liable, are not to be despised.

Any consideration for or allusion to the welfare of this class may be summarily condemned in certain quarters as anti-republican and 'aristocratic' – it being a fashion of your reformers and philanthropists to talk of such people as if they were a set of drones or vipers, to be exterminated without mercy or at least packed out of the country. But it is certain that this class is increasing in numbers as our nation grows older, and that, moreover, being variable from one generation to another, as families and individuals grow rich or poor, its education must in several generations influence that of a very large number of families, and have a very appreciable influence on that of the community. Nor are the rich of one generation to

---

[9]   While writing the above I stumbled upon the assertion (in an English work) that 'A knowledge of Walter Scott and Shakspeare would better qualify a man for the freemasonry of the literary world than a knowledge of Homer.' This is the old fallacy of premise, to which I am not sorry to take an opportunity of alluding once more. It implies that the man who has read Homer is not likely to have read Shakspeare and Scott, whereas he is the very man most likely to read them to the best advantage and enjoy them the most heartily; to luxuriate in Scott's romance without taking it for history, to study Shakspeare and his commentators at home without needing the adventitious excitement of a male lecturer or a lady public-reader.

[10]   [Juvenal, *Satires* 1.80, where the implication is that Cluvienus is a worthless writer.]

be altogether disregarded. Utterly insignificant as his political influence may be, the capitalist or the capitalist's son cannot fail to have social influence. The very Jews of the middle ages, destitute of all political rights and in constant peril of life or liberty, were not without power to control the current of events.

But, to make our position as broad and as practical as may be (for much of the above may seem the exaggeration of professional enthusiasm to those who have not experienced the effects of thorough classical training on a man's ideas, or the different impression made by the society of those who have and those who have not received this training), I now proceed distinctly to maintain that the cultivation of a high classical standard at our colleges would benefit the whole country at large, by correcting two of our prominent national errors.

It has been remarked and shown in a former chapter that the principal and most valuable results of thorough classical study are *accuracy* and *taste*. Now *inaccuracy* and *bad taste* are the most ordinary blemishes of all our intellectual performances. Quicker of apprehension and expression than any other people, our countrymen commit themselves oftener in errors of detail than any other people. Rapid and superficial, with an indistinct knowledge of many things, but not really at home in any one thing except the empirical part of his particular calling; always ready to impart information or to raise a controversy, and more apt to look at the immediate impression than at the ultimate effect to be produced; the American is continually making little slips, his very speed tripping him up. He is too impatient to investigate minutiae. To verify a reference or a quotation is the last thing that occurs to him. He becomes habituated to make assertions, and calling in illustrations merely to point a sentence or fill up a phrase, without taking care to satisfy himself of its correctness; for he trusts to three chances, first that he may be right, secondly that if he is wrong he may not be found out, thirdly that if the error is detected he may be able to make a plausible defence of or apology for it. Look at our newspapers, for instance, the large city no less than the small country sheets; what a mass of blunders every fresh batch of them lets loose upon society. Were I an editor I would have for a standing head of a column, 'Errors of our contemporaries', and such a column would be sure to be always well filled, and not unamusing or uninstructive. One can scarcely pass an hour any morning in a reading-room without making a choice collection of contributions from all parts of the Union towards the perversion of knowledge; blunders in Ancient History and Literature, e.g. that Socrates was put to death by the thirty tyrants, or that Sophocles wrote the Medea; blunders in modern, even in contemporary history, such as that the English excited the revolution in St. Domingo, or that Lord John Russell caused the famine in Ireland; blunders in regard to foreign authors, such as that John Stuart Mill is a Tory writer, or that Albert Smith was the author of the *Rejected Addresses*; blunders about artists, such as that Parodi had the part of *Caliban* in Halévy's *Tempesta*; mis-quotations not only from foreign languages but from the standard English authors, to such an extent that a very precise man may be led into them by sheer force of bad example.[11] Perhaps these inaccuracies have their most ludicrous effect when coming in the form of information to others, as when some enterprising man with a commendable zeal for knowledge, but a very mistaken idea as to the proper source of enlightenment, writes to ask 'Who was the author of the *Prout Papers*' and is told in reply that 'the *Prout Papers*' were written by an English clergyman named *Ingoldsby*.[12]

I might have mentioned among the inaccuracies of our press its habit of calling the authors of leading articles in the London papers 'Penny-a-liners', and representing them as mere hack scribblers sprung from a doubtful class of society. Among these 'penny-a-liners' are, *to my own personal knowledge*, Fellows and Professors of colleges, eminent clergymen, rising barristers, noblemen's sons, and even ladies of good family. A comparison between the stations in society of the persons who write for the English daily press and those who write for ours would not turn out to the disadvantage of the former. These mistakes cannot properly be said to proceed from ignorance. They arise rather from want of reflection, and an inaccurate way of dealing with all subjects of knowledge, encouraged by the conceit of superficial acquirements. To consult a friend, to step into the nearest bookseller's, to investigate the contents of his own library even, are things either beneath the editor's dignity, or a useless waste of time. If a publisher sends him a

---

[11]   I once made a wrong quotation from Shakspeare, entirely through having seen the passage pertinaciously misquoted for years in our journals. It served me right for taking such authority without verification.

[12]   Should any of the fraternity feel wroth with me for speaking so candidly of their attainments, I beg leave to suggest the possibility of their deriving some benefit from the above paragraph. It may at least open their eyes to one cause of the contemptuous way in which foreign writers sometimes speak of them, and which they are so unable to understand as actually in some instances to believe it the disguise of jealousy. [The Prout Papers, written by Revd Francis Mahony, were published in 1834 in *Fraser's Magazine*, for which Bristed himself later wrote; they were collected as *The Reliques of Father Prout*. The confusion is with R.H. Barham's *Ingoldsby Legends*, also published in magazines (in 1837) and also later published in book form.]

work of fiction, he accepts whatever author's name the publisher may put upon the cover, without stopping to think if it may not be a mere trick of the trade to make the book sell (though it is notorious that full ten per cent. of the novels republished here are credited to the wrong authors). If he wants some awful fact to point an anti-English article, he does not cite it by chapter and verse from authentic records, but takes it second or third hand from some Irish or equally imaginative authority.[13]

Similar inaccuracy, though not always so gross, may be traced in other classes of writing and writers; in grave Quarterlies, where haste or want of time cannot be pleaded in excuse; in the works of really able professors; in the speculations of men fond of science, but who have not taken the pains to ground themselves in its first principles. Nor is this looseness confined to subjects of the intellect; there is a great deal of moral inaccuracy among us, not tending to increase our virtue at home or respectability abroad. Most striking individual instances might be given of this but for the fear of introducing personal or partisan reflections. Some general instances may be hinted at. To charge a member of the government with peculation, and be unable to prove the charge, would, in England, cause the accuser to be hooted at by all the respectable men of his own party; here it is passed by as only an ordinary incident of political warfare – a bold speculation, which unfortunately did not succeed. To misquote a literary opponent is disgraceful to a European controversialist; it was one of the things that contributed to the downfall of the Puseyite influence in England, being considered and denounced as conduct unworthy of scholars and gentlemen; here it is apologized for as a slip of the pen or the printer, and the apology is by many deemed sufficient. Nay, I am not sure but the great indulgence afforded to commercial failures, an indulgence often overstepping the bounds of charity, may properly come under this head. The fundamental error is the same in the three cases; *too much leniency shown to gross carelessness.*

An education which teaches men to read, think, and learn slowly, carefully, and deliberately, and which practically convinces them at every step of their fallibility and proneness to be mistaken, is the best calculated to correct this national inaccuracy, mental and moral.

The other great national defect of our national popular literature and oratory, and intellectual public displays generally, is *bad taste*, manifesting itself

---

[13] [The disparaging reference to the Irish, here and below, is typical of Bristed, though he recanted on his deathbed, having been looked after devotedly by his Irish servants.]

in a more than Hibernian tawdriness of style, a violence and exaggeration of language, a forced accumulation of ornament, not growing naturally out of the subject, but stuck violently on for the sake of having it there; and also in a long-winded diffuseness and inane repetition of common-places. Here I can fancy some one starting up and saying – the *tu quoque* is so favorite a form of argument with a certain class, and, without doubt, has a great *ad captandum* effect – 'The author has the driest and most unadorned style himself; how can he appreciate an elegant and florid one?' Now there are few persons who enjoy a *good* ornate style more than myself; I read Macaulay over and over, and have almost some of his essays by heart; the gorgeous word-painting of Ruskin has an exceeding charm for me; but compared with the sentences of such men, richly colored by the allusions of learning, and sedulously polished by critical accuracy, the bulk of what our periodical censors agree to call 'fine writing' seems to me like stage tinsel and paste to real jewelry, or a bouquet of artificial flowers to a posy of natural ones, imitating the original to a cursory inspection, but a worthless sham when you come to look into it. Should any one still join issue on the fact and maintain that our popular style is not a vicious one, it would, I confess, not be very easy to convince him; a question of taste cannot be made matter of demonstration. If I were to cite forty instances of false metaphor, turgidity, bombast, and bathos, he might still consider those very examples as specimens of beautiful writing. But one thing can hardly be denied by anybody – that our writers and speakers are terribly deficient in the faculty of selection; that (with some eminent exceptions) they never know when they have said enough; that a great majority of our sermons, lectures, forensic arguments, anniversary addresses, &c., and our public documents and congregational speeches almost without exception, are a great deal longer than they ought to be.

The remark has been made to me more than once in conversation, that the displays of vulgarity, prolixity, bombast, &c., which deform our popular literature, are chiefly to be set down to the discredit of uneducated southern and western men, who could not be in the most indirect way affected by any condition of or change in our collegiate system. To this it may be replied first that the monopoly of bad taste is not confined to the south and west. There is a great deal of the article in New England. True, there is also much pure and refined taste. There are New Englanders whose works have become acknowledged classics of the English language, acknowledged not only by England but by Europe. There are New Englanders whose speeches will endure as models of oratory while the language endures. But there are also a great many New Englanders who are continually talking and writing all over the country anything but the choicest English. Next, supposing the position admitted to its fullest extent, there are two ways of treating such wild men of the woods, which have very different effects, and are directly dependent on the collegiate system adopted. If you take the ability to make a speech as a sign of education, you put yourself and the uneducated man on something like a footing; for he, knowing only how to read and write perhaps, but having plenty of impudence and self-possession, and acquiring a stock of party common-places from the newspapers or some equally accessible source, can make as fluent and long a speech as you – not as good, no doubt, but he will think it as good, and feel himself your equal. *Make classical knowledge a standard of the educated man, and you put such a person on his level at once.* There is a gulf between you and him that no amount of noisy haranguing can get over.

The critical habits induced by classical study, teaching condensation of thought by rejection of superfluities, purity of style and clearness rather than magniloquence of expression are the best protection against the inroads of bad taste. Abolish the study of Greek and Latin entirely, and we should be delivered over to the Vandals of literature, the heroes of the habit of crying out continually for *more* of it. I, on the contrary, would like to call attention to the desirableness having a *higher order of it* – an education for men of refinement. I think our country has reached that point in national progress when she can afford to attend to refinement. Our common school education is probably much better and more generally diffused than that of any other country; our liberal education is certainly behind that of several countries. Ought we not to take most pains for the improvement of that in which we are most deficient? I put this as a practical question for every man to ask himself who has money to give or leave, or influence to exert or time to spend in the cause of education.

'You want an education for rich men', interposes some patent friend of the people, who disguises his envy of all those that are better off in this world's goods than himself, by a professed sympathy for those who are worse off. Well, I do want an education for rich men. Do they not stand in special need of it? such an education, too, as will give them other sources of pleasure besides the material ones derived from wealth? But perhaps the objector means that I want an education in the advantages of which none but rich men can participate – an assertion disproved at once by the fact that numbers of poor men in England, France, Germany, and other European countries, are enjoying such an education. 'Oh, but you want an education for *gentlemen.*' Exactly – I do; and the gentlemen whom I want to train up should require just wealth enough to enable them to wear clean shirts, and be just 'aristocrats' enough to prefer the company of persons with clean shirts and clean habits to that of persons with dirty ones.

35

What Can and Ought We To Do for our Colleges?

The conclusion of our investigations is that the English system of liberal education possesses some decided advantages over ours; a conclusion from assenting to which the reader need not be prevented by any personal dislike he may feel towards England or Englishmen. Let him profit by the motto of this book,[1] and be wise enough to take a lesson from those whom he does not acknowledge as friends. Still, before we can make any practical use of our result an important inquiry remains. It may be that the peculiar benefits of such an education as an English University affords are dependent on certain political and social conditions peculiar to England, or upon certain antecedents having no counterpart among us. If so, it would be a clear waste of time to suggest any improvements from that quarter. We may be curious about the system or admire it at a distance, but can never rationally hope to imitate it. To seek an impossible combination of advantages is one of the most frequent errors of reformers, and one of the most prolific sources of delusion. Indeed were I asked in what practical wisdom consists, I should not know how to answer better than by defining it as *the faculty of discerning things compatible and incompatible* – that is, I should enlarge Whately's

---

[1] [The title page carries a quotation from Aristophanes: 'But wise men learn much even from their enemies' (Aristophanes, *Birds* 376). As was mentioned in the Introduction, W.G. Clark of Trinity College was incensed by this reference to his countrymen and Bristed's hosts.]

definition, 'a ready perception of analogies', by the addition, *and a ready discrimination of differences*.[2]

If therefore, the peculiar advantages of an English University education are such as to require for their development (1) the influence of an hereditary aristocracy (2) an established church, (3) public schools like the English for the preparatory training of the students, (4) greater wealth on the part of the students than the majority of our undergraduates possess, (5) greater wealth on the part of the institutions themselves – if they involve any one, and a *fortiori* if they involve all of these conditions, then we may copy them in form, but can never hope to reproduce their reality.

It seems to me pretty evident that the first is not. The whole number of noblemen and 'hat Fellow-Commoners'[3] at Cambridge does not exceed thirty, and not one sixth of those reading-men. Their extinction or absence would not diminish both triposes by the average of three a year, nor would it alter anything in the University except that there would be a few showy gowns less on holidays, and that the only unfairness or inequality existing in the examinations (letting noblemen's sons go out in classics without passing the mathematical examination) would be removed.

Equally plain does it seem that the second condition is in no way essential. The ethics and divinity entering into the college Under-graduate studies or the University course, are not necessarily favorable to the peculiar views of any denomination. A Unitarian might read most of it. I was going to say a Romanist could; but the *Index Expurgatorius* may have extended farther than we are aware of. Paley and Butler, the Acts of the Apostles and the Old Testament History, are not remarkably sectarian. The only point where the Established Church acts immediately on the ordinary life and system of the student is attendance at chapel. Now almost every one of our colleges is under the control of some particular denomination, and all our students are compelled to attend daily prayers and much more rigorously too than the Cambridge men; so that in this respect the collegiate institutions of the two countries are already on a similar footing.

The existence of the public schools seems more immediately connected with that of the Universities. I know the opinion to be common among

---

[2] ['... it may be said almost without qualification, that "Wisdom consists in the *ready* and *accurate* perception of Analogies"'. R. Whately, *Elements of Rhetoric* [1828] (1858), 80. The quotation seems to have been a favourite of Bristed, who also used it in his 'Recent English Historians of Ancient Greece', *The American Review* 7 (Feb 1848), pp. 178–90, (March 1848), pp. 286–300, at p. 179.]

[3] [As Bristed explains in Ch. 3, these were the younger sons of noblemen.]

our scholars (having often seen it expressed in print as well as heard it) that whatever benefits result from the English system of education are owing to the schools and *not* to the universities. Some things which have been stated in this book may go a little way towards removing this impression. That the *mathematical* training at Cambridge does not depend on the public schools is clear enough. Few Eton, or Westminster, or Harrow, or Shrewsbury men are high wranglers. The public school men might be taken out of the mathematical tripos altogether without leaving a very serious gap in it. With regard to classics the case is indeed different. Much of the highest technical scholarship, particularly superiority in composition, and more particularly in verse composition, is due to the student from the public schools. Take them away, and you would take away four out of the first five men in every Classical Tripos. Still you would have a high standard left; for a man to be in the first class at all must be a pretty good scholar, and know quite classics enough to bother many of our Professors. And a non-public-school man may make very considerable progress in classics at the University, and derive great benefit from the instruction there. Two instances occurred in my time of the Second Chancellor's Medallist not having been at any public school, and the senior Medallist in 1840 came from King's College, London.[4]

The expense of a University education in England is certainly startling at first sight. That a student spending $750 a year should be called decidedly economical, and one spending $1,500 not extravagant, gives a great shock to the accustomed ideas of an American, German, or Frenchman. But we must remember that England is one of the very dearest countries in the world. All the necessaries of life (except some kinds of clothing) cost about twice as much, not merely at Cambridge but in English country towns, as they do at New Haven; and the comparison with a University town of Continental Europe would probably show a greater difference. Making the proper deductions on, this account, the necessary expenses of a Cantab will, *with the exception of private tuition*, be brought very nearly on a par with those of a Yalensian. And the items which oblige me to add the qualifications *very nearly* are such as I would gladly see added to the American student's account. If, for instance, there were better arrangements for cleaning the men's rooms (every Graduate of Yale College will understand what I allude

---

[4] [The First Classic and Senior Medallist of 1840, Alexander Gooden, in fact came to Cambridge from University College, London.]

to), the *civilization* accruing therefrom would be cheaply purchased by the addition of a few dollars to each term-bill.[5]

The expenses for private tuition, which will not be exaggerated if set down at *$175 per annum* for three years and a half, or above $600 for the whole course, form a large item, one which many of our students would not be able or willing to pay; so that supposing the requisite sort of persons ready to make private tutors, it is very improbable that the system could be established amongst us so as to become at all general, for a long while at least. Here, then, we come directly to the question, whether the peculiar advantages which we have attributed to the Cambridge system of education are inseparable from private tuition? In treating of the private tutors it has been stated that some distinguished members of the University, including the Master of Trinity himself, wished to put them down entirely, or confine them within such limits as would be equivalent to their extinction but that, in the opinion of the majority (wherein I heartily coincide from personal experience), such a step would be very injurious. I certainly do think that the private tutors are an important feature of the University; that they enable a badly-prepared but industrious student to make up his deficiencies in a way that no other mode can, and at the same time prevent the best men from being kept back by the others, thus saving time to all classes of students. But I would not affirm or admit that they are *essential* to the University, or that no improvements from it could be transplanted into any other institution unless they were included in the improvements; nor do I think any one would go so far as to say this. They contribute to the accurate and systematic training of the men, but are not indispensable to it.

There is still another point in which it may be feared that the English system involves a greater outlay on the part of the student than ours will ever admit – the comparatively advanced age to which the English students remain at the University, twenty-two being rather below than above the average. It may be said that our young men cannot afford to stay at college so long; they must be out in the world supporting themselves. Now, in the first place, it by no means follows that our college course may not be

---

[5] One of the grievances of the Trinity Under-Graduates used to be that they had not baths and a water-closet in every staircase (every *entry*, as our students call it), and their complaints actually found their way into the Quarterly Review. This may seem extravagant, but it surely is a failing that leans to virtue's side. [Bristed pressed the case for the provision of lavatories in 1864, when discussing plans for new buildings at Yale with Theodore Woolsey. Bristed to Woolsey, 24 February 1864: Yale University Library, Special Collections, Ms 562.]

made much more full and accurate – in short, altogether better than it is *without* increasing the average age of graduation. In the next place, the persons who have least reason to use this plea seem to be the very ones who take advantage of it. The richer students, those who could very well spend two or three years more in their education and with whom indeed it is often a puzzle to know what to do for the year or two succeeding their graduation, are generally the very youngest in the class. Plenty of Englishmen who have no private fortune, nothing but their profession to look to, remain till the age of twenty-three at the University, thinking that the time and money thus spent are capital well invested. Still we must not keep out of view the fact, that one cause which enables them to do so is the wealth of the individual colleges, which is the last feature on our list to be investigated.

The rich endowments of the colleges enable them to offer the highest rewards for learning – solid rewards as well as distinctions. Putting out of the question those who come up with school 'exhibitions', and also the Sizars, who receive their commons for nothing, and their instruction, public and private, at half price, a tolerably forward student, such a one as is first in a small college and turns out a respectable wrangler or a good double second, will make, by his college scholarship, two fifths or three fifths of his expenses during two thirds of the time he passes at the University. A Trinity Scholar wishing to continue in residence for a year or two as a Bachelor, either with the intention of pursuing his theological studies or of carrying out any other branch, has about a third of his necessary expenditure supplied from a similar source. The student of superior abilities and industry who gains a Fellowship, is provided for during the remainder of his bachelor existence, having an income of about a thousand dollars to depend upon.

Here it must be confessed is our great difficulty. Our colleges want wealth, in the form of specific endowments, foundations to support as well as encourage learning. Very promising young men are often compelled to quit college in the middle of their course, or to be temporarily absent teaching school or raising money in some similar way, to the great detriment of their immediate studies. As for resident Graduates wishing to pursue some literary or philosophical faculty beyond the college course, there is no provision for them whatever, nor any opening beyond the comparatively small number of Professorships and Tutorships. It is the want of funds, and those funds specifically appropriated to these purposes, that prevents, more than anything else, our Colleges and Universities from having such teachers (both in number and quality), giving such systematic instruction, and diffusing about themselves such a classical atmosphere as will in a considerable measure correct the effects of bad previous instruction.

This, then, is the point to which all persons taking an interest in the advancement of our Colleges and Universities should turn their attention. *We want endowments.* For the furtherance of this object public assistance is not to be thought of. The recent act of our own State Legislature in endorsing Noah Webster's barbarous innovations on English orthography is a fair specimen of the capability of such gentry to decide on matters of scholarship and high learning.[6] We must look to private liberality. Many of the College Scholarships and Fellowships, and the majority of the prizes, College and University, at Cambridge, are owing to gifts or legacies from individuals. The generous spirit of our countrymen in such matters is too well known to require enlarging upon; and I feel persuaded that were the subject once definitely brought before them and explained to them, there are many men of substance who would give their $1,000 or $2,000 a piece, each to his respective *Alma Mater,* for the foundation of a Scholarship, and some who would be much more liberal. The first thing to aim at is, to direct their attention clearly to it and show how such gifts have a *certain* tendency to promote learning, and can scarcely by any possibility be misapplied, as vague and general bequests for educational purposes too often are.

All this, however, looks only to the future, and is the work of much time. Does nothing admit of being done *at once* to improve the standard of scholarship and of education generally in our colleges? I think there is *much* which might be done; and shall now proceed to show how I would set about it, supposing myself in the place of a president, professor, or other influential member of the 'Faculty' of a large college or university.

[Bristed added in his final edition:
I am very happy to say that nearly all the rest of this chapter, as originally written, has become an anachronism. Several of the most important changes recommended, such as the introduction of written exercises, the examination of students in passages and authors not forming a part of the regular course, and the abolition of those fearful six-o'clock New England winter-morning chapels have been adopted by several of our principal

---

[6] [Noah Webster was an indefatigable publicist for his dictionaries and spelling books. His attempts to secure a congressional imprimatur for his books had failed, but he managed to secure their official adoption in some states. Webster's most famous innovation was the substitution of *-or* for *-our*.]

colleges. Other suggestions have been rendered unnecessary or impossible by the progress of events. I shall merely say, therefore, in a general way that I would abolish the Junior Exhibition if it could be done without raising a mutiny, that I would continue the *serious* study of Greek and Latin up to the very end of the four years, that I would put the Seniors through a *thorough* course of Logic and that I would make the final standing of the students more dependent on the examinations and less on the daily recitations than it still is in most of our institutions. I also hold to my original opinion that when the 'Beneficiaries' form a numerous class (as at Yale) they should not be mixed up with the younger students, but should be made into a special separate department preparatory to the Theological.]

I should not attempt to raise the limit of age for admission, on account of the pecuniary reason already alluded to. We have adopted the habit of pushing out our youths into the world, as the English run their horses, before they are old and strong, and on the same plea – the expense of the preparatory training. To modify this habit requires a gradual proceeding by other means. But I *would* raise the standard of admission. Not nominally – there should not be another book in classics or mathematics added to those now on the list required of candidates for entrance; but I would insist on something approximating more nearly to a *knowledge* of these books from all the candidates. As we cannot give that particular personal attention to each individual which the private tutorial system allows, it is of great importance that a class should not be kept back and made to lose time by the blunders of the *very* inadequately prepared.

I anticipate the immediate objection that such stringency would bear hard on a particular class of students, the 'beneficiaries', as they are commonly called, men who adopt the intention of becoming clergymen at a comparatively late period of life, and are assisted in their collegiate course by charitable contributions. It is usually considered that the holiness of the object these persons have in view, the benefit which the community is to derive from them, and the actual advantage which the moral and religious tone of the college does derive from them while they are at it, warrant almost any indulgence which can be shown them at the expense of the general progress of the rest. From this form of opinion I must be allowed to express my dissent, and to record my sincere conviction that, on the contrary, it would be, a great benefit to any college *to separate* this class entirely from the main body of the students. On first going up to New Haven a boy of fifteen, the incongruity of mixing up these *opsimatheis*[7]

---

[7] [Mature students.]

with us boys, was about the first thing that struck me, and subsequent experience and reflection have confirmed my belief that it is an incongruity, and a mischievous one.

It is not denied that beneficiaries sometimes acquit themselves with great credit, and attain the highest honors. But every one who has had experience in such matters must admit that the majority of them have by their inadequate preparation the effect of keeping the other students back. If, for instance, all the beneficiaries were removed from a class – say in Yale College – the remainder of the class could be worked along better and faster. And this deterioration of the standard extends beyond the beneficiaries themselves, since for every two of them who are let in on inadequate preparation, there slips in a third candidate as badly off in the rudiments, but who must be admitted because they are, since the examiners manifestly cannot lower the standard for one and put it up again for another. That grown-up men who have not been accustomed to learn, do not learn so readily as youth, is an axiom among teachers. But there is one thing in which any man with an ordinary English education is likely to have the advantage of a boy of fourteen. He will be more ready to express his ideas, good or bad, upon paper, more confident and self-possessed as a public speaker, more ready to fall in with the ordinary business of a debating society. Hence the benefi-ciaries have increased the 'speaking and writing' taste, which even without them would be too prevalent. They interfere doubly with the studies of the college, both by what they *can* and by what they *cannot* do.

Against this there will be a disposition to set off the moral influence and check they have upon the younger students, and particularly their precept and example as Christians. But here the picture may be viewed from two sides. They are sincerely and consistently pious, it is agreed. But is there not something inharmonious in their double position as spiritual guides of and fellow-students along with the younger members of the college? Ought not the pupil's religious teachers to have the advantage and authority of standing somewhat above him in profane learning also? If it be said that their instruction is that of *example* only, not of authority, even here its unmixed benefit may be questioned. We may suspect that the man's example will not be always such as the boy can sincerely follow out; that the seriousness and austerity which animate and direct all the movements of one who at an advanced period of life betakes himself under a sudden call or spiritual impulse to preparation for the ministry, will become an unnatural restraint when copied by the youth just from school. That a lively boy should be shut up in his room for a whole Sunday (except during chapel hours), debarring himself of the exercise which his health requires as much as his inclinations prompt, or if he *does* go out for a walk that he should sneak off to it like one committing a crime – that he should be afraid to join in a game of ball because some of the unconverted may be among the players – that he should carry about habitually the mask of gloom upon the face of youth – all this seems to me an unhealthy feeling, a strained and premature seriousness. But let us grant that it is all a fault on the right side, that it is better for the youthful conscience to be too precocious and tender, than too dull and compliant; there are other less doubtful ills that spring from this association of young and old. Men presuming on their age where talent is supposed to be the test of merit, the 'college church' forming a party in society elections, years held up as a claim for office, the contests of personal ambition rendered fiercer by the introduction of a religious element – such are some of the results which I have witnessed with my own eyes, springing directly from the contact of beneficiaries with the younger students.

It would then on all accounts be a desirable step to form the beneficiaries into a department of their own, connected with and introductory to the Theological Faculty. The studies pursued in this department might resemble those of the ordinary under-graduate one, but not reach so far in mathematics, and perhaps not so far in classics, paying more attention to Greek Testament, and above all going over the first-year studies slowly, carefully, and thoroughly. The motives and intentions of this class of pupils are all that is sacred and honorable. God forbid that I or any other man should throw a straw in their way. I only doubt the expediency of mixing them up with the younger students, and of sacrificing the younger students without doing *them* any real good. For in consequence of the bad preparation of some, and the long absences of others to teach school, &c., full half of them do not receive as good a preliminary education as they would under the plan suggested, and very few a better.

Having argued and explained our first proposal – a virtual elevation of the standard for admission – the next point is, what measures should follow it in the first year.

There are three great difficulties or errors – or *corrigenda* of some kind – things desirable to have altered, whosoever fault or misfortune they may be – which are observable from the first in our colleges; and I appeal to any professor in any large college whether what I am about to state is not confirmed by his own experience. In the first place, those who are better prepared than the rest of the class, and who have more natural capacity for the subjects of study, say the dozen or half dozen best in classics, and the same number in mathematics, have very little to do the first year. The 'recitations' take them hardly so long to prepare for as to sit through, and there is nothing marked out for them during the rest of their time. Thus the most valuable students of the year are doubly injured, immediately by wasting many hours in idle reading or other unprofitable occupation, remotely by forming *half-idle* habits, so that they cannot do themselves justice when harder work comes on in the second and third years. The college seems virtually to say – 'after you have learned the construing and parsing of the page or two in Livy, and the page of Xenophon, and learned the stipulated formulae, or done the stipulated examples in Algebra, we ask nothing more of you. Amuse yourselves for the rest of the time as you like.' That they generally avail themselves of the permission is not to be wondered at.

Secondly. The knowledge which the students continue to acquire both in mathematics and classics, but especially of the latter, is, even in the case of those who recite fluently and stand well for college honors, all *exoteric* – a knowledge not of subjects and language, but of books, nay parts of books. The 'recitations' are learned and recited from day to day, it is scarcely an exaggeration to say from hour to hour, for they are usually committed in the two or three hours previous to their being heard, or at furthest the night before. They are repeated perhaps twice the second time as a 'back-lesson'[8] merely construed, and that is the end of them, for the annual examinations are a mere farce.[9] The learner's actual progress, what he has gained and held fast, is never tested by asking him to apply it. During the whole of his college course, the Under-graduate is never called upon to translate a passage in Greek or Latin, or to solve a problem in mathematics which he is not supposed to have seen and studied before the particular occasions.[10]

Lastly, there is a great difficulty in making cleverness and application go together, in persuading the clever men to work their best at the college studies, and in getting the main body of the students to believe that those who distinguish themselves in the college studies are clever, – or as they might call it, *smart* – men. Nor is this difficulty very surprising, in view of

---

8　['Back-lesson: A lesson which has not been learned or recited; a lesson which has been omitted.' Hall, *College Words and Customs*, pp. 18–19.]

9　It is worth noticing that at Columbia College, where the classical standard both *for* and after admission is higher than at any other similar institution in the country, the Honors are given by semi-annual examinations.

10　This assertion I believe to be strictly predicable of nearly all our colleges. It was true to the letter of Yale in my day, and would be so now but for the Scholarships of which mention has been made.

the two antecedents just mentioned. All three of these evils may be met and remedied by one and the same means, the establishment of an examination which *is* an examination at the end of the year. Let the Latin and Greek authors of the year, or a portion of them, say the First Book of Livy, the First Three Books of the Anabasis, and so on, be made the subjects of written papers, to be delivered to the students only when they are required to answer them, and including not only extracts for translation, with critical and grammatical questions thereon, but all the subject-matter of the author, history, geography, antiquity, law, illustrative extracts from authors not in the course, &c., not omitting translations from English into Latin prose. Let the mathematical papers similarly contain, besides the formulae of the books, original examples, deductions, and problems. Viva voce should enter into the examination, but the chief part of it should be in writing, and its duration ought not to fall short of five days or exceed seven. The examinees should be divided into classes, say four, five, or six, and I would make the first class large – eighteen or twenty per cent. of the whole – and arrange those in it according to order of merit. Did the college finances allow, I would give every one in the first class a prize of books.

By way of previous practice it would be well for the students to have brief written examinations once a month, or six times in all during the first two terms, in the classics and mathematics of each preceding month. During this year there should be *no* English compositions required of them.

Under such an arrangement no student, however well prepared, would have any temptation to idleness, but rather every incentive to industry, as the collateral subjects involved in even one book of Livy or Xenophon open so wide a field that there is no danger of his knowing it too well, if all his spare time is devoted to exploring it. Nor would the students generally look upon good preparation, and 'anticipating', and reading 'books out of the course', in the same light as they do now – as a confession of inferior natural ability, or a means of purchasing idleness beforehand, or a labor of supererogation. The difference between him who mastered his subject and him who merely crammed from day to day would be abundantly shown, and the scope given to general talent in answering the general questions would soon show that clever men had their fair chance.

A brief digression is here necessary. The suggested changes not only recognise the principle of emulation as a legitimate one, but encourage it to its full extent. This may seem to call for some remark, as the doctrine is frequently put forth (though the general practice of our institutions is against it) that all rewards for excellence in college studies are based on an unsound principle and tend to harm, that they excite ill feeling and envy, and bribe students to do that to which a sense of duty should be a sufficient inducement.

Such a 'free trade' in education may not uncharitably be deemed a shrewd device of those enemies who wish to lower the standard of knowledge, and bring the collegians down to their own level. Home learning requires protection and encouragement quite as much as home manufactures. If it be desirable that we should not be entirely dependent on foreigners for rails to ride on and clothes to wear, it is also desirable that a young man should be able to get a thorough and elegant education at home, without having to cross the water for it. Any endowment for the encouragement of classical, mathematical, or other learning, *necessitates* the idea of competition, otherwise you abolish the only test of what they were intended to promote. The difficulty of obtaining proper teachers, already sufficiently formidable, would be ten times augmented by the abolition of all distinctions for academic proficiency, since the public would have no means of judging who were best qualified to teach. Boys will not study mathematics from a sense of duty – that is, not one in a hundred – it is too up-hill work; nor will they indeed, from the same abstract motive, study classics in a sound, regular way, taking the dry matter with the interesting as it comes. They will be apt to work in a *dilettante* way, and pick out the titbits. The example of the German universities is not in point. The German students have been worked hard at their gymnasia, and have passed severe examinations on quitting those. They are, at the university, occupied immediately upon their professional studies, for those of them who will not be lawyers, doctors, or clergymen, will be 'ordinary' professors or government functionaries, immediately after taking their degrees. The fruit of their study is close at hand. With regard to the envy and ill-will supposed to be excited by competition for honors, they certainly are not evils inseparable from the system. You see nothing of them at Cambridge. The two Medallists, or the two Smith's Prizemen, are often warm personal friends, reading with the same tutor, and passing much of their time together. Even with us the extent of it is greatly exaggerated; but, so far as it does exist, it is justly chargeable not on the principle of emulation but on that spirit of envy and impatience of superiority so general in our country, which is expressly generated by our democratic institutions and must be taken as one of the evils of those institutions along with their blessings. According to more general considerations, it is tolerably evident that emulation is one of the main springs of human progress in all departments of life; that individuals and nations become torpid and retrograde without it; that success attending on patient industry and talent combined is the usual rule in this world; that the Divine Law itself is sanctioned by rewards and punishments; that a government without rewards should also in common fairness be one without punishments – which would end in being no government at all – and this perhaps is what some people would prefer. Most of these things are truisms; indeed all the arguments have been presented, or rather alluded to, as briefly as possible, because the common sense of mankind readily agrees to them; and the digression was made merely not to pass over in silence any question that has been started in reference to our subject.

Let us now proceed to the second year, better known by the barbarous term of *Sophomore* (a name to which it is hardly necessary to say there is nothing answering in the colleges of any other country). It is now quite early enough to begin with the exercises in English composition, usually commenced in the first year. Even now it would be well to require them not more frequently than once a month; and the subjects, instead of being of that abstract and general nature which leads the students to write at them vaguely, more with the idea of acquiring or showing a fine style than of expressing their views of anything clearly, should be questions requiring them to *read* as well as write, and supplying them matter to think and write upon – historical or antiquarian for instance. The prizes usually given at the end of each term for a single exercise might be given on an average of the three. This plan would be likely to have the effect of making all the class take some pains with their compositions, and profit by the exercise in more than one way. The monthly *written* examinations should be continued. As to the mathematical studies of the year, they ought to be conducted with more reference to principles, not wasting time in the working of long logarithmic calculations, which neither cultivate nor give scope for any particular faculty except patience. The application of the principles to examples might be sufficiently made in the monthly examinations. In this way the students might go through one third more mathematics than they do in the year, with more profit and less inconvenience to themselves than they now do, and the examination at the end of the year might include not only conic sections and special trigonometry, but also low mechanics. The grateful recollections which all Cambridge classical men have of Newton impel me to put in a word for him here. I could very much wish that the early books of the Principia, according to any standard translation, were generally read in our colleges.

The classical part of the annual examinations should be of the same nature as before; the books read during the year, or such portions of them as would afford sufficient material for six or eight good papers, half extracts for translations, half general questions; and some English to be translated into Latin.

The start gained this year would enable the good mathematicians to carry on their studies much further than at present during the third year. In fact, after the first term the class should be divided; those who pleased might go on with and beyond the Differential Calculus, and the larger portion begin to review their mathematical course from the beginning. The exercises in English composition, or written debates, should still be limited to one a month for two terms. At the end of the year there should be an examination on all the mathematics previously read. The earlier papers of this, containing no problems and only a few simple deductions and examples, besides the regular book formulae, should be a pass examination, and those classical men who got through it should be released from any further mathematical studies. The higher papers, including problems and involving the Calculus, would counterbalance for the good mathematicians the proficiencies of the best classics in the Greek plays and other difficult subjects of the year. To make all the classics of the year, much more all the classics of the three years, the foundation of Pass examinations for the mathematical or for all the students, would be exacting too much of them. As much should be selected as will make three subjects of respectable dimensions (say a Greek play, a book of Tacitus, and an oration of Demosthenes or Cicero), and the six papers in the examination referring to these should be the pass for a Degree, so far as classics are concerned. The student who acquitted himself the best in the whole examination (consisting of all the mathematics of the course and the year's classics, including translation from English into Latin) would be the first man of the year; and the first class should be of liberal dimensions – at least fifteen per cent. of the examinees. The 'Junior Exhibition' I would abolish; that is, if it could be done without raising a mutiny.

During the last year I would not tell the students to be idle, as most of our college authorities do. Every one should continue to study either Classics or Mathematics. The whole senior class ought to be put through a thorough course of Logic – which is now ridiculously neglected, considering the great fondness for and attention to rhetoric and composition. Moral Philosophy comes naturally in connexion with Logic. Compositions and debates might also be more frequent – four or five in each term. The attendance at Lectures on the Natural Sciences I would not make compulsory, or if I did it should not be for only *one* science at the students' option. In the last term of this year, near the end in fact of the whole course, there ought to be two general examinations, one in Classics, the other in Mathematics, and a third and shorter one in Logic and Moral Philosophy. At the risk of carrying out my imaginary details too minutely, and thus interfering with their general applicability, I will proceed to explain the principles on which these examinations might advantageously be conducted, particularly the classical one.

The students should be examined in passages *chiefly* taken from books not in the college course. If, for instance, Cicero's *de Oratore* and *de Officiis* formed part of the course, then give them an extract from the Tusculan Questions; if the Iliad formed part of the course they should have extracts from the Odyssey. The more difficult authors not usually read at our colleges it would not answer to use for some time, *e.g.* Pindar or Aristotle. There should be at least four translation papers with five or six extracts in each, a paper of English prose to turn into Latin, and one or two general papers containing questions on classical history, the ancient government and laws, the elements of prosody and principles of grammar. There would also be some *viva voce* in the examination. The Mathematical Examination should take place sufficiently long after or before the classical, to allow those students who were desirous of taking honors in both (a practice which I would neither encourage nor discourage) to have an opportunity of doing so. The candidates at both examinations, I would divide into four classes, those in the first three should be considered as having *taken honors*, and a list of the three classes (the names in each class arranged in order of merit) should be published by authority. No student should have his degree who was not able to pass in the fourth class of *one* of the examinations.

The Logic and Moral Philosophy examination should be open to all who had taken honors in either of the others. Many of the answers to questions in it would naturally take the form of short extempore essays. It would be a rare chance for really clever men to show themselves, and there need be no danger of political or sectarian party allusions intruding themselves into it.

Such a scheme as this nominally diminishes in many respects the amount of labor required from the students, but really gets a great deal more out of them in one sense and puts a great deal more into them in another. It goes upon the principle that it is better to learn a little at a time and thoroughly, than to pretend to learn a great many things together and learn them very superficially. Very possibly every feature of it can and will be fearfully picked to pieces, but with my present lights I believe it to be all feasible, and have not the slightest doubt that if feasible it would be most beneficial.[11] I am

---

[11] Of the police and government regulations nothing has been said, but there is one point which I cannot refrain from expressing my opinion about. The morning

persuaded that in course of time it would cause the students to enter at a later age and better prepared, attract donations for Prizes, Scholarships, and Fellowships, raise up a class of resident graduates from among whom private tuition could be supplied, and ultimately combine almost all the advantages of the English system, with the proficiency in rhetoric and composition which is in some respects natural and necessary to our people, and which under such a plan, being attained at a later period, and based upon some real training and knowledge, would not then prove so hollow and barren as it now does.

---

recitation between chapel and breakfast, which prevails in many of our colleges, ought most certainly to be done away with. Some of the students are half asleep at it, some of them more than half hungry, some of them less than half dressed. Their bodily discomforts prevent them from really profiting at all by the intellectual exercise they mechanically drag through. Nor is it, in many cases, beneficial to the health to remain so long fasting in the morning. The young men should be allowed another hour of sleep. There is neither reason nor religion in pulling them out of bed at six during a New England winter, with the snow knee-deep, or indeed during winter anywhere. The feelings excited by it are very much the reverse of devotional.

Charles Astor Bristed 1820–1874
An annotated bibliography

Note A complete bibliography of secondary works referred to in the Introduction and notes to this edition will be found at pp. xxi–xxiv.

Abbreviation *PBDC* = *Pieces of a broken-down critic* (see p. 393).

A Printed Works

1 Separately printed works

2 Articles in serial (and other) publications

3 Edited works

4 Translations

B Secondary Literature

A1 Separately printed works

Oratio latina praemio annuo dignata et in Curia Cantabrigiensi recitata: Comitiis Maximis a.d. M.DCCC.XLIII 13 pp. Cantabrigiae: Typis et sumtibus academicis excudit J. Gul. Parker, 1843. Repr. in *Five Years* ed. 1, 1852, 2.251–9. The title is 'Quibusnam e fontibus T. Livius historiam primi libri sui hauserit, et quatenus historia ista vera sit habenda?'

The military orders of the Middle Ages Prize essay, Trinity College, Cambridge, 1843; pr. by J. Hall, Cambridge 1844. pp. 14. Repr. in *Five Years* ed. 1, 1852, 2.184–93.

The principle of liberality: an oration delivered in Trinity College Hall, Friday Dec. 15, 1843, being Commemoration Day. Cambridge: pr. by J. Hall, 1844. pp. 12. Repr. in *Five Years* ed. 1, 1852, 2.208–16.

Was the usurpation of Oliver Cromwell ultimately beneficial to England?: declamation which won the first prize cup, Trinity College, Cambridge, 1843. Cambridge: pr. by J. Hall, 1844. pp. 12. Repr. in *Five years* ed. 1, 1852, 2. 175–83.

American hospitality and English repudiation. Correspondence with the Hon. C.E. Law, MP for Cambridge. London: pr. By W. Clowes, 1850. 4°, pp. 7.
Bowes, *Cambridge Books*, no. 2174. Copy in Forster Collection, National Art Library, London, FP 227. See *Upper Ten Thousand* 53, 56, where the hero Harry Benson (=Bristed) recounts having lent $1000 to an 'Ensign Lawless', who refuses to repay it, and whose father refuses to honour the debt. In the book, Benson publishes a piece of the same title to denounce 'Lawless': Henry Towry Law (1830–1855), youngest son of Charles Law QC, MP for the University of Cambridge, who swindled Bristed out of $1000. Discussed in 'Dishonored drafts on London (Charles Astor Bristed, Charles E. Law)', *Literary World* 7 (3 Aug. 1850) 86–7.

A letter to the Hon. Horace Mann New York: Kernot, 1850 pp. 54 (2nd ed 1850, pp. 54).
A defence of John Jacob Astor against Horace Mann, who in his *Thoughts for a Young Man* (Boston, 1850) had described Astor as 'the most notorious, the most wealthy, and, considering his vast means, the most miserly of his class in the country': p. 64. Repr. *PBDC* 4.4–33.
Reviews:
Harper's New Monthly Magazine 1 (July 1850) 277 ('A pungent letter').
Literary World 6: 586–7; also 641.
Littell's Living Age 26 (13 July 1850).

Five years in an English University ed. 1, 2vv, ii + 423 + 448pp. New York: G.P. Putnam, 1852.
Includes Bristed's Trinity College declamations; those not separately printed are 'On the influence of the political movements of the last half-century on the literature of the same period', n.d., (2.194–207); 'Whether the British government is as favorable to eloquence as the ancient republics', March 1844 (2.217–36); 'The character and conduct of King William III', June 1845 (2.238–51). Also includes a public declamation, 'In legibus ferendis quid propositi haber debeat, qui poenas peccatis irrogat, et quaenam sit adhibenda suppliciorum mensura', 1841 (2.259–65), and an undated declamation, 'Quaenam beneficia a legibus praescriptis diligenter observatis academiae alumni percipiant' (2. 265–73).
Reviews:
Literary World 9 (22 Nov. 1851) 401–3.
The Dollar Magazine 8 (Dec. 1851) 276–9.
Literary World 10 (31 Jan. 1852) 83–4.
Knickerbocker 39 (Mar. 1852):274.
The American Review 15 (Mar. 1852) 283. 'Although disfigured with a great deal of vanity and egotism, this is a decidedly clever book. It gives the most

perfect insight into English university life, both mental and physical, that we have yet had, and is valuable as demonstrating the deficiencies of our own collegiate system.'

Westminster Review 57 (April 1852) 667–9.

The Biblical Repertory and Princeton Review 24 (Apr. 1852) 294–311.

Chambers' Edinburgh Journal (5 June 1852) 366–8; repr. *Littell's Living Age* 34 (17 July 1852) 114.

The Eclectic Magazine 26 (July 1852) 425–8. ('From the Literary Gazette'.)

The North American Review 75 (July 1852) 47–84.

The Southern Quarterly Review 22 ns 6 (Oct. 1852) 414–43; 24 ns 8 (July 1853) 53–9; the first anon., the second signed JGMG, Baltimore.

Yale Literary Magazine 18 (Oct. 1852) 21–5.

Littell's Living Age 8 (13 Jan. 1855) 126. Refers to a review by Dr Samuel Phillips in the *Literary Gazette*; probably the London journal of that name, to which Phillips contributed and which he edited.

Sartain's Union Magazine 10 (April 1852) 356–7.

Boston Review 2 (Mar. 1862) 134–56: 'English and American university life'. Reviewed together with T. Hughes's *Tom Brown's Schooldays* and *Tom Brown in Oxford*. Bristed's insight and detail is praised but the 'black and revolting' picture he paints is deplored.

S.A. Allibone, *A Critical Dictionary of English Literature* vol.1, 1881 (originally 1858): 'The American public are debtors to Mr. Bristed for the valuable information drawn from his own experience in an English university. In a country like America – whilst we make our boast of "a mob of gentlemen who write with ease" – ripe classical scholarship is too apt to be undervalued.'

G. Vapereau's 1858 ed. of *Dictionnaire universel des contemporains*, p. 282: *Five Years* is 'plein de details interessants sur la vie universitaire en Angleterre' ... M. Bristed habite Paris, d'ou il envoie souvent au *Fraser's Magazine* des articles, a la fois spirituels et serieux ... Il est aussi le correspondant francais de divers journaux de New York, entre autres du *Spirit of the Times*. [Repeated almost verbatim in 1870 edition.]

Five years in an English University ed.2, iv, 441pp. New York: G.P. Putnam, 1852. The text of the first edition, minus the Appendices.

Review: 'Philemon Jenkinson', 'Life in Cambridge according to C.A. Bristed', *Fraser's Magazine* 49 (Jan. 1854) 89–100 [ascribed to W.G. Clark in A.T. Bartholomew, *Catalogue & the books and papers ... relating to the university, town and county of Cambridge bequeathed to the university by John Willis Clark*, Cambridge 1912, 59.]

[Frank Manhattan] ***The upper ten thousand: sketches of American society, by a New Yorker***. London: J.W. Parker and Son, 1852, pp. 201; New York: Stringer and Townsend 1852, 274pp. Repr. from *Fraser's Magazine*: see A2, 1850–1.

The Introduction, pp. 1–11, reprints a letter from Bristed to N.P. Willis, editor of the

Home World [i.e. *Home Journal*] acknowledging authorship but denying (p. 8) that he is the leading character of the book, 'Henry Benson'. (The letter was also printed in *International Magazine* 3 (April 1851) 39.) In the body of the book, the main character is called 'Harry Masters' (whom on p. 154 the narrator denies is himself). The writer of the introduction, however, tells us that Bristed denied that the 'Carl Benson' in the book was himself. So we have Carl Benson – Harry Benson – Harry Masters. 'Masters' was presumably used for the USA, where readers might be familiar with Benson = Bristed. The original *Fraser's* articles have 'Carl Benson'. The plates in the US edition of the book still refer to the main character as 'Benson' though the text references have changed to 'Masters'.

> 2nd edn, revised. New York: Stringer and Townsend 1852, 274pp.
> Reviews:
> *Graham's American Monthly Magazine* 41 (Nov. 1852) 547–9. Quotes from the section of *Upper Ten Thousand* which mentions Ensign Lawless, and denounces Bristed for complaining, for bad manners, and for writing a bad book.
> *Peterson's Magazine* 23 (Feb. 1853) 159.
> *Literary World* 11 (7 Aug. 1852) 89.

Pieces of a broken-down critic. Picked up by himself. Baden: pr. by Scotzniovsky, 4 vols in 1, 1858–9, pp. 347 + 81 + 150 + 113. Vols 1–2 1858, vols 3–4 1859.

> Review: *Round Table* 6 (21 Dec. 1867) 417–18, which gives the printers/publishers as Scotzniovsky and Leypoldt & Hoyt of New York. (The latter were in fact merely distributors.)

Now is the time to settle it: suggestions on the present crisis New York: pr. Martin B. Brown 1862, pp. 24; digital reprint by Cornell University Library, 2006.

[Carl Benson] *No surrender* 1863. pp. 8.

A few words of warning to New Yorkers, on the consequences of a railroad in Fifth Avenue: with remarks on city railroads generally, and reflections suggested by the passage of the Broadway Railroad Bill New York: pr. Wm. C. Bryant & Co., 1863. pp. 33.

The cowards' convention New York: Loyal Publication Society, 1864 [no. 68]. pp. 16. On the Democratic Convention.

[Benson, Carl] *A letter to Dr. Henry Halford Jones: concerning his habit of giving advice to everybody, and his qualifications for the task.* New York: pr. Wm. C. Bryant & Co., 1864. pp. 45. Jones was the pseudonym of Josiah Gilbert Holland, editor of the *Wintertown Democrat* and a Springfield republican. Cf. Bristed on Holland (vs. Titcomb) in his 'Fancy signatures': A2, 1869.

[C.A.B.] *That punch!!!*
February 11, 1865. 3pp.
This set of verses celebrates the punch served at the annual artists' receptions in John T. Johnston's art gallery on Fifth Avenue. Opened in 1860 in the stable behind

his house, it was the first gallery to be established in New York, and claimed to be the first anywhere to be open without charge. Its success led in 1870 to the foundation of the Metropolitan Museum of Art, with Johnston as its first president. See H.C. Brown, *Fifth Avenue Old and New, 1824–1924* (New York: Fifth Avenue Association, 1924), 30–31.

The interference theory of government New York: Leypoldt & Holt 1867, pp. 100; 2nd revised edn, New York: Leypoldt & Holt 1868, pp. 109.

   Reported in *Round Table* 6 (16 Nov. 1867) 327–8: The book was printed at Bristed's expense, 500 copies. It was stereotyped; total cost $333.36. 50 copies were given to editors, assuming the others all sold Bristed would get $225; loss to him, $108.36. The maximum profit Leypoldt and Hoyt could make was $45; hence they need to charge high prices for more popular books.
   Reviews:
   [2nd edn] *Putnam's Monthly* 11 (Jan. 1868).
   Nation 5 (7 Nov. 1867) 372. 'A spicy book'.
   Southern Review 3 (1868) 245.

American beauty personified as the nine muses. 27pp. Boston, A.A. Childs & Co., 1870. Title vignette: Description of the muses as personified by nine American ladies (whose names are supplied in pencil under each muse) and painted by Fagnani for the Metropolitan Museum of Art. New York. 'The nine muses' (16th–27th leaves), signed C.A.B., is claimed to be reprinted from the 'Chicago art journal' [not found], July 1869.

On the pronunciation of the ancient languages; practically considered with reference to teaching. 17pp. New York: Little, Rennie & Co., 1870. A paper read at the first annual conference of the American Philological Association, Poughkeepsie, N.Y., July 1869. Pr. for private circulation.

In honorem: Du preux chevalier Eugene Benson, who broke two lances for the ladies of America with the redoubtable Mrs. Uncle Tom. Signed, C.A.B. 100 copies printed for private circulation. pp. 4. New York. N.d., but almost certainly the second half of 1870.
In Jan. 1870 Harriet Beecher Stowe published her *Lady Byron Vindicated*, which aroused a storm of protest by hinting at Byron's incest with his half-sister. In July 1870, Benson published an article in *Revolution* praising George Sand's liberated views on marriage ['George Sand and the marriage question'. *Revolution*, 7 July 1870, 1–23]; Stowe was horrified at the link he made between Sand and the women's movement and sent her brother Henry, since Jan. 1870 editor of the *Christian Union*, a reply to be published editorially. *Revolution* was run by Stowe's allies (at least, until she published her defence of Lady Byron), Susan B. Anthony and Elizabeth Cady Stanton. See J.D. Hedrick, *Harriet Beecher Stowe: A Life* (Oxford, 1994), 371–2.

The origin of morals: temporal tendencies of the progress of scepticism. New York: Little, Rennie & Co., 1870. pp. 20. Pr. for private circulation.

Two essays, 'The origins of morals' and 'The progress of skepticism'. Bristed's prefatory note (August 1870) states that they were 'written for and partly printed in a religious periodical, the suspension of which interrupted their publication'. The periodical has not been traced.

Some notes on Ellis's Early English pronunciation: read at the third annual session of the American Philological Association, July, 1871. Hartford, Conn, revised with additions, 1872. pp. 25. Offprint from the APA's *Transactions.*

[Carl Benson] *Anacreontics.* New York, 1872. Privately printed, pp. 75.

Five years in an English University ed.3, 1873. New York: G.P. Putnam; London: Sampson, Low, Marston, Low & Searle. The US registration statement is dated 1872; some copies are dated 1874. The text of the second ed., with some added material.
Reviews:
New Englander and Yale Review 32 (Jan. 1873) 196.
American Journal of Education 28 (1874) 437.
Spectator [London] 30 Aug. 1873, 1100–1.

On some exaggerations in comparative philology. [Providence?] Pr. for private circulation, 1873. pp. 16.
A paper read for Bristed at the fourth annual meeting of the American Philological Association, July 1872. See *TAPA* 3 (1872) 22.

A2 Articles in serial (and other) publications

1838
[Cebe] Carmen lyricum celeberrimum colonicum: 'Sittin' on a rail', accurate Latine redditum. *Yale Literary Magazine* 4 (Nov. 1838) 36.

1839
[in *Five years* 7–8, Bristed says that in summer 1839 he had just published his first piece in a 'city magazine'.]
[Cebe] Modern Latin anthology. *Yale Literary Magazine* 4 (Feb. 1839) 198–200.
[Cebe] Modern Latin anthology No II. Pasquin and Marforio. *Yale Literary Magazine* 4 (Apr. 1839) 306–8.
[Cebe] Modern Latin anthology No III. Buchanan. *Yale Literary Magazine* 4 (June 1839) 368–74. Three epigrams from this piece repr. *PBDC* 2.37–8 as 'Three epigrams from George Buchanan. New Haven 1839'.
'Mr Ainsworth's Jack Sheppard'. *New Yorker,* 28 Dec. 1839.

1840
Of the summer of 1840, Bristed wrote, 'I … could write newspaper articles in prose or verse': *Five Years* ed.1, 11. He may have been thinking of the three translations from the German published (or republished?) in *PBDC* 2.76–80 in 1858.

The contrabandist. Translated for the Knickerbocker from the French of George Sand. *Knickerbocker* 15 (Jan. 1840) 26–40. Repr. *PBDC* 2, 43–63.

[Anon] Translations from the German: The seven hillocks. *New Yorker* (8 Feb. 1840).

Pungent remarks on punsters. *New Yorker* (29 Feb. 1840).

Niles' Hymn. As originally sung with great applause in the US Senate, to the tune of Greenfields. [Mr Speaker … salt is salt and coal is coal …]. *New Haven Daily Herald* 'during the Spring election of 1840'; repr. in *National Intelligencer*.

Bürger's Leonora. Translated in the metre of the original. *Yale Literary Magazine* 5 (June 1840) 394–7. Repr. *The Evening Post* Jan. 1847; *PBDC* 2, 69–76.

Travelling companions. [short story] *New World* (4 July 1840).

Going on tick. *New World* (15 Aug. 1840).

[Cebe] Human life. A fragment. From the Greek of Simonides. *New World* 1.44 (22 Aug. 1840) p. 2 col. 4.

Epigrams. *New World* 1.45 (29 Aug. 1840), p. 3 col 4.

[Cebe] Ancaeus. From the German. *New Yorker* 9 (12 Sept. 1840) 403.

1841

[C.B.] A university boat race *Yale Literary Magazine* 7 (Nov. 1841) 36–40. Repr. *Five years* ed. 1, 1.59–66.

1842

[Anon] Retrospective review. The man in the moon. *Yale Literary Magazine* 7 (Feb. 1842) 203–7.

Scraps from a projected translation of the Nibelungenlied. *PBDC* 2.66–9. Dated at end 'Trin Coll, Cant. 1842'.

1845

[C.A.B.] English poetry and poets of the present day. Poems by Alfred Tennyson, Miss Elizabeth Barrett, Coventry Patmore, R.H. Horne, and Robert Browning. *Knickerbocker* 25 (June 1845) 534–46.

[Anon] The Scotch school of philosophy and criticism. *The American Review* 2 (Oct. 1845) 386–97. Attributed to Bristed by Sheldon W. Liebman, 'The Origins of Emerson's Early Poetics: His Reading in the Scottish Common Sense Critics', *American Literature* 45 (1973), pp. 23–33, fn. p. 33, but without evidence.

1846

Cooper's 'Indian and Ingin'. *American Review* 4 (Sept. 1846) 276–81. Repr. *PBDC* 1, 1–11.

Translators of Homer. *American Review* 4 (Oct. 1846) 350–72. Repr. *PBDC* 1, 11–57.

[Carl Benson] Short chapters on exotic and novel metres. I: The hexameter and the pentameter. *American Review* 4 (Nov. 1846) 482–5. (Perhaps the first appearance of Bristed's favourite pseudonym.)

1847

[Carl Benson] Short Chapters on Exotic and Novel Metres. Chapter II: Classical Dramatic Metres. *American Review* (Jan. 1847) 72–3.

[Carl Benson] The Hack-Horse Wot Wouldn't Go; or, how the Yankee did the Yorkshireman. *American Review* 5 (Feb. 1847) 159–63. Repr. *PBDC* 3, 48–57. (story)

[Carl Benson] Short Chapters on Rare and Exotic Metres. Chapter III: Classical Lyric Metres. *American Review* 5 (Feb. 1847) 174–5.

[Carl Benson] The Meeting of Siegfried and Chriemhilt. Translated from the third adventure of the Niebelungen Lied. *American Review* 5 (Feb. 1847) 190.

[Carl Benson] English University life. No. 1: The Boat Race. *American Review* 5 (Apr. 1847) 353–6.

'This article was originally prepared for a College magazine some years ago. [See 1841 above.] As it contained several mistakes in statistics and facts it was judged best to re-write it' (353). Incorporated into *Five Years* (ed. 1, 1.59–66).

[C.A.B] Review of Greek–English Lexicons (Liddell & Scott, Pickering). *Knickerbocker* 29 (Apr. 1847) 359–61.

[Carl Benson] Short Chapters on Novel and Exotic Metres. No. III: The New School Metres. *American Review* 5 (May 1847) 502–4. This is 'No III' despite the fact that the Feb. chapter was 'Chapter III'; that chapter also has a slightly different title.

[Carl Benson]. English university life, No. II: A Trinity Supper. *American Review* 5 (Jun. 1847) 629–34. Incorporated, with some introductory text, into *Five years* ed. 1, 1.67–82.

[Carl Benson] Bacchus and Ariadne, from the First Book of Ovid's Ars Amatoria. [verse] *Knickerbocker* 29 (June 1847) 542. Repr *PBDC* 2, 36–7.

[C.A.B.] The *Agamemnon* of Aeschylus, with notes, by C.C. Felton. *Knickerbocker* 29 (June 1847) 543–59. (Itself reviewed, in fact denounced, in *North American Review* 5 (July 1847) 239–55.) A savage critique of the Harvard professor C.C. Felton's edition by a young Yale graduate.

[Letter on national debt] [*New-York?*] *Gazette and Times* (July 1847). Repr. *PBDC* 4, 1–4. Original not found.

[Carl Benson] The Lament for Daphnis, from the First Idyll of Theocritus. (verse) *Literary World* 2 (21 Aug. 1847) 61. Repr *PBDC* 2,25–7.

A reply to Prof. Tayler Lewis's riposte [to Bristed's rev. of Felton]. *Knickerbocker* 30 (Sept. 1847) 246–56. An editorial comment appears at p. 374.

[C.A.B.] The North-American Review and our critique of Felton. *Knickerbocker* 30 (Sept. 1847) 260–70.

[C.A.B.] Classical Criticism. *Knickerbocker* 30 (Oct. 1847) 325–30.

Ladies' Repository 7 (Nov. 1847) 350: 'The Knickerbocker, for September, is on our table. It is to us interesting chiefly for containing an article by Professor Lewis, styled Classical Criticisms, a most pungent reply of that gentleman to an attack made on him in a former number of the Knickerbocker, written, as Professor Lewis thinks, by Charles Astor Bristed.

1848

[Anon] Phonics and phonetics. *Literary World* 2 (8 Jan. 1848) 554–5. Repr. *PBDC* 1, 57–64. A review of three publications by Dr Comstock advocating the use of a phonetic alphabet.

[Anon] The periodical literature of America. *Blackwood's Magazine* 63 (Jan. 1848) 106–12. Repr. *PBDC* 3, 14–24.

The prose writings of André Chenier. *American Review* 7 (Jan. 1848) 71–9. Repr. *PBDC* 1, 64–80.

Recent English Historians of Ancient Greece. *American Review* 7 (Feb. 1848) 178–90, (Mar. 1848) 286–300. Repr. *PBDC* 1, 80–126.

[Ereuneter] Criticism. *Literary World* 3 (18 Mar. 1848) 125–6. Repr. *PBDC* 4, 34–40.

[Carl Benson] Table aesthetics. *Knickerbocker* 31 (Apr. 1848) 292–319. Repr. *PBDC* 1, 126–70. Refers to the disgusting food at Yale, which some men refused to eat.

[Anon, fn. signed C.B.] A talk about the [i.e. Tennyson's] *Princess*. *American Review* 8 (July 1848) 28–39. Repr. *PBDC* 1, 171–95.

[Carl Benson] Bacchus and Ariadne. From the first book of Ovid's Ars Amatoria. *Literary World* 3 (14 Oct. 1848) 733.

[C.A.B.] [Thackeray's] Vanity Fair. *American Review* 8 (Oct. 1848) 421–31. Repr. *PBDC* 1, 195–215.

[Carl Benson] The Vengeance of Eros, imitated from Theocritus [verse]. *American Review* 8 (Nov. 1848) 482–3. Repr. *PBDC* 2, 34–5.

The life and letters of Keats. *The American Review* 8 (Dec. 1848) 603–10. A review of R.M. Milnes's *Life, Letters and Literary Remains of John Keats*.

1849

[Carl Benson] The vengeance of Eros, imitated from Theocritus. (From the *American Review*, Nov. 1848.) *Literary World* 4 (3 Feb. 1849) 104.

[Carl Benson] An Amoebaean from Theocritus. *Literary World* 4 (17 Feb. 1849) 155. Repr. *PBDC* 2,32–4.

'Heus Susanna!' *Knickerbocker* 33 (Mar. 1849) 273–4. Repr. *Literary World* 4 (7 Apr. 1849) 315; repr. *PBDC* 2.80–1. 'O Susanna!' in Latin verse.

[C.A.B.] Oxford hexameters. *Literary World* 4 (9 June 1849) 493–4. Repr. *PBDC* 1, 215–20. A review of Clough's *Bothie*.

Envy and scandal. *Knickerbocker* 33 (June 1849) 527–36. Repr. *PBDC* 3, 1–14.

1850

[Anon] New York society and the writers thereon I. *Literary World* 6 (23 Mar. 1850) 295–7. Repr. *PBDC* 1.22–48, together with Part II below.

Aristophanes. *Literary World* 6 (30 Mar. 1850) 320–3. Repr. *PBDC* 1, 249–62. A review of C.C. Felton's ed. of *The Birds*.

Sketches of American society, by a New Yorker. I, The upper ten thousand. *Fraser's Magazine* 41 (Mar. 1850) 261–71.

[Carl Benson] A joke transferred. *The Literary World* 6 (13 Apr. 1850) 375–6. Discusses an epigram on Mary Wortley Montagu.

[Anon] American society and the writers thereon, II *Literary World* 6 (27 Apr. 1850) 413–15. (Title changed from part 1.) Repr. *PBDC* 1. 220–48, with Part I above.

[Carl Benson] American society and the writers thereon, III. *Literary World* 6 (4 May 1850) 438–40. All three parts repr. as one, *PBDC* 1, 220–48. (Only Part III signed in original publication; note change of title for Parts II-III.)

[Carl Benson] Phillis and Flora. From the 'Walter Mapes' poems. *Knickerbocker* 35 (May 1850) 399–406.

Sketches of American society, by a New Yorker. II, A wedding 'above Bleecker'. *Fraser's Magazine* 41 (May 1850) 523–8.

[Review of Tennyson's *In Memoriam*.] *Literary World* 7 (13 July 1850) 30–31. Possibly by Bristed: see G.J. Kolb, 'Charles Astor Bristed, Henry Hallam and Tennyson's "Timbuctoo"', *Tennyson Research Bulletin* 4 (Nov. 1986), 197–210, at p. 200.

[Anon] American poetry. *Fraser's Magazine* 42 (July 1850) 9–25. Repr. *PBDC* 3, 25–30, abridged. (R.W. Griswold, Bryant, Halleck, Longfellow, Whittier, Poe.)

[Carl Benson] Half a day in Frankfort-on-the-Main. *Literary World* 7 (21 Sept. 1850) 225–6.

Sketches of American society, by a New Yorker. III, Catching a lion. *Fraser's Magazine* 42 (Sept. 1850) 255–66.

Sketches of American society, by a New Yorker. IV, Life at a watering place – accidents will happen. *Fraser's Magazine* 42 (Oct. 1850) 373–9. Repr. *International Monthly Magazine* 2 (Dec. 1850) 81–6.

Sketches of American society, by a New Yorker. V, Life at a watering place – Oldport Springs. *Fraser's Magazine* 42 (Nov. 1850) 562–74. Repr. *International Monthly Magazine* 2 (Jan. 1851) 240–9.

The late Henry Hallam. *Literary World* 7 (Dec. 1850) 451.

Bristed mentions that he had met Hallam the previous June [sc. 1850] in London. He thinks that he was in fact a better man and writer than his lamented elder brother Arthur, whose death had prompted Tennyson's *In memoriam*.

1851

Sketches of American society, by a New Yorker. VI, Life at a watering place – The Lionne. *Fraser's Magazine* 43 (Jan. 1851) 91–101. Repr. *International Monthly Magazine* 2 (1 Mar. 1851) 533–41.

[Anon] A commission of lunacy. *Literary World* 8 (15 Feb. 1851) 125. Repr. *PBDC* 3, 123–6.

Legendary Greece. *Literary World* 8 (15 Feb. 1851) 128–30. A review of vol. 1, *Legendary Greece*, of the US ed. of *Grote's History of Greece* (repr. from 2nd London ed.), 1851.

Letter to N.P. Willis. *Home World* [ie *Home Journal*] ?Feb. 1852. Repr. *Upper Ten Thousand* 8–11.

Sketches of American society, by a New Yorker. VII, Life at a Watering Place. The

Dog of Alcibiades. *Fraser's Magazine* 43 (Mar. 1851) 313–25. Repr. *International Monthly Magazine* 3 (May 1851) 211–21.

Letter to the editor. *International Monthly Magazine* (1 Apr. 1851) 39. On his Sketches.

[Anon] Professor Lincoln's Horace. *Literary World* 8 (19 Apr. 1851) 315–6. Repr. *PBDC* 1, 273–7.

[Carl Benson] The 'Walter Mapes' Poems. *Knickerbocker* 37 (Apr. 1851) 291–7. Repr. *PBDC* 1, 262–72, where it is attributed erroneously to the Apr. 1850 issue.

[Carl Benson] How the twins paid their poet (verse). *Literary World* 8 (14 June 1851) 469–70. Repr. *PBDC* 2, 1–6.

Sketches of American society, by a New Yorker. VIII, The Lion in the Toils. *Fraser's Magazine* 43 (Apr. 1851) 409–17. Repr. *International Monthly Magazine* 3 (June 1851) 366–72.

Sketches of American society, by a New Yorker. IX, A Trot on the Island. *Fraser's Magazine* 43 (June 1851) 648–63. Repr. *International Monthly Magazine* 4 (Aug. 1851) 54–65.

The lay of Sir Lytton. *PBDC* 2.6–9. ('Very much after Macaulay.') No previous publication listed; position in *PBDC* suggests that if such existed it would be June/July 1851. Probably about New York politics.

A specimen of the puff poetical (verse). '*Spirit of the Times* July 1851.' Repr. *PBDC* 2, 9–12. Not found in *Spirit of the Times* June-Aug. 1851.

[Anon] Latin pronunciation. *Literary World* 9 (26 July 1851) 63–5, 9 (23 Aug. 1851) 147–8. The former reviews S.S. Haldeman *Elements of Latin Pronunciation* (1851); the latter replies to the response by Haldeman, *Literary World* 9 (9 Aug. 1851) 108–9. Repr. *PBDC* 1, 277–83 (abridged).

Sketches of American society, by a New Yorker. X, A Country Gentleman at-home. *Fraser's Magazine* 44 (Sept. 1851) 277–90. Repr. *International Monthly Magazine* 4 (Oct. 1851) 389–98. Signed, Frank Manhattan.

[C.A.B.] The Ajax of Sophocles. *Literary World* 9 (11 Oct. 1851) 282–4. Repr. *PBDC* 1, 283–93. Review of an edition by an Englishman, J.B.M. Gray.

[Carl Benson] An Epistle to the editor from 'Carl Benson'. *Knickerbocker* 38 (Oct. 1851) 456–9. Includes several translations from English into Latin.

[Carl Benson] More 'last words' from Carl Benson. *Knickerbocker* 38 (Nov. 1851) 550.

Letter from 'Carl Benson'. *Spirit of the Times* 21 (20 Dec. 1851) 518.

[Carl Benson] Paris unvisited. Not by William Wordsworth. (verse) *Literary World* 9 (27 Dec. 1851) 501.

1852

Letters from 'Carl Benson', number II. *Spirit of the Times* 21 (3 Jan. 1852) 541–2. Paris, 29 Nov. 1851.

Letters from 'Carl Benson', number IV [sic]. *Spirit of the Times* 21 (17 Jan. 1852) 566–7. 38 Ave Gabrielle, Paris, 21 Dec. 1851. Misnumbered: no 'number III' found.

[Carl Benson] The week of the Coup d'Etat. *Literary World* 10 (17 Jan. 1852) 41–3, 10 (24 Jan. 1852), 61–3. Repr. *PBDC* 3, 126–49.

[Frank Manhattan] An election row in New York. *Fraser's Magazine* 45 (Jan. 1852) 104–110. Repr. *International Magazine* 5 (Mar. 1852) 341–5.

[Cranberry Fuster] An Intercepted Parisian Epistle. *Knickerbocker* 39 (Feb. 1852) 185–8. Repr. *PBDC* 4, 55–62. Dated Paris, 10 Nov. 1851.

[Carl Benson] A serious view of the French usurpation. *Literary World* 10 (13 Mar. 1852) 190–1. Repr. *PBDC* 4, 41–55, untitled.

[Carl Benson] Several considerations of the French character. *Literary World* 10 (20 Mar. 1852) 209–10, 10 (27 Mar. 1852) 230–2. Repr. *PBDC* 2, 41–55, with above entry.

Mr Ashburner in New-York. *International Magazine* 5 (Mar. 1852) 324–31.

The French stage. *Literary World* 10 (10 Apr. 1852) 251. A brief account of theatregoing in Paris, reprinted from *Spirit of the Times*.

[Carl Benson] Correspondence. *Literary World* 10 (10 Apr. 1852) 267–8. Dated Paris, Mar. 1852. Reports on the sale of Louis Philippe's library.

[Carl Benson] Prices of some books at the sale of Louis Philippe's library. *Literary World* 10 (29 May 1852) 380.

The fugitive slave. Repr. *PBDC* 3, 76–102, where it is dated '1852', with no location.

1853

[Carl Benson] The Gypsies of Art. Translated from Henry Murger's Scenes de la vie de Boheme. I: how the club was formed. *Knickerbocker* 41 (Jan. 1853) 12–23.

[Carl Benson] The Authors' Quarrel. (Verse: tr. from Molière's *Les Femmes Savantes*.) *Literary World* 12 (5 Feb. 1853) 107–8. Repr. *PBDC* 2, 38–43.

The Gypsies of Art. *Knickerbocker* 41 (Feb. 1853) 218–25.

A synoptical account of the English university commissions and their reports. *Literary World* 12 (19 Mar. 1853) 223–4, 12 (26 Mar. 1853) 245–8, 12 (9 Apr. 1853) 283–6. The first two are general and on Oxford, the third on Cambridge.

[Carl Benson] The Green Monster – a temperance tale. (Tr. from Gerard de Nerval.) *Literary World* 12 (2 Apr. 1853) 270–1. Repr. *PBDC* 3, 118–23.

Our special Paris correspondent at home. *Spirit of the Times* 23 (16 Apr. 1853) 97. Repr. *PBDC* 4, 62–3.

The Gypsies of Art. Chapter two: a good angel. *Knickerbocker* 41 (Apr. 1853) 336–40.

Letter to *Home Journal* on dress, sent from Paris: referred to as recent in *Southern Literary Messenger* 19 (Apr. 1853) 252, which reproduces a paragraph.

The Gypsies of Art. Chapter three: Ali-Rudolphe: or, the Turk perforce. *Knickerbocker* 41 (May 1853) 419–24.

Our special Paris correspondent on the Island. *Spirit of the Times* 23 (18 June 1853) 206. Bedford, RI, 10 June. Repr. *PBDC* 4, 64–8.

[Carl Benson] The three riders (tr. from German), Mr Crow (tr. from French). *Knickerbocker* 41 (June 1853) 561–2.

[Carl Benson] The Incantation of Simoaetha, from the Second Idyll of Theocritus. (Verse) *Literary World* 12 (2 July 1853) 528–9. Repr. *PBDC* 2, 27–32.

'Carl Benson' at Newport. *Spirit of the Times* 23 (10 July 1853) 253. Newport, RI, 9 July.

The untrue and melancholy history [of] Marguerite Gautier (Verse). *Spirit of the Times* 23 (16 July 1853) 254, (23 July 1853) 265. Repr. *PBDC* 2, 12–21.

'Carl Benson' at Newport. *Spirit of the Times* 23 (6 Aug. 1853) 289. Newport, RI, 25 July. Repr. *PBDC* 4, 68–72

[Anon] Poor old Charley. *Knickerbocker* 42 (July 1853) 48–60. Repr. *PBDC* 3, 57–76.

Our special Paris correspondence. *Spirit of the Times* 23 (10 Sept. 1853) 356. Ch Hocquard, Louveciennes 22 August. Repr. *PBDC* 4, 72–81.

The Gypsies of Art. Chapter five: the billows of Pactolus. *Knickerbocker* 42 (Sept. 1853) 227–33.

Our special Paris correspondence. *Spirit of the Times* 23 (15 Oct 1853) 356. Ch Hocquard, Louveciennes 15 Sept.

Our special Paris correspondence. *Spirit of the Times* 23 (29 Oct 1853) 434–5. Ch Hocquard, Louveciennes 6 Oct. Repr. *PBDC* 4, 81–8.

The gypsies of art. Chapter sixth: the white violets. *Knickerbocker* 42 (Oct. 1853) 362–6.

Our special Paris correspondence. *Spirit of the Times* 23 (5 Nov. 1853) 451. Ch Hocquard, 13 Oct.

Our special Paris correspondence. *Spirit of the Times* 23 (19 Nov. 1853) 469. Ch Hocquard, 27 Oct.

Our special Paris correspondence. *Spirit of the Times* 23 (26 Nov. 1853) 481. Ch Hocquard, 2 Nov.

Literary loafings after the manner of Commerson. *PBDC* 3, 149–50. In vol. index called 'Commersoniana'. There dated Nov. 1853; no previous publication given, and none traced. Jean-Louis-Auguste Commerson (1802–79) was a French writer of maxims.

Our special Paris correspondence. *Spirit of the Times* 23 (10 Dec. 1853) 505. 20 Rue Barbet-de-Jouy, 14 Nov.

Our special Paris correspondence. *Spirit of the Times* 23 (17 Dec. 1853) 517. 20 Rue Barbet-de-Jouy, 28 Nov.

Our special Paris correspondence. *Spirit of the Times* 23 (31 Dec. 1853) 552. 20 Rue Barbet-de-Jouy, 8 Dec.

The Gypsies of Art. Chapter seven, The gipsy coffee-house. *Knickerbocker* 42 (Dec. 1853) 596–601.

Walter of Acquitaine's Death-song: a free translation from the French of L. Pichat. (Verse) *Home Journal* 1853. Repr. *PBDC* 2, 63–6, which gives 'Horse Journal' in error.

1854

Our special Paris correspondence. *Spirit of the Times* 23 (7 Jan. 1854) 558–9. 20 Rue Barbet-de-Jouy, 15 Dec.

Our special Paris correspondence. *Spirit of the Times* 23 (14 Jan. 854) 566. 20 Rue Barbet-de-Jouy, 22 Dec.

[Carl Benson] The gypsies of art. Chapter eight: a gypsy at home. *Knickerbocker* 43 (Jan. 1854) 20–30.

Our special Paris correspondence. *Spirit of the Times* 23 (4 Feb. 1854) 602. 20 Rue Barbet-de-Jouy, 5 Jan.

[Carl Benson] The gypsies of art. Chapter nine: the passage of the Red Sea. *Knickerbocker* 43 (Feb. 1854) 165–9.

[Carl Benson] The gypsies of art. Chapter ten: the actress and the Englishman. *Knickerbocker* 43 (Apr. 854) 378–83.

[Carl Benson] Brillat-Savarin: 'Aesthetics of the table.' *Knickerbocker* 43 (Apr. 1854) 422–6.

[Carl Benson] The gypsies of art. Chapter eleven. *Knickerbocker* 43 (May 1854) 485–91.

False Pro-Slavery Analogies. *Evening Post* 1854. Repr. *PBDC* 3, 30–7.

1855

[Carl Benson] The Duchess' Pocket-Handkerchief. A story with several morals, and no particular plot. *Knickerbocker* 45 (Jan. 1855) 1–12. Repr. *PBDC* 3, 102–118.

Paris demolished and Paris embellished: a walk about it and a talk about it. By the author of 'The Upper Ten Thousand'. *Fraser's Magazine* 51 (Jan. 1855) 73–86.

Paris in little, and some of its vanities. By the author of 'The Upper Ten Thousand'. *Fraser's Magazine* 51 (May 1855) 568–86. Repr. *PBDC* 1, 294–331.

[C.A.B.] Possibilities of an Americo-Russian alliance. *Fraser's Magazine* 51 (June 1855) 670–5.

[C.A.B.] The English press and the American public. *Fraser's Magazine* 52 (July 1855) 42–7. Repr. *PBDC* 3, 37–48.

[C.A.B.] American parties, past and present (Part I): national parties to the time of President Pierce. *Fraser's Magazine* 52 (Sept. 1855) 274–85.

[C.A.B.] American parties, past and present (Part II): new opposition parties as now constituted. *Fraser's Magazine* 52 (Nov. 1855) 517–533.

The political press of America. *Fraser's Magazine* 52 (Dec. 1855) 678–85.

Too much of a change. *Knickerbocker Gallery* (New York, 1855) 161. A poem, sgd C.A. Bristed; portrait of Bristed opposite.

The English language in America. In *Cambridge Essays, contributed by Members of the University: 1855*, London: J.W. Parker & Son, 57–78. Described by H. L. Mencken in *The American Language* (1919) as 'to this day the most intelligent brief discussion of the subject ever printed.' (p.79). Review: *Chambers' Journal* ns 25 (1856), 249–51.

1856

Apropos of 'Rachel and the New World'. *Spirit of the Times* 26 (12 July) 259, (19 July) 270–1. Repr. *PBDC* 1, 331–47.

[Carl Benson] Gossip with readers and correspondents: Meister Johann, Carl Benson, W.P.P., F.B.W. Includes An Anathema a la Walter Mapes, on the man who stole my purse in an omnibus. (Verse) *Knickerbocker* 48 (Sept. 1856) 313–15.

[Wanderer] Our Paris Correspondence. *Porter's Spirit of the Times* 1(18 Oct. 1856) 114–15, (8 Nov. 1856) 157, (15 Nov. 1856) 175, (22 Nov. 1856) 191, 20 Dec. 1856) 254. Sport and theatre news.

[Anon] The observations of Mace Sloper, Esq., familiarly narrated by himself. Number nine, telling about different people and Mr Felicien Boutard. *Knickerbocker* 48 (Oct. 1856) 405–8.

Song of the Buchaniers. After the American presidential election. [verse] *Fraser's Magazine* 54 (Dec. 1856) 714–5. Not indexed by Wellesley. Repr. *PBDC* 2, 22–3.

1857

[Wanderer] Our European Correspondence. *Porter's Spirit of the Times* 1 (31 Jan. 1857) 350, 7 Feb. 1857) 367, 14 Feb. 1856) 383. Sport and theatre news.

[C.A.B.] The triumph of barbarism, by a New Yorker. *Fraser's Magazine* 55 (Jan. 1857) 118–26.

Relative speed of American and European racehorses (letter). *Porter's Spirit of the Times* 2 (Mar. 1857) 41.

[Carl Benson] The French spring season. *Porter's Spirit of the Times* 2 (11 Apr. 1857) 87, 2 (6 June 1857) 218.

[Wanderer] Our Paris correspondence. *Porter's Spirit of the Times* 2 (15 Aug. 1857) 372.

[Wanderer returned] Our Paris correspondence. *Porter's Spirit of the Times* 3 (5 Sept. 1857) 6.

[Carl Benson] Our European correspondence. Carl Benson at Baden-Baden – his view of the Goodwood race. *Porter's Spirit of the Times* 3 (19 Sept. 1857) 38.

[Carl Benson] Carl Benson on racing in England – life in Baden-Baden. *Porter's Spirit of the Times* 3 (17 Oct. 1857) 99.

[Carl Benson] Carl Benson in Baden. *Porter's Spirit of the Times* 3 (24 Oct. 1857) 118.

[Carl Benson] Our European correspondence. *Porter's Spirit of the Times* 3 (31 Oct. 1857) 131, (7 Nov. 1857) 151.

[Carl Benson] A Pindaric Ode, inscribed to Richard Ten Broeck, on winning the Cesarewitch. *Porter's Spirit of the Times* 3 (28 Nov. 1857) 205.

1858

Scraps from a projected translation of the Nibelungenlied. *PBDC* 2.66–9. Dated at end 'Trin Coll, Cant. 1842'.

Schiller's Division of the Earth; The maiden's lament; Ancaeus. (Translations from German) *PBDC* 2, 76–80.

1859

Grattan's Civilized America. *Porter's Spirit of the Times* 6 (7 May 1859) 146–7. Repr. *PBDC* 4, 88–113. A review of Thomas Colley Grattan's *Civilized America*, 1859.

1860

[Carl Benson] My friend Mr. Bedlow: or, Reminiscences of American college life (Part I) *Macmillan's Magazine* 2 (July 1860) 218–26. Impressions of Yale in the 1830s.

[Carl Benson] (poem) *Knickerbocker* 56 (Oct. 1860) 441–2. A poem addressed to the magazine.

1861

[Carl Benson] My friend Mr. Bedlow: or, Reminiscences of American college life (Part II). *Macmillan's Magazine* 3 (Feb. 1861) 264–77.

[Carl Benson] Letters from 'Carl Benson'. *Wilkes' Spirit of the Times* 4 (9 Mar. 1861) 3–4, (20 Apr. 1861) 99, (27 Apr. 1861) 125, (18 May 1861) 163, (1 June 1861) 194, (6 July 1861) 275, (22 July 1861) 322.

[Carl Benson] A new theory of Bohemian. *Knickerbocker* 57 (Mar. 1861) 311–17. Repr. *Sharpe's* 50 (1869) 289. [Presumably Sharpe's *London magazine of entertainment and instruction for general reading*.]

[Carl Benson] Laura. *Wilkes' Spirit of the Times* 5 (7 Sept 1861) 4. Dated Baden, August 7; a poem on his wife's death.

1862

[Carl Benson] Letter from 'Carl Benson'. *Wilkes' Spirit of the Times* 5 (18 Jan. 1862) 311.

[Carl Benson] Laura. *Wilkes' Spirit of the Times* 5 (25 Jan 1862) 330. Poem repr. by readers' request.

[Carl Benson] The white lady of Yburg. *Wilkes' Spirit of the Times* 5 (15 Feb. 1862) 369–70. A folk tale of Baden.

Carl Benson] The white lady of Yburg [pt II]. *Wilkes' Spirit of the Times* 5 (22 Feb 1862) 385–6.

[Carl Benson] Growls from an invalid. 1: politeness. *Wilkes' Spirit of the Times* 5 (1 Mar. 1862) 404.

[Carl Benson] T-total gymnastics. *Wilkes' Spirit of the Times* 6 (15 Mar. 1862) 22. Discusses wine, exercise etc.

[Carl Benson] Don't touch the axe! A story of American life. Pt I. *Wilkes' Spirit of the Times* 6 (22 Mar. 1862) 35, (29 Mar. 1862) 54, (5 Apr. 1862) 74, (12 Apr. 1862) 86, (19 Apr. 1862) 102, (26 Apr. 1862) 118, (3 May 1862) 180–1, (10 May 1862) 146.

[Carl Benson] Growls from an invalid. Growl second: our streets. *Wilkes' Spirit of the Times* 6 (22 Mar. 1862) 42.

[Anon] A new French novelist. *Wilkes' Spirit of the Times* 6 (24 May 1862) 178–9. Ascribed to Bristed in editorial comment, ibid p. 184.

[Carl Benson] Trinity. (poem) *Wilkes' Spirit of the Times* 6 (7 June 1862) 211.

[Carl Benson] Growls from an invalid. III – Central Park regulations. *Wilkes' Spirit of the Times* 6 (12 July 1862) 290–1.

[Carl Benson] The equestrian question. *Wilkes' Spirit of the Times* 6 (26 July 1862) 323.

[Carl Benson] Anthony Trollope's North America. *Wilkes' Spirit of the Times* 6 (16 Aug. 1862) 374–5.

[Carl Benson] The first week of August. *Wilkes' Spirit of the Times* 6 (23 Aug. 1862) 386. A poem to mark the anniversary of his wife's death. Dated Lenox, Aug 5.

[Carl Benson] Literary lounges. I – Misquotations, mis-spellings and mistakes generally. *Wilkes' Spirit of the Times* 7 (6 Sept. 1862) 6.

[Carl Benson] To the memory of my friend Philip Kearney (poem). *Wilkes' Spirit of the Times* 7 (13 Sept. 1862) 21.

[Carl Benson] Literary lounges. II – Equestrianism as bearing on the war. Historical parallels and other illustrations. *Wilkes' Spirit of the Times* 7 (4 Oct. 1862) 70.

[Carl Benson] Almost two ghosts: a real ghost story. *Wilkes' Spirit of the Times* 7 (18 Oct. 1862) 102, (25 Oct. 1862) 124–5.

[Carl Benson] Mad dog! *Wilkes' Spirit of the Times* 7 (8 Nov. 1862) 150.

[Carl Benson] The third alternative. *Wilkes' Spirit of the Times* 7 (20 Dec. 1862) 252. On current politics and the War.

1863

[Carl Benson] Carl Benson on Du Chaillu's book. *Wilkes' Spirit of the Times* 7 (3 Jan. 1863) 275. On the attack on Du Chaillu's *Liberty Hall* (a university novel) by Winwood Reade.

[Carl Benson] On the proposed elimination of the Puritan element. *Wilkes' Spirit of the Times* 7 (10 Jan. 1863) 291–2. On post-Civil War politics and culture.

[C A. Bristed] On English insincerity on the slavery question. *New-York Times* (11 Jan. 1863) p. 3 col. 6.

[Carl Benson] Arion. (Poem, tr. from A.W. Schlegel) *Wilkes' Spirit of the Times* 7 (31 Jan. 1863) 343.

[Carl Benson] Carl Benson in reply to C.F.B. *Wilkes' Spirit of the Times* 7 (7 Feb. 1863) 355.

[Carl Benson] Draught of the Seine: queries by Carl Benson. *Wilkes' Spirit of the Times* 7 (7 Feb. 1863) 362.

[Carl Benson] Why call a convention? *Wilkes' Spirit of the Times* 7 (28 Feb. 1863) 402.

[Carl Benson] Two loyal axioms. *Wilkes' Spirit of the Times* 7 (14 Mar. 1863) 22.

[Carl Benson] Carl Benson takes a long lounge, and gives several growls. *Wilkes' Spirit of the Times* 7 (16 May 1863) 170–1. Includes a protest against Webster's rules on spelling.

[Carl Benson] Those blessed Commissioners again! Central Park. *Wilkes' Spirit of the Times* 7 (23 May 1863) 182.

[Carl Benson] Carl Benson sends his compliments from the Island to Sulky. *Wilkes' Spirit of the Times* 7 (20 June 1863) 246–7. About trotting: Sulky was another Spirit correspondent.

[C A. Bristed] On iron pavements and steam carriages. *New-York Times* (6 Sept. 1863) p. 4 col. 6.

[C A. Bristed] On iron pavements and steam carriages. *New-York Times* (27 Sept. 1863) p. 4 col. 6.

[C A. Bristed] On iron pavements and steam carriages. *New-York Times* (18 Oct. 1863).

1864

[Charles Astor Bristed] The probable influence of the new military element on our social and national character. *United States Service Magazine* 1 (June 1864) 594–602.

[C.A.B.] Popular extravagance – its remedies and their limitations. *United States Service Magazine* 2 (Nov. 1864) 435–49.

1865

[Anon] Critics and criticism. *Nation* 1 (6 July 1865) 10–11.

[Anon] Club life. *Nation* 1 (6 July 1865) 12–13.

[Anon] Everett's *On the Cam* (review). *Nation* 1 (10 Aug. 1865) 182–4.

[Anon] A society for improving the condition of the rich. *Nation* 1 (28 Sept. 1865) 399–400.

[C.A.B.] (letter) *Round Table* ns 5 (7 Oct. 1865) 76. Denounces a *Round Table* review of Everett's *On the Cam* for its accusations against Everett (who didn't fight – but he's shortsighted – could not hit an elephant) and Bristed himself.

[Anon] The etiquette of smoking. *Nation* 1 (14 Dec. 1865) 749–50.

[Autobiographical entry] *A quarter-century record of the class of 1839, Yale College*, ed. J.G.E. Larned. New York: pr. Baker & Godwin, 1865, 10–12.

1866

[Anon] Dress and its critics. *Nation* 2 (4 Jan. 1866) 10–11.

[Anon] Some doubts on the supposed popular distinction between wit and humour. *Nation* 2 (18 Jan. 1866) 72–3.

[Carl Benson] A nautical criticism (letter). *Nation* 2 (5 Apr. 1866) 436.

A French sketch of a French girl. *Nation* 2 (23 May 1866) 419.

Translations of Victor Hugo. *New York Evening Post* (25 May 1866).

Victor Hugo's 'Alcove'. *New York Evening Post* (26 May 1866).

[Carl Benson] Baden-Baden. *Galaxy* 1 (15 July 1866) 519–24.

Round Table 4 (23 June 1866) 307. Bristed asks in the Notes and Queries section about 'Lays of the love lorn', a parody of Locksley Hall.

Round Table 4 (18 Aug. 1866) 44. Notes and Queries. Heros von Borcke is a real person – Bristed met him in Paris.

Round Table 4 (13 Oct. 1866) 172–3. A letter on a dispute between Dean Alford and Carl Benson in the *Evening Post*.

'Smalls' and 'little-go'. *Nation* 3 (13 Sept. 1866) 216.

1867

[Carl Benson] The Round Table and the 'Veteran observer'. *Round Table* 5 (23 Mar. 1867) 184–5.

[Carl Benson] Letter on English style. *Round Table* 5 (4 May) 280–1.

[Carl Benson] Letter on French marriage and separation. *Round Table* 5 (25 May 1867) 333.

[Anon] Handicap legislation. *Round Table* 6 (20 July 1867) 36.

The Roman judiciary. *Nation* 5 (26 Sept. 1867) 259.

American neglect of political economy. *Nation* 5 (10 Oct. 1867) 299.

[Carl Benson] Letter on a joke about H. Brougham. *Round Table* 6 (2 Nov. 1867) 297.

The interference theory of government (letter). *Nation* 5 (21 Nov. 1867) 419.

[C.A. Bristed] Letter on German writers in English. *Round Table* 6 (30 Nov. 1867) 356.

1868

Note: a New Orleans upholsterer says the French for armoire is amour. *Round Table* 7 (22 Feb. 1868).

National repudiation (letter). *Nation* 6 (12 Mar. 1868) 209–10, 249–50.

[Carl Benson] Two Alsatian Novelists: Erckmann and Chatrian. *Lippincott's Magazine* 1 (Mar. 1868) 325–30.

[C.A. Bristed] Letter on Publication of Incomes. *New-York Times* (3 May 1868) p. 5 col. 3.

[Carl Benson] Letter on a sarcasm attributed to Dr Holmes – he put it into print himself 12 years ago. Discusses the periodicity of jokes. *Round Table* 8 (11 July 1868) 29.

[Carl Benson] Letter on difference between ancient and modern Greek. *Round Table* 8 (15 Aug. 1868) 109.

The dispute about liberal education. *Lippincott's Magazine* 2 (Sept. 1868) 295–9, (Oct. 1868) 389–95.

1869

[C.A. Bristed] Illustrations of Protection. *New-York Times* (25 January 1869) p. 5 col. 2.

Letter on 'French morals and manners'. *Turf, Field and Farm*. Referred to in *Appletons' Journal* 1 (17 July 1869) 505.

The Drat: A Goblin Story of French Provincial Life. *Appletons' Journal* 1 (24 July 1869) 517–519.

[C.A. Bristed] Letter on Varro, St Augustine, and Mr. Lecky. *Nation* 9 (29 July 1869) 91.

[Carl Benson] Fancy signatures. *Lippincott's Magazine* 4 (July 1869) 106–8. Discusses his own pseudonyms, others', and the fashion for using them.

'American beauty personified as the nine muses', *Chicago art journal*, July 1869. Repr. under the same title as a pamphlet in 1870: see A1.

[C.A. Bristed] Correction on Professorship. *New-York Times* (1 Aug. 1869) p. 5 col. 6.

[Carl Benson] Letter: A mistranslation by Lord Byron. *Nation* 9 (2 Sept. 1869) 190.

[Carl Benson] Letter: A misemendation by Mr. Diez. *Nation* 9 (7 Oct. 1869) 294.

[C.A. Bristed] New-York City: the Astor Library, and the Founder's Fortune. *New-York Times* (31 Oct. 1869) p. 3 col. 5.

1870

[Carl Benson] Letter: Milton's Greek imitations and idioms. *Nation* 10 (3 Feb. 1870) 73.

[Carl Benson] Letter: A Greek but not an Irish bull. *Appletons' Journal* 3 (5 Feb. 1870) 163. On Milton's Hellenisms.

[Carl Benson] Things of To-day. *Galaxy* 9 (Feb. 1870) 267–71. The income tax; cramming; whose fault is it?; anthracite and health.

[Carl Benson] Things of To-day. *Galaxy* 9 (Mar. 1870) 411–17. Our civil service; The Darien expedition; Portable soup; Novels and serials; Climate and industry.

[Carl Benson] Letter: Publishers and copyright. *Nation* 10 (5 May 1870) 319.

[Carl Benson] Things of the Day [*sic*]. *Galaxy* 9 (June 1870) 841–44. The Woman question; accidental suicide and legal infanticide.

[Carl Benson] Letter: The development of Breitmann. *Nation* 11 (14 July 1870) 25–6.

[Carl Benson] Letter: Contrabands. *Nation* 11 (25 Aug. 1870) 122.

[Carl Benson] Reminiscences and speculations, apropos of the turning-point in the King of Prussia's Life. *Galaxy* 10 (Nov. 1870) 604–12.

International Copyright. Part I. Popular delusions on the subject. *Galaxy* 10 (Dec. 1870), 811–18. (Part II not found.)

White on English words. *North American Review* 112 (1870) 469–76. A review of R.G. White, *Words and their Uses, Past and Present* (1870).

1871

Plutarch's Morals. (review) *Nation* 12 (2 Feb. 1871) 77–9.

Trollope's novels. *North American Review* 112 (Apr. 1871) 433–40. A review of *Ralph the Heir, My Daughter Elinor* and *Miss Van Kortlandt*.

[Anon] Jowett's translation of Plato. *Nation* 12 (27 Apr. 1871) 291–3, (4 May 1871) 306–7.

[C.A. Bristed] Letter on terminology of categories of students at Oxford and Cambridge. *Appletons' Journal* 5 (27 May 1871) 623.

[Anon] Forsyth's 'Novels and novelists of the eighteenth century'. *Nation* 13 (13 July 1871) 27–8.

[Carl Benson] Letter on Charles Reade's last plot. *Nation* 13 (27 July 1871) 57.
[Carl Benson] Vatis Testamentum. *Galaxy* 12 (July 1871) 141. Translation of an Irish poem into Latin anacreontics.
[Carl Benson] Popular Fallacies. *Galaxy* 12 (Oct. 1871) 479–87.
[Carl Benson] Popular Fallacies. VI. The Noscitur a Socio Fallacy. *Galaxy* 12 (Nov. 1871) 614–25.
Victor Hugo's 'L'Année terrible'. *Nation* 14 (1871) 393–4. Hugo's poems include two attacking the historian Bancroft and President Grant. See A.L. Rabinowitz, 'Hugo's *Bancroft* and *Le message de Grant*', *Modern Language Notes* (Dec. 1942) 648–52.
Some Notes on Ellis's Early English Pronunciation. *Transactions of the American Philological Association* 2 (1871) 114–137.

1872
[Carl Benson] Johnson and Johnstone. *Nation* 16 (2 Jan. 1872) 9.
[Carl Benson] Letter: The rule of the road. *Appletons' Journal* 7 (6 Jan. 1872) 27.
[Anon] Cranch's Aeneid. *Nation* 16 (30 Jan. 1872) 77–8.
[Charles Astor Bristed] American Criticism; its difficulties and prospects. *North American Review* 114 (Jan. 1872) 23–39.
[C.A. Bristed] Publishing examination papers. *Nation* 16 (6 Feb. 1872) 93–4.
[Carl Benson] Letter: Bridal Tours. *New York Times*. Referred to and quoted editorially in *Appletons' Journal* 7 (24 Feb. 1872) 220–1. An attack on honeymoons.
[Carl Benson] Letter on Post-official redtapery. *Nation* 14 (20 June 1872) 403–4.
[C.A. Bristed] Letter: Irish Brogue. *Appletons' Journal* 8 (17 Aug. 1872) 192.
[C.A. Bristed] Letter: 'Philological conventions'. *Nation* 15 (29 Aug. 1872) 135.
[C.A. Bristed] Letter: The New York Times and the effects of musical vibration. *Nation* 15 (12 Sept. 1872) 167.
[Carl Benson] The horse question and the labor question. *Nation* 15 (7 Nov. 1872) 297–8.
[Carl Benson] Publishers and Authors. *Galaxy* 14 (Nov. 1872) 640–3.
[C.A. Bristed] English authors and American reprints. *Nation* 15 (26 Dec. 1872) 426. Corrects a slip in the third edition of *Five years* (which he twice calls *Two years*).
'On some exaggerations in comparative philology': mentioned in *TAPA* 3 (1872) 22. Published as a pamphlet: see A1, 1873.
[Charles Astor Bristed] 'Erroneous and Doubtful Usages of the Word "Such"'. *Transactions of the American Philological Association* 3 (1872) 55–58.

1873
[Carl Benson] Letter (quoted from editorially) on the inspiration for Tennyson's 'Charge of the Light Brigade'. *Appletons' Journal* 9 (1 Jan. 1873) 27. (An anon. early poem, not Drayton's 'Agincourt'.)
[Carl Benson] Communications on English public schools. The avarice of masters; 'don't'; raw ham. *Appletons' Journal* 9 (18 Jan. 1873) 124–5.
[Carl Benson] Casual Cogitations. *Galaxy* 15 (Feb. 1873) 178–87. I, The unmorality

of the scientific dispensation, 178–81; II, Impoliteness as a national characteristic, 181–7.

[Carl Benson] Literature; Forestier. Rauzan Margaux. To George W. Curtis. (Easter Sunday, 1872.) Stein Wine, The Pertinacious Toper. The Song of the Sorrowful. *The Aldine, A Typographic Art Journal* 6 (Mar. 1873) 68.

[Carl Benson] Casual Cogitations. *Galaxy* 15 (Mar. 1873) 308–18. III, Our Mercantile Spirit 308–12; IV, The 'Labor Question' 312–18.

[Carl Benson] Casual Cogitations. *Galaxy* 15 (May 1873) 625–9. V, Aediles wanted! 625–6; VI, Panurge's sheep 626–8; VII, Color upon color 628–9.

Letter on names. *Appletons' Journal* 9 (7 June 1873) 764. Discusses inter alia his own choice of 'Benson' – to avoid common mis-spellings of 'Bristed'; also 'Carl' – a common name, not royal.

[Carl Benson] Casual Cogitations. *Galaxy* 16 (July 1873) 58–62. VIII, Amateurs and Translations.

[Carl Benson] Casual Cogitations. *Galaxy* 16 (Aug. 1873) 196–201. IX, 'Woman's Rights' Again 196–8; X, Coincidence and Accidents 198–201.

[Carl Benson] Casual Cogitations. *Galaxy* 16 (Sept. 1873) 324–8. XI, Will the Coming American Eat and Drink?

Trench's Plutarch. *Nation* 17 (9 Oct. 1873) 244–5. A review of R.C. Trench, *Plutarch his life, his lives, and his morals* (1873).

1874

[Carl Benson] Physical Impediments to Social Success. *Galaxy* 17 (Jan. 1874) 64–8.

[Carl Benson] My Private Grief against George Sand. *Galaxy* 17 (Apr. 1874) 467–70.

[Aunt Mehitable] My Second Winter in Washington. *Godey's Lady's Book and Magazine* 88 (Apr. 1874) 344–7. Refers to Charles Bristed, who writes as Carl Benson. A slangy account which may reflect Bristed's own second winter in Washington.

A3 Edited works

Selections from Catullus: for the use of classical students. New York: Stanford and Swords, 1849. Ed. W.G. Cookesley; with additional notes by Bristed. pp. 160. Original ed., *Selecta e Catullo, in usum juventutis: notas quasdem Anglice scripta, adjecit G.G. Cookesley.* Eton: E.P. Williams, 1845. pp. 89.

Reviews

American Review 4 (Aug. 1849) 218–19.

Knickerbocker 34 (Sept. 1849) 165–8. (L.G. Clark)

Literary World 5 (11 Aug. 1849) 106–7.

Yale Literary Magazine 14 (July 1849) 376–8 (E.H.R.)

New Englander 7 (Nov. 1849) 625–7.

A4 Translations

[Carl Benson] Victor Cherbuliez, *Prosper, a novel*. NY: Henry Holt & Co., 1874.
Reviews
    Galaxy 17 (Apr. 1874) 573–4. 'The book seems to be well translated, though here
    and there are little bits of English slang which sound strangely'.
    Atlantic Monthly 33 (Apr. 1874) 497. (Thomas S. Parry)
    Appletons' Journal (editorial) 11 (21 Feb. 1874) 251. 'Of the translation it must be
    said that it is admirable – one of the most perfectly successful and spirited
    we remember.'
In his contribution to the Yale Class of 1839 record (see A2, 1865), Bristed claimed
that he had translated 'Peyrat's pamphlet against the Immaculate Conception'. This
must refer to A. Peyrat, *Un nouveau Dogme: histoire de l'Immaculée Conception*. (Paris,
1855). There is no evidence that the translation was published.

B Secondary works

Adam, Adela M., 'Cambridge through an American undergraduate's eyes (C. Bristed,
    1841–46)'. *Report of the Cambridge Antiquarian Society* 1942. Lecture, 27 April.
Bowerman, Sarah G., 'Charles Astor Bristed', *Dictionary of American Biography* 3
    (1929) 53–4.
Patty, James S., 'More light on Baudelaire and Poe: C.A. Bristed, an American in
    Paris', *Romance Quarterly* 6.1 (1996) 166–75.
Searby, P., 'A New Yorker in early Victorian Cambridge', *Cambridge* 33 (Winter
    1993–4) 58–63.
Sherwood, M.E.W., 'Charles Astor Bristed'. *Galaxy* 17 (Apr. 1874) 545–7.
Simmons, M.L. (ed.) *Cyclopaedia of American Literature* (Philadelphia: W.M. Rutter,
    1875) 1. 668–9.
[White, R.G.], 'Linguistic and literary notes and queries, V: Charles Astor Bristed'.
    Galaxy 17 (Apr. 1874) 473–87.
Ward, P.A. and M.B. Raycraft, 'New Notes on C.A. Bristed, Poe, and Baudelaire'.
    Bulletin Baudelairien, 39:1–2 (2004) 111–25.
Obituary, *The Washington Chronicle*, 16 Jan. 1874.
Obituary, *The New York Tribune*, 17 Jan. 1874.
Obituary editorial, *The Evening Star* (Washington), 15 Jan. 1874.

Index

Page numbers in **bold** refer to major sources of information.